AM2   6/2020

D1031751

APPIAN

VI

LCL 544

APPIAN

ROMAN HISTORY

VOLUME VI

CIVIL WARS, BOOK 5
FRAGMENTS

EDITED AND TRANSLATED BY

BRIAN McGING

HARVARD UNIVERSITY PRESS
CAMBRIDGE, MASSACHUSETTS
LONDON, ENGLAND
2020

Library of Congress Control Number 2019940172
CIP data available from the Library of Congress

ISBN 978-0-674-99731-8

Composed in ZephGreek and ZephText by
Technologies 'N Typography, Merrimac, Massachusetts.
Printed on acid-free paper and bound by
Maple Press, York, Pennsylvania

CONTENTS

ΑΠΠΙΑΝΟΥ ΡΩΜΑΪΚΗ ΙΣΤΟΡΙΑ

APPIAN'S ROMAN HISTORY

XVII

ΕΜΦΥΛΙΩΝ ΠΕΜΠΤΗ[1]

1. Μετὰ δὲ τὸν Κασσίου καὶ Βρούτου θάνατον ὁ μὲν Καῖσαρ ἐπὶ τῆς Ἰταλίας ᾔει, ὁ δὲ Ἀντώνιος ἐς τὴν Ἀσίαν, ἔνθα αὐτῷ συμβάλλει Κλεοπάτρα βασιλὶς
2 Αἰγύπτου, καὶ εὐθὺς ὀφθεῖσα ἐκράτει. ὁ δὲ ἔρως ὅδε αὐτοῖς τε ἐκείνοις ἐς ἔσχατον ἔληξε κακοῦ καὶ ἐς ὅλην Αἴγυπτον ἐπ᾽ ἐκείνοις. ὅθεν ἄν τι καὶ Αἰγύπτιον εἴη τῆσδε τῆς βίβλου μέρος, ὀλίγον τε καὶ οὐκ ἄξιον ἐπιγραφῆς πω, διὸ δὴ καὶ τοῖς ἐμφυλίοις πολὺ πλείο-
3 σιν οὖσιν ἐπίμικτον. ἐγίγνετο γὰρ δὴ καὶ μετὰ Κάσ-σιόν τε καὶ Βροῦτον ἕτερα ἐμφύλια ὅμοια, στρατηγοῦ μὲν οὐδενὸς ὄντος ἐπὶ πᾶσιν ὥσπερ ἐκείνοις, κατὰ μέρος δὲ ἑτέρων, μέχρι Πομπήιός τε Σέξτος, ὁ νεώ-τερος παῖς Πομπηίου Μάγνου, λοιπὸς ὢν ἔτι τῆσδε τῆς στάσεως, τοῖς ἀμφὶ τὸν Βροῦτον ἐπανῃρέθη, καὶ Λέπιδος ἐξέπεσε τοῦ μέρους τῆς ἡγεμονίας καὶ ἡ Ῥω-μαίων ἀρχὴ πᾶσα περιῆλθεν ἐς δύο μόνον, Ἀντώνιόν τε καὶ Καίσαρα. ἐγίνετο δὲ αὐτῶν ἕκαστα οὕτως.

4 2. Κάσσιος ὁ Παρμήσιος ἐπίκλην ὑπελέλειπτο μὲν ὑπὸ Κασσίου καὶ Βρούτου περὶ τὴν Ἀσίαν ἐπὶ νεῶν

BOOK XVII

CIVIL WARS, BOOK V

1. After the death of Cassius and Brutus, Octavian went to Italy and Antony to Asia, where Cleopatra, queen of Egypt, meets him and conquered his heart at first sight. This passion ended in complete disaster for them, and for 2 the whole of Egypt in addition. For this reason a part of the book will deal with Egypt—a small part, however, not really worth mentioning in the title, since it is mixed in with the far more substantial narrative of the civil wars. For 3 even after Cassius and Brutus, other similar civil conflicts occurred, but there was no one in overall command as they had been, just different commanders in different sectors. Eventually, Sextus Pompeius, the younger son of Pompey the Great and last remaining member of that faction, was killed, as Brutus and his men had been; Lepidus was removed from his share of the leadership; and the whole government of Rome devolved on two men only, Antony and Octavian. The details of these events are as follows.

2. Cassius of Parma, as he was known, had been left by 4 Cassius and Brutus in Asia in command of ships and troops

---

[1] Ἀππιανοῦ Ῥωμαικῶν ιη′ Ἐμφυλίων πέμπτον L (πέμπτη BJ); Ἀππιανοῦ Ῥωμαικῶν ιη′ Ἐμφυλίων ε′ P

3

καὶ στρατοῦ, χρήματα ἐκλέγειν. Κασσίου δὲ ἀπο-
θανόντος οὐδὲν ἐλπίζων ὅμοιον ἐν Βρούτῳ, Ῥοδίων
ἐπελέξατο νῆας τριάκοντα, ὅσας ἐνόμιζε πληρώσειν,
καὶ τὰς λοιπὰς διέπρησε χωρὶς τῆς ἱερᾶς, ἵνα μὴ δύ-
5 ναιντο νεωτερίσαι. καὶ ὁ μὲν τάδε πράξας ἀνήγετο
ταῖς τε ἰδίαις καὶ ταῖς τριάκοντα, Κλώδιος δὲ ἐκ
Βρούτου πεμφθεὶς ἐς Ῥόδον ἐπὶ νεῶν τρισκαίδεκα,
τοὺς Ῥοδίους νεωτερίζοντας εὑρών (ἐτεθνήκει γὰρ
ἤδη καὶ ὁ Βροῦτος), ἐξήγαγε τὴν φρουράν, οὖσαν
ὁπλιτῶν τρισχιλίων, καὶ ἐς τὸν Παρμήσιον ἐχώρει.
6 ἀφίκετο δὲ αὐτοῖς καὶ Τουρούλιος, ἑτέρας ναῦς ἔχων
πολλὰς καὶ χρήματα, ὅσα προεξείλεκτο ἀπὸ τῆς Ῥόδου. ἐς δὴ τὸ ναυτικὸν τοῦτο ὡς ἐς ἤδη τινὰ ἰσχὺν
συνέθεον, ὅσοι ἦσαν κατὰ μέρη τῆς Ἀσίας ἐπὶ τῶν
ὑπηρεσιῶν, καὶ αὐτὸ ὁπλίταις τε ἐξ ὧν ἐδύναντο ἀν-
επλήρουν καὶ ἐρέταις ἐκ θεραπόντων ἢ δεσμωτῶν,
ἐπιπλέοντες δὲ ταῖς νήσοις καὶ ἀπὸ τῶν νησιωτῶν.
7 ἦλθον δ᾽ εἰς αὐτοὺς καὶ Κικέρων ὁ Κικέρωνος καὶ
ὅσοι ἄλλοι τῶν ἐπιφανῶν ἐκ τῆς Θάσου διεπεφεύγε-
σαν. καὶ ταχὺ πλῆθος ἦν καὶ σύνταξις ἀξιόχρεως
8 ἡγεμόνων τε καὶ στρατοῦ καὶ νεῶν. προσλαβόντες δὲ
καὶ Λέπιδον μεθ᾽ ἑτέρας δυνάμεως, ἢ Βρούτῳ καθ-

---

1 Gaius Cassius Parmensis, a well-known poet and playwright,
had been one of the assassins of Caesar. Quaestor in 43, he made
his way to Sextus Pompeius after the battle of Philippi, then
joined Antony, for whom he fought at the battle of Actium. He
was executed, the last of Caesar's assassins, on Octavian's orders
(Val. Max. 1.7.7; Orosius 6.19.20).

in order to collect money.[1] On the death of Cassius, not expecting a similar fate for Brutus, he selected thirty ships belonging to the Rhodians—which were as many as he intended to man—and apart from the sacred ship,[2] burned the rest to make sure the Rhodians could not revolt. Having done this, he set sail with his own ships and the thirty. Clodius, who had been sent by Brutus to Rhodes in command of thirteen ships, found the Rhodians in revolt. (For Brutus too was now dead.) Clodius removed the garrison of three thousand legionaries, and made his way to Cassius of Parma. They were also joined by Turullius, who had a large number of other ships and the money that had previously been collected from Rhodes.[3] All those who were serving in various parts of Asia hurried to join this fleet, believing it to be now quite powerful, and they manned the ships with what legionaries they could and with rowers taken from among the slaves and prisoners, and after attacking the islands, from the islanders. Cicero, the son of Cicero, also joined them, and those other nobles who had escaped from Thasos.[4] Soon there was a large gathering and a substantial collection of officers, soldiers, and ships. Taking Lepidus too, who had another force, which had

[2] Some Greek states kept ships for special diplomatic and religious missions. At Athens, we know the names of two of them: the Paralos and the Salaminia. [3] Turullius, like Cassius Parmensis, one of the last surviving assassins of Caesar, also met his death on the orders of Octavian (Val. Max. 1.1.19).

[4] Cicero's son, Marcus, served first under Pompey, then Brutus and Sextus Pompeius. In 39 he was reconciled with Octavian. In 30 he was consul with Octavian, and later governor of Syria and of Asia.

ἵστατο Κρήτην, πρὸς Μοῦρκον καὶ Δομίτιον Ἀηνόβαρβον ἐπὶ μεγάλης δυνάμεως ὄντας ἐς τὸν Ἰόνιον
9 διέπλεον. καὶ αὐτῶν οἱ μὲν ἅμα τῷ Μούρκῳ διέπλευ-
σαν ἐς Σικελίαν καὶ τὴν ἰσχὺν Πομπηίῳ Σέξστῳ
συνῆψαν, οἱ δὲ κατέμειναν παρὰ Ἀηνοβάρβῳ καί τιν᾽
αἵρεσιν ἐφ᾽ ἑαυτῶν καθίσταντο.

10 3. Τοιάδε μὲν ἐκ τῶν λειψάνων τῆς παρασκευῆς
Κασσίου τε καὶ Βρούτου πρῶτα συνίστατο, ὁ δὲ Καῖσαρ καὶ ὁ Ἀντώνιος ἐπὶ τῇ νίκῃ τῇ περὶ Φιλίππους
11 ἔθυόν τε λαμπρῶς καὶ τὸν στρατὸν ἐπήνουν. καὶ ἐς
τὴν δόσιν τῶν ἐπινικίων ὁ μὲν ἐς τὴν Ἰταλίαν ἐχώρει,
τήν τε γῆν αὐτοῖς διανεμήσων καὶ ἐς τὰς ἀποικίας
καταλέξων (ὧδε γὰρ αὐτὸς εἵλετο διὰ τὴν ἀρρωστίαν),
ὁ δὲ Ἀντώνιος ἐς τὰ πέραν ἔθνη, συλλέξων τὰ χρή-
12 ματα, ὅσα αὐτοῖς ὑπέσχηντο. διενείμαντο δὲ αὖθις
ὅσα καὶ πρότερον ἔθνη καὶ ἐπελάμβανον τὰ Λεπίδου·
τήν τε γὰρ Κελτικὴν τὴν ἐντὸς Ἄλπεων ἐδόκει Καίσαρος ἀξιοῦντος αὐτόνομον ἀφιέναι γνώμῃ τοῦ προτέρου Καίσαρος, ὅ τε Λέπιδος διεβάλλετο τὰ πράγματα[2] Πομπηίῳ προδιδόναι· καὶ ὥριστο, εἰ Καίσαρι
ψευδὴς ἡ διαβολὴ φανείη, ἕτερα ἀντιδοῦναι τῷ Λε-
13 πίδῳ. ἀφίεσαν δὲ καὶ τῆς στρατείας τοὺς ἐντελῆ χρό-

---

[2] τὰ παρὰ codd.; τὰ πράγματα Bekker; τὰ παρ᾽ αὐτῶν
Schweig.; τὰ πάτρια Étienne-Duplessis

---

[5] The exploits of Lucius Staius Murcus (praetor 45) and
Gnaeus Domitius Ahenobarbus (consul 32) were covered in de-

subjugated Crete for Brutus, they sailed over to the Ionian gulf to Murcus and Domitius Ahenobarbus, who had a large force under their command.[5] Some of these crossed with Murcus to Sicily to combine their strength with that of Sextus Pompeius. The rest remained with Ahenobarbus and pursued an independent policy.

3. Such were the first groups that formed from the remains of Brutus' and Cassius' army. After the victory at Philippi Octavian and Antony offered magnificent sacrifice and commended the army. With a view to distributing the rewards of victory, Octavian made his way to Italy to divide the land among the soldiers and to register them for the colonies—he himself chose this task because of his ill health—while Antony went to the overseas provinces to collect the money they had promised to the soldiers. Once again they divided the provinces among themselves as before and took those of Lepidus besides.[6] For, at the request of Octavian, they decided to make Cisalpine Gaul autonomous, as the elder Caesar had intended, and Lepidus had been accused of betraying their interests[7] to Pompeius. It was also decided that, if Octavian found the accusation to be false, they would recompense Lepidus with other provinces. They also discharged those who had com-

9

10

11

12

13

tail by Appian in Book 4 of the *Civil Wars*. This Lepidus is not the famous triumvir, but Publius Aemilius Lepidus, who is known from coins issued in Crete and Cyrene.

[6] For the original distribution of provinces, see App. *BCiv.* 4.2.7.

[7] Or, possibly, "the interests of the state" (*ta patria* rather than *ta pragmata*): a word seems to have dropped out of the manuscripts.

νον ἐστρατευμένους χωρὶς ὀκτακισχιλίων, οὓς δεηθέν-
τας ἔτι στρατεύεσθαι σφίσιν ἀποδεξάμενοι διείλοντο
14 καὶ συνελόχισαν ἐς στρατηγίδας τάξεις. ὁ δὲ λοιπὸς
αὐτοῖς στρατὸς ἐγένετο, σὺν τοῖς μεταθεμένοις ἀπὸ
Βρούτου, τέλη πεζῶν ἔνδεκα καὶ ἱππέες μύριοις καὶ
τετρακισχίλιοι. καὶ ἔσχεν αὐτῶν ὁ μὲν Ἀντώνιος διὰ
τὴν ἀποδημίαν ἐξ τέλη καὶ ἱππέας μυρίους, ὁ δὲ
Καῖσαρ ἱππέας τετρακισχιλίους καὶ τέλη πέντε· καὶ
τῶνδε δὲ αὐτῶν Ἀντωνίῳ ⟨δύο ἔδωκεν⟩,[3] ἀντιληψόμε-
νος ἐκ τῶν ὑπὸ Καληνῷ τοῦ Ἀντωνίου κατὰ τὴν
Ἰταλίαν ὑπολελειμμένων.

15 4. Ὁ μὲν δὴ Καῖσαρ ἐπὶ τὸν Ἰόνιον ᾔει, ὁ δὲ
Ἀντώνιος ἐν Ἐφέσῳ γενόμενος τῇ θεῷ μεγαλοπρεπῶς
ἔθυε καὶ τοὺς καταφυγόντας ἐκ τῆς Βρούτου καὶ Κασσίου συμφορᾶς ἐς τὸ ἱερὸν ἱκέτας ἀπέλυε, χωρὶς Πε-
τρωνίου, συνεγνωκότος ἐπὶ τῷ φόνῳ Καίσαρος, καὶ
Κοΐντου, προδόντος ἐν Λαοδικείᾳ Κασσίῳ Δολοβέλ-
16 λαν. τοὺς δὲ Ἕλληνας καὶ ὅσα ἄλλα ἔθνη τὴν ἀμφὶ
τὸ Πέργαμον Ἀσίαν νέμονται, κατά τε πρεσβείας
παρόντας ἐπὶ συνθέσει καὶ μετακεκλημένους συν-
17 αγαγὼν ἔλεξεν ὧδε· "Ὑμᾶς ἡμῖν, ὦ ἄνδρες Ἕλληνες,
Ἄτταλος ὁ βασιλεὺς ὑμῶν ἐν διαθήκαις ἀπέλιπε, καὶ
εὐθὺς ἀμείνονες ὑμῖν ἦμεν Ἀττάλου· οὓς γὰρ ἐτελεῖτε

---

3 δύο ἔδωκεν add. Schweig.

---

8 Quintus Fufius Calenus was a partisan of Julius Caesar and
one of his senior officers in the civil wars. Consul in 47, he joined

pleted their full period of service, apart from eight thousand who asked to remain under arms with them. These they accepted, dividing them between themselves, and incorporated into their praetorian cohorts. Their remaining army, along with those who had come over from Brutus, numbered eleven legions of infantry and fourteen thousand cavalry. Of these, Antony kept six legions and ten thousand horse because he was going to be operating abroad, and Octavian five legions and four thousand horse. Two of these, however, he gave to Antony, in exchange for two of Antony's legions that had been left behind in Italy under the command of Calenus.[8] 14

4. So Octavian left for the Ionian gulf. As for Antony, having arrived at Ephesus, he offered splendid sacrifice to the goddess and pardoned those who, after the disaster suffered by Brutus and Cassius, had fled to the sanctuary as suppliants—except for Petronius, who had been implicated in the murder of Caesar, and Quintus, who had betrayed Dolabella to Cassius at Laodicea. He called a meeting of the Greeks and other peoples who live in Asia around Pergamum, both their representatives who were there on a diplomatic mission to conclude an agreement, and others who had been summoned, and delivered a speech as follows: "Men of Greece, your King Attalus bequeathed you to us in his will, and we immediately proved better for you than Attalus.[9] For we remitted the taxes you 15

16

17

Antony after Caesar's death. He commanded eleven legions in Transalpine Gaul for Antony but died in 40, and his son handed over his legions to Octavian.

[9] Attalus III of Pergamum died in 133, leaving his kingdom to Rome.

φόρους Ἀττάλῳ, μεθήκαμεν ὑμῖν, μέχρι δημοκόπων
18 ἀνδρῶν καὶ παρ᾽ ἡμῖν γενομένων ἐδέησε φόρων. ἐπεὶ
δὲ ἐδέησεν, οὐ πρὸς τὰ τιμήματα ὑμῖν ἐπεθήκαμεν, ὡς
ἂν ἡμεῖς ἀκίνδυνον φόρον ἐκλέγοιμεν, ἀλλὰ μέρη
φέρειν τῶν ἑκάστοτε καρπῶν ἐπετάξαμεν, ἵνα καὶ τῶν
19 ἐναντίων κοινωνῶμεν ὑμῖν. τῶν δὲ ταῦτα παρὰ τῆς
βουλῆς μισθουμένων ἐνυβριζόντων ὑμῖν καὶ πολὺ
πλείονα αἰτούντων, Γάιος Καῖσαρ τῶν μὲν χρημάτων
τὰ τρίτα ὑμῖν ἀνῆκεν ὧν ἐκείνοις ἐφέρετε, τὰς δ᾽
ὕβρεις ἔπαυσεν· ὑμῖν γὰρ τοὺς φόρους ἐπέτρεψεν
20 ἀγείρειν παρὰ τῶν γεωργούντων. καὶ τόνδε τοιόνδε
ὄντα οἱ χρηστοὶ τῶν ἡμετέρων πολιτῶν τύραννον ἐκάλουν, καὶ ὑμεῖς αὐτοῖς συνετελεῖτε χρήματα πολλά,
σφαγεῦσί τε οὖσι τοῦ ὑμετέρου εὐεργέτου, καὶ καθ᾽
ἡμῶν τῶν τιμωρούντων ἐκείνῳ.

21   5. "Τῆς δὲ δικαίας τύχης οὐχ, ὡς ἐβούλεσθε, ἀλλ᾽,
ὡς ἦν ἄξιον, κρινάσης τὸν πόλεμον, εἰ μὲν ὡς συν-
αγωνισταῖς τῶν πολεμίων ἔδει χρῆσθαι, κολάσεως
ὑμῖν ἔδει, ἐπεὶ δὲ ἑκόντες πιστεύομεν ὑμᾶς κατὰ ἀνάγκην τάδε πεποιηκέναι, τῶν μὲν μειζόνων ἀφίεμεν,
χρημάτων δὲ ἡμῖν δεῖ καὶ γῆς καὶ πόλεων ἐς τὰ νι-
κητήρια τοῦ στρατοῦ, τέλη δέ ἐστιν ὀκτὼ καὶ εἴκοσιν
ὁπλιτῶν, ἃ μετὰ τῶν συντασσομένων εἰσὶ μυριάδες
ἀνδρῶν ὑπὲρ ἑπτακαίδεκα, καὶ τούτων ἄνευθεν οἱ ἱπ-
22 πέες καὶ ἕτερος ὅμιλος ἑκατέρου⁴ στρατοῦ. ἐκ μὲν δὴ
τοῦ πλήθους τῶν ἀνδρῶν τὸ πλῆθος τῆς χρείας συν-
ορᾶν δύνασθε. τὴν δὲ γῆν καὶ τὰς πόλεις αὐτοῖς δια-
δώσων ὁ Καῖσαρ ἄπεισιν ἐς τὴν Ἰταλίαν, εἰ χρὴ τῷ

had been paying him, until with the rise of populist leaders
among us too, we needed tribute. But when the need   18
arose, we did not tax you according to property valuations,
so that we could collect a sum not subject to fluctuations,
but we required you to pay a percentage of your yearly
harvest in order that we would share with you the bad
harvests too. And when those who bought their contract   19
to collect these taxes from the senate were treating you
violently and demanding much more, Gaius Caesar remitted a third of the sum of money you were paying them,
and brought an end to their assaults. For he entrusted to
you the job of collecting the taxes from the cultivators.
This was the kind of man our 'good' citizens called a tyrant,   20
while you yourselves contributed large amounts of money
to the murderers of your benefactor in opposition to us,
who were seeking to avenge him.

5. "Now that just fortune has decided the war, not as   21
you wished, but as was right, if we were required to treat
you as accomplices of our enemies, we would have to punish you. Since we are willing, however, to believe that you
were forced to act in this way, we will release you from the
heavier penalty, but we need money and land and towns as
the rewards of victory for our soldiers. There are twenty-
eight legions of infantry that, with the auxiliaries, number
more than one hundred and seventy thousand men, not
including the cavalry and other units from the two armies.
You can well imagine the scale of our need from the vast   22
number of men. Octavian is going to Italy to provide them
with the land and the cities—to uproot the Italian popula-

---

4 ἑτέρου codd.; ἑκατέρου Étienne-Duplessis

23 λόγῳ τὸ ἔργον εἰπεῖν, ἀναστήσων τὴν Ἰταλίαν. ὑμᾶς
δ᾽, ἵνα μὴ γῆς καὶ πόλεων καὶ οἰκιῶν καὶ ἱερῶν καὶ
τάφων ἀνίστησθε, ἐς τὰ χρήματα ἐλογισάμεθα, οὐδὲ
ἐς ἅπαντα (οὐδὲ γὰρ ἂν δύναισθε), ἀλλὰ μέρος αὐτῶν
καὶ βραχύτατον, ὃ καὶ πυθομένους ὑμᾶς ἀγαπήσειν
24 οἴομαι. ἃ γὰρ ἔδοτε τοῖς ἡμετέροις ἐχθροῖς ἐν ἔτεσι
δύο (ἔδοτε δὲ φόρους δέκα ἐτῶν), ταῦτα λαβεῖν ἀρκέ-
σει μόνα, ἀλλ᾽ ἑνὶ ἔτει· ἐπείγουσι γὰρ αἱ χρεῖαι. συν-
εῖσι δὲ τῆς χάριτος ὑμῖν τοσοῦτον ἂν ἐπείποιμι, ὅτι
μηδενὸς ἁμαρτήματος ἴσον ἐπιτίμιον ὁρίζεται."

25   6. Ὁ μὲν οὕτως εἶπεν, ἐς ὀκτὼ καὶ εἴκοσι τέλη πεζῶν
τὴν χάριν περιφέρων, ὅτι, οἶμαι, τρία καὶ τεσσαράκοντα ἦν αὐτοῖς, ὅτε ἐν Μουτίνῃ συνηλλάσσοντο ἀλλήλοις καὶ τάδε ὑπισχνοῦντο, ὁ δὲ πόλεμος αὐτὰ ἐς
26 τοσοῦτον ὑπενηνόχει· οἱ δὲ Ἕλληνες ἔτι λέγοντος
αὐτοῦ ταῦτα ἐρρίπτουν ἑαυτοὺς ἐς τὸ ἔδαφος, ἀνάγκην καὶ βίαν ἐς αὐτοὺς ἐκ Βρούτου καὶ Κασσίου
γενομένας ἐπιλέγοντες οὐκ ἐπιτιμίων ἀξίας εἶναι,
ἀλλ᾽ ἐλέου, δόντες δ᾽ ἂν τοῖς εὐεργέταις ἑκόντες ἀπο-
ρεῖν διὰ τοὺς πολεμίους, οἷς οὐ τὰ χρήματα μόνον,
ἀλλὰ καὶ τὰ σκεύη καὶ τοὺς κόσμους ἐσενεγκεῖν ἀντὶ
τῶν χρημάτων, τοὺς δὲ αὐτὰ παρὰ σφίσιν ἐς νόμισμα
27 χαλκεῦσαι. καὶ τέλος παρακαλοῦντες ἔτυχον ἐννέα
ἐτῶν φόρους ἐσενεγκεῖν ἔτεσι δύο. βασιλεῦσι δὲ καὶ
δυνάσταις καὶ πόλεσιν ἐλευθέραις ἄλλα ἐς τὴν ἑκάστων δύναμιν ἐπετάχθη.

28   7. Περιιόντι δ᾽ αὐτῷ τὰ ἔθνη Λεύκιός τε ὁ Κασσίου
ἀδελφὸς καὶ ὅσοι ἄλλοι τῶν δεδιότων ἐπεὶ τῆς ἐν

tion, if we are to call a deed by its real name. So that we   23
do not have to remove you from your land and towns and
homes and sanctuaries and tombs, we have assessed you
for the money, not for all of it (you would not be able to
pay that), but for a part, a very small part, which I think
you will like when you find out what it is. It will be enough   24
if we take simply the same amount as you contributed to
our enemies in two years (and that was the taxes of ten
years), but in one year, since our needs are urgent. You are
well aware of the favor we are doing you, so I would add
only this, that the penalty being fixed is not sufficient for
a single one of the wrongs you have committed."

6. Antony spoke in this way, limiting the reward to   25
twenty-eight legions of infantry, because, I think, they had
forty-three legions when they reached their agreement at
Mutina and made this promise, but the war had reduced
them to this number. While he was still speaking, the   26
Greeks threw themselves on the ground, declaring that, as
they had been subjected to force and violence by Brutus
and Cassius, they deserved pity, not punishment. While
they would willingly contribute to their benefactors, they
did not have the resources. This was because of their enemies, to whom they had delivered not only money, but,
in place of money, their tools and their ornaments, and
who had minted coins from this material in their very
presence. In the end, their pleas were successful: they   27
were to pay the taxes of nine years in two. Tribute was
imposed on kings and princes and free cities in accordance
with the capacity of each to pay.

7. While Antony was touring the provinces, Lucius the   28
brother of Cassius and all the others who feared for their

13

Ἐφέσῳ συγγνώμης ἐπύθοντο, ἱκέται προσῄεσαν. καὶ ἀπέλυε πάντας, πλὴν τοὺς συνεγνωκότας ἐπὶ φόνῳ Καίσαρος· τούτοις γὰρ δὴ μόνοις ἀδιάλλακτος ἦν.

29 παρηγόρει δὲ καὶ τῶν πόλεων τὰς μάλιστα δεινὰ παθούσας, Λυκίους μὲν ἀτελεῖς φόρων ἀφιεὶς καὶ Ξάνθον οἰκίζειν παραινῶν, Ῥοδίοις δὲ διδοὺς Ἄνδρον τε καὶ Τῆνον καὶ Νάξον καὶ Μύνδον, ἃς οὐ πολὺ ὕστε-

30 ρον ἀφῃρέθησαν ὡς σκληρότερον ἄρχοντες. Λαοδικέας δὲ καὶ Ταρσέας ἐλευθέρους ἡφίει καὶ ἀτελεῖς φόρων· καὶ Ταρσέων τοὺς πεπραμένους ἀπέλυε τῆς δουλείας διατάγματι. Ἀθηναίοις δ' ἐς αὐτὸν ἐλθοῦσι μετὰ Τῆνον Αἴγιναν ἔδωκε καὶ Ἴκον καὶ Κέω καὶ

31 Σκίαθον καὶ Πεπάρηθον. ἐπιπαριὼν δὲ Φρυγίαν τε καὶ Μυσίαν καὶ Γαλάτας τοὺς ἐν Ἀσίᾳ Καππαδοκίαν τε καὶ Κιλικίαν καὶ Συρίαν τὴν κοίλην καὶ Παλαιστίνην καὶ τὴν Ἰτουραίαν καὶ ὅσα ἄλλα γένη Σύρων, ἅπασιν ἐσφορὰς ἐπέβαλλε βαρείας καὶ διῇτα πόλεσι καὶ βασιλεῦσιν, ἐν μὲν Καππαδοκίᾳ Ἀριαράθῃ τε καὶ Σισίνῃ, ὧν τῷ Σισίνῃ συνέπραξεν ἐς τὴν βασιλείαν, καλῆς οἱ φανείσης τῆς μητρὸς τοῦ Σισίνου Γλαφύρας· ἐν δὲ Συρίᾳ τοὺς κατὰ πόλεις ἐξῄρει τυράννους.

32 8. Καὶ ἐν Κιλικίᾳ πρὸς αὐτὸν ἐλθούσης Κλεοπάτρας ἐμέμψατο μὲν ὡς οὐ μετασχούσης τῶν ἐπὶ Καίσαρι πόνων· τῆς δὲ οὐκ ἀπολογουμένης μᾶλλον ἢ καταλογιζομένης αὐτοῖς, ὅτι καὶ τὰ παρὰ οἷ τέσσαρα

safety approached him as suppliants when they heard of
his mercy at Ephesus. He released them all, except those
who had been involved in the assassination of Caesar: to
these alone he was unforgiving. He gave relief to those   29
cities that had suffered particularly badly, exempting the
Lycians, on the one hand, from tax and encouraging them
to resettle Xanthus, and granting to Rhodes, on the other,
Andros and Tenos and Naxos and Myndus, which were
taken away from them not long afterward because they
ruled them too harshly. He made Laodicea and Tarsus free   30
cities and released them from taxes, and liberated by de-
cree all those inhabitants of Tarsus who had been sold into
slavery. When the Athenians came to him to make a claim
for Tenos, he gave them Aegina and Icos and Ceos and
Sciathos and Peparethos. He passed through Phrygia and   31
Mysia and Galatia and Cappadocia and Cilicia and Coele-
Syria and Palestine and Ituraea, and the lands of all the
other Syrian peoples, and imposed heavy contributions on
them all. He also acted as arbitrator for kings and cities:
in Cappadocia, for example, in the dispute between Ariarathes and Sisina, he awarded the kingdom to Sisina,
because his mother, Glaphyra, struck him as a beautiful
woman.[10] Or again, in Syria he expelled the city tyrants.

8. When Cleopatra came to meet him in Cilicia, he   32
blamed her for not taking part in the struggles made on
Caesar's behalf. Instead of defending herself, she listed
the things she had done for him and Octavian. She had

[10] Glaphyra was the wife of Archelaus, high-priest ruler of the
temple estate of Comana in Pontus. Antony later had an affair
with her, and she induced him to make Sisina king of Cappadocia.
To do this, Antony had to remove Ariarathes X of Cappadocia.

τέλη πρὸς Δολοβέλλαν αὐτίκα πέμψειε, καὶ στόλον
ἄλλον ἕτοιμον ἔχουσα κωλυθείη ὑπό τε ἀνέμου καὶ
αὐτοῦ Δολοβέλλα, ταχυτέρας ἥσσης τυχόντος, Κασσίῳ τε δὶς ἀπειλοῦντι μὴ συμμαχήσειε καὶ σφίσιν
ἐκείνοις πολεμοῦσιν ἐς τὸν Ἰόνιον αὐτὴ τὸν στόλον
ἔχουσα πλεύσειε μετὰ παρασκευῆς βαρυτάτης, οὔτε
δείσασα Κάσσιον οὔτε φυλαξαμένη Μοῦρκον ναυλο-
χοῦντα, μέχρι χειμὼν τά τε ἄλλα διελυμήνατο καὶ
αὐτὴν ἐς νόσον ἐνέβαλεν, ἧς δὴ χάριν οὐδ᾿ ὕστερον
33 ἐπαναχθῆναι νενικηκότων ἤδη, ὁ Ἀντώνιος ἐπὶ τῇ
ὄψει τὴν σύνεσιν καταπλαγεὶς εὐθὺς αὐτῆς μειρακιω-
δῶς ἑαλώκει, καίπερ ἔτη τεσσαράκοντα γεγονώς, λεγόμενος μὲν ὑγρότατος ἐς ταῦτα ἀεὶ φῦναι, λεγόμενος
δ᾿ ἐς ταύτην καὶ πάλαι, παῖδα ἔτι οὖσαν, ἐρέθισμά τι
τῆς ὄψεως λαβεῖν, ὅτε ἐπὶ τὴν Ἀλεξάνδρειαν Γαβινίῳ
στρατεύοντι νέος ἱππαρχῶν εἵπετο.

34   9. Εὐθὺς οὖν Ἀντωνίῳ μὲν ἡ περὶ ἅπαντα τέως
ἐπιμέλεια ἀθρόα ἠμβλύνετο, Κλεοπάτρα δ᾿ ὅ τι προσ-
τάξειεν, ἐγίγνετο, οὐ διακριδὸν ἔτι περὶ τῶν ὁσίων ἢ
δικαίων, ἐπεὶ καὶ τὴν ἀδελφὴν αὐτῆς Ἀρσινόην, ἱκέτιν
οὖσαν ἐν Μιλήτῳ τῆς Λευκοφρυηνῆς Ἀρτέμιδος, πέμ-
35 ψας ὁ Ἀντώνιος ἀνεῖλε, καὶ Σεραπίωνα, τὸν ἐν Κύπρῳ
στρατηγὸν αὐτῆς, συμμαχήσαντα Κασσίῳ, Τυρίων

---

11 In 55, Aulus Gabinius (consul in 58) led an expedition from
Syria, where he was governor, to Egypt to restore Ptolemy XII
Auletes, who had been deposed. Antony was twenty-seven at the
time and Cleopatra sixteen.

immediately sent the four legions that were with her to
Dolabella; she had prepared another fleet, but had been
frustrated by the wind and by Dolabella himself, who had
been defeated too quickly; although Cassius had threatened her twice, she had not sent him military assistance;
she had personally sailed with her heavily equipped fleet
into the Ionian gulf to assist the triumvirs in their campaign against these men, neither fearing Cassius nor taking precautions against Murcus who was lying in ambush
for her at sea; eventually a storm not only caused general
damage, but also brought on some illness in her, which was
the reason she had not even put to sea again later on when
the triumvirs had already gained their victory. Antony was   33
struck by her intelligence as well as her good looks, and
immediately fell in love with her as if he were a teenager,
although he was forty years old. It is said that he was by
nature always very prone to such behavior, and that he had
been attracted to her a long time ago at first sight when
she was still a girl and he was a young man serving as
cavalry commander on Gabinius' expedition to Alexandria.[11]

9. And so with immediate effect, Antony's former at-   34
tention to detail began to lose its edge completely, and
whatever Cleopatra ordered happened, without regard
any more for what was sacred or just. When, for example,
her sister Arsinoe was a suppliant in Miletus at the temple
of Artemis Leucophryne, Antony sent off to have her
killed; and he ordered the Tyrians to hand over to Cleo-   35
patra her governor of Cyprus, Serapion, who had given

ὄντα ἱκέτην, ἐκέλευσε τοὺς Τυρίους ἐκδοῦναι τῇ Κλεοπάτρᾳ, ἐκδοῦναι δὲ καὶ Ἀραδίους ἕτερον ἱκέτην, ὅν
τινα, Πτολεμαίου τοῦ ἀδελφοῦ τῆς Κλεοπάτρας ἀφα-
νοῦς ἐν τῇ πρὸς Καίσαρα κατὰ τὸν Νεῖλον ναυμαχίᾳ
γενομένου, οἱ Ἀράδιοι εἶχον λέγοντα Πτολεμαῖον εἶ-
36   ναι. καὶ τὸν ἐν Ἐφέσῳ δὲ τῆς Ἀρτέμιδος ἱερέα, ὃν
Μεγάβυζον ἡγοῦνται, ὑποδεξάμενόν ποτε τὴν Ἀρσινόην ὡς βασιλίδα ἀχθῆναι μὲν ἐκέλευσεν, Ἐφεσίων
δ᾽ αὐτὴν Κλεοπάτραν ἱκετευσάντων μεθῆκεν. οὕτω
μὲν ὁ Ἀντώνιος ἐνήλλακτο ταχέως, καὶ τὸ πάθος αὐτῷ
τοῦτο ἀρχὴ καὶ τέλος τῶν ἔπειτα κακῶν ἐγένετο.
37   ἀποπλευσάσης δὲ τῆς Κλεοπάτρας ἐς τὰ οἰκεῖα, ὁ
Ἀντώνιος ἔπεμπε τοὺς ἱππέας Πάλμυρα πόλιν, οὐ μακρὰν οὖσαν ἀπὸ Εὐφράτου, διαρπάσαι, μικρὰ μὲν
ἐπικαλῶν αὐτοῖς, ὅτι Ῥωμαίων καὶ Παρθυαίων ὄντες
ἐφόριοι ἐς ἑκατέρους ἐπιδεξίως εἶχον (ἔμποροι γὰρ
ὄντες κομίζουσι μὲν ἐκ Περσῶν τὰ Ἰνδικὰ ἢ Ἀράβια,
διατίθενται δ᾽ ἐν τῇ Ῥωμαίων), ἔργῳ δ᾽ ἐπινοῶν τοὺς
38   ἱππέας περιουσιάσαι. Παλμυρηνῶν δὲ προμαθόντων
καὶ τὰ ἀναγκαῖα ἐς τὸ πέραν τοῦ ποταμοῦ μετενεγκάν-
των τε καὶ ἐπὶ τῆς ὄχθης, εἴ τις ἐπιχειροίη σκευα-
σαμένων τόξοις, πρὸς ἃ πεφύκασιν ἐξαιρέτως, οἱ ἱππέες τὴν πόλιν κενὴν καταλαβόντες ὑπέστρεψαν, οὔτε
ἐς χεῖρας ἐλθόντες οὔτε τι λαβόντες.

---

12 Both Dio (48.24.2) and Josephus (*AJ* 15.89) indicate that
Arsinoe was a suppliant at the temple of Artemis in Ephesus.
Strabo (14.40) and others refer to a cult of Artemis Leucophryne
at Magnesia-on-the-Meander, rather than at Tyre.

military assistance to Cassius and was now a suppliant at Tyre.[12] He also ordered the Aradians to give up another suppliant, a man they were holding who, after the disappearance of Cleopatra's brother Ptolemy at the naval battle against Caesar on the Nile, claimed to be Ptolemy.[13] He ordered the priest of Artemis at Ephesus, whom they call Megabyzus,[14] to be brought to him for once receiving Arsinoe as queen, but released him when the Ephesians petitioned Cleopatra herself. Such was the way in which Antony changed so quickly, and this passion of his became the beginning and end of his subsequent troubles. When Cleopatra sailed off home, Antony sent his cavalry to plunder Palmyra, which is situated not far from the Euphrates.[15] He brought a trivial accusation against its inhabitants: living on the frontier between Rome and Parthia, they managed both sides with dexterity (and indeed being merchants, they import Indian and Arabian goods from Persia and dispose of them in Roman territory); but in fact, his intention was to enrich his cavalry. The Palmyrenes were forewarned, however, and having carried their essentials over to the other side of the river, stationed themselves on the bank to face any attack, equipped with bows, with which they are exceptionally expert. The cavalry found the city deserted and without fighting returned empty-handed.

36

37

38

13 Cleopatra's brother, Ptolemy XIII Theos Philopator, tried to remove her as joint ruler, but with Caesar's help, she won, and Ptolemy drowned at the battle of the Nile (47).

14 Strabo (14.1.23) says the priests were eunuchs called Megabyzi.

15 It is some 125 miles away.

39   10. Καὶ δοκεῖ τόδε τὸ ἔργον Ἀντωνίῳ τὸν μετ᾽ οὐ
πολὺ Παρθυικὸν πόλεμον ἐξάψαι, πολλῶν ἐκ Συρίας
τυράννων ἐς αὐτοὺς συμφυγόντων. ἡ γὰρ Συρία μέχρι μὲν ἐπ᾽ Ἀντίοχον τὸν Εὐσεβῆ καὶ τὸν τοῦ Εὐσε-
βοῦς υἱὸν Ἀντίοχον ὑπὸ τοῖς ἐκ Σελεύκου τοῦ Νικάτο-
ρος ἐβασιλεύετο, ὥς μοι περὶ Σύρων λέγοντι εἴρηται·
40 Πομπηίου δ᾽ αὐτὴν Ῥωμαίοις προσλαβόντος καὶ
στρατηγὸν αὐτῇ Σκαῦρον ἀποδείξαντος, ἡ βουλὴ
μετὰ Σκαῦρον ἔπεμψεν ἑτέρους καὶ Γαβίνιον τὸν
Ἀλεξανδρεῦσι πολεμήσαντα, ἐπὶ δὲ Γαβινίῳ Κράσσον τὸν ἐν Παρθυαίοις ἀποθανόντα καὶ Βύβλον ἐπὶ
41 τῷ Κράσσῳ. παρὰ δὲ τὴν Γαΐου Καίσαρος ἄρα τελευ-
τὴν καὶ στάσιν ἐπ᾽ αὐτῇ κατὰ πόλεις ὑπὸ τυράννων
εἴχετο, συλλαμβανόντων τοῖς τυράννοις τῶν Παρθυ-
αίων· ἐσέβαλον γὰρ δὴ καὶ ἐς τὴν Συρίαν οἱ Παρθυ-
αῖοι μετὰ τὴν Κράσσου συμφορὰν καὶ συνέπραξαν
42 τοῖς τυράννοις. οὓς ὁ Ἀντώνιος ἐξελαύνων ὑποφεύγον-
τας ἐς τὴν Παρθυηνὴν καὶ τοῖς πλήθεσιν ἐπιβάλλων
ἐσφορὰς βαρυτάτας καὶ ἐς Παλμυρηνοὺς τάδε ἁμαρ-
τών, οὐδ᾽ ἐπέμεινε συστῆσαι τὴν χώραν θορυβου-
μένην, ἀλλὰ τὸν στρατὸν ἐς τὰ ἔθνη διελὼν χειμά-
σοντα αὐτὸς ἐς Αἴγυπτον ᾔει πρὸς Κλεοπάτραν.
43   11. Ἡ δὲ αὐτὸν ἐπεδέχετο λαμπρῶς. καὶ ὁ μὲν
ἐχείμαζεν ἐνταῦθα, ἄνευ σημείων ἡγεμονίας, ἰδιώτου

---

16 Antiochus X Eusebes Philopator ("Pious, Father-loving"),
ruled from 95 and was succeeded by his son, Antiochus XIII

10. It seems that this action lit the fuse on the Parthian 39
war Antony faced shortly afterward, as many of the Syrian
tyrants had taken refuge with the Parthians. For until the
time of Antiochus Eusebes and his son Antiochus, Syria
had been ruled by the descendants of Seleucus Nicator, as
I have related when I was talking about the Syrians.[16]
Pompey annexed it for Rome, and appointed Scaurus to 40
govern it.[17] After Scaurus, the senate sent, among others,
Gabinius, who made war on the Alexandrians, and after
Gabinius, Crassus, who died in Parthia, and after Crassus,
Bibulus. At the time of Caesar's death and the civil unrest 41
that followed, the Syrian cities came under the control of
tyrants, who were supported by the Parthians. For the
latter, of course, invaded Syria after the disaster suffered
by Crassus, and cooperated with the tyrants. Antony ex- 42
pelled these tyrants, who took refuge in Parthia, imposed
very heavy taxes on the ordinary people and met with the
failure already mentioned against the Palmyrenes. He did
not even stay, however, to restore order to the troubled
land, but distributed his army in winter quarters in the
provinces, while he himself went to Egypt to join Cleopatra.

11. She gave him a splendid reception, and he spent 43
the winter there without displaying the insignia of com-

Asiaticus, who was eventually deposed by Pompey in 64. Appian
mentions these last Seleucid kings briefly (*Syr.* 48.248–49), but
he had dealt extensively with the founder of the dynasty, Seleucus
I Nicator (*Syr.* 53.267–63.331).

[17] For Appian's coverage of the first Roman governors from
Marcus Aemilius Scaurus to Marcus Calpurnius Bibulus, see *Syr.*
51.255–59.

σχῆμα καὶ βίον ἔχων, εἴθ' ὡς ἐν ἀλλοτρίᾳ τε ἀρχῇ
καὶ βασιλευούσῃ πόλει, εἴτε τὴν χειμασίαν ὡς παν-
ήγυριν ἄγων, ἐπεὶ καὶ φροντίδας ἀπετέθειτο καὶ
ἡγεμόνων θεραπείαν, καὶ στολὴν εἶχε τετράγωνον
Ἑλληνικὴν ἀντὶ τῆς πατρίου, καὶ ὑπόδημα ἦν αὐτῷ
λευκὸν Ἀττικόν, ὃ καὶ Ἀθηναίων ἔχουσιν ἱερεῖς καὶ
44   Ἀλεξανδρέων, καὶ καλοῦσι φαικάσιον. ἔξοδοί τε ἦσαν
αὐτῷ ἐς ἱερὰ ἢ γυμνάσια ἢ φιλολόγων διατριβὰς μόναι καὶ δίαιτα μεθ' Ἑλλήνων ὑπὸ Κλεοπάτρᾳ, ᾗ δὴ
καὶ μάλιστα τὴν ἐπιδημίαν ἀνετίθει.

45   12. Καὶ τὰ μὲν περὶ Ἀντώνιον ἦν τοιάδε· Καίσαρι
δὲ ἐς τὴν Ῥώμην ἐπανιόντι ἥ τε νόσος αὖθις ἤκμαζεν
ἐν Βρεντεσίῳ μάλιστα ἐπικινδύνως, καὶ φήμη διή-
46   νεγκεν αὐτὸν καὶ τεθνάναι. ῥαΐσας δ' ἐσῆλθεν ἐς τὴν
πόλιν καὶ τοῖς Ἀντωνίου τὰ γράμματα ἐδείκνυε τὰ
Ἀντωνίου. οἱ δὲ Καληνόν τε προσέτασσον ἀποδοῦναι
τὰ δύο τέλη τῷ Καίσαρι καὶ ἐς Λιβύην ἐπέστελλον
47   Σεξτίῳ Λιβύης καὶ αὐτὸν Καίσαρι ἀποστῆναι. καὶ
οἱ μὲν οὕτως ἐποίουν, ὁ δὲ Καῖσαρ οὐδὲν ἀνήκεστον
ἁμαρτεῖν δόξαντι Λεπίδῳ Λιβύην ἀντὶ τῶν προτέρων
ἐθνῶν ἐνήλλασσε καὶ τὰ λοιπὰ τῶν ἐπὶ ταῖς προγρα-
48   φαῖς δεδημευμένων διεπίπρασκε. καταλέγοντι δ' αὐτῷ
τὸν στρατὸν ἐς τὰς ἀποικίας καὶ τὴν γῆν ἐπινέμοντι
δυσεργὲς ἦν. οἵ τε γὰρ στρατιῶται τὰς πόλεις ᾔτουν,
αἳ αὐτοῖς ἀριστίνδην ἦσαν ἐπειλεγμέναι πρὸ τοῦ πολέμου, καὶ αἱ πόλεις ἠξίουν τὴν Ἰταλίαν ἅπασαν ἐπι-

mand, and wearing the clothes and leading the life of a
private person. He did this either because he was in a
kingdom ruled by someone else, in a sovereign city, or
because he was treating the winter as a holiday. He certainly set aside his worries and his commander's retinue,
and wore the square-cut Greek cloak instead of his native
one, and the white Attic sandal also worn by the Athenian
and Alexandrian priests, which they call a *phaecasium*. His   44
only excursions were to temples or gymnasia or the discussions of scholars, and he spent his time with Greeks, in
deference to Cleopatra, to whom he particularly devoted
his stay in Alexandria.

12. Such was the state of affairs with Antony. As for   45
Octavian, while returning to Rome his illness became
acute again at Brundisium to a very dangerous degree, and
a rumor even spread that he had died. After recovering,   46
he made his way to Rome and brought Antony's letters to
the attention of his staff, who ordered Calenus to hand
over the two legions to Octavian, and also wrote to Sextius
in Africa with instructions to turn that province over to
him.[18] Both men acted accordingly. As Lepidus appeared   47
not to have committed any serious offense, Octavian gave
him Africa in exchange for his previous provinces. He also
sold what remained of the property confiscated during the
proscriptions. But the task of registering the soldiers in   48
their colonies and distributing the land was very difficult.
For the soldiers demanded the towns that had been selected for them as prizes for their courage before the war,
and the towns asked that the whole of Italy should share

[18] For Appian's detailed treatment of Titus Sextius (praetor
45), see 4.52.224–56.242. On Fufius Calenus, see above, note 8.

APPIAN

νείμασθαι τὸ ἔργον ἢ ἐν ἀλλήλαις διαλαχεῖν τῆς τε
γῆς τὴν τιμὴν τοὺς δωρουμένους ᾔτουν, καὶ ἀργύριον
49 οὐκ ἦν, ἀλλὰ συνιόντες ἀνὰ μέρος ἐς τὴν Ῥώμην οἵ
τε νέοι καὶ γέροντες ἢ αἱ γυναῖκες ἅμα τοῖς παιδίοις,
ἐς τὴν ἀγορὰν ἢ τὰ ἱερά, ἐθρήνουν, οὐδὲν μὲν ἀδικῆ-
σαι λέγοντες, Ἰταλιῶται δὲ ὄντες ἀνίστασθαι γῆς τε
50 καὶ ἑστίας οἷα δορίληπτοι. ἐφ᾽ οἷς οἱ Ῥωμαῖοι συν-
ήχθοντο καὶ ἐπεδάκρυον, καὶ μάλιστα, ὅτε ἐνθυμη-
θεῖεν οὐχ ὑπὲρ τῆς πόλεως, ἀλλ᾽ ἐπὶ σφίσιν αὐτοῖς
καὶ τῇ μεταβολῇ τῆς πολιτείας τόν τε πόλεμον γεγονότα καὶ τὰ ἐπινίκια διδόμενα καὶ τὰς ἀποικίας συν-
ισταμένας τοῦ μηδ᾽ αὖθις ἀνακῦψαι τὴν δημοκρατίαν,
παρῳκισμένων τοῖς ἄρχουσι μισθοφόρων ἑτοίμων, ἐς
ὅ τι χρῄζοιεν.

51   13. Ὁ δὲ Καῖσαρ ταῖς πόλεσιν ἐξελογεῖτο τὴν
ἀνάγκην, καὶ ἐδόκουν οὐδ᾽ ὡς ἀρκέσειν. οὐδ᾽ ἤρκουν,
ἀλλὰ ὁ στρατὸς καὶ τοῖς γείτοσιν ἐπέβαινε σὺν ὕβρει,
πλέονά τε τῶν διδομένων σφίσι περισπώμενοι καὶ τὸ
ἄμεινον ἐκλεγόμενοι. οὐδὲ ἐπιπλήσσοντος αὐτοῖς καὶ
δωρουμένου πολλὰ ἄλλα τοῦ Καίσαρος ἐπαύοντο,
ἐπεὶ καὶ τῶν ἀρχόντων, ὡς δεομένων σφῶν ἐς τὸ ἐγ-
52 κρατὲς τῆς ἀρχῆς, κατεφρόνουν. καὶ γὰρ αὐτοῖς ἡ
πενταετία παρῴδευε, καὶ τὸ ἀσφαλὲς ἡ χρεία συνῆγεν
ἀμφοτέροις παρ᾽ ἀλλήλων, τοῖς μὲν ἡγεμόσιν ἐς τὴν
ἀρχὴν παρὰ τοῦ στρατοῦ, τῷ στρατῷ δὲ ἐς τὴν ἐπι-
κράτησιν ὧν ἔλαβον, ἡ τῶν δεδωκότων ἀρχὴ παραμέ-
νουσα. ὡς γὰρ αὐτῶν οὐ βεβαίως ‹ἐπικρατήσοντες,

24

the burden of redistribution, or cast lots with each other, and demanded that those who had received grants of land pay for it. But there was no money. People came in groups 49 to Rome, young men and old ones, women along with their children, and went to complain in the Forum, or the temples, saying that they had done nothing wrong, and that even though they were Italians, they were being forced from their land and hearths as if they had been defeated in war. At this, the people of Rome sympathized with them 50 and wept over the situation, especially when they considered that it was not on behalf of the city, but against themselves and the restoration of the constitution that the war had been fought, the rewards of victory given, and the colonies established, so that the democracy should never again lift its head, mercenaries having been settled alongside them, ready to do whatever the men in power needed.

13. Octavian excused himself to the towns on the 51 grounds of necessity, but they thought that even so, there would not be enough land. And there was not enough. The soldiers encroached violently even on their neighbors, seizing more than they had been given and choosing the better land. Nor did they stop when Octavian reprimanded them and gave them many other gifts, since they had low regard even for their rulers, because they knew that the latter needed them to confirm their power. For their five- 52 year term was running out, and both needed each other for their mutual security, the leaders needing the army to retain their power, and the army to confirm possession of what they had received, needing the continuing rule of those who had given it. In the belief that they would not retain secure control of what they had been given unless those who had given it had security of power, the

εἰ μὴ βεβαίως⟩⁵ ἄρχοιεν οἱ δόντες, ὑπερεμάχουν ἀπ᾽
53 εὐνοίας ἀναγκαίου. πολλὰ δὲ καὶ ἄλλα τοῖς ἀπο-
ρουμένοις αὐτῶν ἐδωρεῖτο, δανειζόμενος ἐκ τῶν ἱερῶν,
ὁ Καῖσαρ. ὅθεν τὴν γνώμην ὁ στρατὸς ἐς αὐτὸν ἐπ-
έστρεφε, καὶ πλείων ὑπήντα χάρις ὡς γῆν ἅμα καὶ
πόλεις καὶ χρήματα καὶ οἰκήματα δωρουμένῳ καὶ
καταβοωμένῳ μὲν ἐπιφθόνως ὑπὸ τῶν ἀφαιρουμένων,
φέροντι δὲ τὴν ὕβριν ἐς χάριν τοῦ στρατοῦ.

54   14. Ταῦτα δὲ ὁρῶν ὅ τε ἀδελφὸς ὁ τοῦ Ἀντωνίου
Λεύκιος Ἀντώνιος, ὑπατεύων τότε, καὶ ἡ γυνὴ τοῦ
Ἀντωνίου Φουλβία καὶ ὁ τῆς ἀποδημίας ἐπιτροπεύων
τῷ Ἀντωνίῳ Μάνιος, ἵνα μὴ Καίσαρος δόξειε τὸ ἔργον ἅπαν εἶναι μηδὲ μόνος αὐτοῦ τὴν χάριν ἀπο-
φέροιτο μηδ᾽ ἔρημος ὁ Ἀντώνιος εὐνοίας στρατιωτῶν
γένοιτο, τὰς κατοικίσεις ἐτέχναζον ἐς τὴν ἐπιδημίαν
55 Ἀντωνίου διατρίβειν. οὐ δυνατοῦ δὲ φαινομένου διὰ
τὸν στρατὸν ἐπείγοντα, τοὺς οἰκιστὰς τῶν Ἀντωνίου
τελῶν ἠξίουν Καίσαρα παρὰ σφῶν λαβεῖν, τῆς μὲν
συνθήκης Ἀντωνίου μόνῳ Καίσαρι διδούσης, ἐπιμεμ-
56 φόμενοι δὲ ὡς οὐ παραδόντι⁶ τῷ Ἀντωνίῳ. καὶ ἐς
τὸν στρατὸν αὐτοὶ τήν τε Φουλβίαν παράγοντες καὶ

---

⁵ ἐπικρατήσοντες, εἰ μὴ βεβαίως add. Schweig.
⁶ παραδόντι P; προδόντι L; παρόντι BJ

soldiers fought for them out of forced goodwill. Octavian 53
made many other gifts to the soldiers in difficulty, borrowing money from the temples. For this reason the army
began to turn their favor on him, and greater gratitude
came his way because he was gifting them land along with
towns and money and houses, and being denounced viru-
lently by the dispossessed, but putting up with the insult
for the sake of the army.

14. When he saw this, Antony's brother, Lucius Anto- 54
nius, who was consul at the time, along with Fulvia, Antony's wife, and Manius, his agent during his absence, tried
to devise ways of delaying the founding of the colonies
until Antony's return, so that it would not seem to be entirely the work of Octavian, and he would not be the only
one to get the credit for it, and Antony would not be deprived of the goodwill of the soldiers.[19] As this appeared 55
to be impossible because the army was pressing its demands, they asked Octavian to take those founding the
colonies for Antony's legions from Antony's men, and even
though the agreement with Antony gave the choice to
Octavian alone, they blamed him for not entrusting it to
Antony.[20] Bringing Fulvia and Antony's children before 56

[19] Lucius Antonius was consul in 41 and was captured by Octavian at Perusia in that year but spared and sent to Spain as
governor. Fulvia was one of the most politically active women of
the Roman Republic. She married three populist leaders, Publius
Clodius Pulcher (d. 52), Gaius Scribonius Curio (d. 49), and Marc
Antony. Antony's agent, Manius, is referred to in an epigram of
Martial (11.20).

[20] Or, perhaps (the text is uncertain), "they found fault with
the fact that Antony was not present."

τὰ παιδία τὰ Ἀντωνίου, μάλα ἐπιφθόνως ἱκέτευον μὴ
περιιδεῖν Ἀντώνιον ἢ δόξης ἢ χάριτος τῆς ἐς αὐτοὺς
57 ὑπηρεσίας ἀφαιρούμενον. ἤκμαζε δὲ ἐν τῷ τότε μάλιστα τὸ κλέος τὸ Ἀντωνίου καὶ παρὰ τῷ στρατῷ καὶ
παρὰ τοῖς ἄλλοις ἅπασι· τὸ γὰρ ἔργον τὸ ἐν Φιλίπποις διὰ τὴν τότε Καίσαρος ἀρρωστίαν ἅπαν ἡγοῦντο
58 Ἀντωνίου γεγονέναι. ὁ δὲ Καῖσαρ οὐκ ἠγνόει μὲν
ἀδικούμενος ἐς τὰ συγκείμενα, εἶξε δὲ ἐς χάριν
Ἀντωνίου. καὶ οἱ μὲν τοὺς οἰκιστὰς ἐπὶ τοῖς Ἀντωνίου
τέλεσιν ἀπέφαινον, οἱ δὲ οἰκισταὶ τοῖς στρατιώταις,
ἵνα τι καὶ δοκοῖεν εὐνούστεροι τοῦ Καίσαρος ἐς
59 αὐτοὺς εἶναι, συνεχώρουν ἔτι πλέον ἀδικεῖν. ἄλλο δὴ
πλῆθος ἦν ἑτέρων πόλεων, αἳ ταῖς νενεμημέναις γει-
τονεύουσαί τε καὶ πολλὰ πρὸς τῶν στρατιωτῶν ἀδι-
κούμενοι κατεβόων τοῦ Καίσαρος, ἀδικωτέρας εἶναι
τὰς ἀποικίσεις τῶν προγραφῶν· τὰς μὲν γὰρ ἐπὶ
ἐχθροῖς, τὰς δὲ ἐπὶ μηδὲν ἀδικοῦσι γίγνεσθαι.

60   15. Ὁ δὲ Καῖσαρ οὐκ ἠγνόει ἀδικουμένους. ἀμήχανα δ᾽ ἦν αὐτῷ· οὔτε γὰρ ἀργύριον ἦν ἐς τιμὴν τῆς
γῆς δίδοσθαι τοῖς γεωργοῖς, οὔτε ἀναβάλλεσθαι τὰ
ἐπινίκια διὰ τοὺς ἔτι πολέμους, Πομπηίου μὲν ἐν τῇ
θαλάσσῃ κρατοῦντος καὶ τὴν πόλιν κλείοντος ἐς λιμόν, Ἀηνοβάρβου δὲ καὶ Μούρκου στρατὸν καὶ ναῦς

---

21 It is not clear who the subject of this sentence is. Gram-
matically, "they" seems to refer to Lucius, Fulvia, and Manius,
the subjects of the previous sentence. Similarly in chapter 58, it

the army, they[21] begged the soldiers in particularly malicious terms not to let Antony be deprived of the glory and gratitude he deserved for his service to them. Antony's 57 reputation was then very much at its height, both among the soldiers and everyone else. For they regarded the victory at Philippi as entirely due to him, on account of Octavian's illness at the time. Although Octavian was well 58 aware that he was being mistreated in relation to the agreement, he yielded as a favor to Antony. So they appointed the leaders of the colonies to be founded for his legions, but in order to appear more well disposed to the soldiers than Octavian, the colony leaders allowed the men to commit yet more injustices. And of course a large 59 number of people from other towns, neighboring on the ones that had been resettled and suffering many injustices at the hands of the soldiers, complained loudly against Octavian that the settlements were more unjust than the proscriptions. For the proscriptions, they argued, targeted personal enemies, the settlements those who had done no wrong.

15. Octavian was not unaware that they were the victims of injustice, but he could do nothing about it, because there was no money to pay the farmers the price of the land, and he could not postpone granting the rewards of victory in view of the wars that were still being fought. Pompeius ruled the sea and was causing famine in Rome with his blockade; Ahenobarbus and Murcus were collect-

seems to have been Lucius, Fulvia, and Manius who appointed the colony leaders, but perhaps Appian is referring more generally to Antony's associates.

ἄλλας ἀγειρόντων ἀθυμοτέρων δὲ ἐς τὰ ἐσόμενα ὄντων ⟨τῶν στρατιωτῶν⟩,[7] εἰ μὴ τὰ πρότερα ἐπινίκια
61 λάβοιεν. πολὺ δ᾽ ἦν καὶ τὸ παροδεύειν σφίσιν ἤδη
τὴν τῆς ἀρχῆς πενταετίαν καὶ χρῄζειν αὖθις εὐνοίας
στρατοῦ· διόπερ αὐτῶν καὶ τῆς ὕβρεως ἢ καταφρονή-
62 σεως ἐν τῷ τότε ἑκὼν ὑπερεώρα. ἔν γέ τοι τῷ θεάτρῳ,
παρόντος αὐτοῦ, στρατιώτης ἀπορῶν οἰκείας ἕδρας
παρῆλθεν ἐς τοὺς καλουμένους ἱππέας· καὶ ὁ μὲν
δῆμος ἐπεσημήνατο, καὶ ὁ Καῖσαρ τὸν στρατιώτην
ἀνέστησεν, ὁ δὲ στρατὸς ἠγανάκτησε καὶ περιστάν-
τες αὐτὸν ἀποχωροῦντα τοῦ θεάτρου τὸν στρατιώτην
63 ἀπῄτουν, οὐχ ὁρώμενον ἡγούμενοι διεφθάρθαι. ἐπελ-
θόντα δὲ ἐνόμιζον ἐκ τοῦ δεσμωτηρίου νῦν προαχθῆ-
ναι ἀρνούμενόν τε καὶ τὰ γεγονότα διηγούμενον ψεύ-
δεσθαι διδαχθέντα ἔλεγον καὶ ἐλοιδόρουν ὡς τὰ κοινὰ
προδιδόντα.

64   16. Καὶ τὸ μὲν ἐν τῷ θεάτρῳ γενόμενον τοιόνδε ἦν.
κεκλημένοι δ᾽ ἐπὶ νέμησιν τότε τῆς γῆς ἐς τὸ πεδίον
τὸ Ἄρειον ὑπὸ σπουδῆς ἔτι νυκτὸς ἀφίκοντο, καὶ βρα-
δύτερον αὐτοῖς τοῦ Καίσαρος ἐπιόντος ἠγανάκτουν.
65 Νώνιος δὲ λοχαγὸς ἐπέπλησσεν αὐτοῖς σὺν παρρη-
σίᾳ, τό τε πρέπον τοῖς ἀρχομένοις ἐς τὸν ἄρχοντα
προφέρων καὶ τὴν Καίσαρος ἀσθένειαν, οὐχ ὑπεροψίαν. οἱ δὲ αὐτὸν τὰ μὲν πρῶτα ἔσκωπτον ὡς κόλακα,
πλέονος δὲ ἑκατέρωθεν τοῦ διερεθίσματος γενομένου
ἐλοιδόρουν τε καὶ ἔβαλλον καὶ φεύγοντα ἐδίωκον ἐς

ing a new fleet and an army; and the soldiers would be less enthusiastic in the future if they did not get the rewards of their previous victory. Also very important was the fact 61 that the triumvirs' five-year term of office was running out, and they again needed the goodwill of an army. For this reason Octavian was willing to overlook for the time being their insolence and disrespect. For example, he was pres- 62 ent in the theater when a soldier who could not find a seat in the right place, went over to the section reserved for the so-called equestrians. The people pointed him out and Octavian had him removed. But the soldiers became annoyed, surrounded Octavian as he left the theater, and demanded that he produce the man, as he was nowhere to be seen and they thought he had been killed. When he 63 turned up, they believed he had just been brought out of the prison, but although he denied this, and explained what had happened, they said he had been coached to lie, and abused him for betraying the common cause.

16. Such was the incident in the theater. When the men 64 were called to the Campus Martius for the distribution of land being made at that time, in their enthusiasm they arrived while it was still night, and grew angry at Octavian for being rather slow to join them. Nonius, a centurion, 65 reprimanded them bluntly, urging due deference from subordinates to their superior, and citing Octavian's ill health, not arrogance, as the cause of the delay. They first mocked him as a flatterer, but then with provocation growing from both sides, they abused him, threw stones at him, and chased him as he fled. When he jumped into the river

---

7 τῶν στρατιωτῶν add. Viereck; ἐς τὰ ἐσόμενα τῶν ἐστρατευμένων ὄντων Étienne-Duplessis

τε τὸν ποταμὸν ἐξαλόμενον ἐξειρύσαντες ἔκανον καὶ
66 ἔρριψαν, ἔνθα παροδεύσειν ὁ Καῖσαρ ἔμελλεν. οἱ μὲν
δὴ φίλοι τῷ Καίσαρι παρῄνουν μηδὲ ἐπελθεῖν ἐς
αὐτούς, ἀλλ' ἐκστῆναι μανιώδει φορᾷ. ὁ δ' ἐπῄει μέν,
ἀναθρέψειν ἔτι μᾶλλον αὐτῶν ἡγούμενος τὸ μανιῶδες,
εἰ μὴ ἀφίκοιτο, καὶ τὸν Νώνιον ἰδὼν ἐξέκλινεν, ὡς δὲ
ὀλίγων ταῦτα δρασάντων ἐπεμέμφετο καὶ ἐς τὸ μέλλον ἀλλήλων φείδεσθαι παρῄνει καὶ τὴν γῆν διένεμε,
καὶ δωρεὰς αἰτεῖν τοῖς ἀξίοις ἐπέτρεπε καὶ τῶν οὐκ
ἀξίων ἐνίοις ἐδίδου παρὰ γνώμην, μέχρι τὸ πλῆθος
ἐκπλαγὲν αὐτοῦ τῆς βαρύτητος μετενόει καὶ ᾐδεῖτο
καὶ κατεγίνωσκον αὐτῶν καὶ τοὺς ἐς τὸν Νώνιον
67 ἁμαρτόντας ἠξίουν ἀνευρόντα κολάσαι. ὁ δὲ καὶ γι-
νώσκειν αὐτοὺς ἔφη καὶ κολάσειν "Αὐτῷ τῷ συνειδότι
σφῶν μόνῳ καὶ τῇ παρ' ὑμῶν καταγνώσει." οἱ δὲ
συγγνώμης τε ὁμοῦ καὶ τιμῆς καὶ δωρεῶν ἀξιωθέντες
εὐθὺς αὐτὸν εὐφήμουν ἐκ μεταβολῆς.

68   17. Καὶ δύο μὲν εἰκόνες ἐκ πλεόνων αἵδε ἔστων τῆς
τότε δυσαρχίας· αἴτιον δ' ἦν, ὅτι καὶ οἱ στρατηγοὶ
ἀχειροτόνητοι ἦσαν οἱ πλείους ὡς ἐν ἐμφυλίοις καὶ οἱ
στρατοὶ αὐτῶν οὐ τοῖς πατρίοις ἔθεσιν ἐκ καταλόγου
συνήγοντο οὐδ' ἐπὶ χρείᾳ τῆς πατρίδος, οὐδὲ τῷ δη-
μοσίῳ στρατευόμενοι μᾶλλον ἢ τοῖς συνάγουσιν αὐτοὺς μόνοις, οὐδὲ τούτοις ὑπὸ ἀνάγκῃ νόμων, ἀλλ'
ὑποσχέσεσιν ἰδίαις, οὐδὲ ἐπὶ πολεμίους κοινούς, ἀλλὰ
ἰδίους ἐχθρούς, οὐδὲ ἐπὶ ξένους, ἀλλὰ πολίτας καὶ

they dragged him out, killed him and threw his body down at a spot where Octavian was due to pass. His associates naturally advised Octavian not even to approach the men, but to stay out of the way of their mad rage. But he went anyway, in the belief that he would feed their madness even more if he did not come. When he saw the body of Nonius he turned away from it and, on the assumption that only a small number had committed this act, he rebuked them and advised them to show forbearance to each other in future. He then began to distribute the land, and allowed the deserving to ask for gifts, and unexpectedly gave grants even to some of those who did not deserve them. Eventually the mob were astonished and regretted their heavy-handed behavior: they became ashamed, began to accuse themselves, and asked Octavian to find and punish those who had committed the crime against Nonius. He replied that he knew who they were and would punish them "only with their own guilty conscience and your condemnation." Having all at once been judged worthy of pardon and respect and gifts, the men immediately changed their opinion and began to speak well of him.

17. Let these two instances, among many, serve as examples of the indiscipline prevailing at that time. The cause was that, as happens in civil wars, most of the generals were not elected, and their armies were not recruited from the register in the ancestral manner, nor to meet their country's need; it was not the public interest they served, but only the men who recruited them, and they did not serve these men under constraint of the laws, but in response to private promises; they did not fight against enemies of the state, but against personal adversaries, nor against foreigners, but against fellow citizens who were

66

67

68

APPIAN

69 ὁμοτίμους. τάδε γὰρ πάντα αὐτοῖς τὸν στρατιωτικὸν
φόβον ἐξέλυεν, οὔτε στρατεύεσθαι νομίζουσι μᾶλλον
ἢ βοηθεῖν οἰκείᾳ χάριτι καὶ γνώμῃ, καὶ τοὺς ἄρχοντας ἡγουμένοις ὑπὸ ἀνάγκης αὐτῶν ἐς τὰ ἴδια ἐπιδεῖ-
70 σθαι. τό τε αὐτομολεῖν, πάλαι Ῥωμαίοις ἀδιάλλακτον
ὄν, τότε καὶ δωρεῶν ἠξιοῦτο· καὶ ἔπρασσον αὐτὸ οἵ
τε στρατοὶ κατὰ πλῆθος καὶ τῶν ἐπιφανῶν ἀνδρῶν
ἔνιοι, νομίζοντες οὐκ αὐτομολίαν εἶναι τὴν ἐς τὰ
71 ὅμοια μεταβολήν. ὅμοια γὰρ δὴ πάντα ἦν, καὶ οὐδὲ
ἕτερα αὐτῶν ἐς ἔχθραν κοινὴν Ῥωμαίοις ἀπεκέκριτο·
ἥ τε τῶν στρατηγῶν ὑπόκρισις μία, ὡς ἁπάντων ἐς
τὰ συμφέροντα τῇ πατρίδι βοηθούντων, εὐχερεστέ-
ρους ἐποίει πρὸς τὴν μεταβολὴν ὡς πανταχοῦ τῇ πατρίδι βοηθοῦντας. ἃ καὶ οἱ στρατηγοὶ συνιέντες ἔφερον, ὡς οὐ νόμῳ μᾶλλον αὐτῶν ἄρχοντες ἢ ταῖς
δωρεαῖς.

72 18. Οὕτω μὲν ἐς στάσεις τότε πάντα, καὶ ἐς δυσαρ-
χίαν τοῖς στασιάρχοις τὰ στρατόπεδα ἐτέτραπτο, τὴν
δὲ Ῥώμην λιμὸς ἐπίεζεν, οὔτε τῆς θαλάσσης τι αὐτοῖς
φερούσης διὰ Πομπήιον, οὔτε τῆς Ἰταλίας διὰ τοὺς
πολέμους γεωργουμένης. ὃ δὲ καὶ γένοιτο, ἐς τοὺς
73 στρατοὺς ἐδαπανᾶτο. ἐκλώπευόν τε οἱ πολλοὶ νυκτὸς
ἐν τῇ πόλει καὶ κλοπῆς ἔτι βιαιότερον ἠνώχλουν, καὶ
ἠνώχλουν ἀδεῶς, καὶ ἡ δόξα ἐς τοὺς στρατιώτας
ἐφέρετο. ὁ δὲ λεὼς ἀπέκλειε τὰ ἐργαστήρια καὶ τὰς
ἀρχὰς ἐξανίστη, ὡς οὔτε ἀρχῶν οὔτε τεχνῶν χρήζον-
τες ἐν ἀπορούσῃ καὶ λῃστευομένῃ πόλει.

74 19. Λευκίῳ δὲ ὄντι δημοτικῷ καὶ δυσχεραίνοντι τῇ

34

their equals. All these things undermined military disci- 69
pline among soldiers who thought that they were not serving in the army so much as lending assistance as a favor
and by their own choice, and believed that their leaders
were forced to rely on them for their own personal ends.
Desertion, which had previously been unpardonable for 70
Romans, was now actually rewarded with gifts, and whole
armies resorted to it, as well as some leading figures who
did not consider it desertion to change sides to a similar
cause. For all parties were indeed alike, and none of them 71
had been separated out as a public enemy of Rome. The
common deceit of the generals that they were all contrib-
uting to the best interests of the country made men more
ready to change sides, on the grounds that they were assisting their country whatever side they were on. The generals understood this and put up with it, recognizing that
they controlled the men less by the rule of law than by
donatives.

18. So it was at that time that everything developed into 72
factional strife, and the faction leaders faced insubordina-
tion in the armies. Famine began to squeeze the city of
Rome, as neither the sea brought them anything because
of Pompeius, nor the land of Italy, which was not being
farmed because of the wars. Whatever there was was used
up on the troops. The ordinary people resorted to theft at 73
night in the city, and caused trouble more violent than
theft, and did so with impunity: public opinion attributed
this to the soldiers. The working people closed their work-
shops and made the magistrates leave, since, they alleged,
there was no need of either magistrates or crafts in a city
oppressed by food shortages and robbers.

19. Lucius Antonius, who was a republican and ill dis- 74

τῶν τριῶν ἀρχῇ, οὐδὲ ἐπὶ τῷ χρόνῳ παύσεσθαι νομι-
ζομένῃ, προσκρούσματα ἐς τὸν Καίσαρα ἐγίγνετο
καὶ διαφοραὶ μείζους· τούς τε γεωργούς, ὅσοι τῆς γῆς
ἀφῃροῦντο, ἱκέτας γιγνομένους τῶν δυνατῶν ἑκάστου
μόνος ὑπεδέχετο καὶ βοηθήσειν ὑπισχνεῖτο, κἀκείνων
75 ὑπισχνουμένων ἀμυνεῖν, ἐς ὃ κελεύοι. ὅθεν αὐτὸν ὁ
στρατὸς ὁ Ἀντωνίου κατεμέμφετο καὶ ὁ Καῖσαρ ὡς
ἀντιπράσσοντα Ἀντωνίῳ, καὶ Φουλβία ὡς πολεμο-
ποιοῦντα ἐν ἀκαίρῳ, μέχρι τὴν Φουλβίαν ὁ Μάνιος
πανούργως μετεδίδαξεν ὡς εἰρηνευομένης μὲν τῆς
Ἰταλίας ἐπιμενεῖν Ἀντώνιον Κλεοπάτρᾳ, πολεμουμέ-
νης δ᾽ ἀφίξεσθαι κατὰ τάχος. τότε γὰρ δὴ γυναικὸς
τι παθοῦσα ἡ Φουλβία τὸν Λεύκιον ἐπέτριβεν ἐς τὴν
76 διαφοράν. ἐξιόντος δὲ τοῦ Καίσαρος ἐς τὰ λοιπὰ τῶν
κατοικίσεων, ἔπεμπεν ἑψομένους αὐτῷ τοὺς Ἀντωνίου
παῖδας ἅμα τῷ Λευκίῳ, ὡς μηδὲν ἐκ τῆς ὄψεως ὁ Καῖ-
77 σαρ ἐν τῷ στρατῷ πλέον ἔχοι. ἱππέων δὲ Καίσαρος
ἐκτρεχόντων ἐπὶ τὴν Βρεττίων ἠιόνα, πορθουμένην
ὑπὸ Πομπηίου, δόξας ὁ Λεύκιος ἢ ὑποκρινάμενος ἐφ᾽
ἑαυτὸν καὶ τοὺς Ἀντωνίου παῖδας τόδε τὸ ἱππικὸν
ἀπεστάλθαι, διέδραμεν ἐς τὰς Ἀντωνίου κατοικίας,
συλλεγόμενος φρουρὰν τῷ σώματι, καὶ τὸν Καίσαρα
78 τῷ στρατῷ διέβαλλεν ἐς ἀπιστίαν πρὸς Ἀντώνιον. ὁ
δὲ ἀντεδίδασκεν αὐτούς, ὅτι αὐτῷ μὲν καὶ Ἀντωνίῳ
πάντα εἶναι φίλια καὶ κοινά, Λεύκιον δὲ ὑφ᾽ ἑτέρας
γνώμης αὐτοὺς πολεμοποιεῖν ἐς ἀλλήλους ἀντιπράσσοντα τῇ τῶν τριῶν ἀρχῇ, δι᾽ ἣν οἱ στρατευόμενοι

posed toward the triumvirate, which, it was believed, would not cease to operate at the appointed time, engendered causes of friction with Octavian and more serious disagreements. Those farmers who had been dispossessed of their land were lobbying every man of influence, but Lucius was the only one to listen to them and promise to help, while they on their side promised to protect him in whatever way he might require. For this reason Antony's 75 soldiers and Octavian accused him of working against Antony, and Fulvia blamed him for stirring up war at an awkward time, until Manius deviously changed her mind by pointing out that as long as Italy remained at peace Antony would stay with Cleopatra, but that if war broke out he would be back in a hurry. So then of course Fulvia, moved by the feelings of a wife, incited Lucius to promote disagreement. When Octavian was leaving Rome to found 76 the remaining settlements, she sent Antony's children, along with Lucius, to accompany him, so that the sight of them would prevent Octavian getting any extra credit with the army. And when Octavian's cavalry made a sortie to 77 the coast of Bruttium, which was being raided by Pompeius, Lucius either believed or pretended to believe that this cavalry expedition had been sent against himself and the children of Antony. So he hurried over to the Antonian settlements, collected a bodyguard, and accused Octavian to the soldiers of disloyalty to Antony. Octavian explained 78 to them that on the contrary, relations between himself and Antony were entirely friendly and affable, and that Lucius, in pursuit of a different policy, was trying to stir up a war between them in his opposition to the triumvirate, and that it was because of the triumvirate that those

τὰς ἀποικίας ἔχουσι βεβαίους· καὶ τοὺς ἱππέας εἶναι
καὶ νῦν ἐν Βρεττίοις τὰ ἐντεταλμένα φυλάσσοντας.

79　20. Ὧν οἱ ἡγεμόνες τοῦ στρατοῦ πυνθανόμενοι
διῄτησαν αὐτοῖς ἐν Τεανῷ καὶ συνήλλαξαν ἐπὶ
τοῖσδε, τοὺς μὲν ὑπάτους τὰ πάτρια διοικεῖν μὴ κω-
λυομένους ὑπὸ τῶν τριῶν ἀνδρῶν, μηδενὶ δὲ γῆν ὑπὲρ
τοὺς στρατευσαμένους ἐν Φιλίπποις ἐπινέμεσθαι, τά
τε χρήματα τῶν δεδημευμένων καὶ τιμὰς τῶν ἔτι πι-
πρασκομένων καὶ τὸν στρατὸν Ἀντωνίου τὸν περὶ τὴν
80　Ἰταλίαν ἐπ᾽ ἴσης διανέμεσθαι καὶ μηδέτερον αὐτῶν
ἔτι καταλέγειν ἐκ τῆς Ἰταλίας, στρατεύοντι δὲ ἐπὶ
Πομπήιον τῷ Καίσαρι δύο συμμαχεῖν τέλη παρὰ
Ἀντωνίου, ἀνεῷχθαι δὲ τὰς Ἄλπεις τοῖς ὑπὸ Καίσαρος πεμπομένοις ἐς τὴν Ἰβηρίαν καὶ μὴ κωλύειν
αὐτοὺς ἔτι Ἀσίνιον Πολλίωνα, Λεύκιον δὲ ἐπὶ τοῖσδε
συνηλλαγμένον ἀποθέσθαι τὴν φρουρὰν τοῦ σώμα-
81　τος καὶ πολιτεύειν ἀδεῶς. τάδε μὲν ἦν, ἃ συνέθεντο
ἀλλήλοις διὰ τῶν ἡγεμόνων τοῦ στρατοῦ, ἐπράχθη γε
μὴν αὐτῶν δύο μόνα τὰ τελευταῖα· καὶ Σαλουιδιηνὸς
ἀκωλύτως ⟨εἶχε καὶ ὁ στρατὸς⟩[8] αὐτῷ συμπεριῆλθε
τὰς Ἄλπεις.

82　21. Οὐ γιγνομένων δὲ τῶν ἄλλων ἢ βραδυνόντων,

---

[8] ἄκων αὐτῷ συμπεριῆλθε codd.; ἀκωλύτως Mend.; ἀκωλύτως ⟨εἶχε καὶ ὁ στρατὸς⟩ Étienne-Duplessis

[22] On the historian and politician Gaius Asinius Pollio, see
App. *BCiv.* 2.40.162 note 41.

serving had secure tenure of their settlements. As for the cavalry, they were at that moment in Bruttium, following orders.

20. When the senior army officers heard this, they arbitrated between Lucius and Octavian at Teanum and reconciled them on the following terms: the consuls were to carry out their traditional functions without hindrance from the triumvirs; land was to be assigned to no one who had not fought at Philippi; Antony's troops in Italy were to have an equal share of the money derived from confiscations and of the proceeds from what was still being sold; neither Antony nor Octavian were to recruit in Italy; Antony was to give two of his legions to assist Octavian in his campaign against Pompeius; the Alps were to be opened to the forces being sent by Octavian to Iberia, and Asinius Pollio was to stop obstructing them;[22] and Lucius, on agreeing to this reconciliation, was to disband his bodyguard, and carry out his political functions without having anything to fear. Such were the terms of the agreement they made with each other through the senior officers of the army, but only the last two were actually carried out: Salvidienus encountered no further hindrance and his army accompanied him through the Alps.[23]

21. As the other conditions were not fulfilled, or were

[23] The text is corrupt at this point. I have adopted the reading of the Budé text. Quintus Salvidienus Rufus was an equestrian and one of Octavian's main generals. He was defeated by Sextus Pompeius in 42, sent to Spain by Octavian with six legions in 41, appointed governor of Gaul in 41 and designated consul (even though he was not a senator), but he was eventually denounced by Octavian for plotting against him with Antony.

ἐς Πραινεστὸν ἀνεχώρει Λεύκιος, δεδιέναι λέγων Καίσαρα διὰ τὴν ἀρχὴν δορυφορούμενον, αὐτὸς ἀφρούρητος ὤν. ἀνεχώρει δὲ καὶ Φουλβία, Λέπιδον ἤδη λέγουσα⁹ περὶ τοῖς τέκνοις δεδιέναι· τοῦτον¹⁰ γὰρ ἀντὶ τοῦ Καίσαρος προυτίθει. καὶ τάδε μὲν ἐγράφετο παρ' ἑκατέρων Ἀντωνίῳ, καὶ φίλοι μετὰ τῶν γραμμάτων ἐς αὐτὸν ἐπέμποντο, οἳ διδάξειν ἔμελλον περὶ ἑκάστων. καὶ οὐχ εὗρον ἐρευνώμενος, ὅ τι σαφῶς ἀντεγράφετο αὐτοῖς. οἱ δὲ τῶν στρατῶν ἡγεμόνες συνομόσαντες κρινεῖν τοῖς ἄρχουσιν αὖθις, ὃ δοκοίη δίκαιον εἶναι, καὶ τοὺς ἀπειθοῦντας ἐς αὐτὸ συναναγκάσειν, ἐκάλουν ἐπὶ ταῦτα τοὺς περὶ Λεύκιον. οὐ δεξαμένων δ' ἐκείνων, ὁ Καῖσαρ ἐπιφθόνως αὐτοὺς ἔν τε τοῖς ἡγεμόσι τοῦ στρατοῦ καὶ παρὰ τοῖς Ῥωμαίων ἀρίστοις ἐπεμέμφετο. οἱ δὲ ἐξέθεον ἐς τὸν Λεύκιον καὶ παρεκάλουν οἰκτεῖραι μὲν ἐπὶ τοῖς ἐμφυλίοις τὴν πόλιν καὶ τὴν Ἰταλίαν, δέξασθαι δὲ κοινῷ νόμῳ¹¹ τὴν κρίσιν ἢ ἐπὶ σφῶν ἢ ἐπὶ τῶν ἡγεμόνων γενέσθαι.

22. Αἰδουμένου δὲ τοῦ Λευκίου τά τε λεγόμενα καὶ τοὺς λέγοντας, ὁ Μάνιος μάλα θρασέως ἔφη τὸν μὲν Ἀντώνιον οὐδὲν ἀλλ' ἢ χρήματα μόνα ἀγείρειν ἐν ξένοις ἀνδράσι, τὸν δὲ Καίσαρα καὶ τὴν στρατιὰν καὶ τὰ ἐπίκαιρα τῆς Ἰταλίας ταῖς θεραπείας προκατα-

---

⁹ πρὸς ante Λέπιδον add. BJ; ἀνεχώρει δὲ καὶ Φουλβία, Λέπιδον ⟨ἕνα⟩ ἤδη λέγουσα Étienne-Duplessis; ἀνεχώρει δὲ καὶ Φουλβία πρὸς Λέπιδον, ἤδη λέγουσα Viereck
¹⁰ τοῦτον LBJ; τοῦτο L

delayed, Lucius retired to Praeneste, saying that he was afraid of Octavian, who because of the office he held had a bodyguard, while he himself had no protection. Fulvia also withdrew, now claiming that Lepidus was afraid for her children: for she was using Lepidus as a pretext, instead of Octavian.[24] These issues were written up by both sides in letters to Antony, and associates were sent to him with the letters to explain all the details. Although I have searched, I have not been able to find any clear account of what Antony wrote in reply to them. The senior officers of the armies, having sworn an oath to make a new judgment for their leaders about what they thought was just, and to force any dissidents into compliance, summoned Lucius and his staff for this purpose. But they did not accept the terms, and Octavian criticized them maliciously both among the army commanders and the Roman aristocracy. The latter hurried to Lucius from Rome and implored him to have pity on the city and on Italy, after the civil wars, and to accept that by common agreement the decision should rest with themselves or with the officers.

22. Although Lucius respected the speakers and what was being said, Manius very insolently claimed that while Antony was doing nothing more than collecting money among foreigners, Octavian, because of the services he was providing, was securing in advance both the army and the strategic positions in Italy. For example,

83

84

85

86

87

[24] The text is again uncertain in this sentence, and the meaning far from clear.

---

[11] κοινωνὸν ᾧ codd., κοινῷ νόμῳ Madvig; post κοινωνὸν lacunam indic. Étienne-Duplessis

87 λαμβάνειν· τήν τε γὰρ Κελτικὴν Ἀντωνίῳ πρότερον
δεδομένην ἐλευθεροῦν μετ' ἐξαπάτης Ἀντωνίου, καὶ
τὴν Ἰταλίαν σχεδὸν ἅπασαν ἀντὶ μόνων ὀκτωκαίδεκα
πόλεων τοῖς ἐστρατευμένοις καταγράφειν, τέσσαρσί
τε καὶ τριάκοντα τέλεσιν ἀντὶ ὀκτὼ καὶ εἴκοσι τῶν
συμμαχησάντων ἐπινέμειν οὐ γῆν μόνην, ἀλλὰ καὶ
τὰ ἐκ τῶν ἱερῶν χρήματα, συλλέγοντα μὲν ὡς ἐπὶ
Πομπήιον, ἐφ' ὃν οὐδέ πω παρατάττεται λιμωττούσης
ὧδε τῆς πόλεως, διαιροῦντα δὲ τοῖς στρατοῖς ἐς θεραπείαν κατὰ Ἀντωνίου καὶ τὰ δεδημευμένα οὐ πιπρά-
88 σκοντα μᾶλλον ἢ δωρούμενον αὐτοῖς. χρῆναι δέ, εἰ
τῷ ὄντι εἰρηνεύειν ἐθέλοι, τῶν μὲν ἤδη διῳκημένων
ὑποσχεῖν λόγον, ἐς δὲ τὸ μέλλον, ἃ ἂν κοινῇ βουλευ-
89 ομένοις δοκῇ, μόνα πράσσειν. οὕτω μὲν θρασέως ὁ
Μάνιος ἠξίου μήτε τὸν Καίσαρά τινος εἶναι κύριον
ἔργου μήτε τὴν Ἀντωνίου συνθήκην βέβαιον, ὡρισμέ-
νου τῶν ἐγκεχειρισμένων ἑκάτερον αὐτοκράτορα εἶναι
καὶ τὸ πρασσόμενον ὑπ' ἀλλήλων εἶναι κύριον. πανταχόθεν οὖν ὁ Καῖσαρ ἑώρα πολεμησείοντας αὐτούς,
καὶ παρεσκευάζοντο αὐτῶν ἑκάτεροι.

90   23. Δύο δὲ στρατοῦ τέλη τὰ ἐς Ἀγκῶνα πόλιν ᾠκι-
σμένα, Καίσαρί τε ὄντα πατρῷα καὶ ἐστρατευμένα
Ἀντωνίῳ, τῆς τε ἰδίας παρασκευῆς αὐτῶν πυθόμενοι
καὶ τὴν εἰς ἑκάτερον σφῶν οἰκειότητα αἰδούμενοι,
πρέσβεις ἔπεμψαν ἐς Ῥώμην, οἳ ἔμελλον ἑκατέρων ἐς
91 διαλύσεις δεήσεσθαι. Καίσαρος δ' αὐτοῖς εἰπόντος
οὐκ Ἀντωνίῳ πολεμεῖν, ἀλλ' ὑπὸ Λευκίου πολεμεῖ-
σθαι, συμβαλόντες οἱ πρέσβεις τοῖς ἡγεμόσι τοῦδε

he alleged that Octavian was deceiving Antony by freeing
Gaul, which had previously been granted to Antony; that
he was using almost the whole of Italy to assign land to the
veterans instead of the eighteen cities; that he was distributing to thirty-four legions instead of the twenty-eight that
had fought for him, not only land, but also the money from
the temples he had collected supposedly to fight Pompeius—against whom he was not yet even marshaling his
troops in spite of the fact that Rome was suffering so much
from famine—but that he was in fact distributing to the
soldiers to gain their favor against Antony; and that he was
giving away what had been confiscated rather than selling
it to them. If Octavian really wanted there to be peace, he   88
should account for his administration up to this point, and
in future do only what they decided after consulting together. Such was the audacity with which Manius required   89
that Octavian have no authority for independent action
and that his agreement with Antony be invalid, even
though it had been fixed that each of them would have full
authority over the tasks allotted to them, and that what
either of them did would be validated by the other. So
from all perspectives Octavian could see that they were
warmongering, and both of them began to make their
preparations.

23. Two legions that had been settled at Ancona—Oc-   90
tavian had inherited them from his father, but they had
also served under Antony—on hearing of each side's preparations, and out of respect for their relationship with
both, sent envoys to Rome to ask them to resolve their
differences. When Octavian told them that it was not he   91
who was making war on Antony, but Lucius who was making war on him, the envoys came to an agreement with the

τοῦ στρατοῦ, κοινῇ πάντες ἐς Λεύκιον ἐπρέσβευον,
ἀξιοῦντες αὐτὸν ἐς δίκην Καίσαρι συνελθεῖν· δηλοί τε
ἦσαν, ὃ πράξειν ἔμελλον, εἰ μὴ τὴν κρίσιν ὑποδέ-
92 χοιτο. δεξαμένων δὲ τῶν ἀμφὶ τὸν Λεύκιον, χωρίον τε
ὥριστο τῇ δίκῃ Γάβιοι πόλις ἐν μέσῳ Ῥώμης τε καὶ
Πραινεστοῦ, καὶ συνέδριον τοῖς κρίνουσιν ἐγίνετο καὶ
93 βήματα ἐν μέσῳ δύο τοῖς ἐροῦσιν ὡς ἐν δίκῃ. πρότε-
ρος δ' ὁ Καῖσαρ ἐλθὼν ἱππέας ἔπεμψεν ἐς τὴν πάρ-
οδον τοῦ Λευκίου, ἐρευνησομένους ἄρα, μή τίς ποθεν
ὁρῷτο ἐνέδρα. καὶ οἱ ἱππέες οἵδε ἑτέροις ἱππεῦσι τοῦ
Λευκίου, προδρόμοις ἄρα ἢ καὶ τοῖσδε κατασκόποις,
94 συμβαλόντες ἔκτειναν τινας αὐτῶν. καὶ ἀνεχώρησε
δείσας ὁ Λεύκιος, ὡς ἔλεγεν, ἐπιβουλήν· καλούμενός
τε ὑπὸ τῶν ἡγεμόνων τοῦ στρατοῦ, παραπέμψειν αὐτὸν ὑπισχνουμένων, οὐκέτι ἐπείθετο.

95 24. Οὕτω μὲν ἦσαν αἱ διαλύσεις ἄπρακτοι, καὶ
πολεμεῖν ἐγνώκεσαν καὶ διαγράμμασιν ἤδη πικροῖς
κατ' ἀλλήλων ἐχρῶντο. στρατὸς δὲ ἦν Λευκίῳ μὲν
ὁπλιτῶν ἐξ τέλη, ὅσα αὐτὸς ἐς τὴν ὑπατείαν ἐλθὼν
ἐστράτευσε, καὶ τὰ Ἀντωνίου ἕνδεκα ἕτερα, ὧν ἐστρα-
τήγει Καληνός, σύμπαντα ταῦτα ἀνὰ τὴν Ἰταλίαν·
96 Καίσαρι δὲ ἐν μὲν Καπύῃ τέσσαρα ἦν τέλη, καὶ περὶ
αὐτὸν αἱ στρατηγίδες, ἐξ δὲ ἕτερα Σαλουιδιηνὸς ἦγεν
97 ἐξ Ἰβηρίας. καὶ χρήματα ἦν Λευκίῳ μὲν ἐξ ἐθνῶν
τῶν ὑπὸ τὸν Ἀντώνιον οὐ πολεμουμένων, Καίσαρι δέ,
ἃ εἰλήχει, πάντα χωρὶς Σαρδοῦς <. . .> ἢ[12] ἐπολεμεῖτο,

officers of Lucius' army, and they all sent a joint delegation
to Lucius to ask him to meet with Octavian to settle the
case; and they made it plain what they intended to do if
he did not accept the decision. Lucius and his staff ac-   92
cepted the proposal, and Gabii, a town situated halfway
between Rome and Praeneste, was fixed as the site of the
hearing. There was a council chamber for those judging
the matter, and two tribunals in the middle for the speakers, as in a court case. Octavian arrived first and sent some   93
cavalry along Lucius' route, no doubt to investigate if any
signs of an ambush could be seen anywhere. These troops
encountered another squadron of horse, belonging to Lucius, either his advance guard, I suppose, or scouts like
themselves, and killed some of them. Lucius withdrew, so   94
he claimed, in fear of a trap, and although summoned by
the army's officers, who promised to provide him with an
escort, he could no longer be persuaded.

24. Thus the negotiations came to nothing, and Octa-   95
vian and Lucius decided to go to war and issued what were
now bitter edicts against each other. Lucius had an army
of the six legions he himself had enlisted on entering his
consulship, and the eleven others of Antony commanded
by Calenus. These were all in Italy. Octavian had four le-   96
gions at Capua and his praetorian cohorts escorting him
personally, while Salvidienus was bringing six more legions from Iberia. Lucius had supplies of money from   97
Antony's provinces where there was no fighting, but all the
provinces that Octavian had been allotted except Sardinia

---

¹² ἡ B; ἡ LPJ del. Schweig.; lacunam post Σαρδοῦς indic.
Étienne-Duplessis

ὅθεν ἐκ τῶν ἱερῶν ἐδανείζετο, σὺν χάριτι ἀποδώσειν
ὑπισχνούμενος, ἀπό τε Ῥώμης ἐκ τοῦ Καπιτωλίου καὶ
ἀπὸ Ἀντίου καὶ Λανουβίου καὶ Νεμοῦς καὶ Τίβυρος,
ἐν αἷς μάλιστα πόλεσι καὶ νῦν εἰσι θησαυροὶ χρημάτων ἱερῶν δαψιλεῖς.

98   25. Τετάρακτο δὲ αὐτῷ καὶ τὰ τῆς Ἰταλίας ἔξω.
Πομπήιος γὰρ ἐκ τῶν προγραφῶν καὶ κατοικίσεων
τοῦ στρατοῦ καὶ τῆσδε τῆς Λευκίου διαφορᾶς ἐπὶ
99 μέγα δόξης καὶ δυνάμεως ἦρτο. οἱ γὰρ περὶ σφῶν
δεδιότες ἢ τὰ ὄντα ἀφαιρούμενοι ἢ τὴν πολιτείαν
ὅλως ἀποστρεφόμενοι ἐς αὐτὸν ἐχώρουν μάλιστα· καὶ
ἡ ἄλλη νεότης ὡρμημένη στρατεύεσθαι διὰ τὰ κέρδη
καὶ οὐδὲν ἡγούμενοι διαφέρειν, ὑφ᾽ ὅτῳ στρατεύσον-
ται, Ῥωμαίοις πανταχοῦ συστρατευόμενοι, μᾶλλον ἐς
τὸν Πομπήιον ἐχώρουν ὡς δικαιότερα αἱρούμενον.
100 γεγένητό τε πλούσιος ἐκ τῆς θαλασσίου λείας καὶ
ναῦς εἶχε πολλὰς καὶ πληρώματα ἐντελῆ. Μοῦρκός τε
ἀφῖκτο αὐτῷ δύο ἄγων στρατοῦ τέλη καὶ τοξότας
πεντακοσίους καὶ χρήματα πολλὰ καὶ ναῦς ὀγδοή-
κοντα· καὶ τὸν ἄλλον στρατὸν ἐκ Κεφαληνίας μετ-
101 επέμπετο. ὅθεν τισὶ δοκεῖ τότε ὁ Πομπήιος ἐπελθὼν
εὐμαρῶς ἂν τῆς Ἰταλίας κρατῆσαι, ὑπό τε λιμοῦ καὶ
στάσεως διεφθαρμένης καὶ ἐς αὐτὸν ἀφορώσης. ἀλλὰ
Πομπηίῳ μὲν ὑπὸ ἀφροσύνης οὐκ ἐπιχειρεῖν, ἀλλὰ
ἀμύνεσθαι μόνον ἐδόκει, μέχρι καὶ τοῦδε ἥσσων ἐγέ-
νετο·
102   26. Ἐν δὲ Λιβύῃ Σέξστιος, ὕπαρχος Ἀντωνίου,
παρεδεδώκει μὲν ἄρτι τὸν στρατόν, ὑπὸ Λευκίου κεκε-

were ⟨. . .⟩ or at war.[25] For this reason he borrowed money from the temples—from the Capitol in Rome, from Antium and Lanuvinium and Nemi and Tibur, all towns in which even today there are treasuries full of sacred monies—but he promised to pay it back with interest.

25. Octavian had to face a disturbed situation outside Italy too. For Pompeius, as a result of the proscriptions, the military colonies, and this dispute caused by Lucius, had risen high in reputation and power. Those who feared for their safety or were being robbed of their possessions or were in general alienated from the regime made their way to him especially. And other young men, eager to serve in the military because of the financial rewards, but believing that it made no difference under whom they served, since they would be fighting alongside Romans whichever side they were on, preferred to join Pompeius as representing the more righteous cause. He had become rich from the booty won at sea, and had a large number of ships and full crews. Murcus had joined him with two legions of soldiers, five hundred archers, a large sum of money, and eighty ships; and he was sending for the rest of his army from Cephallenia. This is the reason why some people think that if Pompeius had invaded Italy at that moment, he would easily have taken control of it, as it had been wasted by famine and civil war, and was looking to him. But Pompeius made the foolish decision not to attack, but only to defend, and in the end he could not even manage this.

26. In Africa, Antony's governor Sextius had recently on the orders of Lucius handed over his army to Fango,

98

99

100

101

102

---

[25] There seems to be a small gap in the text in this sentence.

λευσμένος, Φάγγωνι τῷ Καίσαρος, ἐπισταλὲν αὖθις
ἀναλαμβάνειν αὐτὸν οὐκ ἀποδιδόντι τῷ Φάγγωνι ἐπο-
λέμει, συναγαγών τινας τῶν ἀπεστρατευμένων καὶ
Λιβύων πλῆθος ἄλλο καὶ ἑτέρους παρὰ τῶν βασι-
λέων. ἡττηθέντων δὲ τῶν κερῶν ἑκατέρων καὶ ληφθέντων τῶν στρατοπέδων, ὁ Φάγγων ἡγούμενος ἐκ προ-
103 δοσίας τάδε παθεῖν αὐτὸν διεχρήσατο. καὶ Λιβύης
μὲν αὖθις ὁ Σέξστιος ἑκατέρας ἐκράτει· Βόκχον δὲ τὸν
Μαυρουσίων βασιλέα Λεύκιος ἔπεισε πολεμεῖν Καρ-
104 ρίνᾳ τῷ τὴν Ἰβηρίαν ἐπιτροπεύοντι τῷ Καίσαρι. Ἀη-
νόβαρβός τε ἑβδομήκοντα ναυσὶ καὶ στρατοῦ δύο
τέλεσι καὶ τοξόταις καὶ σφενδονήταις τισὶ καὶ ψιλοῖς
καὶ μονομάχοις περιπλέων τὸν Ἰόνιον ἐπόρθει τὰ τοῖς
τρισὶν ἀνδράσιν ὑπήκοα, ἔς τε τὸ Βρεντέσιον ἐπι-
πλεύσας τῶν Καίσαρος τριήρων τὰς μὲν εἷλε, τὰς δὲ
ἐνέπρησε, καὶ τοὺς Βρεντεσίους ἐς τὰ τείχη κατ-
έκλεισε καὶ τὴν χώραν προυνόμευεν.

105   27. Ὁ δὲ Καῖσαρ ἐς τὸ Βρεντέσιον στρατιωτῶν
τέλος ἔπεμπε καὶ Σαλουιδιηνὸν κατὰ σπουδὴν ἐκ τῆς
ἐς Ἰβηρίαν ὁδοῦ μετεκάλει. τούς τε στρατολογήσον-
τας σφίσιν ἀνὰ τὴν Ἰταλίαν ὁ Καῖσαρ καὶ ὁ Λεύκιος
περιέπεμπον· πεῖραί τε τούτων τῶν ξεναγῶν ἦσαν ἐς
ἀλλήλους βραχύτεραι καὶ μείζους καὶ ἐνέδραι πολ-
106 λάκις. ἡ δὲ εὔνοια τῶν Ἰταλῶν ἐς τὸν Λεύκιον παρὰ
πολὺ ἐποίει, ὡς ὑπὲρ σφῶν τοῖς κληρουχουμένοις πολεμοῦντα. καὶ οὐχ αἱ καταγραφόμεναι τῷ στρατῷ

Octavian's governor.[26] On being ordered to resume command of it, he collected some veterans, a large crowd of Africans, and other men sent by the kings, and made war on Fango because he refused to give the troops back. Defeated on both wings and having lost his camps, Fango believed that this had happened to him as a result of treachery, and he committed suicide. Thus Sextius again 103 became master of the two African provinces. Lucius also persuaded Bocchus, king of Mauretania, to make war on Carrinas, who was governing Iberia for Octavian.[27] Ahe- 104 nobarbus, with seventy ships, two legions, some archers and slingers, light-armed troops and gladiators, was sailing around the Ionian gulf devastating the areas subject to the triumvirate. He attacked Brundisium by sea, captured some of Octavian's triremes, burned others, shut the inhabitants up in their walls, and plundered the land.

27. As for Octavian, he sent a legion of soldiers to 105 Brundisium and hurriedly recalled Salvidienus from his march to Spain. Both Octavian and Lucius sent agents all over Italy to recruit troops for them, and there were many engagements and ambushes, both serious and minor, between these mercenary leaders. The goodwill of the Ital- 106 ians was directed very largely to Lucius, as they believed that he was fighting in their interests against the colonists. And it was no longer just the towns assigned to the army

[26] Gaius Fuficius Fango was a centurion in the Roman army, but he was raised to the senate by Julius Caesar (Cass. Dio 48.22.3).   [27] Gaius Carrinas (consul 43) became governor of Gaul in 30 and was awarded a triumph in 28. There is some confusion here and in other sources between Bocchus II of Mauretania and his brother Bogud.

πόλεις ἔτι μόναι, ἀλλ᾽ ἡ Ἰταλία σχεδὸν ἅπασα ἀν-
ίστατο, φοβουμένη τὰ ὅμοια· τούς τε τῷ Καίσαρι κι-
χραμένους ἐκ τῶν ἱερῶν χρημάτων ἐκβάλλοντες ἐκ
τῶν πόλεων ἢ ἀναιροῦντες, τὰ τείχη σφῶν διὰ χειρὸς
εἶχον καὶ πρὸς τὸν Λεύκιον ἐχώρουν. ἐχώρουν δὲ καὶ
οἱ κατοικιζόμενοι τῶν στρατιωτῶν ἐς τὸν Καίσαρα,
ὡς ἐς οἰκεῖον ἤδη πόλεμον ὑπὲρ σφῶν ἑκάτεροι διαι-
ρούμενοι.

107   28. Καὶ τῶνδε γιγνομένων ὁ Καῖσαρ ὅμως ἔτι τήν
τε βουλὴν καὶ τοὺς καλουμένους ἱππέας συναγαγὼν
ἔλεγεν ὧδε· "Καταγινώσκομαι μέν, εὖ οἶδα, ὑπὸ τῶν
περὶ Λεύκιον, οὐκ ἀμυνόμενος αὐτούς, εἰς ἀσθένειαν
ἢ ἀτολμίαν, ἃ καὶ νῦν μου καταγνώσονται διὰ τήνδε
τὴν σύνοδον ὑμῶν· ἐμοὶ δὲ ἔρρωται μὲν ὁ στρατός,
ὅσος τέ μοι συναδικεῖται τὴν κληρουχίαν ἀφαιρούμενος ὑπὸ Λευκίου καὶ ὁ ἄλλος, ὃν ἔχω, ἔρρωται δὲ καὶ
108   τὰ λοιπὰ πλὴν τῆς γνώμης μόνης. οὐ γὰρ ἡδύ μοι
πολεμεῖν ἐμφυλίους πολέμους χωρὶς ἀνάγκης βαρείας, οὐδὲ καταχρῆσθαι τῶν πολιτῶν τοῖς ἔτι λοιποῖς κατ᾽ ἀλλήλων, καὶ μάλιστα τοῦδε τοῦ ἐμφυλίου
οὐκ ἐκ Μακεδονίας ὑμῖν ἢ Θράκης ἀκουσθησομένου,
ἀλλ᾽ ἐν αὐτῇ τῇ Ἰταλίᾳ γενησομένου, ἣν πόσα χρὴ
χωρὶς τῶν ἀπολλυμένων ἀνδρῶν κακοπαθῆσαι, γι-
109   γνομένην στάδιον ἡμῖν. ἐγὼ μὲν δὴ διὰ τάδε ὀκνῶ καὶ
νῦν ἔτι μαρτύρομαι μηδὲν ἀδικεῖν Ἀντώνιον μηδὲ ἀδι-
κεῖσθαι πρὸς Ἀντωνίου· ὑμᾶς δὲ ἐλέγξαι τοὺς ἀμφὶ
τὸν Λεύκιον τάδε δι᾽ ὑμᾶς αὐτοὺς καὶ συναλλάξαι μοι
110   παρακαλῶ. καὶ εἰ μὴ πείθοιντο μηδὲ νῦν, ἐκείνοις μὲν

that rose in revolt, but, because they feared similar treatment, almost the whole of Italy. Those borrowing money
from the temples for Octavian they either drove out of the
towns or killed, and taking control of their own walls, they
went over to Lucius. On the other hand, the troops being
settled in the colonies joined Octavian: on each side men
made their choices in defense of their own interests, as if
they were fighting a personal war.

28. In spite of these events, Octavian still summoned   107
the senate and those called the equestrians, and spoke as
follows: "I am well aware that I stand accused by Lucius'
party of weakness and lack of courage for not defending
myself against them, and that they are going to make the
same accusation against me now because of this meeting
with you. But my army is strong, both the part of it that
shares with me the injustice of being deprived of their land
allotment by Lucius, and the rest of the force I have at my
disposal, and I am strong in all other respects with the sole
exception of my resolve to fight. For I take no pleasure in   108
fighting civil wars unless under pressure of grave necessity, nor in using what survives of our citizenry against
each other, especially in this civil war: for you will not be
hearing from Macedonia or Thrace, but it will take place
in Italy itself which, if it becomes our arena, will inevitably
suffer innumerable miseries, quite apart from the loss of
life. As far as I am concerned, it is for these reasons that I   109
hesitate, and continue even now to assert that I am doing
no wrong to Antony and suffering no wrong at his hands.
For your part, I urge you to convince Lucius' party of this
yourselves, and reconcile him to me. But if, even now, you   110
cannot persuade them, I will immediately show them that

51

αὐτίκα δείξω τὰ μέχρι νῦν εὐβουλίαν, οὐ δειλίαν οὖσαν, ὑμᾶς δὲ καὶ παρ' ὑμῖν αὐτοῖς καὶ πρὸς Ἀντώνιον
ἀξιῶ μάρτυρας εἶναί μοι καὶ συνίστασθαι διὰ τὴν
ὑπεροψίαν Λευκίου."

111　　29. Ταῦτ' εἶπεν ὁ Καῖσαρ. καὶ τούτων οἱ μὲν δὴ
πάλιν ἐς τὸ Πραινεστὸν ἐξέτρεχον· καὶ ὁ Λεύκιος τοσόνδε εἶπεν, ὅτι καὶ τῶν ἔργων ἤδη προειλήφασιν ἀμφότεροι καὶ ὁ Καῖσαρ ὑποκρίνεται, τέλος ἄρτι πέμ-
112　ψας ἐς τὸ Βρεντέσιον κωλύειν Ἀντώνιον ἐπανιόντα. ὁ
δὲ Μάνιος καὶ ἐπιστολὴν ἐδείκνυε τοῦ Ἀντωνίου, εἴτε
πλασάμενος εἴτε ἀληθῆ, πολεμεῖν, ἐάν τις αὐτοῦ τὴν
113　ἀξίωσιν καθαιρῇ. ἐρομένων δὲ τῶν ἀπὸ τῆς βουλῆς,
εἰ καθαιροῖτό τι τῆς ἀξιώσεως Ἀντωνίου, καὶ προκα-
λουμένων ἐς δίκην περὶ τοῦδε, ἕτερα αὖ πολλὰ ἐσοφί-
ζετο ὁ Μάνιος, ἕως οἱ μὲν ἀπῆλθον ἄπρακτοι, καὶ οὐ
συνῆλθον ἐς τὴν ἀπόκρισιν τῷ Καίσαρι, εἴτε καθ'
ἑαυτὸν ἀπαγγείλας ἕκαστος εἴτε δι' ἑτέραν γνώμην
114　εἴτε ὑπὸ αἰδοῦς· ὁ δὲ πόλεμος ἀνέῳκτο, καὶ ὁ Καῖσαρ
ἐπ' αὐτὸν ἐξῄει, φύλακα τῆς Ῥώμης Λέπιδον σὺν δύο
τέλεσι καταλιπών. οἱ δὲ πολλοὶ τῶν ἐπιφανῶν τότε
μάλιστα ἐπεδείκνυον οὐκ ἀρέσκεσθαι τῇ τῶν τριῶν
ἀρχῇ· ἐς γὰρ τὸν Λεύκιον ἐχώρουν.

115　　30. Καὶ ἦν τὰ κεφάλαια τοῦ πολέμου τοιάδε. Λευκίου μὲν δὴ δύο τέλη περὶ Ἄλβην ἐστασίασε καὶ τοὺς
ἄρχοντας ἐκβαλόντα ἐς ἀπόστασιν ἐχώρει· ἐπειγο-
μένων δὲ ἐς αὐτὰ Καίσαρός τε καὶ Λευκίου, φθάσας
τὸν Καίσαρα ὁ Λεύκιος ἀνεσώσατο αὐτὰ χρήμασί τε
116　πολλοῖς καὶ ὑποσχέσεσι μεγάλαις. Φουρνίου δ' ἄλ-

it was goodwill that motivated me up to this point, not cowardice; and I ask you to bear witness on my behalf both among yourselves and before Antony, and to stand with me because of Lucius' arrogance."

29. Such was Octavian's speech. And of course some of his audience hurried off to Praeneste again, where Lucius said only that both sides had already begun hostilities, and that Octavian was putting on an act, as he had just sent a legion to Brundisium to prevent Antony from returning. Manius also produced a letter from Antony, which may have been a forgery or a real letter, giving orders to fight, if anybody tried to damage his reputation. When the delegation from the senate asked if any damage was being done to Antony's reputation, and proposed legal arbitration on the matter, Manius again produced many other sophistries until the senators went away without achieving anything. And they did not hold a meeting with Octavian to give him the answer, either because they had each reported to him individually, or because they held contrary opinions, or because they were ashamed. Open war now broke out and Octavian set off to conduct it, leaving Lepidus with two legions to guard Rome. It was then in particular that most of the aristocracy showed their dissatisfaction with the triumvirate: for they went to join Lucius.

30. The following were the main events of the war. Two of Lucius' legions at Alba mutinied, expelled their officers, and prepared to defect. Both Octavian and Lucius rushed to get to them, but Lucius arrived first and succeeded in keeping them with large sums of money and big promises.

λον στρατὸν ἄγοντος τῷ Λευκίῳ, ὁ Καῖσαρ ἐξήπτετο
τῆς οὐραγίας· ἐς δὲ λόφον ἀναδραμόντι τῷ Φουρνίῳ
καὶ νυκτὸς ἐς ὁμογνώμονα πόλιν ἐπειγομένῳ Σεντίαν,
νυκτὸς μὲν οὐχ ἕσπετο ὁ Καῖσαρ ἐνέδραν ὑποπτεύων,
ἡμέρας δὲ τήν τε Σεντίαν ὁμοῦ καὶ τὸ τοῦ Φουρνίου
117 στρατόπεδον ἐπολιόρκει. Λεύκιος δὲ ἐς Ῥώμην ἐπειγόμενος τρεῖς μὲν τάξεις προύπεμψεν, αἳ νυκτὸς ἔλαθον ἐς τὴν πόλιν ἐσδραμοῦσαι, αὐτὸς δὲ σὺν πολλῷ
118 στρατῷ καὶ ἱππεῦσι καὶ μονομάχοις εἴπετο. καὶ αὐτὸν
Νωνίου τοῦ φύλακος τῶν πυλῶν δεξαμένου τε καὶ τὸν
ὑφ᾽ αὑτῷ στρατὸν ἐγχειρίσαντος, ὁ μὲν Λέπιδος ἐς
Καίσαρα ἔφευγεν, ὁ δὲ Λεύκιος Ῥωμαίοις ἐδημη-
γόρει, Καίσαρα μὲν καὶ Λέπιδον αὐτίκα δώσειν δίκην
ἀρχῆς βιαίου, τὸν δὲ ἀδελφὸν αὐτὴν ἑκόντα ἀποθή-
σεσθαι καὶ ὑπατείαν ἀλλάξεσθαι, νομιμωτέραν ἀρχὴν καὶ πάτριον ἀντὶ παρανόμου καὶ τυραννικῆς.¹³

119   31. Καὶ ὁ μὲν τάδε εἰπών, ἡδομένων ἁπάντων καὶ
ἡγουμένων ἤδη λελύσθαι τὴν τῶν τριῶν ἀρχήν, αὐτο-
κράτωρ ὑπὸ τοῦ δήμου προσαγορευθεὶς ἐπὶ τὸν Καίσαρα ἐχώρει καὶ στρατὸν ἤθροιζεν ἄλλον ἐκ τῶν
120 ἀποικίδων Ἀντωνίου πόλεων καὶ αὐτὰς ἐκρατύνατο. αἱ
δὲ δι᾽ εὐνοίας μὲν ἦσαν Ἀντωνίῳ, Βαρβάτιος δὲ ὁ
Ἀντωνίου ταμίας, Ἀντωνίῳ τι προσκρούσας καὶ διὰ
ταῦτ᾽ ἐπανιών, ἔλεγε πυνθανομένοις τὸν Ἀντώνιον χα-

¹³ νομιμωτέραν ἀρχὴν καὶ πάτριον ἀντὶ παρανόμου καὶ
τυραννικῆς Étienne-Duplessis; νομιμωτέραν ἀρχὴν παρανόμου καὶ πάτριον ἀντὶ τῆς τυραννιξῆς Viereck

While Furnius was bringing another army to Lucius, Oc-   116
tavian attacked his rearguard.[28] Furnius quickly took refuge up a hill and pressed on by night to Sentinum, a town
that shared his political position. Because he was afraid of
an ambush, Octavian did not follow him during the night,
but next day he laid siege to Sentinum and Furnius' camp
at the same time. Lucius, who was hurrying on to Rome,   117
sent three cohorts ahead, which burst into the city at night
without being seen, while he himself followed with a large
force, including cavalry and gladiators. Nonius, who was   118
guarding the gates, let him in and handed over to him the
soldiers under his command. Lepidus fled to Octavian,
and Lucius made a speech to the citizens, saying that Octavian and Lepidus would soon pay the price of their violent rule, and that his brother would willingly resign his
command in exchange for the consulship, a more legiti-
mate and traditional magistracy for an illegal and tyranni-
cal one.

31. Everyone was delighted at this speech of his, and   119
believed that the triumvirate was now dissolved. Lucius
was saluted as Imperator by the people, and set off against
Octavian, collecting a new army from Antony's colonies,
of which he took control. These colonies were well dis-   120
posed toward Antony, but Barbatius, Antony's quaestor,
who had some dispute with him and was returning to
Rome because of it, told those who asked that Antony was

[28] Gaius Furnius was a friend of Cicero and supporter of Marc
Antony. He had been tribune in 50 and was governor of Asia in
36/35. His son reconciled him to Octavian after the battle of
Actium (Sen. *Ben*. 2.25).

APPIAN

λεπαίνειν τοῖς πολεμοῦσι τῷ Καίσαρι κατὰ τῆς κοι-
121 νῆς σφῶν δυναστείας. καὶ οἱ μέν, ὅσοι μὴ τῆς ἐξαπάτης ᾔσθοντο τῆς Βαρβατίου, ἐς τὸν Καίσαρα ἀπὸ
τοῦ Λευκίου μετετίθεντο· ὁ δὲ Λεύκιος ὑπήντα Σαλουιδιηνῷ μετὰ στρατοῦ πολλοῦ πρὸς Καίσαρα ἐκ Κελτῶν ἐπανιόντι. καὶ εἵποντο τῷ Σαλουιδιηνῷ Ἀσίνιός
τε καὶ Οὐεντίδιος, Ἀντωνίου στρατηγοὶ καὶ οἵδε, κω-
122 λύοντες αὐτὸν ἐς τὸ πρόσθεν ἰέναι. Ἀγρίππας δέ, φίλ-
τατος Καίσαρι, δείσας ἐπὶ τῷ Σαλουιδιηνῷ μὴ κυ-
κλωθείη, Σούτριον κατέλαβε, χωρίον τι χρήσιμον τῷ
Λευκίῳ, νομίσας τὸν Λεύκιον ἀπὸ τοῦ Σαλουιδιηνοῦ
περισπάσειν ἐφ᾽ ἑαυτὸν καὶ οἳ τὸν Σαλουιδιηνὸν βο-
123 ηθήσειν, κατόπιν τοῦ Λευκίου γενόμενον. καὶ τάδε
μέν, ὡς προσεδόκησεν ὁ Ἀγρίππας, ἐγίγνετο ἅπαντα·
ὁ δὲ Λεύκιος ἀποτυχὼν ὧν ἐπενόει, πρὸς Ἀσίνιον καὶ
Οὐεντίδιον ᾔει, ἐνοχλούντων αὐτὸν ἑκατέρωθεν Σαλουιδιηνοῦ τε καὶ Ἀγρίππου καὶ φυλασσόντων, ὅτε
μάλιστα περιλάβοιεν ἐν τοῖς στενοῖς.

124 32. Ἐκφανείσης δὲ παρ᾽ αὐτὰ τῆς ἐπιβουλῆς ὁ
Λεύκιος οὐ θαρρῶν ἀμφοτέροις ἑκατέρωθεν οὖσιν ἐς
χεῖρας ἰέναι ἐς Περυσίαν παρῆλθεν, ἐχυρὰν πόλιν,
καὶ παρ᾽ αὐτὴν ἐστρατοπέδευσε, τοὺς περὶ τὸν Οὐεν-
125 τίδιον περιμένων. ὁμοῦ δ᾽ αὐτόν τε καὶ τὴν Περυσίαν
ὁ Ἀγρίππας καὶ ὁ Σαλουιδιηνὸς καὶ ὁ Καῖσαρ ἐπελθὼν τρισὶ στρατοπέδοις ἐκυκλώσαντο· καὶ τὸν ἄλλον
στρατὸν ὁ Καῖσαρ ἐκάλει πανταχόθεν κατὰ σπουδὴν

annoyed with the people who were making war on Octavian contrary to the interests of their joint regime. Some, 121 who failed to see Barbatius' deceit, changed sides from Lucius to Octavian. For his part, Lucius went to confront Salvidienus, who was coming back from Gaul with a large army to join Octavian. Asinius and Ventidius—they too were generals of Antony—were following Salvidienus, trying to prevent him from advancing.[29] Agrippa, Octavi- 122 an's closest associate, was afraid that Salvidienus would be surrounded, and seized Sutrium, a stronghold of importance for Lucius.[30] Agrippa believed that this would draw Lucius away from Salvidienus onto himself, and that Salvidienus, who would then be in the rear of Lucius, would come to his assistance. It all turned out as Agrippa had 123 anticipated. So Lucius, disappointed in his plan, marched off to join Asinius and Ventidius, with Salvidienus and Agrippa harassing him on both flanks, watching for the best opportunity to catch him in the narrows.

32. At this point the plan against Lucius became evi- 124 dent and, as he did not dare to join battle with both of them, located as they were on each of his flanks, he made his way to Perusia, a strongly fortified town and encamped beside it, to wait for Ventidius' men. Agrippa and Salvidi- 125 enus and the newly arrived Octavian surrounded him and Perusia at the same time with their three armies. And Octavian urgently summoned the rest of his forces from

---

[29] For Publius Ventidius Bassus, see App. *BCiv.* 3.66.270 note.   [30] Marcus Vipsanius Agrippa (consul 37, 28, 27), right-hand man of the emperor Augustus, was mentioned in passing at App. *BCiv.* 4.49.213 but only now enters the scene as one of the major players.

ὡς ἐπὶ τοῦτο δὴ κεφάλαιον τοῦ πολέμου, ἐν ᾧ Λεύκιον
126 εἶχε περιειλημμένον. προύπεμπε δὲ καὶ ἑτέρους, ἐμπο-
δὼν εἶναι τοῖς ἀμφὶ τὸν Οὐεντίδιον ἐπιοῦσιν. οἱ δὲ καὶ
αὐτοὶ διὰ σφῶν ὤκνουν ἐπείγεσθαι, τόν τε πόλεμον
ἀποδοκιμάζοντες ὅλως καὶ τὴν Ἀντωνίου γνώμην οὐκ
ἐπιστάμενοι καὶ τὴν ἡγεμονίαν τῆς στρατιᾶς οὐ παρι-
127 έντες ἀλλήλοις κατ' ἀξίωσιν οὐδέτερος. ὁ δὲ Λεύκιος
οὔτ' ἐς μάχην ᾔει τοῖς περικαθημένοις, ἀμείνοσι καὶ
πλέοσιν οὖσι καὶ γεγυμνασμένοις, νεοστράτευτον
ἔχων τὸ πλέον, οὔτε ἐς ὁδοιπορίαν, ἐνοχλησόντων
128 αὐτὸν ὁμοῦ τοσῶνδε. Μάνιον δὲ ἐς τὸν Οὐεντίδιον καὶ
Ἀσίνιον ἔπεμπεν, ἐπείγειν αὐτοὺς βοηθεῖν πολιορ-
κουμένῳ Λευκίῳ, καὶ Τισιηνὸν μετὰ τετρακισχιλίων
ἱππέων, λεηλατεῖν τὰ Καίσαρος, ἵνα ἀνασταίη. αὐτὸς
δὲ παρῆλθεν ἐς τὴν Περυσίαν ὡς ἐν ὀχυρᾷ πόλει χει-
μάσων, εἰ δέοι, μέχρι τοὺς περὶ τὸν Οὐεντίδιον ἀφικέσθαι.

129   33. Καὶ ὁ Καῖσαρ αὐτίκα μετὰ σπουδῆς ἅπαντι τῷ
στρατῷ τὴν Περυσίαν ἀπετείχιζε χάρακι καὶ τάφρῳ,
πεντήκοντα καὶ ἑξ σταδίους περιὼν διὰ τὸ τῆς
πόλεως λοφῶδες καὶ σκέλη μακρὰ ἐπὶ τὸν Τίβεριν
ἐκτείνων, ἵνα τι ἐς τὴν Περυσίαν μὴ ἐσφέροιτο. ἀντε-
πονεῖτό γε μὴν καὶ ὁ Λεύκιος, ἑτέροις ὁμοίοις χαρακώμασι καὶ τάφροις τὴν πέζαν ὀχυρούμενος τοῦ λό-
130 φου. καὶ Φουλβία Οὐεντίδιον καὶ Ἀσίνιον καὶ Ἀτήιον
καὶ Καληνὸν ἐκ τῆς Κελτικῆς ἤπειγε βοηθεῖν Λευκίῳ
καὶ στρατὸν ἄλλον ἀγείρασα Πλάγκον ἔπεμπεν ἄγειν

all quarters, in the belief that here, where he had Lucius trapped, was the key location of the war. He also sent oth-   126
ers ahead to block the advance of Ventidius' men. The latter were, however, reluctant on their own part to press on, as they completely disapproved of the war and did not know what Antony thought about it, and because out of consideration for rank none of them would yield command of their army to each other. Lucius neither engaged the   127
forces surrounding him—who were better, more numerous, and well-trained, while he had mostly new recruits— nor did he resume his march, since so many enemies were harassing him at the same time. He sent Manius to Ven-   128
tidius and Asinius to urge them to come to his assistance as he was under siege, and he sent Tisienus with four thousand cavalry to plunder Octavian's territory and make him abandon the siege.[31] Lucius himself entered Perusia with the intention of wintering in a strong town, if it proved necessary, until Ventidius' men arrived.

33. Octavian, using his whole army, immediately and   129
urgently set about walling off Perusia with a palisade and ditch, creating a perimeter fifty-six stades long because of the location of the town on a hill, and laying out long extensions to the Tiber, so that nothing could be brought into Perusia. Lucius on his part countered Octavian's efforts by fortifying the foot of the hill with new palisades and ditches of a similar sort. Fulvia pressed Ventidius and Asi-   130
nius and Ateius and Calenus to bring help to Lucius from Gaul, and raised a new army, which she instructed Plancus

[31] Tissienus Gallus had repulsed Octavian's attack on the town of Nursia in 41 and succeeded in joining Sextus Pompeius in Sicily (Cass. Dio 48.13, 49.8).

131 Λευκίῳ. Πλάγκος μὲν δὴ τέλος τοῦ Καίσαρος ἐς
Ῥώμην ὁδεῦον διέφθειρεν· Ἀσινίου δὲ καὶ Οὐεντιδίου
σὺν μὲν ὄκνῳ καὶ διχονοίᾳ τῆς Ἀντωνίου γνώμης, διὰ
δὲ Φουλβίαν ὅμως καὶ διὰ Μάνιον ἐς τὸν Λεύκιον
ἰόντων καὶ τοὺς ἀποκλείοντας βιαζομένων, ὁ Καῖσαρ
ὑπήντα σὺν Ἀγρίππᾳ, φυλακὴν τῆς Περυσίας κατα-
132 λιπών. οἱ δὲ οὔτε πω συμβαλόντες ἀλλήλοις οὔτε σὺν
προθυμίᾳ χωροῦντες, ὁ μὲν αὐτῶν ἐς Ῥάβενναν, ὁ δ᾽
ἐς Ἀρίμινον, ὁ δὲ Πλάγκος ἐς Σπωλήτιον συνέφυγον.
133 καὶ ὁ Καῖσαρ αὐτῶν ἑκάστῳ στρατὸν ἐπιστήσας, ἵνα
μὴ πρὸς ἀλλήλους συνέλθοιεν, ἐς τὴν Περυσίαν
ἐπανῆλθε καὶ μετὰ σπουδῆς τὰς τάφρους προσεσταύ-
ρου καὶ ἐδιπλασίαζε τὸ βάθος καὶ πλάτος ὡς τριάκοντα πόδας ἀμφότερα εἶναι, τό τε περιτείχισμα ὕψου
καὶ πύργους ἐπ᾽ αὐτοῦ ξυλίνους δι᾽ ἑξήκοντα ποδῶν
ἵστη χιλίους καὶ πεντακοσίους· καὶ ἐπάλξεις τε ἦσαν
αὐτῷ πυκναὶ καὶ ἡ ἄλλη παρασκευὴ πᾶσα διμέτωπος,
ἔς τε τοὺς πολιορκουμένους καὶ εἴ τις ἔξωθεν ἐπίοι.
134 ἐγίγνετο δὲ ταῦτα σὺν πείραις πολλαῖς καὶ μάχαις,
ἀκοντίσαι μὲν ἀμεινόνων ὄντων τῶν Καίσαρος, συμπλέκεσθαι δὲ τῶν Λευκίου μονομάχων· καὶ πολλοὺς
ἔκτεινον συμπλεκόμενοι.
135   34. Ὡς δὲ ἐξείργαστο πάντα τῷ Καίσαρι, λιμὸς
ἥπτετο τοῦ Λευκίου, καὶ τὸ κακὸν ἤκμαζεν ἀγρίως ἅτε
μηδὲν αὐτοῦ μηδὲ τῆς πόλεως προπαρεσκευασμένης.

to bring to Lucius.[32] Plancus destroyed one of Octavian's   131
legions while it was on its way to Rome, and Asinius and
Ventidius, although hesitant and in disagreement about
Antony's intentions, were nevertheless, thanks to Fulvia
and Manius, heading to Lucius, forcing their way past the
troops blocking them. After leaving a force to keep watch
at Perusia, Octavian went with Agrippa to confront them.
But as they had not yet joined up with each other, and   132
were not advancing with enthusiasm, they simultaneously
took to flight, Asinius to Ravenna, Ventidius to Ariminum,
and Plancus to Spoletium. Octavian stationed a force in   133
front of each, to prevent them from joining forces, and
returned to Perusia, where he quickly added stakes to his
ditches, doubling both their depth and breadth to thirty
feet, and increased the height of the encircling wall, building one thousand five hundred wooden towers on it, sixty
feet apart. It also had continuous battlements, and all the
rest of the structure was double-fronted, facing both in-
ward at the besieged, and outward in case anyone attacked
from there. While these works were under way there were   134
frequent sorties and engagements, Octavian's troops being
better at throwing missiles, Lucius' gladiators at hand-to-
hand fighting; and the latter killed many when engaging
at close quarters.

34. When Octavian had seen to the completion of all   135
these works, famine began to grip Lucius, and the prob-
lem became fiercely intense, since neither he nor the town
had made any preparations beforehand. On learning of

[32] It is not clear who Ateius was. For Quintus Fufius Calenus,
see above, note 8. Lucius Munatius Plancus (consul 42) featured
extensively in Book 3 of the *Civil Wars*.

ὧν ὁ Καῖσαρ αἰσθόμενος ἀκριβεστέρας τὰς φυλακὰς

136 ἐποίει. νουμηνίας δὲ ἔτους ἐς τὴν ἐπιοῦσαν ἡμέραν
οὔσης, φυλάξας ὁ Λεύκιος τὴν ἑορτὴν ὡς ἀμελείας
τοῖς πολεμίοις αἰτίαν ἐξέθορε νυκτὸς ἐπὶ τὰς πύλας
αὐτῶν ὡς διεκπαίσων αὐτοὺς καὶ στρατιὰν ἐπαξόμε-

137 νος ἑτέραν· πολλὴ γὰρ ἦν αὐτῷ πολλαχοῦ. ταχὺ δὲ
τοῦ πλησίον ἐφεδρεύοντος τέλους καὶ τοῦ Καίσαρος
αὐτοῦ σὺν ταῖς στρατηγίσι σπείραις ἐπιδραμόντων,
ὁ Λεύκιος μάλα προθύμως ἀγωνιζόμενος ἀνεώσθη.

138 τῶν δ' αὐτῶν ἡμερῶν ἐν Ῥώμῃ, τοῦ σίτου τοῖς στρατευομένοις φυλασσομένου, τὸ πλῆθος τῷ πολέμῳ καὶ
τῇ νίκῃ φανερῶς ἐπηρῶντο καὶ ἐς τὰς οἰκίας ἐστρέ-
χοντες ἐπὶ ἐρεύνῃ σίτου, ὅσα εὕροιεν, ἥρπαζον.

139   35. Οἱ δ' ἀμφὶ τὸν Οὐεντίδιον αἰδούμενοι λιμῷ
κάμνοντα Λεύκιον περιορᾶν, ἐχώρουν ἐς αὐτὸν ἅπαντες, βιαζόμενοι τοὺς Καίσαρος πανταχόθεν αὐτοὺς

140 περικειμένους καὶ ἐνοχλοῦντας. ὑπαντώντων δ' αὐτοῖς
Ἀγρίππου τε καὶ Σαλουιδιηνοῦ μετὰ δυνάμεως ἔτι
πλείονος, ἔδεισαν, μὴ κυκλωθεῖεν, καὶ ἐς Φουλκίνιόν
τι χωρίον ἐξέκλιναν, ἑξήκοντα καὶ ἑκατὸν σταδίους
τῆς Περυσίας διεστηκός· ἔνθα αὐτοὺς τῶν ἀμφὶ τὸν
Ἀγρίππαν περικαθημένων πυρὰ πολλὰ ἤγειραν, σύμ-

141 βολα τῷ Λευκίῳ. καὶ γνώμην ἐποιοῦντο Οὐεντίδιος
μὲν καὶ Ἀσίνιος βαδίζειν καὶ ὡς μαχούμενοι, Πλάγκος δὲ ἔσεσθαι μέσους Καίσαρός τε καὶ Ἀγρίππου,
χρῆναι δ' ἔτι καραδοκεῖν τὰ γιγνόμενα· καὶ ἐκράτει

142 λέγων ὁ Πλάγκος. οἱ δ' ἐν τῇ Περυσίᾳ τὰ μὲν πυρὰ
ἰδόντες ἥδοντο, τῶν δ' ἀνδρῶν βραδυνόντων εἴκασαν

this, Octavian put his blockading force on closer watch. With the new year starting the next day, Lucius, who had 136 waited on the festival in the belief that it would cause the enemy to be careless, made a sortie against their gates to burst through their lines and get himself another army. For he had many troops everywhere. But the legion sta- 137 tioned nearby, and Octavian himself with his praetorian cohorts, quickly attacked, and Lucius was forced back in spite of his very determined resistance. In the same period 138 at Rome, because the grain was being kept for serving soldiers, the ordinary people began openly to curse the war and the victory, and, after breaking into houses in search of grain, to seize as much of it as they could find.

35. Ventidius and his men, ashamed to look on while 139 Lucius was worn down by hunger, all advanced toward him, forcing back the troops of Octavian in the vicinity who were harassing them from all directions. But when 140 Agrippa and Salvidienus went to meet them with an even larger force, they were afraid that they would be sur- rounded, and changed their route for a place called Ful- ginium, one hundred and sixty stades away from Perusia. Here, with Agrippa's men camped all around them, they lit a large number of fires to signal Lucius. Ventidius and 141 Asinius were of the opinion that they should advance, even in the present circumstances, with the intention of joining battle, but Plancus maintained that, as this would put them between Octavian and Agrippa, they should con- tinue to wait and see what happened. Plancus' words pre- vailed. Those in Perusia were delighted to see the fires, 142 but when the contingent of men was slow in coming, the

καὶ τούσδε ἐνοχλεῖσθαι καὶ παυσαμένου τοῦ πυρὸς
143 διεφθάρθαι. ὁ δὲ Λεύκιος τοῦ λιμοῦ πιέζοντος ἐνυκτο-
μάχησεν αὖθις ἐκ πρώτης φυλακῆς ἐς ἕω περὶ ἅπαν
τὸ περιτείχισμα· καὶ οὐ δυνηθεὶς ἀνέθορεν αὖθις ἐς
τὴν Περυσίαν καὶ τὰς ὑπολοίπους συλλογισάμενος
τροφὰς ἀπεῖπε δίδοσθαι τοῖς θεράπουσι καὶ ἐφύλασσεν αὐτοὺς μηδ' ἐκφυγεῖν, ἵνα μὴ γνωριμώτερον γέ-
144 νοιτο τοῖς πολεμίοις τὸ δεινόν. ἡλῶντο οὖν οἱ θεράπον-
τες κατὰ πλῆθος καὶ κατέπιπτον ἔν τε αὐτῇ τῇ πόλει
καὶ μέχρι τοῦ σφετέρου διατειχίσματος, πόαν εἴ τινα
εὕροιεν ἢ φυλλάδα χλωράν, νεμόμενοι. καὶ τοὺς ἀπο-
ψύχοντας ὁ Λεύκιος ἐς τάφρους ἐπιμήκεις κατώρυσ-
σεν, ἵνα μήτε καιομένων ἐπίδηλον τοῖς ἐχθροῖς γένοιτο, μήτε σηπομένων ἀτμὸς καὶ νόσος.

145   36. Ἐπεὶ δὲ οὔτε τοῦ λιμοῦ τι τέλος ἦν οὔτε τῶν
θανάτων, ἀχθόμενοι τοῖς γιγνομένοις οἱ ὁπλῖται παρεκάλουν τὸν Λεύκιον αὖθις ἀποπειρᾶσαι τῶν τειχῶν,
146 ὡς διακόψοντες αὐτὰ πάντως. ὁ δὲ τὴν ὁρμὴν ἀποδεξάμενος, "Οὐκ ἀξίως," ἔφη, "Πρῴην τῆς παρούσης
ἀνάγκης ἠγωνισάμεθα," καὶ νῦν ἢ παραδιδόναι σφᾶς
ἢ τοῦτο χεῖρον ἡγουμένους θανάτου μάχεσθαι μέχρι
θανάτου. δεξαμένων δὲ προθύμως ἁπάντων καί, ἵνα
μή τις ὡς ἐν νυκτὶ πρόφασις γένοιτο, κατὰ φῶς ἄγειν
147 σφᾶς κελευόντων, ὁ Λεύκιος ἦγε πρὸ ἡμέρας. σίδη-
ρόν τε τειχομάχον εἶχον πολὺν καὶ κλίμακας ἐς εἴδη
πάντα διεσκευασμένας. ἐφέρετο δὲ καὶ τάφρων ἐγχω-
στήρια ὄργανα καὶ πύργοι πτυκτοί, σανίδας ἐς τὰ
τείχη μεθιέντες, καὶ βέλη παντοῖα καὶ λίθοι, καὶ

Perusians guessed that it too was in trouble, and when the
flames died out, that it had been destroyed. With famine   143
pressing him, Lucius again fought a night battle, lasting
from the first watch till dawn, and extending around the
entire fortification; but he failed and hurried back up into
Perusia again. There, having taken stock of his remaining
provisions, he issued an order against any being given to
the slaves, and took precautions to prevent them escaping,
so that his dire situation should not become clearer to the
enemy. The slaves wandered around in crowds, and fell to   144
the ground both in the town itself and right up to their
own cross-wall, feeding on any grass or green leaves they
could find. Those who died Lucius buried in long trenches,
to avoid the situation becoming clear to the enemy by
burning them, and to prevent the stench and disease
caused by rotting corpses.

36. As there was no end to the famine or the deaths,   145
the soldiers, annoyed at what was happening, urged Lucius to make another attempt on the walls, at least to open
a breach in them. Welcoming their eagerness, he said,   146
"Our efforts yesterday were not adequate for our present
desperate situation": now they must, he continued, either
surrender or, if they thought this was worse than death,
then they must fight to the death. They all agreed enthusiastically, and so darkness would provide no excuse, they
demanded that he lead them out in the light of day. So
Lucius marched them out before daybreak. He had a large   147
quantity of iron tools for wall-fighting, and all sorts of ladders, and took with him machines for filling up the ditches,
retractable towers from which gangways could be lowered
onto the walls, all kinds of missiles and stones, and wick-

148 γέρρα τοῖς σκόλοψιν ἐπιρριπτεῖσθαι. προσπεσόντες
δὲ μεθ᾽ ὁρμῆς βιαίου τὴν τάφρον ἐνέχωσαν καὶ τοὺς
σταυροὺς ὑπερέβησαν καὶ τοῖς τείχεσι προσελθόντες
οἱ μὲν ὑπώρυσσον, οἱ δὲ τὰς κλίμακας ἐπῆγον, οἱ δὲ
τοὺς πύργους· ἐνεχείρουν τε ὁμοῦ καὶ ἠμύνοντο λίθοις
καὶ τοξεύμασι καὶ μολυβδαίναις σὺν πολλῇ θανάτου
149 καταφρονήσει. καὶ τάδε ἐγίγνετο κατὰ μέρη πολλά·
ἐπ᾽ εἴδη δέ τινα καὶ[14] ἐς πολλὰ διαιρουμένοις τοῖς πολεμίοις ἀσθενέστερα πάντα ἦν.

150   37. Ἐκταθεισῶν δέ που τῶν σανίδων ἐς τὸ τεῖχος,
βία τότε μάλιστα ἐπικίνδυνος ἦν τῶν Λευκιανῶν ἐπὶ
ταῖς σανίσι μαχομένων, καὶ βέλη πλάγια πάντοθεν
151 ἦν ἐς αὐτοὺς καὶ ἀκόντια. ἐβιάσαντο δὲ ὅμως καὶ ἐς
τὸ τεῖχος ἐξήλαντο ὀλίγοι, καὶ αὐτοῖς εἵποντο ἕτεροι·
καὶ τάχα ἄν τι ἐξείργαστο αὐτοῖς μετὰ ἀπονοίας, εἰ
μή, γνωσθέντος οὐ πολλὰ εἶναι τὰ τοιαῦτα μηχανήματα, οἱ ἄριστοι τῶν Καίσαρος ἐφεδρειῶν ἀκμῆτες
152 ἐπήγοντο κεκμηκόσι. τότε γὰρ δὴ τῶν τειχῶν αὐτοὺς
κατήρειψαν καὶ τὰ μηχανήματα συνέτριψαν καὶ
ἔβαλλον ἄνωθεν ἤδη σὺν καταφρονήσει. τοῖς δὲ τὰ
μὲν ὅπλα καὶ τὰ σώματα ὅλα συνεκέκοπτο, καὶ βοὴ
σφᾶς ἐπελελοίπει, παρέμενον δ᾽ ὅμως τῇ προθυμίᾳ.
153 ὡς δὲ καὶ τὰ νεκρὰ τῶν ἐπὶ τοῦ τείχους ἀνῃρημένων
ἐσκυλευμένα κάτω διερριπτεῖτο, τὴν ὕβριν οὐκ ἔφε-

14 ἐπ᾽ εἴδη δέ τινα καὶ Étienne-Duplessis; ἐπείδη δέ τινας
codd.; post τινας lacunam indic. Schweig.

erwork mats to be thrown onto the pointed stakes. Attack-   148
ing with a violent rush, they filled in the ditch, got over the
stakes, and advancing to the walls, some men began to
undermine them, others placed the ladders against them,
others again the towers. They attacked and at the same
time defended themselves with stones and arrows and
lead slingshots, showing great contempt for death. This   149
happened in many sectors. The whole situation became
less secure for the enemy, divided as they were into many
units to undertake all forms of combat.[33]

37. It was when the gangways had been deployed at   150
various places on the wall that the violent action was particularly dangerous for those of Lucius' men who were
fighting on them and taking missiles and javelins on their
flanks from all directions. They forced their way forward   151
nevertheless, and a few jumped onto the wall followed by
others. And they could perhaps have achieved something
in their desperation if, in the knowledge that Lucius did
not have many such siege engines, Octavian's best re-
serves had not been brought up, fresh troops against exhausted ones. At this point these men threw the enemy   152
down from the walls, shattered their siege engines, and
now disdainfully hurled missiles at them from above. Lucius' men, although their shields and bodies were totally
shattered and their war cry had deserted them, held their
ground all the same with strength of purpose. But when   153
the corpses of those who had been killed on the wall were
stripped and thrown down on them, they could not bear

[33] There is something wrong with the text here. I have followed the Budé edition, but only as an example of what might
make sense in the context.

ρον, ἀλλὰ ἀνετρέποντο ὑπὸ τῆς ὄψεως, καὶ μικρὸν
ἔστησαν ἀποροῦντες ὥσπερ ἐν τοῖς γυμνικοῖς ἀγῶσιν
154 οἱ διαναπαυόμενοι. ὧδε δὲ αὐτοὺς ἔχοντας ἐλεῶν ὁ
Λεύκιος ἐκάλει τῇ σάλπιγγι ἀναχωρεῖν. ἡσθέντων δὲ
τῶν Καίσαρος ἐπὶ τῷδε καὶ τὰ ὅπλα παταγησάντων
οἷον ἐπὶ νίκῃ, ἐρεθισθέντες οἱ τοῦ Λευκίου τὰς κλίμακας αὖθις ἁρπάσαντες (οὐ γὰρ ἔτι πύργους εἶχον)
ἔφερον ἐς τὰ τείχη μετὰ ἀπονοίας, οὐδὲν ἔτι βλάπτον-
τες· οὐ γὰρ ἐδύναντο. περιθέων δ᾽ αὐτοὺς ὁ Λεύκιος
ἐδεῖτο μὴ ψυχομαχεῖν ἔτι καὶ οἰμώζοντας ἀπῆγεν
ἄκοντας.

155   38. Τὸ μὲν δὴ τέλος τῆσδε τῆς τειχομαχίας, ἐκθυ-
μοτάτης γενομένης, ἐς τοῦτο ἐτελεύτα· ὁ δὲ Καῖσαρ,
ἵνα μὴ αὖθις ἐπιτολμήσειαν οἱ πολέμιοι τοῖς τείχεσι,
τὴν στρατιάν, ὅση τοῖς γιγνομένοις ἐφήδρευε, παρ᾽
αὐτὸ τὸ τεῖχος ἵδρυσε καὶ ἐδίδαξεν ἀναπηδᾶν ἐς τὸ
τεῖχος ἄλλους ἀλλαχοῦ κατὰ σύνθημα σάλπιγγος·
συνεχῶς τε ἀπεπήδων οὐδενὸς ἐπείγοντος, ἵνα διδαχῇ
156 τε σφίσι καὶ φόβος εἴη τοῖς πολεμίοις. ἀθυμία δὲ
ἐπεῖχε τοὺς τοῦ Λευκίου, καί, ὅπερ ἐν τοῖς τοιούτοις
εἴωθε γίγνεσθαι, τῆς φυλακῆς οἱ φύλακες ἠμέλουν·
ἐκ δὲ τῆς ἀμελείας αὐτομολίαι πολλῶν ἐγίγνοντο,
καὶ οὐχ οἱ ἀφανέστεροι τοῦτο μόνοι, ἀλλὰ καὶ τῶν
157 ἡγεμονικῶν τινες ἔδρων. ἐνεδίδου τε ὁ Λεύκιος ἤδη
πρὸς διαλύσεις ἐλέῳ τοσοῦδε πλήθους ἀπολλυμένου,
ἐχθρῶν δέ τινων Καίσαρος περὶ σφῶν δεδιότων ἔτι
158 ἐπεῖχεν. ὡς δὲ ὁ Καῖσαρ ὤφθη τοὺς αὐτομόλους φι-
λανθρώπως ἐκδεχόμενος καὶ πλείων ὁρμὴ πᾶσιν ἐς

the insult, but turned away from the sight and stood for a moment not knowing what to do, like athletes taking a rest in the gymnastic games. Lucius had pity on their situation 154 and sounded a retreat by trumpet. Octavian's troops were delighted at this and clashed their arms as if they had won a victory. Infuriated by this, Lucius' men again seized their ladders (for they did not have any towers left), and in desperation carried them to the walls, but inflicted no further damage, as they did not have the strength. Lucius ran from one man to another, begging them not to keep fighting to their last breath, and led them back cursing and reluctant.

38. This was how this hotly contested battle at the walls 155 came to an end. To insure that the enemy did not dare to make any further attempt on his fortifications, Octavian stationed hard by the wall itself those of his troops who were on guard duty, and instructed them to mount the rampart, everyone in their own sector, at a given signal from a trumpet. Even without orders, the men kept doing this, to provide training for themselves and to strike fear into the enemy. Lucius' men began to lose heart, and as 156 usually happens in these situations, the guards became careless. As a result of their negligence, many deserted, and it was not just the ordinary men who did this, but even some of the officer class. Lucius now began to consider a 157 settlement out of distress at such a high casualty rate, but he still held back since some of Octavian's enemies feared for their lives. When it was observed, however, that 158 Octavian received the deserters in a humane manner, and everyone became much more eager for a cessation of

APPIAN

τὰς διαλύσεις ἐγίγνετο, δέος ἥπτετο τοῦ Λευκίου, μὴ
ἀντιλέγων ἐκδοθείη.

159   39. Γενομένης οὖν τινος ἐς τοῦτο πείρας καὶ ἐλπίδος
οὐκ ἀηδοῦς, τὸν στρατὸν συναγαγὼν ἔλεξεν ὧδε·
"Γνώμη μὲν ἦν μοι τὴν πάτριον ὑμῖν ἀποδοῦναι πολιτείαν, ὦ συστρατιῶται, τυρραννίδα τὴν τῶν τριῶν
ἀνδρῶν ἀρχὴν ὁρῶντι καὶ οὐδ', ἐφ' ᾗ συνέστη προ-
φάσει, Κασσίου καὶ Βρούτου τεθνεώτων διαλυθεῖσαν.

160   Λεπίδου γὰρ τὸ μέρος τῆς ἀρχῆς ἀφῃρημένου καὶ
Ἀντωνίου πορρωτάτω χρήματα συλλέγοντος, εἷς οὗτος ἅπαντα πρὸς τὴν ἑαυτοῦ γνώμην διῴκει, τὰ δὲ
πάτρια Ῥωμαίοις πρόσχημα μόνον ἦν καὶ γέλως.

161   ἅπερ ἐγὼ μεταβάλλειν ἐς τὴν ἄνωθεν ἐλευθερίαν τε
καὶ δημοκρατίαν ἐπινοῶν ἠξίουν τῶν ἐπινικίων διαδο-
θέντων ἐκλυθῆναι τὴν μοναρχίαν. ἐπεὶ δὲ οὐκ ἔπειθον,

162   ἐπειρώμην ἐπὶ τῆς ἐμῆς ἀρχῆς καταναγκάσαι. ὁ δέ με
τῷ στρατῷ διέβαλλε, κωλύειν τὰς κληρουχίας ἐλέῳ
τῶν γεωργῶν· καὶ τὴν διαβολὴν ἐγὼ τήνδε ἠγνόησα
ἐπὶ πλεῖστον. ἀλλ' οὐδὲ ἐπιγνοὺς ἐπίστευσά τινα πιστεύσειν, ὁρῶντα τοὺς οἰκιστὰς καὶ παρ' ἐμοῦ δεδο-

163   μένους, οἳ μεριεῖν ἔμελλον ὑμῖν τὰς κληρουχίας. ἀλλὰ
ἐδημαγώγησε γάρ τινας ἡ διαβολή, καὶ πρὸς ἐκεῖνον
ᾤχοντο πολεμήσοντες ὑμῖν, ὡς νομίζουσι, σὺν χρόνῳ

164   δ' εἴσονται στρατευσάμενοι καθ' αὑτῶν. ὑμῖν δ' ἐγὼ
μαρτυρῶ μὲν ἑλομένοις τὰ ἀμείνονα καὶ ὑπὲρ δύναμιν
κακοπαθήσασιν, ἡττήμεθα δὲ οὐχ ὑπὸ τῶν πολεμίων,
ἀλλὰ τοῦ λιμοῦ, ᾧ δὴ καὶ πρὸς τῶν ἡμετέρων στρα-

165   τηγῶν ἐγκαταλελείμμεθα. ἐμοὶ μὲν δὴ καλῶς εἶχεν

70

hostilities, Lucius was seized by a fear that if he opposed them he would be betrayed.

39. Accordingly, after making a tentative move to this end with a reasonable hope of success, he called the men together and spoke as follows: "It was my intention, fellow soldiers, to restore the ancestral constitution to you when I saw that the government of the triumvirs was a tyranny, and was not dissolved even when Cassius and Brutus met their death, which was the excuse on which it was set up. Lepidus was deprived of his share of the government, Antony far away collecting money, and this one man was managing everything according to his own will, and the ancestral constitution was nothing more than a sham and a farce. With the intention of reverting to our previous freedom and democratic government, I asked that after the rewards of victory had been distributed, the monarchy should be dissolved. When persuasion failed, I tried to force the issue by virtue of my office. But Octavian falsely accused me before the army of obstructing the colonies out of pity for the landowners. I knew nothing of this slander for a long time, and even when I found out, I did not think that anybody would believe it, as they could see that the colony leaders, whose job was to distribute the allotments to you, were appointed by me. But the slander misled some people, who went over to Octavian in order to make war against you, so they believe, although in time they will come to see that it was against themselves that they have been campaigning. As for you, I myself bear witness that you, who chose the better course and suffered beyond bearing, have been defeated not by the enemy, but by famine, a fate to which we have in fact been left by our own generals. To be sure, it would have been a fine thing

159

160

161

162

163

164

165

ἀγωνίσασθαι μέχρι τοῦ τελευταίου δαίμονος ὑπὲρ
τῆς πατρίδος· καλὸν γάρ μοι τὸν ἔπαινον ἐπὶ τῇ
γνώμῃ καὶ τὸ τέλος ἐποίει· οὐχ ὑφίσταμαι δὲ δι᾽ ὑμᾶς,
166 οὓς τῆς ἐμῆς προτίθημι εὐκλείας. πέμψω δὴ πρὸς τὸν
κεκρατηκότα καὶ δεήσομαι ἐμοὶ μὲν ἀντὶ πάντων
ὑμῶν εἰς ὃ θέλει καταχρήσασθαι μόνῳ, ὑμῖν δὲ ἀντ᾽
ἐμοῦ ἀμνηστίαν δοῦναι, πολίταις τε οὖσιν αὐτοῦ καὶ
στρατιώταις ποτὲ γενομένοις καὶ οὐδὲ νῦν ἀδικοῦσιν
οὐδὲ πολεμήσασιν ἄνευ καλῆς αἰτίας οὐδὲ ἡσσημένοις πολέμῳ μᾶλλον ἢ λιμῷ."

167   40. Ὁ μὲν οὕτως εἶπε καὶ εὐθὺς ἔπεμπε τρεῖς ἐπι-
λεξάμενος ἐκ τῶν ἀρίστων· ἡ δὲ πληθὺς ἀνώμωζον, οἱ
μὲν ἑαυτῶν χάριν, οἱ δὲ τοῦ στρατηγοῦ, γνώμῃ μὲν
ὁμοῦ σφισιν ἀρίστου καὶ δημοκρατικοῦ φανέντος,
168 ὑπὸ δ᾽ ἐσχάτης ἀνάγκης ἡττημένου. οἱ δὲ τρεῖς ἐντυ-
χόντες τῷ Καίσαρι ἀνεμίμνησκον τοῦ γένους τῶν
στρατῶν ἑνὸς ἑκατέροις ὄντος καὶ στρατειῶν ὁμοῦ
γενομένων καὶ φιλίας τῶν ἐπιφανῶν καὶ ἀρετῆς προ-
γόνων οὐκ ἐς ἀνήκεστον τὰς διαφορὰς προαγαγόν-
των· ὅσα τε εἰκὸς ἦν ἄλλα ἐπαγωγά, τούτοις ὅμοια,
169 ἔλεγον. ὁ δὲ Καῖσαρ εἰδὼς τῶν πολεμίων τοὺς μὲν
ἀπειροπολέμους ἔτι, τοὺς δὲ κληρούχους γεγυμνασμέ-
νους ἔφη τεχνάζων τοῖς ὑπ᾽ Ἀντωνίῳ στρατευσαμένοις διδόναι τὴν ἀμνηστίαν, ὡς χάριν ἐκείνῳ φέρων,
τοὺς δ᾽ ἄλλους ἐπιτρέπειν σφᾶς ἑαυτῷ προσέτασσεν.
170 ταῦτα μὲν εἶπεν ἅπασιν ἰδίᾳ δὲ ἕνα τῶν τριῶν ἀπο-
λαβών, Φούρνιον, ἐς μείζονα φιλανθρωπίαν ἐπήλπισε

for me to have fought for my country until my fated end: for that would have made a noble ending for me and won handsome praise for my decision. But for your sakes, this is a course of action I will not take, since I value your lives more than my own glory. I will send word to the victor and beg that he dispose as he chooses of me alone, instead of all of you, and that he grant an amnesty not to me, but rather to you—you who are his fellow citizens and were once his soldiers, who even now have been doing no wrong, who have not fought without good reason, and who have been defeated not by war but by famine." 166

40. After making this speech he immediately chose three noblemen and sent them off, while the common soldiers grieved, some for themselves, others for their general, whose intentions appeared to them to be at the same time both aristocratic and democratic, and who had been defeated by extreme necessity. The three envoys, when meeting Octavian, reminded him that the armies of both sides belonged to one people, and had campaigned together. They called to mind the friendship of the leading men and the virtue of their ancestors, who had not pushed their differences to breaking point; and they made other arguments similar to these, that were likely to be persuasive. Octavian, knowing that some of the enemy were still without experience of fighting, while the colonists were well trained, replied astutely that he would grant amnesty to those who had served with Antony, as a favor to him, but ordered the others to surrender to himself. This he said in the presence of all, but, taking one of the three envoys, Furnius, aside privately, he led him to expect more 167 168 169 170

τοὺς περὶ Λεύκιον καὶ τοὺς ἄλλους χωρὶς τῶν ἰδίων ἐχθρῶν ἑαυτοῦ.

171   41. Οἵδε οὖν οἱ τοῦ Καίσαρος ἐχθροί, τὴν ἰδίᾳ γενομένην ἔντευξιν τοῦ Φουρνίου ὑπονοοῦντες ἐπὶ σφίσι γενέσθαι, αὐτόν τε τὸν Φούρνιον ἐλοιδόρουν ἐπανελθόντα καὶ τὸν Λεύκιον ἠξίουν ἢ σπονδὰς αὖθις αἰτεῖν ὁμοίας ἅπασιν ἢ πολεμεῖν μέχρι θανάτου· οὐ γὰρ ἴδιόν τινι τὸν πόλεμον, ἀλλὰ κοινὸν ὑπὲρ τῆς

172 πατρίδος γεγονέναι. καὶ ὁ Λεύκιος ἐπῄνει μὲν ἐλεῶν ἄνδρας ὁμοτίμους καὶ πέμψειν ἔλεγεν ἑτέρους, οὐδένα δὲ εἰπὼν ἀμείνονα ἔχειν ἑαυτοῦ, εὐθὺς ἄνευ κήρυκος ᾔει, προθεόντων αὐτοῦ δρόμῳ τῶν ἀπαγγελούντων

173 Καίσαρι κατιέναι Λεύκιον. ὁ δὲ αὐτίκα ὑπήντα. ἑωρῶντο οὖν ἀλλήλοις ἤδη μετὰ τῶν φίλων καὶ περιφανεῖς ἦσαν ἀπὸ τῶν σημείων καὶ τῆς στολῆς οὔσης

174 ἑκατέρῳ στρατηγικῆς. καὶ ὁ Λεύκιος ἀποθέμενος ⟨τὴν στολὴν καὶ ὑπολιπόμενος⟩[15] τοὺς φίλους ᾔει σὺν δύο ῥαβδούχοις μόνοις, ἐπιδεικνὺς ἅμα τὴν γνώμην ἀπὸ τοῦ σχήματος· καὶ ὁ Καῖσαρ συνεὶς ἀντεμιμεῖτο ἐς δεῖγμα καὶ ὅδε τῆς εἰς τὸν Λεύκιον εὐνοίας ἐσομένης·

175 ὡς δὲ καὶ σπεύδοντα εἶδε τὸν Λεύκιον παρελθεῖν ἐς τὸ Καίσαρος χαράκωμα, ἵνα καὶ τῷδε φαίνοιτο ἑαυτὸν ἐπιτρέπων ἤδη, προλαβὼν ὁ Καῖσαρ ἐξῆλθε τοῦ χαρακώμακος, ἵνα ἐλεύθερον εἴη τῷ Λευκίῳ βουλεύε-

[15] τὴν στολὴν καὶ ὑπολιπόμενος add. Étienne-Duplessis; ἀποθέμενος ⟨τὴν στρατηγικὴν στολὴν καὶ ἀποπεμψάμενος⟩ τοὺς φίλους Mend.

humane treatment for Lucius and his men, and for the others, except his own personal enemies.

41. Now, these personal enemies of Octavian, suspecting that Furnius' private meeting was directed against them, abused Furnius himself when he returned, and asked Lucius either to demand new terms that were the same for everybody, or to fight to the death: for, they said, this had not been a private war for anyone, but a common undertaking on behalf of their country. Lucius approved, having pity on them as men of the same rank as himself, and said that he would send new envoys. Arguing that he had no one better for the task than himself, he set off immediately without a herald, just with men running ahead of him to announce that Lucius was coming down to meet Octavian. Octavian immediately went to meet him. So, now they were within sight of each other, accompanied by their associates and conspicuous by their standards and general's uniform they both wore. Then Lucius, after removing ‹his uniform and leaving behind›[34] his associates, went forward with two lictors only, revealing at the same time his intention by his demeanor. Octavian understood and imitated his example, as a demonstration on his part too of the goodwill he would show to Lucius. And when he saw Lucius hurrying to get to his palisade, in order to indicate by this too that he was now surrendering, Octavian anticipated him by advancing out of the palisade, to allow Lucius the freedom to continue to take counsel and

171

172

173

174

175

---

[34] Editors have long agreed on the need for some such addition.

σθαί τε καὶ κρίνειν ἔτι περὶ αὑτοῦ. τοιάδε ἀλλήλοις
προσιόντες ἀπό τε τῆς στολῆς καὶ τῶν σχημάτων
προαπεδείκνυντο.

176   42. Ὡς δὲ ἐπὶ τὴν τάφρον ἀφίκοντο, προσηγόρευσά
τε ἀλλήλους καὶ ὁ Λεύκιος ἔφη· "Εἰ μὲν ξένος ὢν
ἐπολέμησα, ὦ Καῖσαρ, αἰσχρὰν ἂν τὴν τοιαύτην ἧσ-
σαν ἡγούμην καὶ αἰσχίονα ἔτι τὴν παράδοσιν· καὶ
τῆσδε τῆς αἰσχύνης εἶχον ἀπαλλαγὴν εὔκολον παρ'
ἐμαυτοῦ. ἐπεὶ δὲ πολίτῃ διηνέχθην καὶ ὁμοτίμῳ καὶ
ὑπὲρ τῆς πατρίδος, οὐκ αἰσχρὸν ἡγοῦμαι μετὰ τοι-
177   ᾶσδε προφάσεως ὑπὸ τοιοῦδε ἡσσῆσθαι. καὶ τάδε
λέγω οὐ παραιτούμενος παθεῖν, ὅ τι θέλοις (διὰ γάρ
τοι[16] τοῦτο ἐς τὸ στρατόπεδον τὸ σὸν ἄνευ σπονδῶν
ἱέμην), ἀλλ' ἵνα τοῖς ἄλλοις αἰτήσω συγγνώμην δι-
178   καίαν τε καὶ τοῖς σοῖς πράγμασι συμφέρουσαν. δεῖ
δέ με τοῦτο ἐπιδεικνύντα διελεῖν τὸν λόγον ὑπέρ τε
ἐκείνων καὶ ὑπὲρ ἐμαυτοῦ, ἵνα μόνον ἐμὲ τῶν γεγονότων αἴτιον ἐπιγνοὺς εἰς ἐμὲ τὴν ὀργὴν συνα-
γάγῃς. μὴ νομίσῃς δὲ ἐλεγχθήσεσθαι μετὰ παρρη-
σίας (ἄκαιρον γάρ), ἀλλὰ μετὰ ἀληθείας, ἧς οὐκ ἔνι
μοι χωρὶς εἰπεῖν.

179   43. "Ἐγὼ τὸν πρὸς σὲ πόλεμον ἠράμην, οὐχ ἵνα
σε καθελὼν διαδέξωμαι τὴν ἡγεμονίαν, ἀλλ' ἵνα τὴν
ἀριστοκρατίαν ἀναλάβω τῇ πατρίδι, λελυμένην ὑπὸ
τῆς τῶν τριῶν ἀρχῆς, ὡς οὐδ' ἂν αὐτὸς ἀντείποις· καὶ
γὰρ ὅτε συνίστασθε αὐτήν, ὁμολογοῦντες εἶναι παρά-

16 τοι LPJ; σοι B

make a decision about his own fate. Such were the signals as they approached each other they gave in advance by their dress and behavior.

42. When they came to the ditch they greeted each other, and Lucius said: "If I had been a foreigner waging war against you, Octavian, I would consider it disgraceful to have suffered such a defeat and even more shameful to have surrendered in this way; and I would have had an easy means of deliverance from this humiliation at my own hands. But since my dispute was with a citizen, and one of equal rank, and conducted in the cause of our country, I do not consider it a disgrace to be defeated by such a man for such a motive. I say this not to intercede against whatever you may wish me to suffer (and that is, of course, why I came to your camp without a truce being in place), but in order to beg forgiveness for the others, a forgiveness that is both just and serves your own interests. To demonstrate this, I must separate out the case on their behalf from that on my own, so that you may understand that I alone am responsible for what has happened, and direct your anger against me. You should not think that I will make my accusations rudely (it is not the right time for that), but with truthfulness, without which I cannot speak at all.

43. "For my part, I undertook this war against you, not in order to succeed to the leadership by destroying you, but to restore to the country the aristocratic government which had been dismantled by the triumvirate, as not even you yourself would deny. For when you set up the triumvirate you acknowledged that it was unconstitutional, but

176

177

178

179

νομον, ὡς ἀναγκαίαν καὶ πρόσκαιρον ἐτίθεσθε, Κασσίου καὶ Βρούτου περιόντων ἔτι καὶ ὑμῶν ἐκείνοις οὐ
180 δυναμένων συναλλαγῆναι. ἀποθανόντων δὲ ἐκείνων,
οἳ τὸ τῆς στάσεως κεφάλαιον ἦσαν, καὶ τῶν ὑπολοίπων εἴ τινα λείψανα ἔστιν, οὐ τῇ πολιτείᾳ πολεμού-
ντων, ἀλλὰ ὑμᾶς δεδιότων, ἐπὶ δὲ τούτῳ καὶ τῆς
πενταετίας παριούσης, ἀνακύψαι τὰς ἀρχὰς ἐπὶ τὰ
πάτρια ἠξίουν, οὐ προτιμῶν οὐδὲ τὸν ἀδελφὸν τῆς
πατρίδος, ἀλλ᾽ ἐλπίζων μὲν ἐπανελθόντα πείσειν
ἑκόντα, ἐπειγόμενος δὲ ἐπὶ τῆς ἐμῆς ἀρχῆς γενέσθαι.
181 καὶ εἰ κατῆρξας σύ, μόνος ἂν καὶ τὴν δόξαν εἶχες.
ἐπεὶ δὲ δή σε οὐκ ἔπειθον, ᾤμην ἐλθὼν ἐπὶ Ῥώμην
καὶ ἀναγκάσαι, πολίτης τε ὢν καὶ γνώριμος καὶ ὕπα-
182 τος. αἱ μὲν αἰτίαι, δι᾽ ἃς ἐπολέμησα, αὗται μόναι, καὶ
οὔτε ὁ ἀδελφὸς οὔτε Μάνιος οὔτε Φουλβία, οὔτε ἡ
κληρουχία τῶν ἐν Φιλίπποις πεπολεμηκότων οὔτε
ἔλεος τῶν γεωργῶν τὰ κτήματα ἀφαιρουμένων, ἐπεὶ
κἀγὼ τοῖς τοῦ ἀδελφοῦ τέλεσιν οἰκιστὰς ἔδωκα, οἳ τὰ
τῶν γεωργῶν ἀφαιρούμενοι τοῖς στρατευσαμένοις δι-
183 ένεμον. ἀλλά με σὺ τήνδε τὴν διαβολὴν αὐτοῖς δι-
έβαλλες, τὴν αἰτίαν τοῦ πολέμου μεταφέρων ἐπὶ τὴν
κληρουχίαν ἀπὸ σαυτοῦ, καὶ τῷδε μάλιστα αὐτοὺς
ἑλὼν ἐμοῦ κεκράτηκας· ἀνεπείσθησαν γὰρ πολεμεῖ-
184 σθαί τε ὑπ᾽ ἐμοῦ καὶ ἀμύνεσθαί με ἀδικοῦντα. τεχνά-
ζειν μὲν δή σε ἔδει πολεμοῦντα· νικήσας[17] δέ, εἰ μὲν
ἐχθρὸς εἶ τῆς πατρίδος, κἀμὲ ἡγεῖσθαι πολέμιον, ἃ

17 νικήσας Mend.; νικῆσαι LP; νικήσαντα BJ

78

you held it to be necessary and temporary, because Cassius and Brutus were still at large, and you could not come to terms with them. But when they, the leaders of the 180 faction, died, and what was left of the survivors were not at war with the state, but afraid of you, and moreover with the five years' period running out, I demanded that the magistracies should revive in accordance with the custom of our fathers. I did not even value my brother over my country, but hoped to persuade him into willing agreement and pressed hard to make this happen during my own term of office. If you had been the one to take the 181 initiative, you alone would have won the glory. But when I was not able to persuade you, I thought I would proceed to Rome and force you, being, as I was, a citizen and well known and consul. These are the only reasons I made war, 182 and these alone, not my brother, not Manius nor Fulvia, not the allotment of land to those who fought at Philippi, nor pity for the farmers who had their holdings taken from them, for I too appointed colony founders for my brother's legions, and they took the land from the farmers and distributed it to the veterans. But this was the very slander 183 that you, for your part, laid against me to them, transferring the blame for the war from yourself to the allotment of land. It was with this slander in particular that you won them to your side and have defeated me. For they were persuaded that they were being attacked by me and were defending themselves against me as I was the one in the wrong. But since you were the one waging 184 war, you certainly needed to resort to trickery. Now that you are victorious, if you are an enemy of our country, you must consider me an enemy too, since I wished for her

ἔδοξα συνοίσειν αὐτῇ, βουληθέντα μέν, ἡσσηθέντα[18]
δὲ διὰ λιμόν.

185   44. "Λέγω δὲ ταῦτα ἐγὼ ἐγχειρίζων μὲν ἐμαυτόν
σοι, καθάπερ εἶπον, εἰς ὅ τι θέλοις, ὑποδεικνὺς δέ, οἷα
καὶ πρότερον καὶ νῦν ἐφρόνησα περὶ σοῦ καὶ φρονῶν
186   ἔτι μόνος ἀφικόμην. καὶ περὶ μὲν ἐμοῦ τοσαῦτα· περὶ
δὲ τῶν φίλων καὶ τοῦ στρατοῦ παντός, εἰ μὲν οὐχ
ὑποπτεύσεις με λέγοντα, συμβουλεύσω τὰ σοὶ μάλιστα ὠφελιμώτατα, μηδὲν δεινὸν αὐτοὺς ἐργάσασθαι
διὰ τὴν ἐμὴν καὶ σὴν φιλονικίαν, μηδὲ ἄνθρωπον
ὄντα καὶ τύχῃ χρώμενον, οὐ βεβαίῳ πράγματι, κωλῦ-
σαι τοὺς κινδυνεύειν ἐν τύχαις ἢ χρείαις ἐθελήσοντάς
ποτε ὑπὲρ σοῦ, μαθόντας ἐκ τοῦδε τοῦ σοῦ νόμου
187   δυσέλπιστον σῴζεσθαι μὴ κατορθοῦσιν. εἰ δὲ ὕπο-
πτος ἢ ἄπιστος ἐχθροῦ πᾶσα συμβουλή, οὐκ ὀκνῶ
καὶ παρακαλεῖν σε μὴ τοὺς φιλοὺς τίνυσθαι τῆς ἐμῆς
ἁμαρτίας καὶ τύχης, ἀλλ' εἰς ἐμὲ συναγαγεῖν πάντα,
τὸν πάντων αἴτιον. ἀφ' ἧς δὴ γνώμης αὐτοὺς ὑπελι-
πόμην, ἵνα μὴ δόξαιμι, σοὶ τάδε λέγων ἐκείνων ἀκου-
όντων, ὑπὲρ ἐμαυτοῦ τεχνάζων εἰπεῖν."

188   45. Τοιαῦτα δὲ εἰπόντος τοῦ Λευκίου καὶ σιωπήσαν-
τος ὁ Καῖσαρ ἔλεξεν· "Ἄσπονδον μέν σε κατιόντα
πρὸς ἐμὲ ὁρῶν, ὦ Λεύκιε, ὑπήντησα τῶν ἐμῶν ἐρυ-
μάτων ἔτι ἐκτὸς ὄντι κατὰ σπουδήν, ἵνα ἔτι κύριος ὢν
σεαυτοῦ βουλεύοιο καὶ λέγοις καὶ πράττοις, ἃ νομί-
ζεις σοι συνοίσειν. ἐπεὶ δ', ὅπερ ἐστὶ τῶν ἀδικεῖν ὁμο-

---

[18] ἡσσηθέντα P; οὐ δυνηθέντα BJ

what I thought would be of benefit, but was defeated by famine.

44. "In saying this, I place myself in your hands, for you 185 to do whatever you wish. I have demonstrated my opinion of you both before and now, an opinion I still hold, since I have come here alone. But enough about myself. Con- 186 cerning my associates and my whole army, if you will not look with suspicion on what I say, the most useful advice I can give you is to inflict no harsh treatment on them on account of our mutual rivalry. As you are human and sub- ject to fate, an unreliable thing, do not put off those who might be willing one day to face danger on your behalf when fate or necessity demands, by having them find out from this practice of yours that there is no hope of safety for those who fail. Even if any advice from an enemy is 187 suspect or untrustworthy, I do not hesitate to implore you not to take vengeance on my associates for my mistake and my ill fortune, but to blame everything on me, as I am responsible for it all. It was precisely with this intention that I left them behind, so that I would not appear, by saying these things in their presence, to be speaking in some calculating manner on my own behalf."

45. After this speech, Lucius relapsed into silence, and 188 Octavian spoke: "When I saw you coming down to me, Lucius, without a truce in place, I hurried to meet you while you were still outside my defenses, so that while still master of your own fate, you could plan, speak, and act in accordance with what you regard as your best interests. Since you are surrendering to me, which is what people

λογούντων, σαυτὸν ἡμῖν ἐπιτρέπεις, οὐδὲν ἔτι δέομαι
189 διελέγχειν, ὅσα σὺν τέχνῃ μου κατεψεύσω. ἐξ ἀρχῆς
δέ με βλάψειν ἑλόμενος καὶ νῦν ἔβλαψας. σπονδὰς
γάρ μοι τιθέμενος ἔτυχες ἂν ἠδικημένου καὶ νενικη-
κότος· ἄσπονδον δὲ σαυτόν τε καὶ τοὺς φίλους ἐπιτρέπων ἡμῖν καὶ τὸν στρατόν, ἀφαιρῇ μὲν πᾶσαν
ὀργήν, ἀφαιρῇ δὲ καὶ τὴν ἐξουσίαν, ἣν σπενδόμενος
190 ἂν ἔδωκας ὑπ᾽ ἀνάγκης. συμπέπλεκται γὰρ οἷς ἄξιον
ὑμᾶς παθεῖν, τὸ προσῆκον ὧν ἐμὲ δίκαιόν ἐστι ποιεῖν·
ὃ δὴ προτιμήσω διά τε τοὺς θεοὺς καὶ δι᾽ ἐμαυτὸν καὶ
διὰ σέ, ὦ Λεύκιε, καὶ οὐ ψεύσω σε τῆς προσδοκίας,
191 ἣν ἔχων περὶ ἐμαυτοῦ κατελήλυθας." ταῦτα μὲν ἔλε-
ξαν ἀλλήλοις, ὡς ἐκ τῶν ὑπομνημάτων ἦν ἐς τὸ δυνατὸν τῆσδε τῆς φωνῆς μεταβαλεῖν τεκμαιρομένῳ
τῆς γνώμης τῶν λελεγμένων. καὶ διεκρίθησαν, ὁ μὲν
Καῖσαρ ἐν ἐπαίνῳ καὶ θαύματι τὸν Λεύκιον ἔχων, οὐδὲν ὡς ἐν συμφοραῖς ἀγεννὲς οὐδ᾽ ἀσύνετον εἰπόντα,
ὁ δὲ Λεύκιος τὸν Καῖσαρα τοῦ τε ἤθους καὶ βραχυ-
λογίας. οἱ λοιποὶ δ᾽ ἐτεκμαίροντο τῶν εἰρημένων ἐκ
τῆς ὄψεως ἑκατέρων.

192   46. Καὶ ὁ Λεύκιος ἔπεμπε τοὺς χιλάρχους τὸ σύνθημα τῷ στρατῷ ληψομένους παρὰ τοῦ Καίσαρος. οἱ
δὲ ἔφερον αὐτῷ τὸν ἀριθμὸν τοῦ στρατοῦ, καθὰ καὶ
νῦν ἔθος ἐστὶ τὸν αἰτοῦντα τὸ σύνθημα χιλίαρχον
ἐπιδιδόναι τῷ βασιλεῖ βιβλίον ἐφήμερον τοῦ ἀριθμοῦ
193 τοῦ παρόντος. οἱ μὲν δὴ τὸ σύνθημα λαβόντες τὰς

do who admit that they are in the wrong, I have no need to disprove the false allegations you cleverly make against me. But from the start you chose to inflict damage on me, 189 and now you have succeeded in doing so. For if you were negotiating a truce with me, you would have been dealing with a man both wronged and victorious. But by surrendering yourself, your associates, and your army to me without seeking a truce, you rob me of all anger, and you rob me of the power which you would necessarily have given me in negotiating terms. What you deserve to suffer 190 and the appropriateness of what it is right that I do, are interwoven. And to be sure, I will prioritize the latter, for the sake of the gods, of myself, and of you, Lucius, and I will not disappoint you in the expectation you had of me in coming down here." This is what they said to each other, 191 insofar as it was possible for somebody trying to assess the substance of what was said, to translate from the memoirs into what could be rendered in the Greek language.[35] They then parted, Octavian praising and admiring Lucius for not saying anything unworthy or unwise, as happens in times of adversity, and Lucius feeling the same toward Octavian for his character and economy with words. The others made their assessment of what had been said from the expression of the two men.

46. Lucius sent the tribunes to get the watchword for 192 the army from Octavian, and they took the army roll to him, just as it is even still the practice for the tribune who asks for the watchword to deliver to the emperor the daily register of the number of troops present. After receiving 193

[35] This is presumably another reference to Octavian's autobiography, mentioned at *BCiv.* 4.110.463, *Ill.* 15.42.

φυλακὰς ἔτι διὰ χειρὸς εἶχον, οὕτω κελεύσαντος αὐτοῦ Καίσαρος, νυκτοφυλακεῖν ἑκατέρους τὰ ἴδια· ἅμα
δὲ ἡμέρᾳ ὁ μὲν Καῖσαρ ἔθυεν, ὁ δὲ Λεύκιος αὐτῷ τὸν
στρατὸν ἔπεμπε, τὰ μὲν ὅπλα φέροντα, ἐσκευασμένον
194 δ᾽ ὡς ἐν ὁδοιπορίᾳ. οἱ δὲ τὸν Καίσαρα πόρρωθεν ὡς
αὐτοκράτορα ἠσπάσαντο καὶ ἔστησαν ἐν μέρει κατὰ
τέλος, οὗ προσέταξεν ὁ Καῖσαρ, ἐφ᾽ ἑαυτῶν, οἵ τε
195 κληροῦχοι καὶ οἱ νεοστράτευτοι κεχωρισμένοι. ὁ δὲ
Καῖσαρ ἐκτελεσθείσης τῆς θυσίας στεψάμενος δά-
φνῃ, συμβόλῳ νίκης, προυκάθητο ἐπὶ βήματος καὶ
προσέταξε μὲν ἅπασι θέσθαι τὰ ὅπλα, ἔνθα εἱστήκεσαν, θεμένων δὲ τοὺς κληρούχους ἐκέλευσεν ἐγγυ-
τέρω προσελθεῖν, διεγνωκὼς ἄρα ὀνειδίσαι τῆς ἀχα-
196 ριστίας καὶ φοβῆσαι. προέγνωστο δὲ μέλλων ὧδε
ποιήσειν, καὶ ὁ στρατὸς ὁ τοῦ Καίσαρος, εἴτε ἐξ-
επίτηδες, οἷα προδιδάσκονται πολλάκις, εἴτε ὑπὸ
πάθους ὡς πρὸς οἰκείους ἄνδρας, ἀκρατεῖς τῆς δεδο-
μένης σφίσι τάξεως γενόμενοι, προσιοῦσι τοῖς Λευ-
κιανοῖς οἷα συνεστρατευμένοις ποτὲ περιχυθέντες
ἠσπάζοντο καὶ συνέκλαιον καὶ τὸν Καίσαρα ὑπὲρ
αὐτῶν παρεκάλουν καὶ οὔτε βοῶντες ἔτι ἐπαύοντο
οὔτε συμπλεκόμενοι, κοινωνούντων ἑκατέροις τοῦ πάθους ἤδη καὶ τῶν νεοστρατεύτων· οὐδὲ ἦν τι διακεκρι-
μένον ἔτι οὐδ᾽ εὔκριτον.

197   47. Ὅθεν οὐδὲ ὁ Καῖσαρ ἔτι τῆς γνώμης ἐκράτει,
ἀλλὰ μόλις τὴν βοὴν καταπαύσας εἶπε τοῖς ἰδίοις.
"Ὑμεῖς μέν, ὦ συστρατιῶται, οὕτως ἀεί μοι προσενή-
198 νεχθε ὡς μηδενὸς ἀτυχῆσαι παρ᾽ ἐμοῦ δύνασθαι· ἐγὼ

the watchword they still kept their guards on hand, Octavian himself having given orders to this effect that both armies should mount their own guard at night. At dawn, Octavian offered sacrifice, and Lucius sent his soldiers to him carrying their weapons, but equipped as if for a march. From a distance they saluted Octavian as imperator, and took up position separately legion by legion on its own where Octavian had ordered, the colonists being separated from the new recruits. With the sacrifice completed, Octavian, crowned with laurel, the symbol of victory, took his seat on the tribunal in front of them, and ordered them all to lay down their arms where they stood. When they had done so he instructed the colonists to approach closer, having decided, of course, to rebuke them for their ingratitude and strike fear into them. It was discovered beforehand that he was intending to do this, and his own army, either by design, as soldiers are often tutored beforehand, or moved by sympathy for men who were their own kin, became unable to keep the ranks assigned to them and crowded around Lucius' men as they approached, greeting them as former companions in arms. They wept with them, pleaded with Octavian on their behalf, and would not stop shouting and embracing, the new recruits now sharing in the emotion on both sides, so that there was nothing to distinguish or discriminate between them.

47. As a result, not even Octavian could enforce his decision, but after bringing the shouting to an end with some difficulty, he addressed his own men. "You, my fellow soldiers, have always behaved toward me in such a way that you can ask nothing of me in vain. My own belief is

δὲ τοὺς μὲν νεοστρατεύτους ὑπ' ἀνάγκης ἐστρατεῦ-
σθαι Λευκίῳ νομίζω, τουτωνὶ δὲ τῶν συνεστρατευ-
μένων τε πολλάκις ὑμῖν καὶ νῦν ὑφ' ὑμῶν σῳζομένων
ἐπενόουν πυθέσθαι, τί παθόντες ἐξ ἡμῶν ἢ τίνος
χάριτος οὐκ ἀξιωθέντες ἢ τί μεῖζον παρ' ἑτέρου προσδοκῶντες ἐναντία ὅπλα ἤραντο καὶ ἐμοὶ καὶ ὑμῖν καὶ
ἑαυτοῖς; ἃ γὰρ ἔκαμνον ἐγώ, πάντα ἦν ὑπὲρ τῆς κληρουχίας, ἧς τοῦ μέρους καὶ τούτοις μετῆν. καὶ εἰ συγ-
199 χωρεῖτέ μοι, καὶ νῦν πεύσομαι." οὐκ ἐπιτρεπόντων
δέ, ἀλλὰ ἀπαύστως παρακαλούντων, "Συγχωρῶ ὑμῖν,
ὅσα βούλεσθε," ἔφη, "Καὶ ἀφείσθωσαν ἀπαθεῖς τῶν
ἡμαρτημένων, ἂν ἐς τὸ μέλλον ὑμῖν ὅμοια φρονῶσιν."
200 ὑπισχνουμένων δ' ἑκατέρων βοαί τε καὶ χάριτες ἦσαν
ἐς τὸν Καίσαρα· καί τισιν αὐτῶν ἐπέτρεψέ τινας καὶ
ὑποδέξασθαι, τὸ δὲ πλῆθος ἐκέλευε σκηνοῦν, ἔνθα
περ εἱστήκεσαν, ἄπωθεν, ἕως ὁ Καῖσαρ αὐτοῖς πόλεις
τε ἐς χειμασίαν καὶ τοὺς ἀπάξοντας ἐς τὰς πόλεις
δοίη.

201   48. Καθεζόμενος δ' ἐπὶ τοῦ βήματος ἐκάλει τὸν
Λεύκιον ἐκ τῆς Περυσίας μετὰ τῶν ἐν τέλει Ῥωμαίων.
καὶ κατῄεσαν πολλοὶ μὲν ἀπὸ τῆς βουλῆς, πολλοὶ δὲ
ἀπὸ τῶν καλουμένων ἱππέων, ἐν ὄψει πάντες ⟨ὄντες⟩[19]
202 οἰκτρᾷ καὶ ὀξείᾳ μεταβολῇ. ἅμα δὲ ἐξῄεσαν οὗτοι τῆς
Περυσίας, καὶ φρουρὰ τὴν πόλιν περιέστη. ἐπεὶ δὲ
ἀφίκοντο, Λεύκιον μὲν ὁ Καῖσαρ ἑαυτῷ παρεστή-
σατο, τῶν δὲ ἄλλων τοὺς μὲν οἱ φίλοι Καίσαρος, τοὺς

---

[19] ὄντες add. Étienne-Duplessis

that the new recruits fought for Lucius under compulsion, but it was my intention to ask these men here, who have often campaigned alongside you and whom you are now in the process of protecting, what they have suffered at our hands, or what favor they were refused, or what greater favors they are expecting from somebody else, that they have taken up arms against me, against you, against themselves. For the issues that have caused me difficulty all arose from the assignment of lands, in which they too have had their share. And now, if you will permit me, I will put these questions to them." As they would not allow him to   199
do this, but continued to make their entreaties, he said, "I yield to all your wishes. Let them be released without punishment for their crimes, on condition that in future they display the same attitude as you." Both sides made   200
their promises, and there were cheers and expressions of gratitude for Octavian, who allowed some of his own men to look after particular individuals among their men. He ordered the ordinary soldiers, however, to pitch their tents where they stood, away from his own men, until he could assign them towns for winter quarters and appoint persons to lead them off to those towns.

48. Then, seated on his tribunal, Octavian summoned   201
Lucius from Perusia along with those Romans who had official positions in his entourage. Many senators and those called knights came down to him, all exposed to view by their bitter and sudden change of fortune. As soon as   202
they left Perusia, a guard was stationed around it. When they arrived, Octavian put Lucius standing beside him, and of the rest, Octavian's associates took charge of some, and the centurions of others, but all had been instructed

δὲ οἱ λοχαγοὶ διέλαβον, προδεδιδαγμένοι πάντες ἐς
203 τιμὴν ἀπάγειν ἅμα καὶ φυλακὴν ἄσημον. τοὺς δὲ Πε-
ρυσίους ἀπὸ τοῦ τείχους παρακαλοῦντας ἐκέλευσεν
ἥκειν, ἄνευ τῆς βουλῆς μόνης· καὶ ἐλθοῦσι συνέγνω.
οἱ δὲ βουλευταὶ τότε μὲν φύλαξι παρεδόθησαν, μετ᾽
οὐ πολὺ δὲ ἀνῃρέθησαν, χωρὶς Αἰμιλίου Λευκίου, ὃς
ἐν Ῥώμῃ δικάζων ἐπὶ τῷ φόνῳ Γαΐου Καίσαρος τὴν
καταδικάζουσαν ἤνεγκε φανερῶς καὶ πάντας φέρειν
ἐκέλευεν ὡς ἐκλυομένους μύσος.

204 49. Τὴν δὲ Περυσίαν αὐτὴν ἐγνώκει μὲν ὁ Καῖσαρ
ἐς διαρπαγὴν ἐπιτρέψαι τῷ στρατῷ, Κέστιος δέ τις
αὐτῶν ὑπομαργότερος, ἐν Μακεδονίᾳ πεπολεμηκὼς
καὶ ἐκ τοῦδε Μακεδονικὸν αὐτὸν ὀνομάζων, ἐνέπρησε
τὴν οἰκίαν καὶ ἑαυτὸν ἐς τὸ πῦρ ἐνέβαλε, καὶ ἄνεμοι
τὴν φλόγα ὑπολαβόντες περιήνεγκαν ἐς ὅλην Περυσίαν, καὶ ἐνεπρήσθη χωρὶς τοῦ Ἡφαιστείου μόνου.
205 τόδε μὲν δὴ τῇ Περυσίᾳ τέλος ἦν, δόξαν ἀρχαιότητος
ἐχούσῃ καὶ ἀξιώσεως· ὑπὸ γὰρ Τυρρηνῶν πάλαι φα-
σὶν αὐτὴν ἐν ταῖς πρώταις δυώδεκα πόλεσιν ἐν Ἰταλίᾳ
206 γενέσθαι. διὸ καὶ τὴν Ἥραν ἔσεβον, οἷα Τυρρηνοί·
τότε δὲ ὅσοι τὰ λείψανα τῆς πόλεως διέλαχον, τὸν
Ἥφαιστον σφίσιν ἔθεντο θεὸν εἶναι πάτριον ἀντὶ τῆς
207 Ἥρας. τῆς δ᾽ ἐπιούσης ὁ μὲν Καῖσαρ ἐσπένδετο ἅπασιν, ὁ δὲ στρατὸς οὐκ ἐπαύετο ἐπί τισι θορυβῶν, ἕως
ἀνῃρέθησαν· καὶ ἦσαν οἱ μάλιστα Καίσαρος ἐχθροί,

beforehand to treat them honorably while at the same time keeping a discreet watch on them. As for the Perusians who were making their appeal for mercy from the walls, he ordered them, with the exception of the town council, to approach, and when they came he pardoned them. The council members were put under guard at the time, but were executed shortly after, apart from Lucius Aemilius, who, while acting as a juror at Rome in the trial of the murderers of Gaius Caesar, had voted openly for condemnation, and urged all the others to do the same in an attempt to expiate pollution. 203

49. As for Perusia itself, Octavian had intended to turn it over to the soldiers to plunder, but one of the citizens, a certain Cestius, who was somewhat deranged and called himself "the Macedonian" because he had fought in Macedonia, set fire to his house and threw himself into the flames. The wind caught the fire and spread it to the whole of Perusia, which was burned to the ground, except the temple of Vulcan. Such was the end of Perusia, a town renowned for its antiquity and importance. They say that in the past under Etruscan rule, it became one of the twelve major towns of Italy.[36] That is why they used to worship Hera in the Etruscan manner. But at this time, those who inherited the remains of the town took Vulcan as their patron god instead of Hera. Next day Octavian made peace with everyone, but the army would not stop raising a clamor against certain people, until they were executed. These were the particular personal enemies 204 205 206 207

[36] Perusia may have been one of the twelve towns in the Etruscan League that, according to Livy (6.2), met in the temple of Voltumna at Volsinii.

Καννούτιός τε καὶ Γάιος Φλάνιος καὶ Κλώδιος ὁ Βι-
θυνικὸς καὶ ἕτεροι.

208   50. Τοῦτο μὲν δὴ τέλος ἦν τῆς ἐν Περυσίᾳ Λευκίου
πολιορκίας, καὶ ὁ πόλεμος ὧδε ἐξελέλυτο, χαλεπώτα-
τός τε καὶ χρόνιος ἐλπισθεὶς ἔσεσθαι τῇ Ἰταλίᾳ. καὶ
γὰρ Ἀσίνιος αὐτίκα καὶ Πλάγκος καὶ Οὐεντίδιος καὶ
Κράσσος καὶ Ἀτήιος καὶ ὅσοι τῆσδε τῆς γνώμης
ὄντες ἕτεροι στρατὸν εἶχον οὐκ εὐκαταφρόνητον, ἀλλ᾽
εἰς τρισκαίδεκα τέλη γεγυμνασμένα καὶ ἱππέας ἑξα-
κισχιλίους ἐπὶ πεντακοσίοις, ἡγούμενοι τὸ κεφάλαιον
τοῦ πολέμου Λεύκιον γεγονέναι ἐπὶ θάλασσαν ᾖσαν,
209 ἕτερος ἑτέρας ὁδούς, οἱ μὲν ἐς Βρεντέσιον, οἱ δ᾽ ἐπὶ
Ῥαβέννης, οἱ δ᾽ ἐς Τάραντα καὶ οἱ μὲν ἐς Μοῦρκον ἢ
Ἀηνόβαρβον, οἱ δὲ ἐς Ἀντώνιον, διωκόντων αὐτοὺς
τῶν Καίσαρος φίλων καὶ σπονδὰς προτεινόντων καὶ
οὐκ ἐθέλουσιν ἐνοχλούντων τὰ πεζὰ μάλιστα· ὧν δὴ
καὶ μόνων Ἀγρίππας ἔπεισε μεταθέσθαι δύο τέλη
210 Πλάγκου, ἀποληφθέντα ἐν Καμερίᾳ. ἔφευγε δὲ καὶ
Φουλβία μετὰ τῶν τέκνων ἐς Δικαιάρχειαν καὶ ἀπὸ
Δικαιαρχείας ἐς τὸ Βρεντέσιον, μετὰ τρισχιλίων
ἱππέων οἳ αὐτῇ παρὰ τῶν στρατηγῶν πομποὶ ἀπ-
211 εστάλησαν. ἐν δὲ τῷ Βρεντεσίῳ νεῶν πέντε μακρῶν
ἐκ Μακεδονίας οἱ μεταπέμπτων γενομένων ἐπιβᾶσα
ἀνήγετο· καὶ αὐτῇ Πλάγκος συνέπλει, τὸν ἔτι λοιπὸν
αὐτοῦ στρατὸν ἐκλιπὼν ὑπὸ δειλίας. οἱ δὲ Οὐεντίδιον

---

[37] None of these figures has been securely identified. There
was a Tiberius Cannutius who was tribune of the plebs in 44, but

of Octavian, Cannutius and Gaius Flavius and Clodius
Bithynicus, among others.[37]

50. Such, then, was the end of the siege of Lucius in   208
Perusia, and it also brought the war to an end, a war that
had been expected to be extremely difficult and long for
Italy. The reason it ended was that Asinius and Plancus
and Ventidius and Crassus and Ateius, and all the others
of this party, although they had an army not to be despised,
numbering some thirteen trained legions and six thousand
five hundred cavalry, thought that Lucius had become the
vital person in the war, and they now made for the coast.[38]
They all took different routes, some to Brundisium, some   209
to Ravenna, some to Tarentum, some to join Murcus and
Ahenobarbus, and still others to Antony. Octavian's associates pursued them, offering a truce, and, when they refused, harassed them, particularly the infantry. In fact,
from this force, Agrippa was only able to persuade two of
Plancus' legions, who had been abandoned at Cameria, to
come over to his side. Fulvia also fled with her children to   210
Dicaearchia, and from there to Brundisium, accompanied
by three thousand cavalry, who had been dispatched by
the generals to escort her. At Brundisium she embarked   211
on the five warships that had been summoned from Macedonia for her, and put to sea. Plancus sailed with her,
having abandoned the remains of his army out of coward-

Appian himself (*BCiv.* 3.41.167–69) refers to him as a staunch
partisan of Octavian. There was also a Publius Cannutius whom
Cicero regarded as the most eloquent of senators (*Brut.* 56.205).

[38] Publius Canidius Crassus (suffect consul 40) was a loyal
supporter of Antony to the very end: he was executed by Octavian
after the battle of Actium.

212 σφῶν εἵλοντο ἄρχειν. Ἀσίνιος δὲ Ἀηνοβάρβῳ συν-
ετίθετο φιλίαν εἶναι πρὸς Ἀντώνιον· καὶ ἐπέστελλον
ἄμφω τάδε τῷ Ἀντωνίῳ καὶ ἀποβάσεις αὐτῷ καὶ
ἀγορὰν ὡς αὐτίκα ἥξοντι εὐτρέπιζον ἀνὰ τὴν Ἰταλίαν.

213 51. Ἄλλῳ δ᾽ Ἀντωνίου στρατῷ πολλῷ περὶ Ἄλπεις,
οὗ Φούφιος Καληνὸς ἡγεῖτο, ὁ Καῖσαρ ἐπεβούλευεν,
ἤδη μὲν τὸν Ἀντώνιον ὑπονοῶν, ἐλπίζων δὲ ἢ φίλῳ
ἔτι ὄντι φυλάξειν ἢ πολεμοῦντος μεγάλην ἰσχὺν
214 προσλήψεσθαι. διαμέλλοντος δὲ ὅμως ἔτι αὐτοῦ καὶ
τὸ εὐπρεπὲς περιορωμένου, ὁ Καληνὸς ἐτελεύτησε·
καὶ ὁ Καῖσαρ, ὡς ἐς ἀμφότερα πρόφασιν εὑρών, ᾔει
καὶ παρελάμβανε τόν τε στρατὸν καὶ τὴν Κελτικὴν
ἐπ᾽ αὐτῷ καὶ Ἰβηρίαν, καὶ τάσδε οὔσας ὑπὸ Ἀντωνίῳ,
Φουφίου τοῦ παιδὸς Καληνοῦ καταπλαγέντος τε
215 αὐτὸν καὶ παραδόντος ἅπαντα ἀμαχεί. ὁ μὲν δὴ Καῖσαρ ἑνὶ τῷδε ἔργῳ ἕνδεκα τέλη στρατοῦ καὶ χώρας
τοσάσδε λαβὼν τοὺς ἡγεμόνας αὐτῶν παρέλυε τῆς
ἀρχῆς καὶ ἰδίους ἐπιστήσας ἐς Ῥώμην ἀνέστρεφεν·

216 52. Ὁ δὲ Ἀντώνιος χειμῶνος μὲν ἔτι τοὺς πρέσβεις
κατεῖχε τοὺς ἀπὸ τῶν κληρουχιῶν πρὸς αὐτὸν ἐλθόντας, ἔτι[20] ἐπικρύπτων, ἃ ἐφρόνει, ἦρι δ᾽ ἐκ μὲν Ἀλεξ-
ανδρείας ἐς Τύρον ὥδευεν, ἐκ δὲ Τύρου διαπλέων ἐπὶ
Κύπρου καὶ Ῥόδου καὶ Ἀσίας ᾔσθετο τῶν ἐν τῇ Περυσίᾳ γεγονότων καὶ τὸν ἀδελφὸν ἐμέμφετο καὶ

20 ἔτι BJ; εἴτε LP.; post ἐλθόντας lacunam indic. Étienne-
Duplessis

92

ice; these soldiers now chose Ventidius as their com- 212
mander. Asinius came to an agreement with Ahenobarbus
to make a pact of friendship with Antony. Both Asinius and
Ventidius wrote to inform Antony of this, and they prepared landing places and store depots for him throughout
Italy, in the expectation that he would come immediately.

51. Octavian now began to make plans to acquire an- 213
other large army belonging to Antony stationed in the
Alpine region under the command of Fufius Calenus. He
was on the one hand already suspicious of Antony, and on
the other he hoped to keep this army for Antony if he
remained friendly, or, if war broke out, to get for himself
a large additional force. However, while he was still hesi- 214
tating and looking around for a decent excuse, Calenus
died; and Octavian, having found his pretext for both
eventualities, went and took possession both of this army
and of Gaul and Iberia as well—these too were under
Antony's control—for Fufius, the son of Calenus, was terrified of him, and handed over everything without a fight.
So with this one stroke Octavian acquired an army of 215
eleven legions and very extensive territory. He relieved
the governors of their command, installed his own men,
and returned to Rome.

52. While it was still winter, Antony detained the rep- 216
resentatives who had come to him from the colonists,
keeping his intentions to himself for the time being,[39] but
in spring he journeyed from Alexandria to Tyre, and sailed
from Tyre across to Cyprus and Rhodes and Asia. Hearing
of the events in Perusia, he blamed his brother and Fulvia,

[39] It is possible that Antony keeping his intentions to himself
is the second part of an either/or construction, in which case
something is missing from the text.

217 Φουλβίαν καὶ μάλιστα πάντων Μάνιον. Φουλβίαν
μὲν οὖν εὗρεν ἐν Ἀθήναις, ἐκ Βρεντεσίου φυγοῦσαν·
Ἰουλίαν δ' αὐτῷ τὴν μητέρα Πομπήιος, ἐς αὐτὸν δια-
φυγοῦσαν, ἔπεμπεν ἐκ Σικελίας ἐπὶ νεῶν μακρῶν, καὶ
παρέπεμπον αὐτὴν οἱ τῶν ἀμφὶ τὸν Πομπήιον ἄριστοι, Λεύκιός τε Λίβων, ὁ κηδεστὴς τοῦ Πομπηίου,
καὶ Σατουρνῖνος καὶ ἕτεροι, ὅσοι χρῄζοντες τῆς
Ἀντωνίου μεγαλοπραγίας ἠξίουν αὐτὸν συναλλα-
γέντα Πομπηίῳ σύμμαχον ἐπὶ Καίσαρι λαβεῖν Πομ-
218 πήιον. ὁ δὲ αὐτοῖς ἀπεκρίνατο χάριν μὲν ἐπὶ τῇ μητρὶ
γιγνώσκειν Πομπηίῳ καὶ ἀποτίσειν ἐν χρόνῳ, αὐτὸς
δέ, εἰ μὲν πολεμοίη Καίσαρι, χρήσεσθαι Πομπηίῳ
συμμάχῳ, εἰ δ' ἐμμένοι τοῖς πρὸς αὐτὸν ὡμολογημέ-
νοις ὁ Καῖσαρ, πειράσεσθαι καὶ Πομπήιον Καίσαρι
συναλλάξαι.

219 53. Ὁ μὲν ὧδε ἀπεκρίνατο, ὁ δὲ Καῖσαρ ἐς Ῥώμην
ἀπὸ Κελτῶν ἐπανιὼν ᾔσθετο μὲν τῶν ἐς Ἀθήνας δια-
πεπλευκότων, τὸ δὲ τῆς ἀποκρίσεως ἀκριβὲς ἄρα οὐκ
εἰδὼς ἐξώτρυνε τοὺς κληρούχους ἐπὶ τὸν Ἀντώνιον ὡς
κατάγοντα μετὰ τῶν γεωργῶν Πομπήιον, ὧν αὐτοὶ τὰ
χωρία ἔχουσιν· ἐς γὰρ δὴ Πομπήιον οἱ πλέονες τῶν
220 γεωργῶν ἐπεφεύγεσαν. καὶ πιθανοῦ τοῦ διερεθίσματος ὄντος, οὐδ' ὡς οἱ κληροῦχοι προθύμως ἐπὶ τὸν
Ἀντώνιον ἐστράτευον· οὕτως ἡ δόξα τῶν ἐν Φιλίπποις

---

40 Lucius Scribonius Libo (praetor 50) was a supporter of
Pompey in the civil war against Julius Caesar, with whom he was
reconciled after the battle of Pharsalus. Although not part of the

but most of all Manius. He found Fulvia at Athens, after   217
her flight from Brundisium. His mother, Julia, had escaped to Pompeius, who sent her to him from Sicily in a
convoy of warships, and she was escorted by leading figures of Pompeius' entourage, including his father-in-law,
Lucius Libo, Saturninus, and others who needed Antony's
capacity for great undertakings, and asked him to come to
an agreement with Pompeius and take him as an ally
against Octavian.[40] Antony replied that he was grateful to   218
Pompeius for what he had done for his mother, and would
repay him in time. As for himself, if he waged war against
Octavian he said he would treat Pompeius as an ally, but
if Octavian adhered to the terms of their agreement, he
would try to reconcile Pompeius too with Octavian.

53. Such was his answer. When Octavian returned from   219
Gaul to Rome, he found out about the deputation that
had sailed to Athens, but as he did not really have accu-
rate information about the reply, he roused the colonists
against Antony, alleging that he was intending to restore
Pompeius along with the farmers whose land they themselves were holding. For it was certainly the case that most
of the farmers had taken refuge with Pompeius. Although   220
this provocation was plausible, the colonists were not even
then keen to take up arms against Antony, so popular had

conspiracy against Caesar, he was proscribed in 43. Octavian married his sister in 40 to secure a peace with Sextus Pompeius, Libo's
son-in-law. After abandoning Pompeius in 35, he held the consulship with Marc Antony in 34. Saturninus is probably Gaius Sen-
tius Saturninus Vetulo, who was proscribed in 43. His son, also
proscribed in 43, became a loyal supporter of Augustus and held
the consulship in 19.

221 γεγονότων ἐδημαγώγει τὸν Ἀντώνιον. ὁ δὲ Καῖσαρ
Ἀντωνίου μὲν καὶ Πομπηίου καὶ Ἀηνοβάρβου κατὰ
πλῆθος ὁπλιτῶν ὑπεροίσειν ἐνόμιζεν (ἦρχε γὰρ τελῶν
ἐς τότε τεσσαράκοντα πλεόνων), ναῦν δὲ οὐδεμίαν
ἔχων οὐδὲ καιρὸν ἐς ναυπηγίαν ὠρρώδει, ναῦς ἐκείνων
ἐχόντων πεντακοσίας, μὴ τὴν Ἰταλίαν περιπλέοντες

222 ἐς λιμὸν περιενέγκαιεν. ὧν ἐνθυμούμενος (ἐλέλεκτο δὲ
αὐτῷ περὶ πολλῶν παρθένων ἐς γάμον) ἐπέστελλε
Μαικήνα συνθέσθαι Σκριβωνίᾳ, τῇ Λίβωνος ἀδελφῇ,
τοῦ κηδεύοντος Πομπηίῳ, ἵν’ ἔχοι καὶ τήνδε ἀφορμὴν
ἐς διαλύσεις, εἰ δεήσειεν. καὶ πυθόμενος ὁ Λίβων
ἐπέστελλε τοῖς οἰκείοις ἐγγυᾶν αὐτὴν τῷ Καίσαρι

223 προθύμως. ὁ δὲ Καῖσαρ τῶν Ἀντωνίου φίλων καὶ
στρατῶν ὅσους ὑπώπτευε, διέπεμπεν ἐπὶ προφάσεων
ἄλλους ἀλλαχοῦ καὶ Λέπιδον ἐς τὴν ἐψηφισμένην
αὐτῷ Λιβύην, ἄγοντα τῶν Ἀντωνίου τελῶν τὰ ὑπ-
οπτότατα ἕξ.

224 54. Λεύκιον δὲ καλέσας ἐπῄνει μὲν ἐς φιλαδελφίαν,
εἰ τῇ Ἀντωνίου γνώμῃ ὑπομεμενηκὼς ἴδιον τὸ ἁμάρτημα ποιοῖτο, ὠνείδιζε δὲ ἐς ἀχαριστίαν, εἰ τοιούτου
τυχὼν αὐτοῦ μηδὲ νῦν ὁμολογοίη περὶ Ἀντωνίου, σα-

225 φῶς ἤδη καὶ Πομπηίῳ συνθέσθαι λεγομένου. “Ἐγὼ
δέ σοι πιστεύων,” ἔφη, “Καληνοῦ τελευτήσαντος τά

---

41 Scribonia was the sister of Lucius Scribonius Libo (consul
34), who was aligned for most of this period against Octavian.

his reputation for the events at Philippi made him. Octa- 221
vian thought that he would have the better of Antony,
Pompeius, and Ahenobarbus in the number of soldiers, for
he commanded more than forty legions at that time, but
as he did not have a single ship nor the opportunity to
build any, while they had five hundred, he was afraid that
they would reduce Italy to famine by patrolling its coasts.
With these matters on his mind, and having had proposals 222
made to him about many young women he could marry,
he wrote to Maecenas to arrange an engagement for him
with Scribonia, the sister of Libo, the father-in-law of
Pompeius, so that he might have this as the basis for a
settlement with Pompeius, if it should prove necessary.[41]
When Libo heard of this he wrote to his family telling
them to betroth her to Octavian without hesitation. Those 223
of Antony's associates and armed forces Octavian did not
trust he found excuses to send to various different places;
and he dispatched Lepidus to Africa, the province officially assigned to him, bringing with him the six most suspect of Antony's legions.

54. Then he summoned Lucius and praised him for his 224
loyalty to his brother, if it was the case that he had taken
the blame on himself while carrying out Antony's policy,
but reproached him with ingratitude, if it was the case
that, after meeting with such a response from himself, he
refused to admit the truth about Antony even now when
he was spoken of openly as having made an agreement with
Pompeius. "Because I trusted you," Octavian said, "when 225

After two previous marriages, she was married to Octavian in 40,
who divorced her on the birth of their daughter, Julia, in 39.

τε ἔθνη τὰ ὑπ' αὐτῷ καὶ τὸν στρατόν, ἵνα μὴ ἄναρχος
εἴη, διὰ τῶν ἐμαυτοῦ φίλων διῴκουν Ἀντωνίῳ. ἀλλὰ
νῦν ἐκφανείσης τῆς ἐνέδρας ἐκεῖνά τε ἐμαυτοῦ πάντα
ποιοῦμαι καὶ σοὶ πρὸς τὸν ἀδελφὸν ἀπιέναι θέλοντι
226 συγχωρῶ μετὰ ἀδείας." ὁ μὲν οὕτως εἶπεν, εἴτε πειρώμενος τοῦ Λευκίου, εἴτε τὸ λεχθὲν ἐκπεσεῖν ἐθέλων ἐς
τὸν Ἀντώνιον· ὁ δὲ οἷα καὶ πρότερον εἶπε· "Φουλβίας
μὲν ᾐσθόμην οὔσης μοναρχικῆς, ἐγὼ δὲ συνεχρώμην
τοῖς τοῦ ἀδελφοῦ στρατοῖς ἐς τὴν ἁπάντων ὑμῶν καθ-
227 αίρεσιν. καὶ νῦν, εἰ μὲν ἐπὶ καταλύσει τῆς μοναρχίας
ἔρχοιτο ὁ ἀδελφός, καὶ φανερῶς καὶ λαθὼν οἰχήσο-
μαι πρὸς αὐτόν, ἀγωνιούμενος αὖθις ὑπὲρ τῆς πατρί-
228 δος πρὸς σέ, καίπερ ἤδη μοι γενόμενον εὐεργέτην. εἰ
δ' ἐπιλέγοιτο κἀκεῖνος καὶ διακρίνοι τοὺς συμμοναρ-
χήσοντας αὐτῷ, πολεμήσω σὺν σοὶ πρὸς αὐτόν, ἕως
ἂν ἡγῶμαι μηδὲ σὲ μοναρχίαν καθίστασθαι· τὸ γὰρ
τῆς πατρίδος αἰεὶ προθήσω καὶ χάριτος καὶ γένους."
229 ὧδε μὲν ὁ Λεύκιος εἶπεν, ὁ δὲ Καῖσαρ αὐτὸν καὶ
τέως ἐν θαύματι ἄγων οὐκ ἔφη μὲν οὐδὲ βουλόμενον
ἐπάξεσθαι κατὰ ἀδελφοῦ, πιστεύσειν δὲ ὡς τοιῷδε
ἀνδρὶ πᾶσαν Ἰβηρίαν καὶ τὸν ἐν αὐτῇ στρατόν, ὑπο-
στρατηγούντων αὐτῷ τῶν νῦν ἡγουμένων αὐτῆς Πε-
δουκαίου τε καὶ Λευκίου.[21]
230 55. Οὕτω μὲν δὴ καὶ Λεύκιον ὁ Καῖσαρ ἀπέπεμπε

---

[21] Post Λευκίου indic. lacunam Schweig.

Calenus died I took on the administration of the provinces under his command and of his army, so that it would not be without a leader, using my own associates, and acting on behalf of Antony. But now that this plot has come to light, I claim all these for myself, and if you wish to go off to join your brother, I grant you safe conduct to do so." He 226 said this either to test Lucius, or because he wanted his words to reach Antony's ears. Lucius replied as before, saying, "I was aware that Fulvia was a proponent of monarchic government, but as far as I was concerned, I collaborated with my brother's forces in order to destroy all of you. And now if my brother comes to abolish the mo- 227 narchic regime, I will go to join him, either openly or secretly, and, on behalf of our country, I will renew my struggle against you, even though you have now become my benefactor. On the other hand, if he too is merely 228 choosing and setting apart people to share sole rule with him, I will fight on your side against him, as long as I think that you are not also trying to establish a monarchy. For I will always set the interests of my country above favor and family." Such was Lucius' reply, and Octavian, who already 229 admired him before, said that he would not take him as an ally against his brother, even if he was willing, but, because he was a man of such character, he would entrust to him the whole of Iberia and the army stationed there, with its present governors, Peducaeus and Lucius, acting as his subordinates.[42]

55. In this way Octavian removed Lucius to a distance 230

[42] There was a Titus Peducaeus who was suffect consul in 35. It is odd that the second man only has a praenomen, and there may be something wrong with the text.

σὺν τιμῇ καὶ διὰ τῶν ὑποστρατήγων ἐφύλασσεν
ἀφανῶς· Ἀντώνιος δὲ Φουλβίαν μὲν ἐν Σικυῶνι νοση-
λευομένην ἀπέλιπεν, ἀπὸ δὲ Κερκύρας ἐς τὸν Ἰόνιον
ἔπλει, στρατῷ μὲν οὐ πολλῷ, ναυσὶ δὲ διακοσίαις, ἃς
231   ἐν Ἀσίᾳ πεποίητο. πυθόμενος δὲ Ἀηνόβαρβον ἀπαντᾶν αὐτῷ ναυσὶ καὶ στρατῷ πολλῷ, οὐ δοκοῦντά τισιν οὐδ᾽ ἐπὶ ταῖς διαπεμφθείσαις σπονδαῖς εἶναι βέβαιον (ἦν γὰρ Ἀηνόβαρβος τῶν κατεγνωσμένων τε
ἐκ δίκης ἐπὶ Γαΐῳ Καίσαρι φόνου καὶ προγεγραμμένων ἐπὶ τῇ καταδίκῃ καὶ ἐν Φιλίπποις Ἀντωνίῳ καὶ
Καίσαρι πεπολεμηκότων), ὅμως ἔπλει, πέντε ναυσὶν
ἐπιβὰς ταῖς ἀρίσταις, ἵνα φαίνοιτο πιστεύων, καὶ τὰς
232   λοιπὰς ἐκ διαστήματος ἕπεσθαι κελεύσας. καθορωμέ-
νου δὲ ἤδη τοῦ Ἀηνοβάρβου παντί τε τῷ στρατῷ καὶ
παντὶ τῷ στόλῳ μετ᾽ ὀξείας εἰρεσίας προσπλέοντος,
ἔδεισεν ὁ Πλάγκος Ἀντωνίῳ παρεστὼς καὶ ἐπισχεῖν
αὐτὸν ἠξίου τὸν πλοῦν καὶ προπέμψαι τινὰς ἐς πεῖραν
ὡς πρὸς ἀμφίβολον ἄνδρα. ὁ δὲ εἰπὼν αἱρεῖσθαι
παρασπονδούμενος ἀποθανεῖν μᾶλλον ἢ σῴζεσθαι
233   δειλὸς ὀφθείς, ἔπλει. πλησίον τε ἦσαν ἀλλήλων ἤδη,
καὶ αἱ ναυαρχίδες ἐκ τῶν σημείων ἐφαίνοντο καὶ ἀλλήλαις προσέπλεον· καὶ τῶν ῥαβδούχων ὁ ἡγούμενος
Ἀντωνίῳ, κατὰ τὴν πρῷραν, ὥσπερ ἔθος ἐστίν, ἑστώς,
εἶτ᾽ ἐκλαθόμενος, ὅτι ἀμφίβολος ἀνὴρ καὶ στρατοῦ
κἀκεῖνος ἡγούμενος ἰδίου προσπλέοι, εἴτε ἀπὸ εὐγενε-

---

43 This is a mistake: as Appian himself observed (*BCiv.*

with honor, but kept a discreet watch on him through his lieutenants. Antony left Fulvia in need of medical attention at Sicyon, and sailed from Corcyra into the Ionian gulf with a not very large army, but with two hundred ships which he had had built in Asia. When he was informed 231 that Ahenobarbus was coming to meet him with a fleet and a large army, although some regarded Ahenobarbus as unreliable, even after the terms exchanged between them—for not only was he one of the people condemned in court for the murder of Gaius Caesar, but was also proscribed after the verdict, and had fought against Antony and Octavian at Philippi[43]—nevertheless, Antony embarked on five of his best ships and sailed on, in order to present the appearance of trusting him, and ordered the rest to follow at a distance. But when Ahenobarbus was 232 now observed rowing toward them at full speed with his whole army and fleet, Plancus, who was standing beside Antony, was frightened, and asked him to heave to and send some men ahead to investigate, as you would against a man whose intentions were unclear. Antony replied that he would rather die as a result of a treaty violation than be seen as a coward and live, and he maintained his course. They were now close to each other, and the flagships, 233 which could be recognized by their ensigns, sailed toward each other. Antony's chief lictor stood in the prow, as is the custom, and either forgetting that sailing toward them was a man of uncertain intention who also commanded his own army, or adopting an aristocratic attitude, ordered

4.115.479), Ahenobarbus did not fight at Philippi, but was involved on the day of the battle in a naval engagement with Domitius Calvinus.

στέρου φρονήματος, ὡς ὑπηκόοις ἢ ἐλάσσοσιν ἀνδράσιν ὑπαντῶσι, προσέταξε καθελεῖν τὸ σημεῖον.

234 οἱ δὲ καθήρουν τε καὶ τὴν ναῦν ἐς τὰ πλάγια τῆς
Ἀντωνίου νεὼς περιέστρεφον. ὡς δὲ καὶ συνιδόντες
ἀλλήλους ἠσπάσαντο καὶ ὁ στρατὸς ὁ τοῦ Ἀηνοβάρβου τὸν Ἀντώνιον ἡγεμόνα προσεῖπεν, ὁ μὲν Πλάγκος ἀνεθάρρει μόλις, ὁ δὲ Ἀντώνιος ἐς τὴν ἑαυτοῦ
ναῦν τὸν Ἀηνόβαρβον ἀναδεξάμενος ἐς Παλόεντα
κατέπλευσεν, ἔνθα ἦν Ἀηνοβάρβῳ καὶ τὸ πεζόν. καὶ
ὁ Ἀηνόβαρβος τῆς σκηνῆς ἐξίστατο Ἀντωνίῳ.

235 56. Ἐντεῦθεν ἐπὶ Βρεντεσίου διέπλεον, φυλασσομένου πρὸς πέντε Καίσαρος τάξεων, καὶ οἱ Βρεντέσιοι
τὰς πύλας ἀπέκλειον, Ἀηνοβάρβῳ μὲν ὡς ἐκ πολλοῦ
236 πολεμίῳ, Ἀντωνίῳ δὲ ὡς πολέμιον ἐπάγοντι. ὁ δὲ
ἀγανακτῶν καὶ ἡγούμενος εἶναι τάδε καλλωπίσματα,
τὸ δ' ἀληθὲς ἀποκλείεσθαι πρὸς τῶν Καίσαρος φρουρῶν γνώμῃ Καίσαρος, διετάφρευε τῆς πόλεως τὸν
237 ἰσθμὸν καὶ ἀπετείχιζεν. ἔστι δ' ἡ πόλις χερρόνησος
ἐν μηνοειδεῖ λιμένι, καὶ οὐκ ἦν ἔτι τοῖς ἐξ ἠπείρου
προσελθεῖν ἀνάντει λόφῳ, διατετμημένῳ τε καὶ διατε-
τειχισμένῳ. ὁ δὲ Ἀντώνιος καὶ τὸν λιμένα μέγαν ὄντα
φρουρίοις πυκνοῖς περιεφράξατο καὶ τὰς νήσους τὰς
ἐν αὐτῷ. ἔς τε τὰ παράλια τῆς Ἰταλίας περιέπεμπεν,
238 οἷς εἴρητο τὰ εὔκαιρα καταλαμβάνειν. ἐκέλευε δὲ καὶ
Πομπήιον ἐπιπλεῖν τῇ Ἰταλίᾳ καὶ δρᾶν, ὅ τι δύναιτο.
ὁ δὲ ἄσμενος αὐτίκα Μηνόδωρον σὺν ναυσὶ πολλαῖς
καὶ στρατοῦ τέσσαρσι τέλεσιν ἐκπέμψας Σαρδὼ Καίσαρος οὖσαν καὶ τὰ ἐν αὐτῇ δύο τέλη περιέσπασε τὴν

them, as if it were subjects or inferior beings he was encountering, to lower their ensign. They did so, and turned   234
their ship to bring it alongside Antony's. When the two
commanders saw each other they exchanged greetings,
and the army of Ahenobarbus saluted Antony as Imperator. Plancus just about managed to recover his nerve, and
Antony received Ahenobarbus on his own ship and sailed
to Paloeis, where Ahenobarbus had his infantry, and here
he gave up his tent to Antony.

56. From there they sailed to Brundisium, which was   235
garrisoned by five cohorts of Octavian's troops. The citizens closed their gates against Ahenobarbus, because he
was an old enemy, and against Antony because he was
bringing an enemy against them. Antony was annoyed,   236
and believing that these were just fancy words and that he
was in fact being shut out by Octavian's garrison as a result
of Octavian's decision, he dug a ditch across the isthmus
on which the town was located, and walled it off. The town   237
is situated on a peninsula in a crescent-shaped harbor, and
it was no longer possible for those coming from the mainland to get to it up a steep hill that had been cut through
and walled off. Antony also set closely spaced guard posts
to enclose the harbor, which is large, and the islands in it,
and sent men along the coasts of Italy with orders to seize
the advantageous positions. He instructed Pompeius too   238
to attack Italy by sea, and do whatever he could. Pompeius
was delighted to dispatch Menodorus immediately with
numerous ships and four legions of soldiers, and seized
Sardinia, which was under Octavian's control, and the
two legions there, who were unnerved by his cooperation

239 συμφροσύνην Ἀντωνίου καταπλαγέντας. τῆς δὲ Ἰταλίας Σιποῦντα μὲν τῆς Αὐσονίας οἱ τοῦ Ἀντωνίου
κατέλαβον, Θουρίους δὲ καὶ Κωνσεντίαν Πομπήιος
ἐπολιόρκει καὶ τὴν χώραν ἐπενέμετο τοῖς ἱππεῦσιν.

240 57. Ὁ δὲ Καῖσαρ, ὀξείας καὶ πανταχοῦ τῆς ἐπι-
χειρήσεως γενομένης, ἐς μὲν τὴν Αὐσονίδα ἔπεμπεν
Ἀγρίππαν ἐπικουρεῖν τοῖς πονουμένοις. καὶ ὁ Ἀγρίππας τοὺς ἐν ὁδῷ κληρούχους ἦγεν, ἐκ διαστήματος
ἑπομένους ὡς ἐπὶ Πομπήιον ἰόντας· μαθόντες δὲ Ἀντωνίου γνώμῃ τὰ γιγνόμενα εἶναι, ἀνέστρεφον αὐτίκα
διαλανθάνοντες. καὶ τοῦτο μάλιστα κατέπληξε τὸν

241 Καίσαρα. ὁδεύων δ᾽ ὅμως ἐς τὸ Βρεντέσιον αὐτὸς μεθ᾽
ἑτέρου στρατοῦ, τοῖς κληρούχοις αὖθις ἐνετύγχανε
καὶ μετεδίδασκε καὶ τοὺς ὑφ᾽ ἑαυτοῦ συνῳκισμένους
ἦγεν, αἰδουμένους καὶ γνώμην ἐν ἀπορρήτῳ ποιουμέ-
νους Ἀντώνιον καὶ Καίσαρα συναλλάσσειν, εἰ δ᾽ ὁ

242 Ἀντώνιος ἀπειθῶν πολεμοίη, Καίσαρι ἀμύνειν. ὁ δὲ
Καῖσαρ ἐν μὲν Καννυσίῳ τινὰς ἡμέρας ἐνοσηλεύετο,
παντὶ δὲ ὢν ἔτι κρείσσων Ἀντωνίου κατὰ τὸ πλῆθος,
εὗρε τὸ Βρετέσιον ἀποτετειχισμένον καὶ οὐδὲν ἄλλ᾽ ἢ
παρεστρατοπέδευε καὶ τοῖς γιγνομένοις ἐφήδρευεν.

243 58. Ὁ δ᾽ Ἀντώνιος ἐκράτει μὲν τοῖς ὀχυρώμασιν ὡς
πολὺ μείονας[22] ἔχων ἀσφαλῶς ἀπομάχεσθαι, ἐκάλει
δὲ τὸν στρατὸν ἐκ Μακεδονίας κατὰ σπουδὴν καὶ ἐτέ-

22 μείονας BJ; πλέονας LP

104

with Antony.[44] In Italy Antony's men captured the town of   239
Sipuntum in Ausonia, while Pompeius besieged Thurii
and Consentia, and used their territory as grazing for his
cavalry.

57. In response to this fierce and general attack, Octa-   240
vian sent Agrippa to Ausonia to help those in difficulty.
Agrippa brought with him the colonists settled along his
route who followed at a distance in the belief that they
were marching against Pompeius. But when they learned
that things were happening on Antony's initiative, they
immediately turned back without drawing attention to
themselves. Octavian was particularly alarmed by this.
Nevertheless, while making his way to Brundisium with   241
another army, he again fell in with the colonists, got them
to change their mind, and brought with him the men he
himself had settled in their colonies. They were ashamed
and made a secret decision to reconcile Antony and Octavian, but to support Octavian if Antony could not be persuaded and waged war instead. Octavian was ill for some   242
days at Canusium, but although he continued to enjoy
complete numerical superiority over Antony, he found
Brundisium cut off by defensive walls, and so did nothing
more than camp opposite it and await events.

58. In spite of having considerably fewer men, Antony   243
succeeded in using his strongholds to defend himself
safely, but he urgently summoned his army from Macedo-

44 Menodorus, or Menas, was called a pirate by Plutarch (*Ant.*
1), and it is often surmised that he was captured by Pompey the
Great in his campaign of 67 and freed by him. Although he
changed sides many times, he ended up fighting for Octavian and
died in 35 on the Illyrian campaign (Cass. Dio 49.37.6).

χναζεν ἑσπέρας ἀφανῶς ἀνάγεσθαι ναῦς μακράς τε
καὶ στρογγύλας ἰδιωτικοῦ πλήθους, οἳ μεθ᾽ ἡμέραν
ἄλλοι μετ᾽ ἄλλους κατέπλεον ὡπλισμένοι καθάπερ ἐκ
Μακεδονίας ἐπιόντες, ἐφορῶντος αὐτῶν τὸν ἐπίπλουν
τοῦ Καίσαρος. ἤδη δ᾽ αὐτῷ καὶ τὰ μηχανήματα γεγένητο, καὶ ἐπιχειρήσειν ἔμελλε τοῖς Βρεντεσίοις,
ἀχθομένου τοῦ Καίσαρος, ὅτι μὴ εἶχεν ἐπαμύνειν.
244 περὶ δὲ ἑσπέραν ἑκατέροις ἀγγέλλεται Σιποῦντα μὲν
Ἀγρίππας ἀναλαβών, Πομπήιος δὲ Θουρίων μὲν ἀπε-
ωσμένος, Κωνσεντίαν δ᾽ ἔτι περικαθήμενος, ἐφ᾽ οἷς ὁ
245 Ἀντώνιος ἐδυσχέραινεν. ὡς δὲ καὶ Σερουίλιος ἀπηγ-
γέλθη προσιὼν τῷ Καίσαρι μετὰ χιλίων καὶ πεντα-
κοσίων ἱππέων, οὐ κατασχὼν τῆς ὁρμῆς ὁ Ἀντώνιος
εὐθὺς ἀπὸ τοῦ δείπνου, μεθ᾽ ὧν εὗρεν ἑτοίμων φίλων
καὶ ἱππέων τετρακοσίων, μάλα θρασέως ἐπειχθεὶς
ἐπέπεσε τοῖς χιλίοις καὶ πεντακοσίοις εὐναζομένοις
ἔτι περὶ πόλιν Ὑρίαν καὶ ἐκπλήξας ἀμαχεὶ παρέλαβέ
τε καὶ αὐτῆς ἡμέρας ἐς τὸ Βρεντέσιον ἐπανήγαγεν.
οὕτω τὸν Ἀντώνιον ὡς ἄμαχον ἐκ τῆς ἐν Φιλίπποις
δόξης ἔτι κατεπεπλήγεσαν.

246   59. Αἵ τε στρατηγίδες αὐτοῦ τάξεις, ὑπὸ τῆσδε τῆς
δόξης ἐπαιρόμεναι, προσεπέλαζον τῷ χάρακι τῷ Καίσαρος κατὰ μέρη καὶ τοὺς συνεστρατευμένους σφίσιν
ὠνείδιζον, εἰ πολεμήσοντες ἥκοιεν Ἀντωνίῳ τῷ πάν-
247 τας αὐτοὺς περισώσαντι ἐν Φιλίπποις. τῶν δὲ ἀντεπι-
καλούντων, ὅτι αὐτοὶ σφίσιν ἥκουσι πολεμήσοντες,
λόγοι συνισταμένων ἐγίγνοντο, καὶ τὰ ἐγκλήματα
ἀλλήλοις προύφερον, οἱ μὲν τὴν ἀπόκλεισιν τοῦ

nia, and devised a stratagem of sending out warships and merchantmen filled with civilians in the evening without being seen, who returned the next day, one group after another, in arms as though they were arriving from Macedonia, while Octavian watched them dock. Antony now had siege engines available and was on the point of making an attack on Brundisium much to Octavian's annoyance, since he did not have the means to protect them. But toward evening the news reaches both armies that Agrippa had recaptured Sipuntum and that Pompeius had been pushed back from Thurii, although he was still investing Consentia. Antony was annoyed at this, and when it was reported to him that Servilius was coming to Octavian with one thousand five hundred cavalry, he could not hold his impatience in check and, rising straight from dinner, pressed ahead very daringly with whatever associates he found ready and four hundred cavalry, and fell on the one thousand five hundred who were still asleep near the town of Hyria. Having struck panic into them he won them over without a fight, and brought them back to Brundisium the same day. To such an extent were they still browbeaten by Antony's reputation for invincibility won at Philippi.

59. Antony's praetorian cohorts, confident in this reputation of his, approached Octavian's palisade in groups and criticized their fellow veterans for coming to make war on Antony who had saved them all at Philippi. When they made the counterclaim that Antony's men were coming to make war on them, arguments arose as they stood around and accused each other. The Antonians complained that

244

245

246

247

Βρεντεσίου καὶ τὴν ἀφαίρεσιν τοῦ Καληνοῦ στρατοῦ,
οἱ δὲ τὴν ἀποτείχισιν τοῦ Βρεντεσίου καὶ πολιορκίαν
καὶ τὴν τῆς Αὐσονίδος καταδρομὴν καὶ τὸ συνθέσθαι
μὲν Ἀηνοβάρβῳ σφαγεῖ Γαΐου Καίσαρος, συνθέσθαι
248 δὲ Πομπηΐῳ κοινῷ πολεμίῳ. καὶ τέλος οἱ τοῦ Καίσαρος τὴν γνώμην σφῶν τοῖς ἑτέροις ἀνεκάλυπτον, ὅτι
Καίσαρι συνέλθοιεν οὐκ ἀμνημονοῦντες Ἀντωνίου
τῆς ἀρετῆς, ἀλλὰ διαλλαγὰς ἐπινοοῦντες ἀμφοτέροις
ἢ Ἀντώνιον ἀπειθοῦντα καὶ πολεμοῦντα ἀμυνούμενοι.
καὶ τάδε καὶ αὐτοὶ προσπελάζοντες τοῖς Ἀντωνίου
249 χαρακώμασι προύλεγον. γιγνομένων δὲ τούτων ἀγγέλλεται Φουλβία τεθνεῶσα, λεγομένη μὲν ἐπὶ ταῖς
Ἀντωνίου μέμψεσιν ἀθυμῆσαι καὶ ἐς τὴν νόσον ἐμπεσεῖν, νομιζομένη δὲ καὶ τὴν νόσον ἑκοῦσα ἐπιτρῦψαι
διὰ τὴν ὀργὴν Ἀντωνίου· νοσοῦσάν τε γὰρ αὐτὴν
250 ἀπολελοίπει καὶ οὐδὲ ἀπολείπων ἑωράκει. ἐδόκει δ'
ἀμφοτέροις ἐς πολλὰ συνοίσειν ὁ θάνατος, γυναίου
φιλοπράγμονος ἀπηλλαγμένοις, ἢ διὰ τὸν Κλεοπάτρας ζῆλον ἐξερρίπισε τοσόνδε πόλεμον. τό γε μὴν
πάθος ἀσθενῶς ἤνεγκεν ὁ Ἀντώνιος, ἡγούμενός τι καὶ
αἴτιος γεγονέναι.

251   60. Λεύκιος δὲ ἦν Κοκκήιος ἑκατέρῳ φίλος καὶ ὑπὸ
Καίσαρος ἐς Φοινίκην τοῦ προτέρου θέρους πρὸς τὸν
Ἀντώνιον ἀπέσταλτο μετὰ Καικίνα, ἐπανιόντος δὲ τοῦ
252 Καικίνα παρὰ Ἀντωνίῳ κατέμενεν. οὗτος τότε ὁ Κοκ-

---

[45] Lucius Cocceius Nerva, presumably an ancestor of the fu-

Brundisium had been closed to them and Calenus' army taken from them, while Octavian's men cited the investment and siege of Brundisium, the attack on Ausonia, the agreement with Ahenobarbus, one of Caesar's murderers, and the agreement with Pompeius, their common enemy. In the end, Octavian's men revealed their plan to the others: they had united with Octavian not because they had forgotten Antony's courage, but because they intended to reconcile both parties, or to fight Antony if he refused and made war. They in their turn approached Antony's palisade and issued the same warning. While these events were happening, the news is announced that Fulvia was dead. She was said to have become depressed and fallen ill as a result of Antony's criticisms, and it was believed that she deliberately aggravated her illness because of Antony's anger. For even though she was ill, he had left her, and had not even visited her when he was going away. Both men found her death very much to their advantage, freed as they were of a meddlesome woman, who, because of her jealousy of Cleopatra, had kindled such a great war. All the same, Antony took the event badly, as he thought he was partly responsible for it.

60. There was a certain Lucius Cocceius, a friend of both men, who had been sent the previous summer by Octavian, along with Caecina, to Antony in Phoenicia, where he had remained with Antony after Caecina's return.[45] Not letting the opportunity pass, this Cocceius

ture emperor Nerva, was later one of those accompanying Horace on his famous journey to Brundisium in 38 or 37 (*Sat.* 1.5.29, where Horace refers to his important role as go-between for Octavian and Antony).

κήιος, τὸν καιρὸν οὐ μεθείς, ὑπεκρίνατο μεταπεμφθῆ-
ναι πρὸς Καίσαρος ἀσπασόμενος αὐτόν. συγχωροῦ-
ντος δ᾽ ἀπιέναι τοῦ Ἀντωνίου πειρώμενος ἤρετο, εἴ τι
καὶ αὐτὸς ὁ Ἀντώνιος ἐπιστέλλει τῷ Καίσαρι, κεκο-
253 μισμένος δι᾽ αὐτοῦ Κοκκηίου γράμματα. καὶ ὁ Ἀντώνιος, "Νῦν μέν," ἔφη, "Τί ἂν ἀλλήλοις γράφοιμεν,
ὄντες ἐχθροί, εἰ μὴ κακῶς ἀγορεύοιμεν ἀλλήλους;
ἀντέγραψα δὲ τοῖς πάλαι διὰ Καικίνα· καὶ εἰ βούλει,
254 λάβε τὰ ἀντίγραφα." ὁ μὲν οὕτως ἐπεχλεύασεν, ὁ δὲ
Κοκκήιος οὐκ εἴα πω τὸν Καίσαρα καλεῖν ἐχθρόν, ἔς
τε Λεύκιον καὶ τοὺς ἄλλους Ἀντωνίου φίλους τοιόνδε
255 γεγενημένον. ὁ δέ, "Ἐκ Βρεντεσίου με," φησίν, "Ἀπο-
κλείων καὶ τὰ ἐμὰ ἔθνη καὶ τὸν Καληνοῦ στρατὸν
ἀφαιρούμενος ἔτι τοῖς φίλοις ἐστὶν εὔνους μόνοις·
οὐδὲ τοὺς φίλους ἐμοὶ περισῴζειν ἔοικεν, ἀλλὰ ταῖς
εὐεργεσίαις ἐχθροποιεῖν." καὶ ὁ Κοκκήιος, ἃ μὲν ἐπεμέμφετο μαθών, οὐδὲν δὲ ἔτι ὀξυτέραν φύσιν ἐπερεθί-
σας, ᾤχετο πρὸς τὸν Καίσαρα.

256   61. Ὁ δὲ αὐτὸν ἰδὼν ἐν θαύματι ἐποιεῖτο, ὅτι μὴ
θᾶσσον ἔλθοι· "Οὐ γάρ," ἔφη, "Καὶ τὸν σὸν ἀδελφόν,
ἵν᾽ ἐχθρὸς ᾖς μοι, περιέσωσα." ὁ δέ, "Πῶς," ἔφη,
"Τοὺς μὲν ἐχθροὺς φίλους ποιῇ, τοὺς δὲ φίλους
ἐχθροὺς ἀποκαλεῖς τε καὶ τὸν στρατὸν ἀφαιρῇ καὶ τὰ
257 ἔθνη;" καὶ ὁ Καῖσαρ, "Οὐ γάρ," ἔφη, "Καληνοῦ τελευτήσαντος ἐχρῆν ἐπὶ μειρακίῳ τῷ Καληνοῦ παιδὶ γενέσθαι τοσαύτας ἀφορμάς, ἀπόντος ἔτι Ἀντωνίου· αἷς
καὶ Λεύκιος ἐπαρθεὶς[23] ἐμάνη, καὶ Ἀσίνιος καὶ Ἀηνό-

---

[23] ἐπαρθεὶς BJ; ἀνιαθεὶς LP

now pretended that he had been sent for by Octavian to pay his respects to him. Antony gave him permission to leave, but Cocceius sounded him out by asking if, since he had been in receipt of a letter from Octavian through Cocceius himself, he had any message for Octavian. Antony 253 replied: "Why would we write to each other in the present circumstances when we are enemies, except to exchange insults? I replied to his earlier letters through Caecina. Take the copies of them, if you like." He was being offhand 254 in this, but Cocceius would not allow him to call Octavian an enemy yet, after his generous behavior toward Lucius and Antony's other associates. Antony replied: "He has 255 shut me out of Brundisium and taken from me my provinces and the army of Calenus. He is well disposed only to my associates, and he is probably not even trying to keep them as my friends, but make them my enemies by his kindnesses." Having learned what his complaints were, Cocceius annoyed him no further, as he was by nature rather irritable, but went off to Octavian.

61. On seeing him, Octavian said he was surprised he 256 had not come more quickly: "For I did not save your brother too," he said, "in order for you to be my enemy."[46] Cocceius replied, "How is it that you turn your enemies into friends, but call your friends enemies and rob them of their army and provinces?" "Because it was necessary," 257 replied Octavian, "that after the death of Calenus such great resources should not be left in the hands of Calenus' son, a mere boy, while Antony was still away. It was encouraged by these resources that Lucius lost his senses, while Asinius and Ahenobarbus, who were in the vicinity,

[46] His brother was Marcus Cocceius Nerva, governor of Asia 38–37 and consul in 36.

βαρβος γειτονεύοντες ἐχρῶντο καθ' ἡμῶν. ἐπεὶ καὶ τὰ
Πλάγκου τέλη κατὰ σπουδὴν κατέλαβον, ἵνα μὴ οἴχοιτο πρὸς Πομπήιον· οἱ γοῦν ἱππέες αὐτῶν διέπλευ-
258 σαν ἐς Σικελίαν." καὶ ὁ Κοκκήιος, "'Ετέρως," ἔφη,
"Τάδε λογοποιούμενα οὐδὲ Ἀντώνιος ἐπίστευεν, ἕως
259 ἀπεκλείσθη τοῦ Βρεντεσίου καθάπερ πολέμιος." καὶ ὁ
Καῖσαρ οὐδὲν μὲν αὐτὸς ἔφη περὶ τοῦδε προστάξαι
(οὐδὲ γὰρ προμαθεῖν προσπλέοντα οὐδ' ἀφικέσθαι
μετὰ πολεμίων προσδοκῆσαι), Βρεντεσίους δὲ αὐτοὺς
καὶ τὸν ὑπολελειμμένον αὐτοῖς διὰ τὰς Ἀηνοβάρβου
καταδρομὰς ταξίαρχον αὐτοκελεύστους ἀποκλεῖσαι
τὸν Ἀντώνιον, "Συνθέμενον μὲν ἐχθρῷ κοινῷ Πομπηίῳ, ἐπαγαγόντα δὲ Ἀηνόβαρβον φονέα τοῦ ἐμοῦ
πατρός, ψήφῳ καὶ κρίσει καὶ προγραφῇ κατεγνωσμέ-
νον καὶ πολιορκήσαντα μὲν τὸ Βρεντέσιον μετὰ Φιλίππους, πολιορκοῦντα δὲ ἔτι τὸν Ἰόνιον ἐν κύκλῳ,
ἐμπρήσαντα δὲ τὰς ἐμὰς ναῦς καὶ τὴν Ἰταλίαν λεη-
λατήσαντα."

260   62. Ὁ δέ, "Σπένδεσθαι μέν," ἔφη, "Συνεχωρήσατε
ἀλλήλοις, πρὸς οὓς ἂν ἐθέλητε· καὶ οὐδενὶ τῶν ἀνδροφόνων Ἀντώνιος ἐσπείσατο, οὐδὲν ἔλασσον ἢ αὐτὸς
261 σὺ τὸν σὸν πατέρα τιμῶν. Ἀηνόβαρβος δὲ οὐκ ἔστι
τῶν ἀνδροφόνων, ἡ δὲ ψῆφος αὐτῷ κατ' ὀργὴν ἐπῆ-
κται· οὐδὲ γὰρ τῆς βουλῆς πω τότε μετεῖχεν. εἰ δ' ὡς
φίλῳ Βρούτου μὴ συγγνῶναι νομίζοιμεν, οὐκ ἂν φθά-
262 νοιμεν ὀλίγου δεῖν ἅπασι χαλεπαίνοντες; Πομπηίῳ δὲ

[47] Ahenobarbus did not play any part in the Perusine war,

were beginning to use them against us.[47] That is why I also quickly took possession of Plancus' legions, so that they would not go over to Pompeius. And indeed their cavalry did cross over to Sicily." "Different constructions have 258 been put on these matters," said Cocceius, "but not even Antony believed them until he was shut out of Brundisium like an enemy." Octavian responded that he personally 259 gave no order to that effect, since he did not know beforehand that Antony was approaching by sea, and did not expect him to arrive in the company of enemies. The people of Brundisium themselves and the military tribune assigned to them because of the attacks of Ahenobarbus made their own decision to shut Antony out, "because he had allied himself with our common enemy Pompeius and was bringing with him Ahenobarbus, my father's murderer, who had been condemned by vote, court judgment and proscription, who besieged Brundisium after Philippi, and is still blockading the whole circuit of the Ionian gulf, and who burned my ships and plundered Italy."

62. "But it was agreed between you," said Cocceius, 260 "that you could come to terms with anyone you liked. Antony made no peace with any of the assassins, and he holds your father in no less honor than you do. Ahenobar- 261 bus is not one of the assassins, and the vote was cast against him out of personal animosity, for he had no role whatever in the plot at that time. If we refuse to pardon him on the grounds that he is an associate of Brutus, wouldn't we lead the way in quarreling with virtually everybody? Antony 262

above, 32.124–49.207, and it has been suggested that his name might be a mistake for Ventidius, who did operate in that campaign with Asinius.

οὐ συνέθετο μὲν συμμαχήσειν ὁ Ἀντώνιος, πολεμού-
μενος δ' ὑπὸ σοῦ προσλήψεσθαι σύμμαχον ἢ καὶ σοὶ
συναλλάξειν, οὐδὲν ἀνήκεστον οὐδ' ἐκεῖνον εἰργασμέ-
νον. σὺ δὲ καὶ τῶνδε τὴν αἰτίαν ἔχεις· εἰ γὰρ οὐκ
ἐπολεμήθη κατὰ τὴν Ἰταλίαν, οὐδ' ἂν οὗτοι πρεσβεύ-
263 εσθαι ταῦτα πρὸς τὸν Ἀντώνιον ἐθάρρουν." καὶ ὁ Καῖσαρ ἔτι ἐπικαλῶν, "Τὴν μὲν Ἰταλίαν," ἔφη, "Κἀμὲ
σὺν αὐτῇ, Μανιος καὶ Φουλβία καὶ Αεύκιος ἐπο-
λέμουν· ὁ δὲ Πομπήιος οὐ πρότερον, ἀλλὰ νῦν
264 Ἀντωνίῳ θαρρῶν ἐπιβέβηκε τῆς παραλίου." καὶ ὁ
Κοκκήιος, "Οὐκ Ἀντωνίῳ θαρρῶν," εἶπεν, "Ἀλλὰ ὑπ'
Ἀντωνίου πεμφθείς. οὐ γὰρ ἐπικρύψω σε, ὅτι καὶ τὴν
ἄλλην Ἰταλίαν ἐπιδραμεῖται ναυτικῷ πολλῷ ναυτικὸν
265 οὐκ ἔχουσαν, εἰ μὴ διαλύσεσθε ὑμεῖς." ὁ δὲ Καῖσαρ
(οὐ γὰρ ἀμελῶς ἤκουσε τοῦ τεχνάσματος) ἐπισχὼν
ὀλίγον εἶπεν· "Ἀλλ' οὐ χαιρήσει Πομπήιος, κακὸς κα-
266 κῶς καὶ νῦν ἐκ Θουρίων ἐξελαθείς." καὶ ὁ Κοκκήιος
τὰ ἀμφίλογα πάντα κατιδὼν ἐπῆγε τὸν Φουλβίας θάνατον καὶ τρόπον αὐτοῦ, ὅτι πρὸς τὴν ὀργὴν Ἀντω-
τίου δυσχεράνασά τε νοσήσειε καὶ τὴν νόσον ἐπιτρί-
ψειεν ὑπὸ τῆς δυσθυμίας, οὐκ ἰδόντος αὐτὴν οὐδὲ
νοσοῦσαν Ἀντωνίου, ⟨μεμφόμενος Ἀντώνιον⟩[24] ὡς αἴτιον τῇ γυναικὶ θανάτου γενόμενον· "Ἐκποδὼν δὲ
κἀκείνης γενομένης, οὐδενὸς ὑμῖν ἐνδεῖν ἔτι," ἔφη,
"Πρὸς ἀλλήλους πλὴν ἀληθεῦσαι, περὶ ὧν ὑπενοή-
σατε."

[24] μεμφόμενος Ἀντώνιον add. Étienne-Duplessis

did not agree to give military assistance to Pompeius, but only to take him as an ally if you attacked Antony, or to reconcile him to you, since even he has done nothing irreparable. It is you who are to blame for this situation, for if there had been no war in Italy, those men would not have dared to make these diplomatic approaches to Antony." But Octavian continued his accusations: "It was 263 against Italy," he said, "and against me along with Italy, that Manius, Fulvia, and Lucius made war; and although Pompeius did not do so before, he has now made attacks on our coast, because he has confidence in Antony." "Not 264 because he has confidence in Antony," Cocceius replied, "but because he was sent by Antony. For I will not hide from you the fact that he will use his large fleet to overrun the rest of Italy, which has no fleet to defend it, unless you two reconcile your differences." Octavian, after a brief 265 silence (for he listened carefully to this clever suggestion), said, "But Pompeius will regret it, a cowardly man even now ignominiously driven out of Thurii." Then Cocceius, 266 having identified all points of dispute, brought up the death of Fulvia, and the manner in which it happened: namely, how she had taken Antony's anger badly and fallen ill, making her illness worse because of depression at the fact that Antony had not visited her even when she was ill, <accusing Antonius>[48] of being responsible for his wife's death. "Now that she too is out of the way," he continued, "it only remains for you to speak frankly with each other about the suspicions you have harbored."

[48] This is added to the text by the Budé editor, as the grammar is strained without it.

267   63. Οὕτω καθομιλῶν τὸν Καίσαρα ὁ Κοκκήιος
ἐκείνην τε τὴν ἡμέραν ἐξενίζετο παρ' αὐτῷ καὶ ἐδεῖτο
ἐπιστεῖλαί τι τῷ Ἀντωνίῳ, νεώτερον ὄντα πρεσβυ-
τέρῳ. ὁ δὲ πολεμοῦντι μὲν ἔτι οὐκ ἔφη γράψειν· οὐδὲ
γὰρ ἐκεῖνον· μέμψεσθαι δ' αὐτοῦ τῇ μητρί, ὅτι συγ-
γενὴς οὖσα καὶ προτιμηθεῖσα ἐκ πάντων ὑφ' αὐτοῦ,
φύγοι τὴν Ἰταλίαν καθάπερ οὐ τευξομένη πάντων ὡς
268   παρ' υἱοῦ. ὧδε μὲν καὶ ὁ Καῖσαρ ἐτέχναζε καὶ ἐπέστελλε τῇ Ἰουλίᾳ. ἐξιόντι δὲ τοῦ στρατοπέδου τῷ
Κοκκηίῳ πολλοὶ τῶν ταξιάρχων τὴν γνώμην ἐξέφε-
ρον τοῦ στρατοῦ. ὁ δὲ καὶ τἆλλα καὶ τόδε αὐτὸ τῷ
Ἀντωνίῳ μετέφερεν, ἵνα εἰδείη πολεμήσοντας οὐ συν-
269   τιθεμένῳ. συνεβούλευεν οὖν Πομπήιον μὲν ἐς Σικελίαν ἐξ ὧν ἐπόρθει μετακαλεῖν, Ἀηνόβαρβον δέ ποι
270   πέμπειν, ἕως αἱ συνθῆκαι γένοιντο. παρακαλούσης δὲ
καὶ τῆς μητρὸς ἐς ταῦτα τὸν Ἀντώνιον (γένει γὰρ ἦν
ἐκ τῶν Ἰουλίων), ᾐσχύνετο Ἀντώνιος, εἰ μὴ γενομένων τῶν συμβάσεων τὸν Πομπήιον αὖθις ἐς συμ-
271   μαχίαν καλοίη. τῆς δὲ μητρὸς οὐκ ἀπελπιζούσης
αὐτὰς ἔσεσθαι καὶ Κοκκηίου ἰσχυριζομένου τε περὶ
αὐτῶν καὶ ἐλπιζομένου τι πλέον εἰδέναι, ὁ Ἀντώνιος
ἐνεδίδου καὶ τὸν Πομπήιον ἀναχωρεῖν ἐκέλευεν ἐς Σικελίαν, ὡς ἐπιμελησόμενος τῶν συγκειμένων, καὶ Ἀηνόβαρβον ἔπεμπεν ἡγεῖσθαι Βιθυνίας.

272   64. Ὧν ὁ στρατὸς ὁ τοῦ Καίσαρος αἰσθανόμενοι
πρέσβεις εἵλοντο τοὺς αὐτοὺς ἐς ἀμφοτέρους, οἳ τὰ
μὲν ἐγκλήματα αὐτῶν ἐπέσχον ὡς οὐ κρῖναι σφίσιν,

63. In this way Cocceius reconciled himself to Octa- 267
vian, and was entertained hospitably by him that day. Although Cocceius asked him to make some written com-
munication, as the younger man, to his senior, Antony,
Octavian refused to write to someone who was still waging
war; and he said that Antony had not written to him either.
He would, however, complain about him to Antony's
mother, because in spite of being related to himself and
honored by him above all, she had fled from Italy as
though she would not have had all her wishes fulfilled by
him as by her own son. Such was the strategy Octavian 268
devised as he wrote to Julia. When Cocceius was leaving
the camp, many of the military tribunes informed him of
the soldiers' attitude, and he communicated this and the
other information to Antony, so that he would know they
would fight against him if he did not come to an agreement. Accordingly, he advised Antony to recall Pompeius 269
to Sicily from the areas he was ravaging, and to send Ahenobarbus somewhere else, until the agreement was in
place. When his mother made the same request of him 270
(for by birth she belonged to the Julian family), Antony
was ashamed at the idea of asking Pompeius for military
assistance again if no agreement took place. But as his 271
mother did not lose hope that this would happen, and with
Cocceius both insistent on this score and holding out hope
that he knew more than he was saying, Antony relented:
he ordered Pompeius to withdraw to Sicily, implying that
he himself would take care of their mutual interests, and
sent Ahenobarbus to govern Bithynia.

64. On hearing this, Octavian's army chose delegates, 272
the same ones to send to both men; and the delegates put
a stop to their mutual accusations, since they had been

ἀλλὰ διαλλάξαι μόνον ᾑρημένοι, σφίσι δ᾽ αὐτοῖς
προσελόμενοι Κοκκήιον μὲν ὡς κοινὸν ἀμφοῖν, ἐκ δὲ
τῶν Ἀντωνίου Πολλίωνα καὶ Μαικήναν ἐκ τῶν Καίσαρος, ἔγνωσαν Καίσαρι καὶ Ἀντωνίῳ πρὸς ἀλλήλους ἀμνηστίαν εἶναι τῶν γεγονότων καὶ φιλίαν
273 ἐς τὸ μέλλον. ὑπογύως δὲ Μαρκέλλου τεθνεῶτος, ὃς
τὴν ἀδελφὴν Καίσαρος εἶχεν Ὀκταουίαν, ἐδικαίουν οἱ
διαλλακταὶ τὴν Ὀκταουίαν Ἀντωνίῳ τὸν Καίσαρα ἐγ-
γυῆσαι. καὶ ὁ μὲν αὐτίκα ἐνηγγύα, καὶ ἠσπάζοντο
ἀλλήλους, καὶ βοαὶ παρὰ τοῦ στρατοῦ καὶ εὐφημίαι
πρὸς ἑκάτερον αὐτῶν ἦσαν ἄπαυστοι δι᾽ ὅλης τε τῆς
ἡμέρας καὶ ἀνὰ τὴν νύκτα πᾶσαν.

274   65. Ὁ δὲ Καῖσαρ καὶ ὁ Ἀντώνιος τὴν Ῥωμαίων
αὖθις ἀρχὴν ἐφ᾽ ἑαυτῶν ἐμερίσαντο ἅπασαν, ὅρον
μὲν εἶναι σφίσι Σκόδραν πόλιν τῆς Ἰλλυρίδος, ἐν
μέσῳ τοῦ Ἰονίου μυχοῦ μάλιστα δοκοῦσαν εἶναι, ταύ-
της δ᾽ ἔχειν τὰ μὲν πρὸς ἕω πάντα τὸν Ἀντώνιον ἔθνη
τε καὶ νήσους ἕως ἐπὶ ποταμὸν Εὐφράτην ἄνω, τὰ δὲ
ἐς δύσιν τὸν Καίσαρα μέχρι ὠκεανοῦ. Λιβύης δὲ Λέ-
275 πιδον ἄρχειν, καθὰ Καῖσαρ ἐδεδώκει. πολεμεῖν δὲ
Πομπηίῳ μὲν Καίσαρα, εἰ μή τι συμβαίνοι, Παρθυαίοις δὲ Ἀντώνιον, ἀμυνόμενον τῆς ἐς Κράσσον
παρασπονδήσεως. Ἀηνοβάρβῳ δ᾽ εἶναι πρὸς Καίσαρα συμβάσεις τὰς πρὸς Ἀντώνιον γενομένας.
στρατὸν δὲ ἐκ τῆς Ἰταλίας προσκαταλέγειν ἀκω-

---

49 Gaius Claudius Marcellus had been consul in 50 and a de-

chosen not to judge between them, but solely to bring about their reconciliation. The delegates added Cocceius to their number as a friend of both men, together with Pollio from Antony's party and Maecenas from that of Octavian. Their decision was that there should be an amnesty between Antony and Octavian with regard to what had happened in the past, and friendship for the future. Mar- 273 cellus, who was married to Octavia, the sister of Octavian, had died recently, and the mediators recommended that Octavian should betroth her to Antony.[49] He did so immediately, both men embraced each other, and cheers and congratulations were offered by the army continuously all day and throughout the night.

65. Octavian and Antony now, on their own authority, 274 made a new division of the whole Roman empire, the boundary between them to be the town of Scodra in Illyria, which was thought to be about midway on the Ionian gulf. Antony was to have all provinces and islands east of this, as far as the river Euphrates, and Octavian everything to the west, as far as the Atlantic. Lepidus would govern Africa, in accordance with the grant Octavian had made. Octavian was to wage war against Pompeius, 275 unless he reached some accommodation with him, and Antony against the Parthians to avenge their treachery toward Crassus. Ahenobarbus would have the same arrangement with Octavian as that agreed with Antony. And both Antony and Octavian would be allowed to recruit equal numbers of additional troops in Italy without hin-

termined opponent of Julius Caesar, although he did not take part in the civil war between Pompey and Caesar, and Caesar pardoned him. He died in 40.

276 λύτως ἴσον ἑκάτερον. αἵδε μὲν ἦσαν αἱ τελευταῖαι
Καίσαρί τε καὶ Ἀντωνίῳ γενόμεναι συμβάσεις. καὶ
εὐθὺς ἐς τὰ ἐπείγοντα τοὺς φίλους ἑκάτερος αὐτῶν
περιέπεμπεν, Οὐεντίδιον μὲν ἐς τὴν Ἀσίαν Ἀντώνιος,
ἀναστέλλειν Παρθναίους τε καὶ Λαβιηνὸν τὸν Λαβι-
ηνοῦ, μετὰ τῶν Παρθναίων ἐν ταῖσδε ταῖς ἀσχολίαις
Συρίαν τε καὶ τὰ μέχρι τῆς Ἰωνίας ἐπιδραμόντα. ἃ
μὲν δὴ Λαβιηνός τε καὶ Παρθναῖοι δράσαντες ἔπα-
θον, ἡ Παρθνικὴ δηλώσει γραφή.

277   66. Ἕλενον δὲ στρατηγὸν Καίσαρος, σὺν ὁρμῇ
κατασχόντα Σαρδοῦς αὖθις ἐξέβαλε τῆς Σαρδοῦς
Μηνόδωρος ὁ Πομπηίου, καὶ τῷδε μάλιστα χαλεπαίνων ὁ Καῖσαρ οὐκ ἐδέχετο τὰς πείρας Ἀντωνίου
278 συνάγοντος αὐτῷ Πομπήιον. ἐς δὲ Ῥώμην παρελθόν-
τες ἐτέλουν τοὺς γάμους. καὶ ὁ Ἀντώνιος Μάνιον μὲν
ἔκτεινεν ὡς ἐρεθίσαντά τε Φουλβίαν ἐπὶ διαβολῇ
Κλεοπάτρας καὶ τοσῶνδε αἴτιον γενόμενον, Καίσαρι
δὲ ἐνέφηνε Σαλουιδιηνόν, τὸν ἡγούμενον τῷ Καίσαρι
τοῦ περὶ Ῥοδανὸν στρατοῦ, ἀπόστασιν ἰδίᾳ βουλεῦ-
σαι καί οἱ περὶ τοῦδε προσπέμψαι περικαθημένῳ τὸ
279 Βρεντέσιον. καὶ ὁ μὲν τόδε ἐξεῖπεν οὐ πρὸς πάντων
ἐπαινούμενον, εὐφυὴς ὢν ἄρα καὶ ταχὺς ἐς εὔνοιαν· ὁ
δὲ Καῖσαρ αὐτίκα τὸν Σαλουιδιηνὸν ἐκάλει κατὰ

---

50 Titus Labienus (Tribune of the People 63) was Caesar's
legate during his campaigns in Gaul, but he went over to Pompey
in the civil war and died in 45 at the battle of Munda. His son,
Quintus Labienus, had been sent by Brutus and Cassius in 43 to

drance. These were the final terms agreed between Octa-   276
vian and Antony. Both of them immediately sent their
associates off to deal with pressing matters. Antony dispatched Ventidius to Asia to drive off the Parthians and
Labienus, the son of Labienus, who, in company with the
Parthians, had raided Syria and territory as far as Ionia in
those troubled times.[50] But of course my Parthian book
will show what Labienus and the Parthians did and what
happened to them.

66. With regard to Octavian's general, Helenus, who   277
had made a sudden attack and retaken possession of Sardinia, Menodorus, Pompeius' lieutenant, drove him out.[51]
Octavian was particularly angry at this and rejected Antony's attempts to reconcile him with Pompeius. But they   278
did go to Rome and celebrate the marriage. Antony had
Manius executed because he had provoked Fulvia by his
slanders against Cleopatra and been the cause of such
enormous consequences. He also revealed to Octavian the
fact that Salvidienus, who was in command of Octavian's
army on the Rhone, was secretly planning to desert, and
had sent him advance notice of this while he was besieging
Brundisium. Not everyone approved of Antony speaking   279
out on this matter, but he did so presumably because he
was naturally obliging and quick to do a favor. Octavian
immediately summoned Salvidienus with urgency, pre-

negotiate an alliance with the king of Parthia and invaded Syria
with the king's son, Pacorus. He was defeated and killed by Ventidius in 39.

[51] Gaius Julius Helenus, a freedman of Octavian, was captured by Menodorus but returned to Octavian without ransom
(Cass. Dio 48.30.8).

σπουδήν, ὡς ἐπὶ δή τι μόνου χρῄζων καὶ εὐθὺς ἐκπέμψων αὖθις ἐς τὸν στρατόν, καὶ ἐλθόντα ἔκτεινε διελέγξας καὶ τὸν ὑπ' αὐτῷ στρατὸν ὡς ὕποπτον ὄντα ἔχειν ἔδωκεν Ἀντωνίῳ.

280   67. Ῥωμαίους δ' ὁ λιμὸς ἐπίεζεν, οὔτε τῶν ἑῴων ἐμπόρων ἐπιπλεόντων δέει Πομπηίου καὶ Σικελίας, οὔτε τῶν ἐκ δύσεως διὰ Σαρδὼ καὶ Κύρνον ἐχομένας ὑπὸ τῶν Πομπηίου, οὔτ' ἐκ τῆς περαίας Λιβύης διὰ
281 τοὺς αὐτοὺς ἑκατέρωθεν ναυκρατοῦντας. ἐπετίμητο δὴ πάντα, καὶ τῶνδε τὴν αἰτίαν ἐς τὴν ἔριν τῶν ἡγεμόνων ἀναφέροντες ἐβλασφήμουν αὐτοὺς καὶ ἐς διαλύσεις πρὸς Πομπήιον ἐπέσπερχον. οὐκ ἐνδιδόντος δὲ τοῦ Καίσαρος οὐδ' ὥς, ὁ Ἀντώνιος αὐτὸν ἠξίου ταχύνειν
282 γε τὸν πόλεμον διὰ τὴν ἀπορίαν. χρημάτων δ' ἐς αὐτὸν οὐκ ὄντων προυτέθη διάγραμμα, εἰσφέρειν ἐπὶ μὲν τοῖς θεράπουσι τοὺς κεκτημένους ὑπὲρ ἑκάστου τὸ ἥμισυ τῶν πέντε καὶ εἴκοσι δραχμῶν ὡρισμένων ἐς τὸν πόλεμον τὸν Κασσίου τε καὶ Βρούτου, ἐσφέρειν δὲ καὶ μοῖραν τοὺς ἐκ διαθήκης τι καρπουμένους.
283 τοῦτο τὸ γράμμα σὺν ὁρμῇ μανιώδει καθεῖλεν ὁ δῆμος ἀγανακτῶν, εἰ τὰ κοινὰ ταμιεῖα κεκενωκότες καὶ τὰ ἔθνη σεσυληκότες καὶ τὴν Ἰταλίαν αὐτὴν ἐσφοραῖς καὶ τέλεσι καὶ δημεύσεσι καταβαρήσαντες οὐκ ἐς πολέμους[25] οὐδ' ἐς ἐπίκτητον ἀρχήν, ἀλλ' ἐς ἰδίους ἐχθροὺς ὑπὲρ οἰκείας δυναστείας, ὑπὲρ ἧς δὴ καὶ προγραφὰς καὶ σφαγὰς καὶ λιμὸν ἐκ τῶνδε πανώδυνον γεγονέναι, ἔτι καὶ τὰ λοιπὰ περιδύοιεν αὐτούς.

---

[25] πολέμους codd.; πολεμίους Mend.

tending that he needed to see him alone about something, and that he would send him straight back to the army. When he arrived, Octavian had him convicted and executed. As he did not trust the army that had been under Salvidienus' orders, he gave it to Antony to command.

67. Famine was now pressing the people of Rome, 280 since neither the eastern merchants would sail to Italy, out of fear of Pompeius and Sicily, nor the merchants from the west, because Sardinia and Corsica were held by Pompeius' men, nor those from Africa on the opposite coast, because the seas on both sides of them were controlled by the same men. The price of all commodities had 281 risen, and the Romans ascribed the cause of this to the quarreling of the leaders whom they cursed and urged to come to terms with Pompeius. Octavian refused to yield, even in these circumstances, and Antony asked him to speed up the war because of the food shortage. As there 282 was no money for this, an edict was published requiring owners to pay a tax on their slaves at a rate per head of half the twenty-five drachmas that had been set for the war against Cassius and Brutus; and those benefiting from wills were to contribute a proportion. The people tore 283 down the edict in a surge of fury. They were indignant that, after exhausting the public treasury, stripping the provinces, burdening Italy itself with contributions, taxes, and confiscations, not for the purpose of fighting foreign wars or extending the empire, but to use against their personal enemies for the benefit of their own dominance— and it was, of course, this that had given rise to the proscriptions, the killings, and now this appalling famine— the triumvirs would deprive them of what was left of their

284 συνιστάμενοί τε ἐβόων καὶ τοὺς οὐ συνισταμένους
ἔβαλλον καὶ ἠπείλουν διαρπάσειν αὐτῶν τὰς οἰκίας
καὶ καταπρήσειν, ἕως τὸ μὲν πλῆθος ἅπαν ἠρέθιστο,
ὁ δὲ Καῖσαρ σὺν τοῖς φίλοις καὶ ὀλίγοις ὑπασπι-
σταῖς ἐς μέσους ἦλθεν, ἐντυχεῖν τε βουλόμενος καὶ
τὴν μέμψιν ἐκλογίσασθαι.

285   68. Οἱ δὲ αὐτὸν εὐθὺς ὀφθέντα ἔβαλλόν τε ἀφειδῶς
πάνυ καὶ οὐδ᾽ ὑπομένοντα καὶ ἑαυτὸν ἐμπαρέχοντα
286 καὶ τιτρωσκόμενον ᾐδοῦντο. πυθόμενος δ᾽ ὁ Ἀντώνιος
ἐβοήθει κατὰ σπουδήν. οἱ δὲ καὶ τόνδε, κατιόντα τὴν
ἱερὰν ὁδόν, οὐκ ἔβαλλον μὲν ὡς ἕτοιμον ἐς τὰς Πομπηίου διαλύσεις, ἀναχωρεῖν δὲ ἐκέλευον· καὶ οὐ πει-
287 θόμενον, τότε ἔβαλλον. ὁ δὲ ὁπλίτας πλέονας, οἳ ἦσαν
ἔξω τοῦ τείχους, ἐκάλει. καὶ οὐ παριέντων οὐδ᾽ ὡς
αὐτόν, οἱ μὲν ὁπλῖται διαιρεθέντες ἐς τὰ πλάγια τῆς
ὁδοῦ καὶ τῆς ἀγορᾶς ἐπεχείρουν ἐκ τῶν στενωπῶν καὶ
τὸν ἐντυχόντα ἀνήρουν· οἱ δ᾽ οὐκέτι εὐμαρῶς οὐδὲ φυγεῖν ἐδύναντο, βεβυσμένοι τε ὑπὸ πλήθους καὶ δια-
δρομὴν οὐκέτι ἔχοντες, ἀλλὰ φόνος ἦν καὶ τραύματα
288 καὶ ἀπὸ τῶν τεγῶν οἰμωγαὶ καὶ βοαί. καὶ ὁ Ἀντώνιος
μόλις τε παρῆλθε, καὶ τοῦ κινδύνου τὸν Καίσαρα
περιφανῶς δὴ τότε μάλιστα οὗτος ἐξείλετο καὶ ἐς τὴν
οἰκίαν περιέσωσε. διαφυγόντος δέ ποτε τοῦ πλήθους
τὰ νεκρά, ἵνα μὴ ἐνοχλοίη θεωρούμενα, ἐς τὸν πο-
289 ταμὸν ἀπερριπτεῖτο· καὶ ἕτερον πένθος ἦν ὁρωμένων
ἀνὰ τὸ ῥεῦμα, καὶ περιδυόντων αὐτὰ τῶν στρατιωτῶν
καὶ ὅσοι μετ᾽ αὐτῶν κακοῦργοι τὰ εὐσχήμονα μάλιστα ὡς οἰκεῖα ἔφερον. ἀλλὰ ταῦτα μὲν ἐπαύετο σὺν

possessions. Crowds gathered shouting, and threw stones   284
at those who would not join in, threatening to loot and
burn their houses, until the whole populace was agitated,
and Octavian appeared in public with his associates and a
few bodyguards, wishing to meet with the people and discuss their complaints.

68. As soon as they saw him, the crowd stoned him with   285
a complete lack of restraint, and showed no shame even
when he stood his ground, put himself in their power, and
was getting hurt. When Antony heard what was going on,   286
he hurried to his assistance. Although they did not stone
him too as he made his way down the Via Sacra in view of
his readiness to make peace with Pompeius, they told him
to go back, but when he refused, that is when they began
to stone him. He called in a larger force of legionaries,   287
who were outside the city walls, but even then the crowd
did not let him pass, and so the soldiers split up on either
side of the street and of the Forum, and made their attack
from the narrow lanes, killing anyone they met. The people could no longer even find an easy way to flee, but
hemmed in as they were by the crowd and no longer having anywhere to run to, they met with death and injury,
and there was shouting and groaning from the rooftops.
Antony reached the Forum with difficulty, and it was he   288
personally who on this occasion very publicly rescued Octavian from the danger and brought him safely home.
Once the crowd had made their escape, the bodies of the
dead were thrown into the river so that the sight of them
would not cause annoyance. But it was another grievance   289
when they were seen floating in the stream and being
stripped by the soldiers, and the accompanying criminals
carrying off the well-dressed ones as if they were their own
relations. The affair was brought to an end in an atmo-

φόβῳ τε καὶ μίσει τῶν ἡγουμένων, ὁ δὲ λιμὸς ἤκμαζε,
καὶ ὁ δῆμος ἔστενε καὶ ἡσύχαζεν.

290   69. Ὁ δ' Ἀντώνιος ἐδίδασκε τοὺς Λίβωνος οἰκείους
Λίβωνα καλεῖν ἐκ Σικελίας ἐπὶ συνθέσει[26] τοῦ κήδους,
ἐργασόμενόν τι καὶ μεῖζον· τὸ δ' ἀσφαλὲς τῷ Λίβωνι
ἀνεδέχετο αὐτός. οἱ μὲν δὴ ταχέως ἐπέστελλον, καὶ ὁ
291   Πομπήιος τῷ Λίβωνι συνεχώρει. ἀφικόμενος δὲ ὁ Λίβων ἐς νῆσον ὡρμίσθη τὰς Πιθηκούσας, ἢ νῦν ἐστιν
Αἰναρία. καὶ μαθὼν ὁ δῆμος αὖθις ἠθροίζετο καὶ
παρεκάλει σὺν ὀλοφύρσει τὸν Καίσαρα πέμψαι Λίβωνι πίστιν, πρεσβεύειν ἐθέλοντι πρὸς αὐτὸν ὑπὲρ
εἰρήνης. καὶ ὁ μὲν ἄκων ἔπεμπεν, ὁ δὲ δῆμος καὶ
Μουκίαν, τὴν μητέρα τοῦ Πομπηίου, καταπρήσειν
292   ἀπειλοῦντες, ἐξέπεμπον ἐργασομένην διαλύσεις. Λίβων μὲν δὴ συνεὶς τῶν ἐχθρῶν ἐνδιδόντων ἠξίου τοὺς
ἡγεμόνας αὐτοὺς συνελθεῖν ὡς ἀλλήλοις ἐνδώσοντας,
ὅ τι ἂν δοκῇ· βιασαμένου δὲ καὶ ἐς τοῦτο τοῦ δήμου,
ἐξῄεσαν ἐς Βαΐας ὁ Καῖσαρ καὶ ὁ Ἀντώνιος.

293   70. Πομπήιον δὲ οἱ μὲν ἄλλοι πάντες ὁμαλῶς ἔπειθον ἐς τὴν εἰρήνην, Μηνόδωρος δὲ ἀπὸ Σαρδοῦς ἐπέστελλεν ἢ πολεμεῖν ἐγκρατῶς ἢ βραδύνειν ἔτι, ὡς

---

[26] συνησθήσει codd.; συνθέσει Musgrave

[52] The text makes it difficult to understand exactly what Appian is saying here. I take it (with Étienne-Duplessis in the Budé
edition) to mean that Libo was to come in order to secure the
marriage of his sister Scribonia with Octavian, and thus help to
achieve the more important objective of a reconciliation between

sphere of fear and loathing of the leaders, but the famine became worse, and the people complained, but remained peaceful.

69. Antony suggested to Libo's family that they sum- 290 mon Libo from Sicily to secure their marriage relation-ship, and thus achieve something even more important;[52] and he himself undertook to guarantee Libo's safety. His relatives wrote without delay and Pompeius gave Libo his permission. On his arrival, Libo dropped anchor at the 291 island of Pithecoussai, which is now called Aenaria. When the people learned this, they gathered again and made a pathetic plea to Octavian to send a letter of safe-conduct to Libo, as he wanted to negotiate peace with him. Oc-tavian reluctantly sent the letter, and after threatening to burn her out, the people dispatched Mucia, Pom-peius' mother, to bring about the reconciliation.[53] Libo, of 292 course, understood that his enemies were yielding, and invited the leaders themselves to meet in order to make whatever concessions to each other they decided. With the people also forcing them into this course of action, Octa-vian and Antony left for Baiae.

70. Everyone was united in trying to persuade Pom- 293 peius to make peace, except Menodorus who wrote a let-ter from Sardinia advising him either to prosecute the war

Octavian and Libo's son-in-law, Sextus Pompeius. Appian has mentioned this plan already (above, 53.222), but not that it had been carried out.   [53] Mucia was the daughter of Quintus Mucius Scaevola (consul 95), one of the most famous legal experts of the Republic. She married Pompey the Great in 80 and bore him two sons and a daughter. Pompey divorced her for adultery, allegedly with Julius Caesar.

τοῦ λιμοῦ σφῶν προπολεμοῦντος καὶ τῶν συμβάσεων, εἰ καραδοκοίη, κρεισσόνων ἐσομένων· Μοῦρκόν
τε τούτοις ἐνιστάμενον ὑποβλέπειν ἐκέλευεν ὡς ἀρχὴν
294 αὑτῷ περικτώμενον. ὁ δὲ καὶ τέως τὸν Μοῦρκον διά
τε ἀξίωμα καὶ γνώμην ἐγκρατῆ βαρυνόμενος ἔτι μᾶλλον ἐκ τῶνδε ἀπερρίπτει, καὶ οὐδὲν ἦν, ὅ τι Μούρκῳ
προσεῖχεν, ἕως ὁ μὲν Μοῦρκος ἀχθόμενος ἐς Συρα-
κούσας ὑπεχώρει καί τινας ἰδὼν φύλακας ἑπομένους
ἐκ Πομπηίου, φανερῶς αὐτὸν ἐν τοῖς φύλαξιν ἐλοι-
295 δόρει. ὁ δὲ χιλίαρχον καὶ λοχαγὸν αὐτοῦ Μούρκου
διαφθείρας ἔπεμψεν ἀνελεῖν αὐτὸν καὶ φάσκειν ὑπὸ
θεραπόντων ἀνῃρῆσθαι· ἔς τε πίστιν τῆς ὑποκρίσεως
296 τοὺς θεράποντας ἐσταύρου. οὐ μὴν ἐλάνθανε δεύτερον
ἐπὶ Βιθυνικῷ τόδε μύσος ἐργασάμενος, περὶ ἄνδρα
καὶ τὰ πολέμια λαμπρὸν καὶ τῆς αἱρέσεως ἐγκρατῆ
φίλον ἀπ' ἀρχῆς καὶ ἐς αὐτὸν Πομπήιον εὐεργέτην τε
ἐν Ἰβηρίᾳ γενόμενον καὶ ἑκόντα ἐλθόντα ἐς Σικελίαν.
297 71. Μοῦρκος μὲν δὴ τεθνήκει, τῶν δ' ἄλλων τὸν
Πομπήιον ἐς τὰς διαλύσεις ἐπειγόντων καὶ τὸν Μηνόδωρον διαβαλλόντων ἐς φιλαρχίαν ὡς οὐκ εὐνοίᾳ
τοῦ δεσπότου μᾶλλον ἢ ὅπως αὐτὸς ἄρχοι στρατοῦ
καὶ χώρας ἐνιστάμενον, ἐνδοὺς ὁ Πομπήιος ἐς τὴν
Αἰναρίαν διέπλει ναυσὶ πολλαῖς ἀρίσταις, ἐξήρους
298 λαμπρᾶς ἐπιβεβηκώς. καὶ Δικαιάρχειαν μὲν οὕτω σο-

54 Aulus Pompeius Bithynicus (no relation of Sextus Pompeius) was governor of Sicily in 44 and 43 and was executed by
Sextus in 42, according to Dio (48.19.1), for plotting against him.

vigorously or to continue delaying, for the reason that famine was fighting on their side, and the terms of agreement, if he were to wait on events, would be more favorable. Menodorus also urged him to keep an eye on Murcus, who opposed these views, alleging that he was seeking power for himself. Pompeius, who even before this had been finding it difficult to put up with Murcus because of his high rank and opinionated views, kept him at a distance even more after this, and consulted him on nothing. Eventually, Murcus indignantly withdrew to Syracuse, where on seeing some men sent by Pompeius to watch him, he openly abused Pompeius in front of the guards. Then Pompeius bribed one of Murcus' own military tribunes and one of his centurions, and sent them to kill him and say that he had been murdered by slaves. To give credibility to this sham, he crucified the slaves. But he had already perpetrated this crime against Bithynicus, and did not succeed in concealing it a second time, against a man who had been a brilliant warrior, a determined supporter of the party from the beginning, and someone who had rendered valuable service to Pompeius himself in Iberia, and had joined him in Sicily voluntarily.[54]

71. With Murcus now dead, his other advisers urged Pompeius to come to terms, and accused Menodorus of lust for power, as he was opposing the treaty not out of goodwill for his patron, but rather to get command himself of an army and province. So Pompeius gave in and sailed across to Aenaria with many of his best ships, having embarked himself on a magnificent one with six banks of oars. In this style, toward evening, he sailed proudly past Di-

APPIAN

βαρῶς παρέπλευσε περὶ ἑσπέραν, ἐφορώντων τῶν
πολεμίων· ἅμα δὲ ἕῳ, καταπηχθέντων σταυρῶν ἐξ
ὀλίγου διαστήματος ἐν τῇ θαλάσσῃ, σανίδες τοῖς
σταυροῖς ἐπετέθησαν, καὶ διὰ τῶνδε τῶν καταστρω-
μάτων ὁ μὲν Καῖσαρ καὶ ὁ Ἀντώνιος παρῆλθον ἐς τὸ
πρὸς τῇ γῇ πεποιημένον, ὁ δὲ Πομπήιος καὶ ὁ Λίβων
ἐς τὸ πελαγιώτερον, ὀλίγου ῥεύματος αὐτοὺς διείργον-
299   τος μὴ κεκραγότας ἀλλήλων ἀκούειν. ἐπεὶ δὲ ὁ μὲν
Πομπήιος ἐπὶ κοινωνίᾳ τῆς ἀρχῆς ἥκειν ᾤετο ἀντὶ
Λεπίδου, οἱ δὲ ὡς κάθοδον αὐτῷ δώσοντες μόνην,
τότε μὲν ἐπ᾽ οὐδενὶ ἔργῳ διεκρίθησαν, διαπομπαὶ δὲ
συχναὶ τῶν φίλων ἦσαν ἐπὶ ποικίλαις ἑκατέρων προ-
300   κλήσεσιν. ᾔτει δ᾽ ὁ Πομπήιος τῶν προγεγραμμένων
τε καὶ οἳ συνόντων τοῖς μὲν ἀνδροφόνοις Γαΐου Καίσαρος φυγὴν ἄδολον, τοῖς δὲ λοιποῖς κάθοδόν τε ἔντι-
301   μον καὶ τὰς οὐσίας, ἃς ἀναλώκεσαν. ἐπειγόμενοι δὲ
ἐς τὰς συμβάσεις ὑπό τε τοῦ λιμοῦ καὶ ὑπὸ τοῦ
δήμου, ἐς τὸ τέταρτον μόλις ἐνεδίδουν ὡς ὠνησόμενοι
παρὰ τῶν ἐχόντων· καὶ τοῖς προγεγραμμένοις αὐτοῖς
περὶ τούτων ἐπέστελλον, ἐλπίζοντες αὐτοῖς αὐτοὺς
302   ἀγαπήσειν. οἱ δὲ ἐδέχοντο πάντα, ἐπεὶ καὶ Πομπήιον
αὐτὸν ἐδεδοίκεσαν ἤδη διὰ τὸ Μούρκου μύσος· καὶ
προσιόντες τῷ Πομπηίῳ συνθέσθαι παρεκάλουν, ὅτε
καὶ τὴν ἐσθῆτα κατερρήξατο ὁ Πομπήιος ὡς καὶ
τῶνδε προδιδόντων αὐτόν, ὧν προμάχεται, καὶ θαμινὰ
τὸν Μηνόδωρον ὡς στρατηγικὸν καὶ μόνον εὔνουν
ἀνεκάλει.

303   72. Μουκίας δὲ αὐτὸν τῆς μητρὸς καὶ Ἰουλίας τῆς

130

caearchia with his enemies looking on. At dawn, after piles
had been driven into the seabed a short distance apart, and
planks placed upon them, they went separately to these
platforms, Octavian and Antony to the one constructed
near the land, Pompeius and Libo to the more seaward
one. A narrow strip of water separated them so that they
could hear each without having to shout. But as Pompeius   299
thought that he had come to get a share of the government
in place of Lepidus, while the others were going to con-
cede nothing but his recall from exile, they separated for
the time being without accomplishing anything, although
constant negotiations continued to be carried out by their
associates on detailed proposals from both sides. Pom-   300
peius demanded for the proscribed who were his followers
a safe exile for the assassins of Gaius Caesar, and for the
others recall from exile with the restoration of honors and
the property they had lost. With the famine, and the peo-   301
ple exerting pressure to reach an accommodation, Octavian and Antony reluctantly agreed to buy back up to a
quarter of this property from the current holders, and
wrote to this effect to the proscribed themselves, hoping
that this would satisfy them. The latter accepted all the   302
terms, for they were now also afraid of Pompeius himself
on account of his foul crime against Murcus. They approached Pompeius begging him to make the agreement,
and it was at this point that he tore his clothes, accusing
even those for whom he had fought of betraying him,
and repeatedly invoking Menodorus as someone with
the qualities of a general and the only one well disposed
to him.

72. On the insistence of his mother, Mucia, and of Julia,   303

γυναικὸς[27] ἐναγουσῶν, αὖθις οἱ τρεῖς συνῆλθον ἐς τὸ
ἀμφίκλυστον Δικαιαρχέων χῶμα, περιορμουσῶν τῶν
304 φυλακίδων νεῶν, καὶ συνέβησαν ἐπὶ τοῖσδε· λελύσθαι μὲν τὸν πόλεμον αὐτοῖς καὶ κατὰ γῆν καὶ κατὰ
θάλασσαν καὶ τὰς ἐμπορίας ἀκωλύτους εἶναι πανταχοῦ, Πομπήιον δὲ τὰς φρουρὰς ἐξαγαγεῖν, ὅσαι κατὰ
τὴν Ἰταλίαν εἰσί, καὶ μηκέτι τοὺς ἀποδιδράσκοντας
οἰκέτας ὑποδέχεσθαι μηδ’ ἐφορμεῖν ναυσὶ τὴν ἀκτὴν
305 τῆς Ἰταλίας, ἄρχειν δὲ Σαρδοῦς καὶ Σικελίας καὶ
Κύρνου καὶ ὅσων ἄλλων εἶχεν ἐς τότε νήσων, ἐς ὅσον
ἄρχοιεν τῶν ἑτέρων Ἀντώνιός τε καὶ Καῖσαρ, πέμ-
ποντα Ῥωμαίοις τὸν ἐκ πολλοῦ τεταγμένον αὐταῖς
φέρειν σῖτον, ἐπιλαβεῖν δὲ καὶ Πελοπόννησον ἐπὶ
ταύταις, ὑπατεῦσαι δ’ ἀπόντα, δι’ ὅτου κρίνοι τῶν
φίλων, καὶ τῆς μεγίστης ἱερωσύνης ἐς τοὺς ἱερέας
306 ἐγγραφῆναι. καὶ τάδε μὲν εἶναι Πομπηίῳ, κάθοδον δὲ
τοῖς ἔτι φεύγουσι τῶν ἐπιφανῶν, πλὴν εἴ τις ἐπὶ τῷ
φόνῳ Γαΐου Καίσαρος ψήφῳ καὶ κρίσει κατέγνωσται·
καὶ τῆς περιουσίας τοῖς μὲν ἄλλοις, ὅσοι κατὰ φόβον
ἔφευγον καὶ τὰ ὄντα αὐτοῖς ἐκ βίας ἀπωλώλει, τὸ
ἐντελὲς ἀποδοθῆναι χωρὶς ἐπίπλων, τοῖς δὲ προγε-
307 γραμμένοις μοῖραν τετάρτην. καὶ τῶν ἐστρατευμένων
τῷ Πομπηίῳ τοὺς μὲν οἰκέτας ἐλευθέρους εἶναι, τοῖς
δ’ ἐλευθέροις, ὅτε παύσαιντο τῆς στρατείας, τὰ αὐτὰ

[27] τῆς ⟨Ἀντωνίου καὶ Σκριβωνίας τῆς⟩ γυναικὸς prop.
Étienne-Duplessis

his wife, the three men met again on the mole at Dicaearchia, with the waves washing all round and the guard
ships anchored nearby, and they came to an agreement on
the following terms:[55] the war between them was finished,   304
and trade was to proceed unhindered everywhere; Pompeius was to remove all the garrisons he had in Italy, and
no longer take in runaway slaves or blockade the Italian
coast with his ships; he was to have authority over Sardinia,   305
Sicily, and Corsica, and any other islands then in his possession, as long as Antony and Octavian had authority over
the other territories; he was to send to Rome the grain that
had long been required of these places to pay in tax; in
addition he was to have the Peloponnese; he was to hold
the consulship in absentia through whichever of his associates he chose, and be appointed one of the priests of the
most important priesthood. These were the terms that   306
applied to Pompeius, while the nobles who were still in
exile were to be allowed to return, except those who had
been condemned by vote or court verdict for the murder
of Gaius Caesar. The entirety of their possessions, except
for movables, was to be restored to everyone else who had
fled out of fear and whose property had been seized by
violence, but only a quarter to the proscribed. Of those   307
who had served under Pompeius, slaves were to be free,
and free persons were to receive on discharge the same

[55] Sextus' wife was in fact Scribonia (aunt of the Scribonia
married to Octavian). Julia was the name of Antony's mother, and
it is possible that something has fallen out of the text identifying
the correct relationships; or Appian may simply have made a
mistake.

δοθῆναι γέρα τοῖς ἐστρατευμένοις Καίσαρί τε καὶ
Ἀντωνίῳ.

308   73. Ἐς ταῦτα συνέβησαν καὶ ταῦτα συνεγράψαντο
καὶ ἐσημήναντο καὶ ταῖς ἱεραῖς παρθένοις φυλάσσειν
ἔπεμψαν ἐς Ῥώμην. ἐξένιζον δ᾽ ἀλλήλους αὐτίκα, περὶ
τῆς τάξεως διαλαχόντες, πρῶτος μὲν ἐπὶ ἑξήρους
Πομπήιος περιωρμισμένης ἐς τὸ χῶμα, ταῖς δὲ ἑξῆς
Ἀντώνιός τε καὶ Καῖσαρ, σκηνοποιησάμενοι καὶ οἵδε
ἐπὶ τοῦ χώματος, πρόφασιν μὲν ὡς ἅπαντες ἐπὶ ἀκτῆς
309   ἑστιῶντο, τάχα δ᾽ ἐς ἀσφάλειαν ἀνύποπτον. οὐδὲ γὰρ
οὐδ᾽ ὡς εἶχον ἀμελῶς, ἀλλ᾽ αἵ τε νῆες αὐτοῖς παρώρ-
μουν, καὶ οἱ φύλακες περιειστήκεσαν, καὶ οἱ περὶ τὸ
310   δεῖπνον αὐτὸ ἀφανῶς εἶχον ὑπεζωσμένα ξιφίδια. λέ-
γεται δὲ Μηνόδωρος ἑστιωμένων ἐν τῇ νηὶ τῶν ἀνδρῶν πέμψαι Πομπηίῳ, προτρέπων αὐτὸν ἐπιθέσθαι
τοῖς ἀνδράσι καὶ τίσασθαι μὲν τῆς ἐς τὸν πατέρα καὶ
τὸν ἀδελφὸν ἁμαρτίας, ἀναλαβεῖν δὲ τὴν ἀρχὴν τὴν
πατρῴαν δι᾽ ὀξυτάτης ἀφορμῆς· ἐπιμελήσεσθαι γὰρ
311   αὐτὸς ἐν ταῖς ναυσὶν ὢν μηδένα διαφυγεῖν. ὁ δ᾽ ἀπο-
κρίνασθαι τοῦ γένους ἅμα καὶ τῆς χρείας ἀξίως,
"Εἴθε Μηνόδωρον ἦν ἐργάσασθαι ταῦτα χωρὶς ἐμοῦ·"
312   Μηνοδώρῳ γὰρ ἁρμόζειν ἐπιορκεῖν, οὐ Πομπηίῳ. ἥρ-
μοσαν δ᾽ ἐν τῷδε τῷ δείπνῳ τὴν Πομπηίου θυγατέρα,
Λίβωνος οὖσαν θυγατριδῆν, Μαρκέλλῳ τῷ προγόνῳ
313   μὲν Ἀντωνίου, ἀδελφιδῷ δὲ Καίσαρος. ἀπέφηναν δὲ
τῆς ἐπιούσης ὑπάτους ἐς τετραετὲς Ἀντώνιον μὲν καὶ
Λίβωνα πρώτους, ἀντικαθιστάντος ὅμως Ἀντωνίου,

rewards as those who had served under Octavian and Antony.

73. Such were the terms on which they agreed, drew   308
up in writing, signed, and sent to Rome for safekeeping with the Vestal Virgins. They immediately provided hospitality to each other, drawing lots to decide the order. First Pompeius hosted them on his six-banked ship anchored at the mole, then on the following days Antony and Octavian, who erected tents also on the mole, supposedly so that everyone might celebrate the feast on shore, but perhaps really for risk-free security. For even in these   309
circumstances they did not fail to act cautiously, but their ships were moored alongside, guards were stationed on the perimeter, and those attending the banquet itself carried daggers hidden under their clothing. There is a story   310
that while the men were feasting on board, Menodorus sent a message to Pompeius urging him to attack the triumvirs, avenge the wrong done to his father and brother, and take back his father's power by means of the swiftest stroke: for as he was on the ships himself he would take care that no one escaped. But Pompeius replied, in a man-   311
ner worthy of his family and at the same time in keeping with his dangerous situation, "If only Menodorus could have done this without asking me!" In other words, it was fitting for a Menodorus to break his oath, but not for a Pompeius. At this banquet the daughter of Pompeius,   312
granddaughter of Libo, was betrothed to Marcellus, the stepson of Antony and nephew of Octavian.[56] On the fol-   313
lowing day they designated the consuls for the next four years, first Antony and Libo (with Antony, however, al-

[56] They were both still young children at this point.

ὃν ἂν βούλοιτο, ἐπὶ δ' ἐκείνοις Καίσαρά τε καὶ Πομπήιον, εἶτα Ἀηνόβαρβον καὶ Σόσιον, εἶτ' αὖθις Ἀντώνιόν τε καὶ Καίσαρα, τρίτον δὴ τότε μέλλοντας ὑπα-
τεύσειν καὶ ἐλπιζομένους τότε καὶ ἀποδώσειν τῷ
δήμῳ τὴν πολιτείαν.

314   74. Τάδε μὲν ἔπραξαν, καὶ διακριθέντες ἀλλήλων
ὁ μὲν ἐς Σικελίαν ἔπλει, Καῖσαρ δὲ καὶ Ἀντώνιος
ὥδευον ἐς Ῥώμην. πυθόμεναι δὲ ἥ τε πόλις καὶ ἡ
Ἰταλία, ἐπαιάνιζον αὐτίκα ἅπαντες ὡς ἐπὶ εἰρήνῃ, πολέμου τε ἀπαλλαγέντες ἐπιχωρίου καὶ ξεναγήσεως
υἱῶν καὶ φρουρῶν ὕβρεως καὶ θεραπόντων αὐτομολίας καὶ λεηλασίας πεδίων καὶ γεωργίας ἀργίας,
ὑπὲρ ἅπαντα δὲ τοῦ λιμοῦ, πιέσαντος αὐτοὺς ἐς ἔσχατον, ὥστε παροδεύουσιν αὐτοῖς οἷα σωτῆρσιν ἐγί-
315   γνοντο θυσίαι· καὶ τὸ ἄστυ ἔμελλεν ὑποδέξεσθαι
περιφανῶς, εἰ μὴ νυκτός, ἐκκλίνοντες τὸ φορτικόν,
316   ἔλαθον ἐς τὴν Ῥώμην ἐσελθόντες. μόνοι δὲ ἤχθοντο,
ὅσοι τὰ τῶν ἐλευσομένων σὺν Πομπηίῳ χωρία κεκλη-
ρουχήκεσαν, ἡγούμενοι σφίσι τοὺς γεωμόρους ἀδιαλ-
λάκτους ἐχθροὺς παροικήσειν καί, εἴ ποτε δυνηθεῖεν,
317   ἐπιθήσεσθαι. οἱ δ' ἀμφὶ τὸν Πομπήιον φυγάδες
αὐτίκα, χωρὶς ὀλίγων, οἱ πλείους ἐν τῇ Δικαιαρχείᾳ
τὸν Πομπήιον ἀσπασάμενοι κατέπλεον ἐς τὴν Ῥώμην.
καὶ ἕτερα τοῦ πλήθους ἦν ἡδονὴ καὶ βοαὶ ποικίλαι,
τοσῶνδε οὕτως ἐπιφανῶν ἐξ ἀέλπτου περισεσωσμέ-
νων.

---

[57] This sequence of consuls is correct, but it started in 34, not,
as Appian seems to be indicating, in 38. Pompeius did not hold

lowed to substitute whomever he liked); after them, Octavian and Pompeius; then Ahenobarbus and Sosius; and, finally, Antony and Octavian again; and as they would then be about to hold the consulship for the third time, it was also expected that they would at that time restore the constitution to the people.[57]

74. Having finished this business, they went their separate ways, Pompeius to Sicily by sea, while Octavian and Antony traveled by road to Rome. As soon as the people of Rome and Italy heard the news, everyone immediately began to sing their praises as if at the return of peace: for they had won relief from civil war, from the conscription of their sons, the violence of garrisons, the desertion of slaves, the pillaging of fields, the stagnation of agriculture, and, above all, from the famine that had reduced them to the last extremity. So, as the triumvirs proceeded on their way people sacrificed to them as if to savior gods. The city was ready to give them a magnificent reception, if they had not entered Rome unobserved at night to avoid vulgarity. The only aggrieved group were those who had received allocations of land belonging to people about to return from exile with Pompeius: they thought the returnees would settle beside them as uncompromisingly hostile landowners, and would, if they ever could, take aggressive action against them. With a few exceptions, most of the exiles with Pompeius took their leave of him at Dicaearchia, and sailed for Rome. It was a new source of delight and all sorts of shouting for the crowd that so many nobles had been saved in this way.

314

315

316

317

the consulship with Octavian in 33, as he was dead by then. Gaius Sosius was a loyal supporter of Antony and fought for him at the battle of Actium, but he was pardoned by Octavian.

318   75. Ἐπὶ δὲ τούτοις ὁ μὲν Καῖσαρ ἐς τὴν Κελτικὴν
ἐξώρμα ταρασσομένην, ὁ δὲ Ἀντώνιος ἐπὶ τὸν πόλεμον τῶν Παρθυαίων. καὶ αὐτῷ τῆς βουλῆς ψηφι-
σαμένης εἶναι κύρια, ὅσα ἔπραξέ τε καὶ πράξει, αὖθις
στρατηγοὺς πανταχῇ περιέπεμπε καὶ τἆλλα ὡς ἐπε-
319   νόει πάντα διεκόσμει. ἵστη δέ πη καὶ βασιλέας, οὓς
δοκιμάσειεν, ἐπὶ φόροις ἄρα τεταγμένοις, Πόντου μὲν
Δαρεῖον τὸν Φαρνάκους τοῦ Μιθριδάτου, Ἰδουμαίων
δὲ καὶ Σαμαρέων Ἡρῴδην, Ἀμύνταν δὲ Πισιδῶν καὶ
Πολέμωνα μέρους Κιλικίας καὶ ἑτέρους ἐς ἕτερα ἔθνη.
320   τὸν δὲ στρατόν, ὅσος ἔμελλεν αὐτῷ συγχειμάσειν,
περιουσιάσαι τε βουλόμενος καὶ γυμνάσαι, τοὺς μὲν
αὐτῶν ἐπὶ Παρθηνοὺς ἔπεμπεν, Ἰλλυρικὸν ἔθνος Ἐπι-
δάμνῳ πάροικον, προθυμοτάτους γενομένους Βρούτῳ,
τοὺς δ' ἐπὶ Δαρδανέας, ἕτερον Ἰλλυριῶν γένος, αἰεὶ
Μακεδονίαν ἐπιτρέχοντας· τοὺς δ' ἐν Ἠπείρῳ μένειν
ἐκέλευεν, ὡς ἂν ἐν κύκλῳ πάντας ἔχῃ, μέλλων αὐτὸς
321   ἐν Ἀθήναις χειμάσειν. ἔπεμπε δὲ καὶ Φούρνιον ἐς Λιβύην, τὰ ὑπὸ Σεξτίῳ τέλη τέσσαρα ἄξοντα ἐπὶ Παρ-
θυαίους· οὐ γάρ πω πέπυστο αὐτὰ Λέπιδον ἀφῃρῆσθαι Σεξτίου.

---

58 Appian summarizes the reign of Mithridates Eupator's son,
Pharnaces, as king of Bosporus at *Mith.* 120.590–95. It is perhaps
strange not to mention the Jews in connection with their famous
king, Herod, but at this stage he had not yet taken possession of
Judaea. Amyntas had supported Brutus and Cassius at first, but
he went over to Antony, who rewarded him with extensive terri-

75. After this, Octavian set out for Gaul, which was in   318
a state of disturbance, and Antony for the war against the
Parthians. As the senate had voted to ratify all that Antony
had done or would do in the future, he again dispatched
his lieutenants in all directions and ordered everything
else in accordance with his plans. He established kings of   319
whom he approved in various places, on condition, of
course, that they paid a prescribed tribute: in Pontus,
Darius, the son of Pharnaces and grandson of Mithridates:
in Idumea and Samaria, Herod: in Pisidia, Amyntas; in
part of Cilicia, Polemon;[58] and others in other countries.
Wishing to enrich as well as exercise those soldiers who   320
were about to go into winter quarters with him, he sent
some of them against the Partheni, an Illyrian people living near Epidamnus, who had been very enthusiastic supporters of Brutus; others against the Dardanians, another
Illyrian people, who were constantly making incursions
into Macedonia. Others again he ordered to remain in
Epirus, in order to have them all in a circle round him, as
he intended to pass the winter himself in Athens. He also   321
sent Furnius to Africa to get the four legions under Sextius' command for service against the Parthians, for he had
not yet heard that Lepidus had taken them away from
Sextius.

tories in Asia Minor. Before the battle of Actium, he deserted to
Octavian, who extended his kingdom. He died fighting in 25.
Having staunchly resisted the Parthian invasion of 40–39, Pole-
mon, son of the famous rhetorician, Zeno, was rewarded by An-
tony with Cilicia, and then made king of Pontus. Augustus added
Bosporus in 15. Polemon was killed in 8.

322 76. Ταῦτα διαθέμενος ἐχείμαζεν ἐν ταῖς Ἀθήναις
μετὰ τῆς Ὀκταουίας, καθὰ καὶ ἐν Ἀλεξανδρείᾳ μετὰ
τῆς Κλεοπάτρας, τὰ μὲν ἐκ τῶν στρατοπέδων ἐπιστελ-
λόμενα ἐφορῶν μόνα, ἀφέλειαν δὲ ἰδιωτικὴν αὖθις ἐξ
ἡγεμονίας καὶ σχῆμα τετράγωνον ἔχων καὶ ὑπόδημα
323 Ἀττικὸν καὶ θύρας ἠρεμούσας. ἔξοδοί τε ἦσαν ὁμοίως
ἄνευ σημείων αὐτῷ, σὺν δύο φίλοις καὶ σὺν ἀκο-
λούθοις δύο, ἐς διδασκάλων διατριβὰς ἢ ἀκροάσεις.
καὶ τὸ δεῖπνον ἦν Ἑλληνικὸν καὶ μεθ᾽ Ἑλλήνων ἡ
γυμνασία πανηγύρεις τε σὺν θυμηδίᾳ μετὰ τῆς
Ὀκταουίας· πολὺς γὰρ καὶ ἐς τήνδε ἐρρύη, ταχὺς ὢν
324 ἐς ἔρωτας γυναικῶν. λήγοντος δὲ τοῦ χειμῶνος,
ὥσπερ ἑτέρῳ γενομένῳ, ἥ τε ἐσθὴς αὖθις καὶ μετὰ τῆς
ἐσθῆτος ἡ ὄψις ἐνηλλάσσετο, καὶ πλῆθος ἦν ἀμφὶ
τὰς θύρας αὐτίκα σημείων τε καὶ ἡγεμόνων καὶ δορυφόρων, καὶ φόβου πάντα μεστὰ καὶ καταπλήξεως·
πρεσβεῖαί τ᾽ ἐσεδέχοντο, αἱ τέως ἠρέμουν κεκελευ-
σμέναι, καὶ δίκαι διεκρίνοντο, καὶ νῆες καθείλκοντο,
καὶ ἡ ἄλλη παρασκευὴ πᾶσα συνεκινεῖτο.

325 77. Καὶ Ἀντώνιος μὲν ἀμφὶ ταῦτα ἦν, Καίσαρι δὲ
καὶ Πομπηίῳ διελύθησαν αἱ γενόμεναι σπονδαί, κατὰ
μὲν αἰτίας, ὡς ὑπενοεῖτο, ἑτέρας, αἱ δὲ ἐς τὸ φανερὸν
326 ὑπὸ τοῦ Καίσαρος ἐκφερόμεναι αἵδε ἦσαν. Πελοπόννησον Ἀντώνιος μὲν ἐδίδου Πομπηίῳ, κελεύων, ὅσα
ἔτι ὤφειλον αὐτῷ Πελοποννήσιοι δόντα ἢ αὐτὸν ἀνα-
δεξάμενον ἀποδώσειν παραλαβεῖν ἢ περιμεῖναι τὴν
327 πρᾶξιν αὐτῶν. ὁ δὲ οὐκ ἐδέχετο μὲν ἐπὶ τοῖσδε τὴν
χώραν, ἡγούμενος αὐτῷ σὺν τοῖς ὀφλήμασι δεδό-

76. Having made these arrangements, Antony spent   322
the winter at Athens with Octavia, just as he had at Alexandria with Cleopatra, merely looking over the reports
sent from the armies, once again adopting the simple life
of a private citizen in place of military command, wearing
the square-cut pallium and the Attic shoe, and with no
crowd at his doors. He would go out, in similar manner,   323
without the insignia of his office, accompanied by two
friends and two attendants, to the discussions and lectures
of the public teachers. He took his meals in the Greek
fashion, exercised with Greeks, and enjoyed their festivals
in Octavia's company: for he was very much in love with
her too, being quick to fall in love with women. But when   324
winter came to an end, he was a different person: he
changed his clothing again, and with his clothing his whole
appearance. Immediately his door was crowded with standards and officers and bodyguards, and fear and appre-
hension were everywhere. Embassies were received which
had previously been told to wait, and lawsuits were decided, and ships were launched, and all other preparations
were put in motion.

77. While Antony was occupied in these matters, the   325
agreement reached between Octavian and Pompeius
broke down, for different reasons, it was suspected, but
the ones publicly put forward by Octavian were as follows.
Antony was ceding the Peloponnese to Pompeius, but he   326
stipulated that Pompeius would get it, either after giving
him all the taxes the Peloponnesians still owed Antony, or
having undertaken to pay them personally, or he must wait
until the collection had been made. But Pompeius did not   327
accept the territory on these conditions. He thought that

141

APPIAN

σθαι· χαλεπαίνων δέ, ὡς ὁ Καῖσαρ ἔλεγεν, εἴτε ἐπὶ
τούτοις εἴτε κατὰ γνώμην ἄπιστον εἴθ᾽ ὑπὸ ζήλου τῶν
ἑτέρων μεγάλους στρατοὺς ἐχόντων εἴτε Μηνοδώρου
διερεθίζοντος αὐτὸν ἀνοχὰς μᾶλλον ἢ βεβαίους
σπονδὰς εἶναι νομίζειν, ναῦς ἄλλας ἐποιεῖτο καὶ ἐρέτας συνέλεγε καὶ τῷ στρατῷ ποτε ἐδημηγόρησε χρῆ-
328 ναι παντὸς οὕνεκα παρασκευάζεσθαι. ληστήριά τε
αὖθις ἀφανῆ τὴν θάλασσαν ἠνώχλει, καὶ μικρὸν ἢ
οὐδὲν ἄκος τοῦ λιμοῦ γεγένητο Ῥωμαίοις, ὥστε ἐβόων
οὐκ ἀπαλλαγὴν τῶν κακῶν, ἀλλ᾽ ἐπίληψιν τετάρτου
329 τυράννου κατὰ σπονδὰς γεγονέναι. καὶ ὁ Καῖσάρ
τινα ληστήρια συλλαβὼν ἐβασάνιζεν, οἳ Πομπήιον
σφᾶς ἔλεγον ἐπιπέμψαι· καὶ τάδε αὐτὰ ὁ Καῖσαρ τῷ
δήμῳ προσέφερε καὶ ἐπέστελλεν αὐτῷ Πομπηίῳ. ὁ δὲ
ἐξελογεῖτο μὲν ὑπὲρ τούτων, ἀντενεκάλει δὲ Πελοπον-
νήσου χάριν.

330   78. Ὅσοι δὲ τῶν ἐπιφανῶν ἦσαν ἔτι παρὰ τῷ Πομπηίῳ, ὁρῶντες αὐτὸν αἰεὶ πειθόμενον τοῖς ἀπελευ-
θέροις, διέφθειραν ἐνίους τῶν ἀπελευθέρων, εἴτε ἀπὸ
σφῶν αὐτῶν εἴτε ἐς χάριν Καίσαρος, ἐξοτρύνειν ἐπὶ
Μηνοδώρῳ, Κύρνου καὶ Σαρδοῦς ἔτι ἄρχοντι, τὸν
331 δεσπότην. οἱ δὲ καὶ αὐτοὶ φθόνῳ τῆς Μηνοδώρου δυνάμεως ἑκόντες ἐποίουν. καὶ Πομπήιος μὲν ἐς ἀλ-
λοτρίωσιν ὑπήγετο τοῦ Μηνοδώρου, τῶν δ᾽ αὐτῶν
ἡμερῶν Φιλάδελφος, ὁ Καίσαρος ἀπελεύθερος, πρὸς
τὸν Μηνόδωρον διέπλευσε σίτου κομιδῆς οὕνεκα καὶ
Μικυλίων ὁ πιστότατος τῷ Μηνοδώρῳ πρὸς Καίσαρα
332 περὶ αὐτομολίας τοῦ Μηνοδώρου· ὑπισχνεῖτο δὲ ἐγ-

it had been given to him along with the outstanding arrears. Annoyed, according to Octavian, either for this reason or because he had a suspicious disposition, or out of jealousy of the others who had large armies, or because Menodorus was prompting him to think of the agreement as a truce rather than a lasting peace, he began to build new ships and recruit rowers, and on one occasion he gave a speech to his soldiers, telling them they must be prepared for every eventuality. Clandestine pirate bands 328 again disturbed the sea, and the people of Rome had little or no relief from the famine, with the result that they began to complain loudly that the treaty had not brought relief from their troubles, but the addition of a fourth tyrant. When Octavian captured some pirate bands and tortured them, they said it was Pompeius who had sent them out to raid. So Octavian reported these facts to the people and wrote to Pompeius himself, who denied involvement, and made countercomplaints about the Peloponnese.

78. All the nobles who were still with Pompeius could 330 see that he constantly deferred to the advice of his freedmen, so either in their own interests or as a favor to Octavian, they bribed some of these freedmen to incite their master against Menodorus, who was still governing Corsica and Sardinia. The freedmen, for their part, did this 331 willingly, as they were jealous of Menodorus' power. At the same time as Pompeius was being manipulated into an estrangement from Menodorus, Philadelphus, a freedman of Octavian, sailed over to Menodorus to secure the transport of grain, and Micylio, Menodorus' most trusted adviser, made his way to Octavian to discuss the possible desertion of Menodorus. Menodorus promised to hand 332

χειριεῖν Σαρδὼ καὶ Κύρνον καὶ τρία τέλη στρατοῦ
καὶ ψιλῶν πλῆθος ἕτερον. καὶ τόδε ὃν ἔργον εἴτε Φι-
λαδέλφου εἴτε τῶν ἐς Μηνόδωρον παρὰ Πομπηίου
διαβολῶν, ὁ Καῖσαρ οὐκ εὐθὺς μέν, ἐδέξατο δ᾽ ὅμως,
333 ἡγούμενος ἔργῳ τὴν εἰρήνην λελύσθαι. καὶ Ἀντώνιον
ἐξ Ἀθηνῶν ἐς τὸ Βρεντέσιον ἐς ἡμέραν ῥητὴν παρεκάλει, συμβουλευσόμενος αὐτῷ περὶ τοῦδε τοῦ πο-
λέμου· ναῦς τε μακρὰς ἐκ Ῥαβέννης καὶ στρατὸν ἐκ
τῆς Κελτικῆς καὶ παρασκευὴν ἄλλην ἐς τὸ Βρεντέσιον καὶ ἐς Δικαιάρχειαν ὀξέως περιέπεμπεν, ὡς ἑκατέρωθεν ἐπιπλευσούμενος τῇ Σικελίᾳ, ἢν Ἀντωνίῳ
συνδοκῇ.

334   79. Ὁ δὲ ἦλθε μὲν ἐς τὴν τεταγμένην ἡμέραν σὺν
ὀλίγοις, Καίσαρα δὲ οὐχ εὑρὼν οὐ περιέμεινεν, εἴτε
τὴν γνώμην τοῦ πολέμου μεμψάμενος ὡς παράσπονδον εἴτε τὴν Καίσαρος παρασκευὴν ἰδὼν πολλὴν οὖσαν (οὐ γάρ ποτε αὐτοὺς ἀνέπαυε φόβων ἡ τῆς μο-
335 ναρχίας ἐπιθυμία), εἴτε τι σημεῖον δεδισάμενος. τῶν
γὰρ περικοιμωμένων αὐτοῦ τῇ σκηνῇ πρὸς θηρίων τις
εὑρέθη δεδαπανημένος, ἄνευ τοῦ προσώπου μόνου,
καθάπερ ἐς ἐπίδειξιν παραλελειμμένου, οὔτε τι βοή-
σας οὔτε τινὸς τῶν συναναπαυομένων ᾐσθημένου· καὶ
λύκον ἔλεγον οἱ Βρεντέσιοι πρὸ ἕω φανῆναι τῶν σκη-
336 νωμάτων ἐκθέοντα. ἔγραφέ γε μὴν τῷ Καίσαρι μὴ
λύειν τὰ συγκείμενα καὶ ἠπείλει Μηνόδωρον ἀπάξειν
ὡς ἑαυτοῦ δραπέτην· γεγένητο γὰρ Πομπηίου Μάγνου, τὴν δὲ τοῦ Μάγνου περιουσίαν ὁ Ἀντώνιος
ἐώνητο νόμῳ πιπρασκομένην ὡς πολεμίου.

over to him Sardinia, Corsica, three legions of soldiers, and a another large number of light-armed troops. Whether this was the work of Philadelphus, or was a consequence of the accusations against Menodorus made to Pompeius, Octavian accepted the offer, although not immediately, since he considered that the peace had in fact been broken. He invited Antony to come from Athens and 333 meet him at Brundisium on a specified day to consult with him about this war. He quickly sent orders around for warships from Ravenna, an army from Gaul, and other war materiel to be assembled at Brundisium and Dicaearchia, with the intention of sailing against Sicily from both places, if Antony agreed.

79. Antony came on the appointed day with a small 334 escort, but not finding Octavian he did not wait, either because he did not approve of the decision to go to war, regarding it as a violation of the treaty, or because he observed the scale of Octavian's armament (the desire for sole rule never allowed them a respite from fear), or because he had been frightened by an omen. For one of the 335 men sleeping near his tent was found to have been devoured by wild animals, except only for his face, which had been left as if for the purpose of identifying the man; he had not cried out at all and none of those sleeping beside him heard a thing. The people of Brundisium said that a wolf had been seen just before daybreak running away from the tents. Nevertheless, Antony wrote to Octavian 336 telling him not to break their agreement, and he threatened to repossess Menodorus as a runaway slave belonging to himself; for he had been owned by Pompey the Great, whose property Antony had bought when it was put up for sale by law as belonging to a public enemy.

145

337   80. Ὁ δὲ Καῖσαρ ἔπεμπεν ἐς Σαρδόνα καὶ Κύρνον
τοὺς παραληψομένους, ἃ Μηνόδωρος ἐνεχείριζεν,
ἐκρατύνετο δὲ τὰ παράλια τῆς Ἰταλίας φρουρίοις
338   πολλοῖς, μὴ αὖθις αὐτὰ ὁ Πομπήιος ἐπιδράμοι. τρι-
ήρεις δὲ ἑτέρας ἐν Ῥώμῃ καὶ ἐν Ῥαβέννῃ προσέτασσε
γίγνεσθαι καὶ στρατὸν πολὺν ἐκ τῆς Ἰλλυρίδος μετ-
επέμπετο· Μηνόδωρόν τε ἐλθόντα ἐλεύθερον εὐθὺς
ἀπέφηνεν ἐξ ἀπελευθέρου και ὧν αὐτὸς ἤγαγε νεῶν,
ἐπέτρεπεν ἡγεῖσθαι, ὑποστρατηγοῦντα τῷ ναυάρχῳ
339   Καλουισίῳ. ταῦτα μὲν δὴ καθιστάμενος ὁ Καῖσαρ
καὶ παρασκευὴν ἔτι πλέονα συνάγων ἐβράδυνε καὶ
τὸν Ἀντώνιον οὐ περιμείναντα ἐμέμφετο, τὴν δ᾽ οὖσαν
ἤδη παρασκευὴν ἐκέλευε Κορνιφίκιον ἐκ Ῥαβέννης
340   μεταγαγεῖν ἐς Τάραντα. Κορνιφικίῳ μὲν δὴ χειμὼν
περιπλέοντι ἐπιγίγνεται, καὶ μόνη τῶν νεῶν ἡ ναυαρ-
χὶς ἡ γενομένη Καίσαρι διεφθάρη· καὶ ἔδοξε τοῦτ᾽ ἐς
341   τὰ μέλλοντα σημῆναι. ἐπιπολαζούσης δὲ ὑπονοίας
ἔτι, ὡς παρασπόνδως ὁ πόλεμος ὅδε γίγνοιτο, τὴν
ὑπόνοιαν ὁ Καῖσαρ ἐκλύων ἐπέστελλε τῇ πόλει καὶ
τὸν στρατὸν αὐτὸς ἐδίδασκεν, ὅτι τὰς σπονδὰς ὁ
Πομπήιος ληστεύων τὴν θάλασσαν ἀναλύσειε καὶ
τοῦθ᾽ οἱ λῃσταὶ κατείποιεν αὐτοῦ, κατείποι δὲ καὶ Μηνόδωρος τὴν ὅλην γνώμην, μάθοι δὲ καὶ Ἀντώνιος καὶ
διὰ τοῦτο Πελοπόννησον οὐ δοίη.

---

59 Gaius Calvisius Sabinus had tried to protect Julius Caesar
from his assassins in 44. Consul in 39, he later governed Spain
and celebrated a triumph in 28.

80. Octavian, however, sent officers to Sardinia and 337 Corsica, to take possession of what Menodorus was turning over to him, and reinforced the Italian coastline with numerous guard posts in case Pompeius attacked it again. He also ordered the building of new triremes at Rome and 338 Ravenna, and sent for a large army from Illyria. When Menodorus came he immediately declared him a freeborn man rather than an ex-slave, and put him in command of the ships he himself was bringing, as a subordinate of the admiral Calvisius.[59] Having made these arrangements and 339 collected even more substantial military resources, Octavian played for time and blamed Antony for not waiting for him. He ordered Cornificius to bring with him from Ravenna to Tarentum the armament already in place.[60] While Cornificius was making the voyage a storm overtook 340 him, but only the flagship intended for Octavian was destroyed. This was considered a portent for the future. As 341 the suspicion still prevailed that this war was a violation of the treaty, Octavian, seeking to dispel the suspicion, wrote a letter to Rome and told the troops in person that Pompeius was the one who had broken the treaty by committing acts of piracy on the sea, and that the pirates had accused him of this; furthermore Menodorus had revealed the whole plan, and Antony too knew of it, and for that reason had refused to give up the Peloponnese.

[60] Lucius Cornificius was a loyal supporter of Octavian. As tribune in 43 he had prosecuted Brutus for the murder of Julius Caesar. Consul in 35, he then governed Africa and was awarded a triumph in 32.

342   81. Ὡς δὲ αὐτῷ τὰ ἐν χερσὶν ἕτοιμα γεγένητο,
ἐπέπλει τῇ Σικελίᾳ, αὐτὸς μὲν ἐκ Τάραντος, Καλουίσιος δὲ Σαβῖνος καὶ Μηνόδωρος ἀπὸ Τυρρηνίας·
περιῄει δὲ καὶ τὸ πεζὸν ἐς Ῥήγιον, καὶ μετὰ σπουδῆς
343   ἐταχύνετο ἅπαντα. ὁ δὲ Πομπήιος τῆς μὲν αὐτομολίας τοῦ Μηνοδώρου ἐπιπλέοντος ἤδη Καίσαρος
ᾔσθετο, πρὸς δὲ τὸν ἑκατέρωθεν ἐπίπλουν αὐτὸς μὲν
ὑπέμεινεν ἐν Μεσσήνῃ τὸν Καίσαρα, Καλουισίῳ δὲ
καὶ Μηνοδώρῳ τὸν ἔχθιστον τῷ Μηνοδώρῳ μάλιστα
τῶν ἐξελευθέρων ἑαυτοῦ Μενεκράτη προσέτασσεν
344   ἀπαντᾶν ἐπὶ στόλου πολλοῦ. ὅδε οὖν ὁ Μενεκράτης
ἐπιφαίνεται τοῖς πολεμίοις περὶ δείλην ἑσπέραν πελάγιος. καὶ οἱ μὲν ἐς τὸν κόλπον τὸν ὑπὲρ Κύμης συνέφυγον καὶ τὴν νύκτα ἀνεπαύοντο, καὶ Μενεκράτης ἐς
Αἰναρίαν παρῆλθεν· ἠοῦς δὲ ἀρχομένης οἱ μὲν τὸν
κόλπον ἐν χρῷ παρὰ τὴν γῆν αὐτὴν μηνοειδεῖ στόλῳ
παρέπλεον, ἵνα μὴ αὐτοὺς διεκπλέοιεν οἱ πολέμιοι, ὁ
δὲ Μενεκράτης αὐτοῖς αὖθις ἐπιφαίνεταί τε καὶ εὐθὺς
ἐπλησίαζεν ὑπὸ ῥύμης καὶ τάχους· δρᾶν δὲ οὐκ ἀνα-
γομένους ἐς τὸ πέλαγος οὐδὲν μέγα ἔχων, ἐς τὴν γῆν
ἐγχρίμπτων ἐξεώθει. οἱ δὲ ἐξώκελλόν τε ὁμοῦ καὶ τὰς
345   ἐμβολὰς ἀπεμάχοντο. ἦν δὲ τοῖς μὲν ἐς τὸ πέλαγος
ἀναχώρησίς τε καὶ ἐφόρμησις, ὅτε βούλοιντο, καὶ
σκαφῶν ἑτέρων ἀλλαγὴ παρὰ μέρος· οἱ δὲ ἔκαμνον ἔκ
τε τῶν πετρῶν, ἐφ' ἃς ἐπώκελλον, καὶ ὑπὸ τῆς ἀκινη-
σίας τῶν νεῶν· πεζομαχεῖν γὰρ πρὸς ναυμαχοῦντας
ἐῴκεσαν, οὔτε διώκειν οὔτε ἐκκλίνειν ἔχοντες.
346   82. Ἐν δὲ τούτῳ Μηνόδωρος καὶ Μενεκράτης καθ-

148

81. When the forces at his disposal were all ready, he 342
set sail to attack Sicily, he himself leaving from Tarentum,
Calvisius Sabinus and Menodorus from Etruria. The infantry too made their war round to Rhegium, and everything was expedited with urgency. Pompeius learned of 343
Menodorus' desertion when Octavian was already sailing
to the attack, and to face this naval assault from both
fronts, he himself waited for Octavian at Messena and
ordered Menecrates, who of all his freedmen was by far
the most hostile to Menodorus, to meet Calvisius and
Menodorus with a large fleet. This Menecrates then is 344
sighted by his enemies in the late afternoon on the open
sea. They took refuge in the bay above Cumae, where they
passed the night, while Menecrates made his way to Aenaria. At daybreak they sailed along the bay in crescent
formation hard by the land in order to prevent the enemy
breaking through their line. Menecrates again comes into
view, and immediately closed with them furiously and fast,
but being unable to do them any great harm as long as they
refused to come out to the open sea, he pressed hard to
drive them against the shore. They ran aground together
and fought off his attempts to ram them. For one side it 345
was possible to withdraw to the open sea and attack again
whenever they wanted, and bring in fresh boats by turns,
while the other side was in difficulty from the rocks on
which they had grounded and from the fact that they could
not move their ships. They were like land forces fighting
a battle against sea forces, unable either to pursue or retreat.

82. Meanwhile, Menodorus and Menecrates catch 346

ορῶσιν ἀλλήλους καὶ τὸν ἄλλον πόνον ἀφέντες
αὐτίκα μετ᾽ ὀργῆς καὶ βοῆς ἀλλήλοις ἐπέπλεον, ἐν
τῷδε τὴν νίκην καὶ τὸ κεφάλαιον τοῦ πολέμου τιθέμε-
347 νοι, ἐν ᾧ τις αὐτῶν κρατήσειν ἔμελλεν. αἱ μὲν δὴ νῆες
ἀλλήλαις ὑπὸ ῥύμης ἐνέπεσον καὶ συνέτριψαν ἡ μὲν
τὸν ἔμβολον τῆς Μηνοδώρου νεώς, ἡ δὲ τὸν ταρσὸν
τῆς Μενεκράτους· ἐπεὶ δὲ αὐταῖς ἑκατέρωθεν χεῖρες
ἐπεβλήθησαν σιδηραῖ, τῶν μὲν νεῶν οὐδὲν ἔτι ἔργον
ἦν, συνεστηκυίας ἑκατέρας, οἱ δὲ ἄνδρες ὥσπερ ἐν γῇ
348 πόνου καὶ ἀρετῆς οὐδὲν ἀπέλειπον. ἀκόντιά τε γὰρ ἦν
ἀθρόα καὶ λίθοι καὶ τοξεύματα ἐπ᾽ ἀλλήλους, καὶ ἐπὶ
τὰς ναῦς καταρράκτας ἐρρίπτουν ἐς τὸ ἐπιέναι δι᾽
αὐτῶν. ὑψηλοτέρας δ᾽ οὔσης τῆς Μηνοδώρου νεώς, οἵ
τε καταρράκται τοῖς τολμῶσιν ἦσαν εὐεπιβατώτεροι
349 καὶ τὰ βαλλόμενα ὡς ἀφ᾽ ὑψηλοῦ βιαιότερα. τεθνεώτων δ᾽ ἤδη πολλῶν καὶ τῶν ὑπολοίπων κατατετρω-
μένων, ὁ μὲν Μηνόδωρος ὀβελῷ τὸν βραχίονα ἐτρώθη,
καὶ ὁ ὀβελὸς ἐξῃρέθη, ὁ δὲ Μενεκράτης τὸν μηρὸν
ἀκοντίῳ πολυγλώχινι Ἰβηρικῷ ὁλοσιδήρῳ, καὶ οὐκ
350 ἦν ἐξελεῖν αὐτὸ σὺν ἐπείξει. ἀχρεῖος οὖν ὁ Μενεκράτης ἐς μάχην γενόμενος ἐπέμενε καὶ ὥς, τοὺς ἄλλους ἐποτρύνων, μέχρι λαμβανομένης τῆς νεὼς ἐς τὸν
βυθὸν τοῦ πελάγους ἑαυτὸν ἔρριψεν. καὶ τὴν μὲν ναῦν
ὁ Μηνόδωρος ἀνεδήσατο καὶ ἐς τὴν γῆν ἀπέπλευσεν,
οὐδὲν ἔτι δρᾶν οὐδὲ ἐκεῖνος δυνάμενος.

351   83. Καὶ τὸ μὲν λαιὸν τῆς ναυμαχίας οὕτως ἐπεπρά-
χει. ἐκ δὲ τοῦ δεξιοῦ Καλουίσιος μέν, διαπλέων ἐς τὸ
λαιόν, ἀπετέμετό τινας τῶν Μενεκράτους νεῶν καὶ

sight of each other, and, ignoring the rest of the fight, immediately set course against each other, roaring angrily and regarding victory and the decisive moment of the war as dependent on this encounter, in which one of them would be victorious. Their ships collided violently, and 347 Menodorus' lost its ram, and Menecrates' its oars. When grappling irons were thrown by both, the ships were no longer of service, stuck together as they were, but the men showed no lack of effort or courage, fighting as if they were on land. There were volleys of javelins, stones, and arrows 348 released against each other, and they threw gangways onto each ship to use for boarding. As Menodorus' was higher, his gangways were easier to use for those who ventured onto them, and his missiles had greater impact as they were thrown from a height. Many were already dead and 349 the rest wounded, when Menodorus was wounded in the arm by a dart, which was extracted, and Menecrates in the thigh by a multibarbed Iberian javelin made of solid iron, which was impossible to pull out quickly. Although 350 Menecrates could no longer take part in the fight, he remained there all the same, encouraging the others, until his ship was captured, and he threw himself into the depths of the sea. Menodorus took the ship in tow and sailed to shore; not even he could do anything more.

83. Such was the outcome of the sea battle on the left 351 wing. While sailing from the right wing across to the left, Calvisius cut off some of Menecrates' ships and chased

ἐκφυγούσας εἰς τὸ πέλαγος ἐδίωκε, Δημοχάρης δ', ὁ
τοῦ Μενεκράτους συνεξελεύθερός τε καὶ ὑποστράτη-
γος, ταῖς λοιπαῖς τοῦ Καλουισίου συμπεσών, τὰς μὲν
ἐς φυγὴν ἐτρέπετο, τὰς δὲ ἐς πέτρας συνήραξε, καὶ
τῶν ἀνδρῶν ἐξαλομένων ἐνεπίμπρα τὰ σκάφη, μέχρι
Καλουίσιος ἐκ τῆς διώξεως ἐπανιὼν τάς τε φευγού-
σας τῶν ἰδίων ἐπανήγαγε καὶ τὰς ἐμπιπραμένας εἵλκυσε.[28] καὶ νυκτὸς ἐπιλαβούσης ηὐλίσαντο πάντες,
352 ἔνθα καὶ τῆς προτέρας. ἡ μὲν δὴ ναυμαχία ἐς τοῦτο
ἐτελεύτα, καὶ προῦχεν ἐν αὐτῇ τὰ Πομπηίου παρὰ
πολύ· Δημοχάρης δὲ βαρυθυμῶν ἐπὶ τῷ θανάτῳ Μενεκράτους ὡς ἐπὶ ἥττῃ μεγίστῃ (δύο γὰρ οἴδε ἦσαν
μάλιστα τῷ Πομπηίῳ θαλάσσης ἐργάται, Μενεκράτης τε καὶ Μηνόδωρος), ἅπαντα μεθεὶς ἐκ χειρῶν
εὐθὺς ἐς Σικελίαν ἔπλει, καθάπερ οὐ τὸ Μενεκράτους
σῶμα καὶ ναῦν μίαν, ἀλλὰ τὸν στόλον ὅλον ἀπο-
βαλών.

353   84. Ὁ δὲ Καλουίσιος ἕως μὲν ἐπιπλευσεῖσθαι τὸν
Δημοχάρην προσεδόκα, παρέμενεν, ἔνθαπερ ὥρμιστο,
ναυμαχεῖν οὐ δυνάμενος· αἵ τε γὰρ κράτισται τῶν
νεῶν αὐτῷ διωλώλεσαν, καὶ αἱ ἕτεραι πρὸς ναυμαχίαν
εἶχον ἀχρείως· ἐπεὶ δὲ ἔμαθεν οἰχόμενον ἐς Σικελίαν,
ἐπεσκεύαζε τὰς ναῦς καὶ παρέπλει τὴν γῆν, τοὺς κόλ-
354 πους ἐξελίσσων. ὁ δὲ Καῖσαρ ἐκ μὲν Τάραντος ἐς
τὸ Ῥήγιον διεπεπλεύκει ναυσὶ πολλαῖς καὶ στρατῷ
πολλῷ καὶ Πομπήιον περὶ Μεσσήνην κατειλήφει
ναῦς ἔχοντα τεσσαράκοντα μόνας, ὥστε αὐτῷ παρή-
νουν οἱ φίλοι, ὡς ἐν καιρῷ μάλιστα, ἐπιθέσθαι τῷ

them as they made their escape into the open sea, while
Demochares, who was a fellow freedman of Menecrates
and his lieutenant, fell upon the remainder of Calvisius'
squadron. He put some of them to flight, shattered others
on the rocks, and set fire to them after the crews had
jumped off. Eventually Calvisius returned from his pursuit, brought back those of his own ships that were in
flight, and towed the ones that were burning. With the
onset of night, all parties camped in the same place as the
previous night. That was the end of the sea battle, in which   352
the forces of Pompeius had much the better of it. Demochares, however, was as grief-stricken over the death of
Menecrates as if it had been the worst of defeats (for it
was these two, Menecrates and Menodorus, who had been
Pompeius' special naval experts), and he let everything
slip from his hands and sailed straight for Sicily as if he
had lost not merely the body of Menecrates and one ship,
but his whole fleet.

84. As long as he expected Demochares to attack, Cal-   353
visius stayed where he had anchored, being incapable of
fighting a battle. For his most powerful ships had been
destroyed and the others were unfit for combat. But when
he learned that Demochares had left for Sicily, he refitted
his ships and sailed along the coast, following the curve of
the bays. Octavian had sailed from Tarentum to Rhegium   354
with a large number of ships and soldiers, and near Messena encountered Pompeius, who only had forty ships. So
Octavian's associates advised him, in such a favorable situ-

---

28 ἐκώλυσε codd.; εἵλκυσε Étienne-Duplessis

Πομπηίῳ μετὰ τοσοῦδε στόλου, ναῦς ἔχοντι ὀλίγας,
355 μέχρι τὸ λοιπὸν ἐκείνῳ ναυτικὸν οὐ πάρεστιν. ὁ δ᾽
οὐκ ἐπείθετο, Καλουίσιον περιμένων καὶ λέγων οὐκ
εὔβουλον εἶναι τὸ ῥιψοκίνδυνον, ἔνθα συμμαχίαν ἄλ-
356 λην προσδοκῴη. ὡς δὲ Δημοχάρης ἐς Μεσσήνην
κατέπλευσεν, ὁ μὲν Πομπήιος αὐτόν τε Δημοχάρην
καὶ Ἀπολλοφάνην, καὶ τόνδε ἀπελεύθερον ἑαυτοῦ,
ναυάρχους ἀπέφηνεν ἀντὶ Μηνοδώρου καὶ Μενεκράτους.

357   85. Ὁ δὲ Καῖσαρ περὶ τῶν συμβεβηκότων ἀμφὶ τῇ
Κύμῃ πυθόμενος ἐξέπλει τὸν πορθμόν, ὑπαντήσων τῷ
Καλουισίῳ. ἀνύσαντι δ᾽ αὐτῷ τοῦ πόρου τὸ πλέον καὶ
Στυλίδα ἤδη παραπλέοντι καὶ ἐς τὸ Σκύλλαιον ἐπικά-
μπτοντι, ἐκθορὼν ἐκ τῆς Μεσσήνης ὁ Πομπήιος ἐξήπτετο τῶν ὑστάτων καὶ τὰς πρόπλους ἐδίωκε καὶ πά-
358 σαις ἐνέβαλλε καὶ ἐς μάχην προυκαλεῖτο. αἱ δὲ
καίπερ ἐνοχλούμεναι ἐς μὲν ναυμαχίαν οὐκ ἐπέστρε-
φον, Καίσαρος οὐκ ἐῶντος, εἴτε δείσαντος ἐν στενῷ
ναυμαχεῖν εἴτ᾽ ἐπιμένοντος οἷς ἀπ᾽ ἀρχῆς διεγνώκει,
μὴ ναυμαχεῖν δίχα τοῦ Καλουισίου· γνώμῃ δὲ αὐτοῦ
παρά τε τὴν γῆν ὑπεχώρουν ἅπασαι καὶ ἐπ᾽ ἀγκυρῶν
ἐσάλευον καὶ κατὰ πρῷραν ἀπεμάχοντο τοὺς ἐπιό-
359 ντας. Δημοχάρους δ᾽ ἐπιστήσαντος δύο ναῦς περὶ
ἑκάστην ἐθορυβοῦντο ἤδη, πρός τε τὰς πέτρας ἀρασσόμεναι καὶ πρὸς ἀλλήλας, θαλάσσης τε ἐνεπίμπλα-
ντο· καὶ διεφθείροντο μετὰ ἀργίας καὶ αἵδε ὥσπερ αἱ

ation, and with such a large fleet, to attack Pompeius and his small number of ships, while the rest of the latter's naval force was absent. Octavian, however, did not follow 355 this advice, but waited for Calvisius, saying that it was unwise to court danger when he was expecting further military assistance. When Demochares arrived at Mes- 356 sena, Pompeius appointed him and Apollophanes, another of his freedmen, admirals in place of Menodorus and Menecrates.

85. On hearing of what had happened at Cumae, Oc- 357 tavian sailed out of the straits to go to meet Calvisius. He had completed most of the passage and was already sailing past Stylis and turning course for Scyllaeum, when Pompeius darted out of Messena, harassed the rearmost ships, chased after the leading ones, attacked the whole fleet and challenged them to fight. Although in trouble, Octavian's 358 ships did not face about for battle, as he would not allow it, either because he was afraid to fight in narrow waters, or because he was sticking to his original decision not to fight without Calvisius. It was his decision that all ships withdrew near the land and rode at anchor, fighting off the attackers from the prows. But when Demochares set two 359 of his ships against each one of theirs, they were then thrown into confusion, crashing against the rocks and each other, and beginning to fill with water. And so these ships too, like those at Cumae, were lost without being able to

περὶ Κύμην, ὁρμοῦσαί τε καὶ ἐμβαλλόμεναι πρὸς
ἐχθρῶν ἐπιπλεόντων καὶ ἀναχωρούντων.²⁹

360   86. Ὁ μὲν δὴ Καῖσαρ ἐξήλατο τῆς νεὼς ἐπὶ τὰς
πέτρας καὶ τοὺς ἐκνέοντας ἐκ τῆς θαλάσσης ἀνελάμβανε καὶ ἐς τὸ ὄρος ἄνω παρέπεμπε· Κορνιφίκιος δὲ
καὶ ὅσοι ἄλλοι στρατηγοὶ ἦσαν αὐτοῦ, παρακαλέσαν-
τες ἀλλήλους, ἄνευ προστάγματος ἀπέρρηξαν τὰ
ἀγκύρια καὶ ἀνήχθησαν ἐπὶ τοὺς πολεμίους, ὡς δέον
τι δρῶντας παθεῖν μᾶλλον ἢ ἑστῶτας ἀμαχεὶ τοῖς
361   ἐπιχειροῦσι προκεῖσθαι. τόλμῃ τε παραβόλῳ πρῶτον
ὁ Κορνιφίκιος τὴν ναυαρχίδα τοῦ Δημοχάρους κατέσεισε καὶ εἷλε. καὶ Δημοχάρης μὲν ἐς ἑτέραν ἐξήλατο, τοιούτου δὲ ὄντος τοῦ πόνου καὶ τοῦ φθόρου
ἐπεφαίνοντο ἐκ πόντου προσπλέοντες ἤδη Καλουί-
362   σιός τε καὶ Μηνόδωρος. καὶ αὐτοὺς οἱ μὲν τοῦ Καίσαρος οὐχ ἑώρων οὔτε ἀπὸ γῆς οὔτε ἐκ θαλάσσης,
πελαγιώτεροι δὲ ὄντες οἱ τοῦ Πομπηίου κατεῖδον καὶ
ἰδόντες ἀνεχώρουν· συνεσκόταζε γὰρ ἤδη, καὶ κεκμη-
κότες ἀκμῆσιν οὐκ ἐθάρρουν συμπλέκεσθαι.

363   87. Τοῦτο μὲν δὴ συγκύρημα τοῖς ὑπολοίποις ἐκ
τοῦ τέως ἀχρείου χρηστὸν ἐπιγίγνεται· νυκτὸς δὲ ἐπιλαβούσης οἱ μὲν ἐκ τῶν νεῶν ἐκπεσόντες ἐς τὰ ὄρη
συνέφευγον καὶ πυρὰ πολλὰ ἔκαιον σύμβολα τοῖς ἔτι
οὖσιν ἐν τῇ θαλάσσῃ καὶ διενυκτέρευον οὕτως ἄσιτοι
364   καὶ ἀθεράπευτοι καὶ πάντων ἐνδεεῖς. καὶ αὐτοὺς ὁ

---

²⁹ ἔμελλ᾽ ἐπεὶ οὐδέπω κακὸν γ᾽ ἀπώλετο (Soph. Phil. 446)
interp. P; seclusit Schweig.

take action, since they were anchored and facing the attacks of an enemy who could advance and withdraw.[61]

86. Octavian jumped from his ship onto the rocks and 360
pulled out of the water those who were swimming to land,
and brought them to the high ground above. Cornificius,
however, and the other generals present, encouraged each
other and, without orders to do so, cut their anchor lines
and put to sea against the enemy, thinking that they should
die in action rather than stand exposed to their attackers
without retaliating. First, with reckless daring, Cornificius 361
rammed the flagship of Demochares and captured it. Demochares jumped onto another vessel, but at this point in
the battle and destruction, Calvisius and Menodorus now
appeared, making their approach from the seaward side.
Octavian's men did not see them, either from the land or 362
the water, but the Pompeian forces, being further out to
sea, did spot them and having done so, withdrew. For it
was now getting dark, and they were tired, and did not
dare to engage with fresh forces.

87. This combination of events served Octavian's sur- 363
viving men well after their previous helplessness. At nightfall those who had been forced ashore took refuge in the
mountains and lit many fires as a signal to those still at sea,
and spent the night without food, unattended and lacking
everything they needed. Octavian himself was in the same 364

[61] One manuscript has taken into the text what was obviously
a marginal comment by an educated reader quoting a line from
Sophocles (*Phil.* 446): "For nothing evil is ever destroyed."

Καῖσαρ, ὁμοίως ἔχων, παρεκάλει περιθέων ἐς τὴν ἔω
κακοπαθῆσαι. ταλαιπωρουμένῳ δὲ αὐτῷ περὶ ταῦτα
Καλουίσιος μὲν οὐδ᾽ ὡς ἐγιγνώσκετο προσπλέων,
οὐδὲ ἀπὸ τῶν νεῶν τι χρηστὸν ἐγίγνετο, ἀσχολου-
365 μένων περὶ τὰ ναυάγια· ὑπὸ δὲ ἑτέρου δαίμονος ἀγα-
θοῦ τὸ τρισκαιδέκατον τέλος ἐπλησίαζε διὰ τῶν ὀρῶν
καὶ περὶ τοῦ κακοῦ πυθόμενοι τοὺς κρημνούς, τῷ πυρὶ
τῆς ὁδοῦ τεκμαιρόμενοι, διέδραμον καὶ καταλαβόντες
τὸν αὐτοκράτορα σφῶν καὶ τοὺς συμφυγόντας ὧδε
ἔχοντας καμάτου καὶ τροφῶν ἀπορίας ἐθεράπευον,
ἄλλους ἄλλῃ διαλαβόντες, οἱ δὲ ταξίαρχοι τὸν αὐτοκράτορα ἐς αὐτοσχέδιον σκηνὴν ἐσαγαγόντες, οὐδενὸς τῶν οἰκετῶν αὐτῷ θεραπευτήρων παρόντων, ὡς
366 ἐν νυκτὶ καὶ τοσῷδε ταράχῳ διερριμμένων. περιπέμ-
ψας δ᾽ εὐθὺς πανταχῇ τοὺς ἐξαγγελοῦντας, ὅτι σῴζοιτο, πυνθάνεται Καλουίσιον σὺν ταῖς πρόπλοις
καταπλέοντα καὶ ὡς ἐπὶ δύο χρηστοῖς καὶ ἀδοκήτοις
ἀνεπαύετο.

367   88. Ἅμα δ᾽ ἡμέρᾳ τὴν θάλασσαν ἐφορῶν ἐθεᾶτο
ναῦς ἐμπεπρησμένας τε καὶ ἡμιφλέκτους ἔτι καὶ ἡμι-
καύστους ἄλλας τε λελυμασμένας ἱστίων τε ὁμοῦ καὶ
πηδαλίων καὶ σκευῶν ἔμπλεων τὸ πέλαγος καὶ τῶν
368 ἔτι σῳζομένων τὰ πολλὰ πεπονηκότα. προστησάμε-
νος οὖν τὸν Καλουισίου στόλον, ἐπεσκεύαζε τὰ ἐπείγοντα τῶν σκαφῶν πλαγιάσας, ἠρεμούντων καὶ τῶν
πολεμίων, εἴτε διὰ Καλουίσιον εἴτε αὖθις ἀναγομένοις
369 ἐπιθέσθαι διεγνωκότων. ὧδε δὲ ἐχόντων ἑκατέρων, ἐκ
μέσης ἡμέρας νότος ἐμπεσὼν ἤγειρε κῦμα βίαιον ἐν

situation, and moved around encouraging his men to endure their troubles until dawn. In spite of being in such difficulties, it was still not known that Calvisius was sailing in, nor were his own ships of any use at all, busy as they were with the wrecks. But with the help of another benign   365
divinity, the thirteenth legion was approaching their position through the mountains, and on hearing of the disaster, hurried across the crags using torches to find the route. They discovered their commander in chief and those who had escaped with him suffering from fatigue and lack of food, and took care of them, dividing them up among different groups. The military tribunes brought the commander in chief to an improvised tent, none of his own slaves being present, because they had been scattered in the darkness and such great confusion. Octavian immedi-   366
ately sent round messengers everywhere to announce that he was safe, and then he learns of Calvisius' arrival with the vanguard of his fleet; and in view of two helpful and unexpected events, he took some rest.

88. At dawn, when Octavian looked out over the sea,   367
the spectacle that met him was one of ships consumed by flames, or still half burning, or half reduced to ashes, and others utterly shattered, and of the sea filled with sails and rudders and tackle; and most of the ships still being salvaged were seriously damaged. So he positioned Calvisius'   368
fleet in front for protection, and, having put them on their side, repaired those of his ships in most urgent need, while the enemy did nothing, either because of Calvisius, or because they had decided to attack when the ships put to sea again. Such was the situation on each side when after   369
midday a south wind burst on them, stirring up a violent

ῥοώδει καὶ στενῷ χωρίῳ. Πομπήιος μὲν οὖν ἐν Μεσσήνῃ λιμένων ἔνδον ἦν, αἱ δὲ τοῦ Καίσαρος νῆες αὖθις περὶ τραχεῖαν ἀκτὴν καὶ δύσορμον ἀρασσόμεναι ταῖς τε πέτραις καὶ ἀλλήλαις ἐπεφέροντο, οὐδὲ τῶν πληρωμάτων σφίσιν ὥστε διακρατεῖν ἐντελῶν ὄντων.

370   89. Μηνόδωρος μὲν οὖν, ἀρχόμενον τὸ δεινὸν ἐλπίσας πλεονάσειν, ἐς τὸ πελαγιώτερον ἀνήχθη καὶ ἐπ' ἀγκυρῶν διεσάλευεν· ἀσθενέστερον δὲ ἔχων τὸ κῦμα διὰ τὸν βυθόν, εἰρεσίᾳ ὅμως καὶ πρὸς τόδε ἐνίστατο
371   καρτερᾷ μὴ παραφέρεσθαι, καί τινες αὐτὸν ἐμιμοῦντο ἕτεροι. τὸ δὲ λοιπὸν πλῆθος, οἰόμενοι ταχέως τὸ πνεῦμα ἐνδώσειν ὡς ἐν ἔαρι, τὰς ναῦς ἑκατέρωθεν ἀγκύραις ἔκ τε τοῦ πελάγους καὶ ἀπὸ τῆς γῆς διε-
372   κράτουν καὶ κοντοῖς ἐξεώθουν ἀπ' ἀλλήλων. τραχυτέρου δὲ τοῦ πνεύματος γενομένου συνεκέχυτο πάντα καὶ συνετρίβοντο αἱ νῆες, τὰς ἀγκύρας ἀπορρηγνύουσαι καὶ ἐς τὴν γῆν ἢ ἐπ' ἀλλήλας τινασσόμεναι· βοή τε ἦν παμμιγὴς δεδιότων ὁμοῦ καὶ οἰμωζόντων καὶ παρακαλούντων[30] ἀλλήλους ἐς ἀνήκοον· οὐ γὰρ ἐφικνοῦντο ἔτι τῶν λεγομένων, οὐδὲ κυβερνήτης ἰδιώτου
373   διέφερεν οὔτε κατ' ἐπιστήμην οὔτε προστάσσων. ἀλλ' ὁ φθόρος ἦν ὅμοιος ἔν τε ταῖς ναυσὶν αὐταῖς καί, ὅτε τις αὐτῶν ἐκπέσοι κύματι καὶ κλύδωνι καὶ ξύλοις ἀρασσομένων· ἔγεμεν γὰρ ἡ θάλασσα ἱστίων καὶ ξύλων καὶ ἀνδρῶν καὶ νεκρῶν. εἰ δέ τις καὶ τάδε διαφυγὼν ἐκνήχοιτο ἐπὶ τὴν γῆν, συνηράσσοντο καὶ οἵδε

sea in the confined space with its powerful currents. Pompeius, at least, was inside the harbor at Messena, but Octavian's ships were again pounded onto a rough shore with poor anchorage, and thrown against the rocks and each other, without even having full crews to hold them steady.

89. Now Menodorus, when the storm began, expected it to get worse, and moved more into the open sea and rode at anchor. Although he faced less violent waves because of the deep water, nevertheless he held his position against them by rowing hard to avoid being carried away. Some of the others followed his example, but the remaining majority thought that the wind would soon die down, as it usually does in the spring, and held their ships with anchors from both bow and stern, on the seaward and on the landward side, pushing each other off with poles. But the wind grew stronger and everything was thrown into confusion: the ships were shattered when they broke their anchors and were smashed onto the shore or against each other. Cries of alarm were mixed together from terrified men, lamenting their fate or urging each other on, but they fell on deaf ears. For voices could no longer reach their hearer, and there was nothing to distinguish a helmsman from an ordinary seaman, whether in terms of technical knowledge or in issuing orders. The same death awaited those who stayed on the ships themselves and those who fell overboard, crushed by swell and surf and timber. For the sea was full of sails and pieces of wood and men and corpses. And if anyone avoided these things and managed to swim to shore, they too were pulverized

370

371

372

373

---

30 παρακελευόντων codd.; παρακαλούντων Étiennne-Duplessis

374 ἐπὶ τὰς πέτρας ὑπὸ τοῦ κύματος. ὡς δὲ καὶ τὸ σπά-
σμα τὴν θάλασσαν ἐλάμβανεν, ὃ συνήθως ἐπιγίγνεται τῷδε τῷ πορθμῷ, τοὺς μὲν ἀήθεις καὶ τόδε ἐξ-
έπλησσε, τὰ δὲ σκάφη τότε μάλιστα περιφερόμενα
συνέπιπτεν ἀλλήλοις. καὶ τὸ πνεῦμα ἐς νύκτα χαλε-
πώτερον ἐγίγνετο, ὥστε μηδὲ κατὰ φῶς ἔτι, ἀλλ᾽ ἐν
σκότῳ διόλλυσθαι.

375 90. Οἰμωγαί τε ἀνὰ τὴν νύκτα πᾶσαν ἦσαν καὶ τῶν
οἰκείων μετακλήσεις ἀνά τε τὴν γῆν διαθεόντων καὶ
τοὺς ἐν τῇ θαλάσσῃ καλούντων ἐξ ὀνόματος καὶ θρη-
νούντων, ὅτε μὴ ἐπακούσειαν, ὡς ἀπολωλότας· ἔμ-
παλίν τε ἑτέρων ἀνὰ τὸ πέλαγος ὑπερκυπτόντων τὸ
κῦμα καὶ ἐς βοήθειαν τοὺς ἐν τῇ γῇ παρακαλούντων.

376 ἀμήχανα δὲ πάντα ἦν ἑκατέροις· καὶ οὐχ ἡ θάλασσα
μόνη τοῖς ἐς αὐτὴν ἐσελθοῦσιν καὶ ὅσοι τῶν νεῶν
ἐπεβεβήκεσαν ἔτι, ἀλλὰ καὶ ἡ γῆ τοῦ κλύδωνος οὐχ
ἧσσον ἦν ἀπορωτέρα, μὴ σφᾶς τὸ κῦμα συναράξειεν

377 ἐπὶ τὰς πέτρας. ἐμόχθουν τε χειμῶνι τῶν πώποτε
μάλιστα καινοτρόπῳ, γῆς ὄντες ἀγχοτάτω καὶ τὴν
γῆν δεδιότες καὶ οὔτε ἐκφυγεῖν αὐτὴν ἔχοντες ἐς τὸ
πέλαγος οὔτε ὅσον ἀλλήλων διαστῆναι· ἡ γὰρ στε-
νότης ἥ τοῦ χωρίου καὶ τὸ φύσει δυσέξοδον αὐτοῦ καὶ
κλύδων ἐπιπεσὼν καὶ τὸ πνεῦμα, ὑπὸ τῶν περικειμένων ὀρῶν ἐς θυέλλας περικλώμενον, καὶ ὁ τοῦ βυ-
θοῦ σπασμὸς ἐπὶ πάντα εἰλούμενος οὔτε μένειν οὔτε
φεύγειν ἐπέτρεπε· τό τε σκότος ἠνώχλει νυκτὸς μάλι-

378 στα μελαίνης· ὅθεν ἔθνησκον οὐδὲ καθορῶντες ἀλλήλους ἔτι, οἱ μὲν θορυβούμενοι καὶ βοῶντες, οἱ δ᾽

against the rocks by the waves. When the maelstrom af-   374
fected the sea in the way that was usual in these straits,
this both terrified the men who were not used to it, and
also tossed the ships around then more than ever, and
threw them against each other. With the arrival of night,
the wind became more difficult to withstand, so that destruction no longer came in the light, but in the darkness.

90. There was wailing all night long, and the cries of   375
friends and relatives running along the shore as they called
by name to those in the water and grieved for them in the
belief that they had been killed when there was no reply.
Conversely, there were others in the sea who kept their
head above the waves and called for help to those on the
land. But nothing could be done for either group. And it   376
was not just the sea that was unmanageable for those who
went into it or those who were still on board the ships, but
the land too was no less intractable than the deep, for fear
of the waves dashing men on the rocks. They were strug-   377
gling with a storm quite unparalleled up to that time, in
that they were very near the shore but also afraid of it, and
unable to get away from it into the open sea or put enough
distance between each other. For the narrowness of the
place, and the innate difficulty of getting out of it, and the
surge of the waves, and the wind whipped into gusts by
the surrounding mountains, and the maelstrom in the
deep water churning everything up, made it impossible to
stay or escape. And the darkness of a particularly black
night was unnerving. As a result, they died no longer even   378
able to see each other, some confused and shouting out,

ἐφ' ἡσυχίας παριέμενοι καὶ τὸ δεινὸν ἐκδεχόμενοι καὶ
συνεργοῦντες ἐς αὐτὸ ἔνιοι ὡς ἀπολούμενοι πάντως.
379 γενόμενον γὰρ τὸ κακὸν κρεῖσσον ἐπινοίας καὶ τὴν ἐκ
τῶν παραλόγων αὐτοὺς ἐλπίδα ἀφῃρεῖτο, μέχρι ποτὲ
ἄφνω τὸ πνεῦμα προσιούσης ἡμέρας διελύετο καὶ
380 μεθ' ἡλίου ἐπιτολὴν πάμπαν ἐμαραίνετο. καὶ τὸ κῦμα
ὅμως καὶ τότε, τοῦ πνεύματος ἐκλυθέντος, ἐπὶ πολὺ
ἐτραχύνετο. καὶ τὸ δεινὸν οὐδ' ὑπὸ τῶν ἐγχωρίων
ποτὲ τηλικοῦτον ἐμνημονεύετο γενέσθαι· γενόμενον δὲ
ἔθους τε καὶ νόμου κρεῖσσον διέφθειρε τῶν Καίσαρος
νεῶν καὶ ἀνδρῶν τὸ πλέον.

381 91. Ὁ δὲ καὶ τῆς προτεραίας ἡμέρας πολλὰ τῷ
πολέμῳ βλαβεὶς καὶ δύο τοῖσδε συμπτώμασιν ὁμοῦ
συνενεχθεὶς ἐπὶ τὸ Ἱππώνειον εὐθὺς ᾔει διὰ τῶν ὁρῶν
νυκτὸς αὐτῆς ἐκείνης κατὰ σπουδήν, οὐχ ὑφιστάμε-
382 νος τὴν συμφοράν, ἐν ᾧ μηδὲν εἶχεν ἐπικουρεῖν. καὶ
φίλοις καὶ στρατηγοῖς ἐπέστελλε πᾶσι διὰ χειρὸς
εἶναι, μή τις αὐτῷ καὶ ἑτέρωθεν ὡς ἐν κακοπραγίᾳ
γένοιτο ἐπιβουλή. περιέπεμπε δὲ καὶ ἐς τὴν ἀκτὴν
ἅπασαν τῆς Ἰταλίας τὰ παρόντα πεζά, μὴ ἐπιτολμή-
383 σειε καὶ τῇ γῇ διὰ τὴν εὐτυχίαν ὁ Πομπήιος. ὁ δὲ
οὔτε περὶ τῆς γῆς ἐνενόησεν οὔτε τοῖς λειψάνοις τοῦ
ναυαγίου παροῦσιν ἢ ἀπιοῦσι καταστάντος τοῦ κλύδωνος ἐπεχείρησεν, ἀλλ' ὑπερεῖδεν ἐκ τῶν δυνατῶν
διαζωννυμένους τὰ σκάφη καὶ ἀνέμῳ διαπλέοντας ἐς
τὸ Ἱππώνειον, εἴτε τὴν συμφορὰν ἀρκεῖν οἱ νομίζων
εἴτ' ἄπειρος ὢν νίκην ἐπεξελθεῖν εἴθ', ὥσπερ εἴρηταί

others yielding and accepting the horror in silence, and some even assisting it, convinced that they were totally lost. For because the disaster was worse than they could 379 imagine, it even deprived them of the hope of unexpected safety. Eventually, with the approach of day the wind suddenly began to moderate, and when the sun rose it dropped completely. Even then, however, the waves continued to 380 make the sea rough for a long time after the wind died. Not even the local inhabitants could remember there ever being such a terrible storm. In exceeding what was usual and normal, it destroyed most of Octavian's ships and men.

91. Having sustained serious losses in the fighting the 381 previous day and met with these two disasters at the same time, Octavian immediately that very night hurried off through the mountains to Hipponium, having been unable to deal with the catastrophe at a time when he had no source of assistance. He wrote to all his associates and 382 commanders telling them to be on the alert for any move against him that might arise from a different quarter, as happens when things go wrong. He also stationed the infantry he had at his disposal around the whole coast of Italy in case Pompeius used his good fortune to venture an attack by land as well. But Pompeius had no thoughts 383 about the mainland, nor did he attack those who survived the wreckage, either while they were still present or as they departed when the swell subsided. Indeed, he ignored them while they secured the ships' hulls with ropes as best they could and sailed on the wind across to Hipponium. He did this either because he thought that their misfortune was enough for him, or because he did not know how to follow up a victory, or, as I have said else-

μοι καὶ ἑτέρωθι, ἐπιχειρεῖν ὅλως μαλακὸς ὢν καὶ μόνον ἐγνωκὼς ἀμύνεσθαι τοὺς ἐπιπλέοντας.

384   92. Καίσαρι δὲ οὐδ' ἐς ἥμισυ τῶν νεῶν περιεσώθη,
καὶ τοῦτο σφόδρα πεπονηκός. καταλιπὼν δ' ὅμως
αὐτοῦ τινας ἐπιμελεῖσθαι, ἐπὶ Καμπανίαν ἤει δυσ-
φορῶν· οὔτε γὰρ ἄλλας ναῦς εἶχεν, δεόμενος πολλῶν,
οὔτε χρόνον ἐς ναυπηγίαν, ἐπειγόμενος ὑπὸ τοῦ λιμοῦ
καὶ τοῦ δήμου περὶ συμβάσεων αὖθις ἐνοχλήσαντος
καὶ τὸν πόλεμον ἐπιτωθάσαντος ὡς παράσπονδον.
χρημάτων τ' ἔχρῃζε καὶ ἠπόρει, Ῥωμαίων οὔτε εἰσ-
φερόντων οὔτε τοὺς πόρους ἐώντων, οὓς ἐπινοήσειε.

385 δεινὸς δὲ ὢν ἀεὶ τὸ συμφέρον συνιδεῖν ἔπεμπε Μαικήναν ἐς Ἀντώνιον, μεταδιδάξοντα περὶ ὧν ἔναγχος
ἐπεμέμφοντο ἀλλήλοις, καὶ ἐς συμμαχίαν ὑπαξόμε-
νον. εἰ δὲ μὴ πείσειεν, ἐπενόει τοὺς ὁπλίτας ὁλκάσιν
ἐπιβήσας ἐς Σικελίαν περαιοῦν καὶ τὴν θάλασσαν

386 μεθεὶς κατὰ γῆν πόλεμον συνίστασθαι. οὕτω δ' ἀθύ-
μως ἔχοντι αὐτῷ ἀγγέλλεται ὁ Ἀντώνιος συνθέμενος
συμμαχήσειν καὶ νίκη κατὰ Κελτῶν τῶν Ἀκυιτανῶν
ἐπιφανής, ἣν Ἀγρίππας ἄγων,[31] ἐφάνη. οἵ τε φίλοι καὶ
τῶν πόλεών τινες αὐτῷ ναῦς ὑπισχνοῦντο καὶ ἐποίουν·
ὁ μὲν δὴ καὶ τῆς λύπης ἀνίη καὶ λαμπροτέραν τῆς
προτέρας παρασκευῆς συνεπήγνυτο.

387   93. Ἀρχομένου δ' ἦρος ὁ μὲν Ἀντώνιος ἐξ Ἀθηνῶν
ἐς Τάραντα διέπλει ναυσὶ τριακοσίαις, τῷ Καίσαρι

---

[31] Post ἄγων lac. indicavit Étienne-Duplessis

where,[62] because he was completely ineffective at taking the offensive, and had decided only to defend himself against those who attacked by sea.

92. Not even half of Octavian's ships were saved, and these were badly damaged. Nevertheless he left some men in place to take charge of them, and despondently made his way to Campania. For he had no other ships, but needed a great many, and had no time to build them because he was being pressed by the famine and by the people, who were again harassing him about an agreement and showing scorn for the war, as being in breach of the treaty. He also needed money, but did not have enough, since the Romans were neither paying their taxes, nor allowing him to raise the revenues he had planned. But he was always good at seeing where his interests lay, and he sent Maecenas to Antony to change his mind about the issues on which they had recently reproached each other, and to draw him into giving military assistance. If Maecenas could not persuade him, Octavian intended to embark his infantry on merchant vessels, cross over to Sicily, abandon the sea, and wage war on land. While he was in a state of such dejection, news reaches him that Antony had agreed to give military assistance, and a sparkling victory over the Gauls of Aquitania had been reported, won under Agrippa's command. His associates and certain cities also promised him ships, and began to build them. So Octavian recovered from his depression, and set about constructing an armament even more splendid than the previous one.

93. At the beginning of spring, Antony sailed from Athens to Tarentum with three hundred ships to assist Octa-

384

385

386

387

[62] See above, 25.101.

συμμαχήσων, ὡς ὑπέσχητο, ὁ δ' ἐνήλλακτο τὴν
γνώμην καὶ ἐς τὰς ἔτι γινομένας αὐτῷ ναῦς ἀνεβάλ-
388 λετο. καλούμενος δὲ αὖθις ὡς ἐπὶ ἔτοιμα καὶ ἀρκοῦντα
τὰ Ἀντωνίου, ἑτέρας ἀσχολίας προύφερε καὶ δῆλος
ἦν ἢ αὖθις ἐπιμεμφόμενός τι τῷ Ἀντωνίῳ ἢ τῆς συμ-
389 μαχίας διὰ τὴν εὐπορίαν τὴν οἰκείαν ὑπερορῶν. χαλεπαίνων δ' ὁ Ἀντώνιος ἐπέμενεν ὅμως καὶ αὖθις αὐτὸν ἐκάλει· τῇ τε γὰρ χορηγίᾳ τοῦ ναυτικοῦ κάμνων
καὶ στρατοῦ χρῄζων ἐπὶ Παρθναίους Ἰταλοῦ, Καίσαρι τὰς ναῦς ἐπενόει διαλλάξαι, εἰρημένον μὲν ἐν
ταῖς συνθήκαις ἑκάτερον ξενολογεῖν ἐκ τῆς Ἰταλίας,
δυσχερὲς δ' ἐσόμενον αὐτῷ καὶ βαρὺ Καίσαρος τὴν
390 Ἰταλίαν εἰληφότος.[32] Ὀκταουΐα οὖν ἐχώρει πρὸς Καίσαρα διαιτήσουσα αὐτοῖς. καὶ ὁ μὲν ἐγκαταλελεῖφθαι
τοῖς κινδύνοις ἔλεγε τοῖς ἐν πορθμῷ καταλαβοῦσιν, ἡ
391 δὲ ἐκλελύσθαι τοῦτο διὰ Μαικήνα. ὁ δὲ τὸν Ἀντώνιον
ἔφη καὶ Καλλίαν ἀπελεύθερον ἐς Λέπιδον ἐκπέμψαι,
συντιθέμενον τῷ Λεπίδῳ κατὰ Καίσαρος, ἡ δὲ συνει-
δέναι Καλλίαν περὶ γάμων ἀπεσταλμένον· βουληθῆ-
ναι γὰρ Ἀντώνιον πρὸ τῶν Παρθικῶν ἐκδεδόσθαι
τὴν θυγατέρα τῷ παιδὶ Λεπίδου, καθάπερ ὡμολόγητο.
392 καὶ τάδε μὲν ἡ Ὀκταουΐα, Ἀντώνιος δὲ καὶ τὸν Καλλίαν ἔπεμπεν, ἐς βάσανον τῷ Καίσαρι διδούς· ὁ δὲ

---

[32] εἰληχότος codd.; εἰληφότος Étienne-Duplessis

[63] The manuscripts say that Italy had been "allotted" (*eilecho-tos*) to Octavian. Other sources do not support this, and a small

vian as he had promised, but the latter had changed his mind and was putting things off while waiting for the ships that were still being built for him. When invited a second time, Antony's forces being ready and large enough, Octavian made excuses that he had other business, and it was clear that he was either blaming Antony for something again, or was not interested in his military assistance because of the abundance of his own resources. Antony was annoyed, but nevertheless he stayed where he was, and issued another invitation to Octavian. For he was laboring under the expense of maintaining his fleet and needed Italian soldiers to use against the Parthians, so he intended to exchange ships for men with Octavian, because although it was permitted in the terms of the treaty that either man could recruit in Italy, it was going to be difficult and expensive for him to do so when Octavian had taken possession of Italy.[63] Octavia therefore went to Octavian to act as mediator between them. He said that he had been abandoned while in the middle of the dangers that overtook him in the straits, but she replied that this matter had been resolved through the intervention of Maecenas. Octavian then said that Antony also sent a freedman to Lepidus named Callias, who was in the process of making an agreement with him against Octavian, but she replied that she knew that Callias had been sent to arrange a marriage, because Antony wanted his daughter to be betrothed to Lepidus' son before the Parthian war, as had been agreed. So much for Octavia's role. As for Antony, he sent Callias with permission for Octavian to question him under tor-

388

389

390

391

392

textual change (*eilephotos*) leaves Octavian "taking" Italy—which is what he seems to have done.

οὐκ ἐδέξατο μέν, ἀφίξεσθαι δὲ ἔφη καὶ συμμίξειν
Ἀντωνίῳ μεταξὺ Μεταποντίου καὶ Τάραντος, μέσον
ἔχων ποταμὸν τὸν ἐπώνυμον.

393   94. Κατὰ δαίμονα δ' ἀμφοτέρων προσιόντων τῷ
ῥεύματι, Ἀντώνιος ἐκ τῆς ἀπήνης καταθορὼν ἔς τι
τῶν παρορμούντων σκαφῶν ἐσήλατο μόνος καὶ ἐπέρα
πρὸς τὸν Καίσαρα, πιστεύων ὡς φίλῳ. καὶ ὁ Καῖσαρ
ἰδὼν ἀντεμιμεῖτο, καὶ ξυμβάλλουσιν ἀλλήλοις κατὰ
τὸ ῥεῦμα καὶ διήριζον, ἑκάτερος ἐκβῆναι βουλόμενος
394   ἐς τὴν ὄχθην τοῦ ἑτέρου. ἐνίκα δὲ ὁ Καῖσαρ, ὡς καὶ
πρὸς τὴν Ὀκταουίαν ἥξων ἐς Τάραντα, ἐπί τε τῆς
ἀπήνης Ἀντωνίου συνήδρευεν αὐτῷ καὶ ἐν Τάραντι ἐς
τὴν καταγωγὴν αὐτοῦ παρῆλθέ τε ἀφύλακτος καὶ τὴν
νύκτα ὁμοίως ἀνεπαύετο χωρὶς δορυφόρων παρ' αὐτῷ.
395   τὰ δ' ὅμοια καὶ παρ' Ἀντωνίου τῆς ἐπιούσης ἐπεδεί-
κνυτο. οὕτως αὐτοῖς ἦν συνεχὴς ἡ μεταβολή, πρός τε
τὰς ὑπονοίας διὰ φιλαρχίαν καὶ ἐς τὰς πίστεις ὑπὸ
χρείας.

396   95. Τὸν μὲν οὖν ἐπίπλουν τὸν ἐπὶ Πομπήιον ὁ Καῖσαρ ἐς νέωτα ἀνεβάλλετο· ὁ δ' Ἀντώνιος ἐπιμένειν
διὰ Παρθυαίους οὐ δυνάμενος, ἀντέδοσαν ὅμως ἀλλήλοις, Καίσαρι μὲν ὁ Ἀντώνιος ναῦς ἑκατὸν εἴκοσι,
ἃς αὐτίκα πέμψας εἰς Τάραντα παρέδωκεν, Ἀντωνίῳ
δὲ ὁ Καῖσαρ δισμυρίους Ἰταλοὺς ὁπλίτας, οὓς ἐπι-
397   πέμψειν ὑπισχνεῖτο· ἐδωρήσατο δὲ καὶ Ὀκταουία τὸν
ἀδελφόν, αἰτήσασα παρ' Ἀντωνίου, δέκα φασήλοις
τριηριτικοῖς, ἐπιμίκτοις ἔκ τε φορτίδων νεῶν καὶ μα-

ture. But Octavian refused, and said that he would come and meet with Antony between Metapontum and Tarentum, with the river from which Tarentum gets its name between them.[64]

94. As fate would have it, they both approached the river at the same time. Antony bounded down from his carriage, jumped unaccompanied onto one of the boats moored alongside and began to cross over to Octavian, trusting him as a friend. When Octavian saw this he copied what Antony was doing, and they met on the water and argued, as they both wanted to disembark on each other's bank. Octavian won the argument, as he said he that in going to Tarentum he was also going to Octavia. He sat beside Antony in the latter's carriage and went to Antony's quarters with no guard present and likewise slept the night there without bodyguards beside him. Next day there was a similar display of trust from Antony. And so their behavior kept changing the whole time, moving from suspicion caused by love of power to trust brought about by necessity.

95. Octavian, accordingly, intended to postpone his expedition against Pompeius until the following year. Although Antony could not stay on account of the Parthians, nevertheless they made a mutual exchange, Antony giving Octavian one hundred and twenty ships which he immediately sent and handed over at Tarentum, Octavian giving Antonius twenty thousand Italian legionaries, whom he promised to send on. Octavia also presented her brother with a gift, which she had begged from Antony, of ten trireme-like skiffs, which were a composite of warship and

393

394

395

396

397

---

[64] The river Taras.

κρῶν, καὶ τὴν Ὀκταουίαν ὁ Καῖσαρ χιλίοις λογάσι
398 σωματοφύλαξιν, οὓς ἐπιλέξαιτο Ἀντώνιος. ἐπεὶ δὲ ὁ
χρόνος αὐτοῖς ἔληγε τῆς ἀρχῆς, ἣ τοῖς τρισὶν ἐψή-
φιστο ἀνδράσιν, ἑτέραν ἑαυτοῖς ὥριζον πενταετίαν,
399 οὐδὲν ἔτι τοῦ δήμου δεηθέντες. οὕτω μὲν οὖν διεκρίθησαν ἀπ᾽ ἀλλήλων, καὶ ὁ Ἀντώνιος εὐθὺς ἐς τὴν Συρίαν
ἠπείγετο, τὴν Ὀκταουίαν παρὰ τῷ ἀδελφῷ καταλιπὼν
μετὰ θυγατρὸς ἤδη γενομένης αὐτοῖς.

400   96. Μηνόδωρος δέ, εἴτε τις ὢν φύσει παλιμπρο-
δότης εἴτε δείσας τήν ποτε ἀπειλὴν Ἀντωνίου, ἀπάξειν αὐτὸν εἰπόντος ὡς ἀνδράποδον πολεμοποιόν, εἴτε
ἐλασσόνων ἀξιοῦσθαι νομίζων παρ᾽ ἃ προσεδόκησεν,
εἴτε τῶν ἄλλων αὐτὸν ἐξελευθέρων τοῦ Πομπηίου
συνεχῶς ὀνειδιζόντων ἐς ἀπιστίαν δεσπότου καὶ
παρακαλούντων ἐπανελθεῖν Μενεκράτους ἀποθανόν-
τος, πίστιν αἰτήσας καὶ λαβὼν ηὐτομόλησε πρὸς
Πομπήιον σὺν ἑπτὰ ναυσί, Καλουίσιον τὸν ναύαρχον
τοῦ Καίσαρος διαλαθών. ἐφ᾽ ᾧ τὸν Καλουίσιον ὁ Καῖσαρ ἀπέλυσε τῆς ναυαρχίας καὶ ἀντικατέστησεν
401 Ἀγρίππαν. ἐπεὶ δ᾽ ἕτοιμος ἦν ὁ στόλος, ἐκάθαιρεν
αὐτὸν ὁ Καῖσαρ ὧδε. οἱ μὲν βωμοὶ ψαύουσι τῆς
θαλάσσης, καὶ ἡ πληθὺς αὐτοὺς περιέστηκε κατὰ
ναῦν μετὰ σιωπῆς βαθυτάτης· οἱ δὲ ἱερουργοὶ θύουσι
μὲν ἑστῶτες ἐπὶ τῇ θαλάσσῃ καὶ τρὶς ἐπὶ σκαφῶν
περιφέρουσιν ἀνὰ τὸν στόλον τὰ καθάρσια, συμπερι-

merchantman, and Octavian gave her in return one thousand elite troops as a bodyguard, to be selected by Antony. Since the term of the power voted to them as triumvirs was running out, they designated another five-year period for themselves, without asking anything further of the people.[65] And so it was that they went their separate ways, Antony immediately hurrying off to Syria, leaving Octavia, along with the daughter already born to them, with her brother.

96. As for Menodorus, either because repeated betrayal was part of his nature, or because he was afraid of the threat Antony issued on one occasion when he said he would bring him to justice as a warmongering slave, or because he was less valued than he expected, or because Pompeius' other freedmen were constantly rebuking him for disloyalty to his master and urging him to come back, now that Menecrates was dead, having asked for and been granted a personal assurance, he deserted to Pompeius with seven ships, without being noticed by Octavian's admiral, Calvisius. As a result, Octavian relieved the latter of his naval command and appointed Agrippa in his place. When the fleet was ready, Octavian purified it in the following manner. The altars are adjacent to the water, and the crews take up station round about in their ships, in the deepest silence. The priests who perform the ceremony offer sacrifice while standing at the water's edge, and carry the expiatory offerings in skiffs three times round the fleet,

---

[65] The first period of triumviral power had run out almost certainly on December 31, 38. This renewal, now some time in the middle of 37, must have been backdated to the beginning of the year, and so would run until December 31, 32.

πλεόντων αὐτοῖς τῶν στρατηγῶν καὶ ἐπαρωμένων ἐς τάδε τὰ καθάρσια, ἀντὶ τοῦ στόλου, τὰ ἀπαίσια τρα-

402 πῆναι. νείμαντες δὲ αὐτά, μέρος ἐς τὴν θάλασσαν ἀπορρίπτουσι καὶ μέρος ἐς τοὺς βωμοὺς ἐπιθέντες ἅπτουσι, καὶ ὁ λεὼς ἐπευφημεῖ. οὕτω μὲν Ῥωμαῖοι τὰ ναυτικὰ καθαίρουσιν.

403   97. Ἔμελλε δ᾽ ὁ μὲν Καῖσαρ ἐκ Δικαιαρχείας, ὁ δὲ Λέπιδος ἐκ Λιβύης, Ταῦρος δ᾽ ἐκ Τάραντος ἐπιπλευ- σεῖσθαι τῇ Σικελίᾳ, ὡς ἂν αὐτὴν ἐξ ἠοῦς ὁμοῦ καὶ

404 δύσεως καὶ μεσημβρίας περιλάβοιεν. καὶ τῆς ἀναγω- γῆς τοῦ Καίσαρος ἡ ἡμέρα προείρητο πᾶσι, καὶ ἦν δεκάτη τροπῶν θερινῶν, ἥν τινα Ῥωμαῖοι νουμηνίαν ἔχουσι τοῦ μηνός, ὃν ἐπὶ τιμῇ τοῦ Καίσαρος τοῦ προ- τέρου Ἰούλιον ἀντὶ Κυιντιλίου καλοῦσι. τήνδε μὲν ὁ Καῖσαρ ὥρισε τὴν ἡμέραν, αἰσιούμενος ἴσως διὰ τὸν

405 πατέρα νικηφόρον ἀεὶ γενόμενον· ὁ δὲ Πομπήιος Λε- πίδῳ μὲν ἀντέταττε Πλένιον ἐν Λιλυβαίῳ, τέλος ὁπλι- τῶν ἔχοντα καὶ ἄλλο πλῆθος ἐσκευασμένον κούφως, τὴν δὲ πρὸς ἕω καὶ δύσιν ἀκτὴν τῆς Σικελίας πᾶσαν ἐφρούρει, καὶ νήσους μάλιστα Λιπάραν τε καὶ Κοσ- σύραν, ἵνα μήτε Κοσσύρα Λεπίδῳ μήτε Λιπάρα Καί- σαρι ἐνορμίσματα ἢ ναύσταθμα γένοιτο εὔκαιρα ἐπὶ τῇ Σικελίᾳ. τὸ δ᾽ ἄριστον τοῦ ναυτικοῦ ἐν Μεσσήνῃ συνεῖχεν ἐπεδρεῦον ὅπῃ δεήσειεν.

---

[66] According to Velleius Paterculus (2.127), Titus Statilius Taurus was Augustus' second most important general after

the generals accompanying them as they sail around, and praying that the bad omens be turned against these victims, not against the fleet. Then, dividing the victims, they 402 throw part of them into the sea, and place part on the altars and burn them, while the people shout their assent. This is how the Romans purify their naval forces.

97. The intention was that Octavian would sail against 403 Sicily from Dicaearchia, Lepidus from Africa and Taurus from Tarentum with the purpose of surrounding it from east, west and south simultaneously.[66] The day Octavian 404 was to set sail had been communicated beforehand to everyone: it was the tenth day after the summer solstice, which the Romans keep as the kalends of the month they call July instead of Quintilis, in honor of the first Caesar. Octavian fixed on this day, perhaps because he considered it of good omen in view of the fact that his father was always victorious. Pompeius stationed Plinius at Lilybaeum 405 with one legion of infantry and a considerable number of light-armed troops, to oppose Lepidus.[67] He garrisoned the whole east and west coast of Sicily, and in particular the islands of Lipara and Cossyra, to prevent them from becoming convenient anchorages and harbors for an attack on Sicily, Cossyra for Lepidus and Lipara for Octavian. The best part of his naval force he kept together at Messena to watch for situations where it might be needed.

Agrippa. He was suffect consul in 37 and held a second consulship, with Augustus himself as his colleague, in 26. When Augustus went west in 16, he left Statilius in charge of Rome as *Praefectus Urbi*.

[67] Lucius Plinius Rufus is known from an inscription to have been praetor designate in 36.

406   98. Οὕτω μὲν ἑκάτεροι παρασκευῆς εἶχον, γενομένης δὲ τῆς νουμηνίας ἀνήγοντο πάντες ἅμα ἠοῖ,
Λέπιδος μὲν ἐκ Λιβύης χιλίαις ὁλκάσι καὶ μακραῖς
ἑβδομήκοντα καὶ τέλεσι στρατοῦ δυώδεκα καὶ ἱππεῦσι Νομάσι πεντακισχιλίοις καὶ ἑτέρᾳ παρασκευῇ
πολλῇ, Ταῦρος δ᾽ ἐκ Τάραντος ταῖς Ἀντωνίου ναυσὶν
ἐξ ἑκατὸν καὶ τριάκοντα δύο μόναις καὶ ἑκατόν, ἐπεὶ
τῶν λοιπῶν οἱ ἐρέται χειμῶνος ἐτεθνήκεσαν, ὁ δὲ
Καῖσαρ ἐκ Δικαιαρχείας, θύων ἅμα καὶ σπένδων ἀπὸ
τῆς ναυαρχίδος νεὼς ἐς τὸ πέλαγος ἀνέμοις εὐδίοις
καὶ Ἀσφαλείῳ Ποσειδῶνι καὶ ἀκύμονι θαλάσσῃ,
συλλήπτορας αὑτῷ κατὰ ἐχθρῶν πατρῴων γενέσθαι.
407   πρόπλοι δ᾽ αὐτῷ τινες τοὺς μυχοὺς τῆς θαλάσσης
διηρεύνων, καὶ Ἄππιος μετὰ πλήθους νεῶν ὀπισθοφυ-
408   λακῶν εἵπετο. τρίτῃ δὲ τῆς ἀναγωγῆς ἡμέρᾳ νότος
ἐμπεσὼν Λεπίδου μὲν ὁλκάδας ἀνέτρεψε πολλάς, ὡρμίσθη δὲ ὅμως ἐς Σικελίαν καί, Πλένιον ἐν Λιλυβαίῳ
πολιορκῶν, τινὰς τῶν πόλεων ὑπήγετο καὶ ἑτέρας
ἐβιάζετο· Ταῦρος δὲ ἀρχομένου τοῦ πνεύματος ἐς
409   Τάραντα ἐπαλινδρόμει. Ἀππίου δ᾽ ἄρτι τὸ Ἀθηναῖον
ἄκρον περιπλέοντος αἱ μὲν συνετρίβοντο τῶν νεῶν
ἀμφὶ ταῖς πέτραις, αἱ δ᾽ ἐς τέλματα ἐξώκελλον ὑπὸ
410   ῥύμης, αἱ δὲ καὶ διερρίφησαν οὐκ ἀσινεῖς. ὁ δὲ Καῖσαρ ἀρχομένου μὲν τοῦ χειμῶνος ἐς τὸν Ἐλεάτην
κόλπον ἐρυμνὸν ὄντα συμπεφεύγει, χωρὶς ἐξήρους
μιᾶς, ἣ περὶ τῇ ἄκρᾳ διελύθη· λιβὸς δὲ τὸν νότον
μεταλαβόντος ὁ κόλπος ἐκυκᾶτο, ἐς τὴν ἑσπέραν
ἀνεῳγμένος, καὶ οὔτε ἐκπλεῦσαι δυνατὸν ἦν ἔτι πρὸς

98. Such were the preparations on each side. When the 406
day of the kalends arrived, they all set sail at dawn, Lepidus from Africa with one thousand transports, seventy
warships, twelve legions of infantry, five thousand Numidian cavalry and a large additional armament; Taurus from
Tarentum with only one hundred and two of Antony's one
hundred and thirty ships because the rowers of the other
ones had died during the winter; and Octavian from Dicaearchia, offering sacrifices and pouring libations from
his flagship into the sea to Gentle Winds, to Neptune the
Savior, and to Waveless Sea, in order to secure their assistance for himself against his father's enemies. Some 407
ships sailed ahead inspecting the inlets of the sea for him,
and Appius followed with numerous ships to guard the
rear. On the third day after their departure a south wind 408
hit them and capsized many of Lepidus' transports. Nevertheless, he reached safe anchorage in Sicily, and while
besieging Plinius in Lilybaeum, won over some towns by
persuasion and others by force. When the wind began
to blow, Taurus ran back to Tarentum. Appius was just 409
rounding the promontory of Minerva, and some of his
ships were shattered against the rocks, others ran aground
in the shoals, driven by the force of the wind, and others
were dispersed, not without being damaged. At the begin- 410
ning of the storm, Octavian took refuge in the bay of Elea,
which was sheltered, apart from one six-banked ship,
which was wrecked on the promontory. When the south
wind was followed by a southwester, the bay, being open
to the west, was churned up, and it was no longer possible
to sail out of it into a headwind blowing straight into the

ἐναντίον τοῦ κόλπου τὸ πνεῦμα, οὔτε κῶπαι κατεῖχον
οὔτε ἄγκυραι, ἀλλ᾽ ἐς ἀλλήλας ἢ ἐς τὰς πέτρας ἐνη-
ράσσοντο αἱ νῆες. καὶ νυκτὸς ἦν ἔτι τὸ δεινὸν ἀτο-
πώτερον.

411   99. Ἐνδόντος δέ ποτε τοῦ κακοῦ τὰ νεκρὰ ἔθαπτεν
ὁ Καῖσαρ, καὶ τοὺς τραυματίας ἐθεράπευε, καὶ τοὺς
ἐκνέοντας ἐνέδυε, καὶ ὥπλιζεν ἑτέροις ὅπλοις, καὶ τὸν
στόλον ἅπαντα ἐκ τῶν ἐνόντων ἀνελάμβανε. διεφθάρατο δ᾽ αὐτῷ νῆες βαρεῖαι μὲν ἕξ, κουφότεραι δὲ ἐξ
412   καὶ εἴκοσι, λιβυρνίδες δὲ ἔτι πλείους. καὶ ἐς τάδε δι-
ορθούμενα τριάκοντα ἡμέρας ἀναλώσειν ἔμελλεν, ἤδη
τοῦ θέρους προκόπτοντος· ὅθεν ἦν ἄριστον αὐτῷ τὸν
413   πόλεμον ἐς τὸ μέλλον θέρος ἀναβαλέσθαι. ἐνοχλουμέ-
νου δὲ τοῦ δήμου ταῖς ἀπορίαις, ἐπεσκεύαζε τὰς ναῦς
ἐς τὴν γῆν ἀνέλκων μετὰ ἐπείξεως καὶ τὰ πληρώματα
τῶν διεφθαρμένων ἐς τὰς παρὰ Ταύρῳ ναῦς κενὰς
414   ἐξέπεμπεν. ὡς δὲ ἐπὶ συμφορᾷ μείζονι, Μαικήναν μὲν
ἐς Ῥώμην ἐξέπεμπε διὰ τοὺς ἐπτοημένους ἔτι πρὸς
τὴν μνήμην Πομπηίου Μάγνου· οὐ γὰρ αὐτοὺς ἐξέλι-
πεν ἡ δόξα τοῦ ἀνδρὸς τούτου· τοὺς δὲ κληρούχους
αὐτὸς ἀνὰ τὴν Ἰταλίαν ἐπέτρεχε καὶ ἐκ τοῦ φόβου
415   τῶν γεγονότων ἀνελάμβανε. διέδραμε δὲ καὶ ἐς Τάραντα καὶ τὸ ναυτικὸν εἶδε τὸ ὑπὸ Ταύρῳ, καὶ ἐς Ἱππώνειον ἦλθε καὶ τὰ πεζὰ παρηγόρησε καὶ τὴν τῶν
νεῶν ἐπισκευὴν ἐπέσπερχεν. καὶ πλησίον ἦν ἤδη καὶ
ὁ δεύτερος ἐς Σικελίαν ἐπίπλους.

416   100. Ὁ δὲ Πομπήιος οὐδ᾽ ἐπὶ τοιᾷδε εὐκαιρίᾳ
τοσοῖσδε ναυαγίοις ἐπιχειρεῖν ἠξίου, ἀλλ᾽ ἔθυε μόνον

bay, nor could oars or anchors hold the ships in position with the wind still ahead. They crashed into each other or against the rocks, and at night the horror was even more abnormal.

99. Once the storm subsided, Octavian buried the dead, tended to the wounded, clothed those who had swum to land and equipped them with new weapons, and repaired the whole fleet with his existing resources. Six of his heavy ships, twenty-six lighter ones, and even more Liburnians had been destroyed. To put the situation right was going to take thirty days, and with the end of summer now approaching, it would have been best for him to postpone the war until the following summer. But as the people were suffering from the shortages, he hauled his ships onto land and began repairing them with urgency, and sent the crews of the ships that had been destroyed to the ones that had no crews with Taurus. This being a major disaster, he sent Maecenas to Rome because of the people who were still very excited at the memory of Pompey the Great: for this man's fame had not lost its effect over them. Octavian himself visited the colonists throughout Italy and calmed their fears over what had happened. He also hurried over to Tarentum and inspected the naval force under Taurus, and then proceeded to Hipponium, where he addressed the infantry and hastened the repair of the fleet. The second expedition against Sicily was now at hand.

100. As for Pompeius, he did not think it suitable to take the offensive, even when presented with such a good

θαλάσσῃ καὶ Ποσειδῶνι καὶ υἱὸς αὐτῶν ὑφίστατο κα-
λεῖσθαι, πειθόμενος οὐκ ἄνευ θεοῦ δὶς οὕτω θέρους
417 πταῖσαι τοὺς πολεμίους. φασὶ δ᾽ αὐτόν, ὑπὸ τῶνδε
χαννούμενον, καὶ τὴν συνήθη τοῖς αὐτοκράτορσι
χλαμύδα ἐκ φοινικῆς ἐς κυανῆν μεταλλάξαι, εἰ-
418 σποιούμενον ἄρα ἑαυτὸν τῷ Ποσειδῶνι. ἐλπίσας δ᾽
ἀναζεύξειν τὸν Καίσαρα, ὡς ἐπύθετο ναυπηγούμενόν
τε καὶ ἐπιπλευσούμενον αὖθις αὐτοῦ θέρους, ἐξεπλήσ-
σετο μὲν ὡς ἀμάχῳ γνώμῃ καὶ παρασκευῇ πολεμῶν,
Μηνόδωρον δὲ μετὰ νεῶν ἑπτὰ ὧν ἤγαγεν ἔπεμπε
κατασκεψόμενον τὰ νεώλκια τοῦ Καίσαρος καὶ δρά-
419 σοντα, ὅ τι καὶ δύναιτο. ὁ δὲ καὶ τέως ἀχθόμενος οὐκ
ἀποδοθείσης αὐτῷ τῆς ναυαρχίας καὶ τότε αἰσθόμενος, ὅτι σὺν ὑποψίᾳ μόνων ἠξίωτο ὧν ἤγαγε νεῶν,
ἐπεβούλευεν αὖθις αὐτομολίαν.

420   101. Ἐπινοῶν δὲ πρότερον, ὡς ἐς πάντα οἱ συνοῖ-
σον, ἀνδραγαθίσασθαι, διέδωκε τοῖς συμπλέουσιν,
ὅσον εἶχε χρυσίον, καὶ διέπλευσεν εἰρεσίᾳ τρισὶν
ἡμέραις πεντακοσίους ἐπὶ χιλίοις σταδίους καὶ τοῖς
προφύλαξι τῶν ναυπηγουμένων Καίσαρι νεῶν οἷα
σκηπτὸς ἀφανῶς ἐμπίπτων καὶ ἐς ἀφανὲς ἀναχωρῶν
ᾕρει κατὰ δύο καὶ τρεῖς ναῦς τῶν φυλακίδων καὶ τὰς
ὁλκάδας, αἳ τὸν σῖτον ἔφερον, ὁρμούσας ἢ παραπλε-
ούσας κατέδυεν ἢ ἀνεδεῖτο ἢ ἐνεπίμπρη. θορύβου δὲ
πάντα μεστὰ διὰ Μηνόδωρον ἦν, Καίσαρος ἀπόντος

opportunity provided by so many shipwrecks. He merely offered sacrifice to Sea and to Neptune, and decided to be called their son, persuading himself that it was not without divine intervention that his enemies had failed twice during the summer. They say that these events made him so   417 vain that he exchanged the purple cloak customarily worn by Roman commanders for a dark blue one, to signify, of course, that he was the adopted son of Neptune. Having   418 expected Octavian to withdraw, when he heard that he was having ships built and was going to launch a new expedition that very summer, he became alarmed at finding himself at war with such irresistible spirit and military resources, and sent Menodorus along with the seven ships he had brought with him to reconnoiter Octavian's dockyards and do whatever damage he could. Menodorus,   419 however, who had been annoyed beforehand that he had not been compensated with command of the fleet, was now aware that he was under suspicion, being regarded as suitable to command only the ships he had brought with him. So he planned a new desertion.

101. Intending first to perform acts of outstanding in-   420 dividual courage, as he thought this would be to his advantage in all circumstances, he distributed all the money he had to the men on board with him, and traveled one thousand five hundred stades in three days of rowing. By falling invisibly with the speed of a thunderbolt on the squadron guarding the ships Octavian was constructing and retiring into invisibility, he captured in twos and threes the ships on guard, and sank or towed away or burned the merchantmen that were carrying the grain as they rode at anchor or sailed along the coast. With Octavian and Agrippa still away—Agrippa had gone off to collect tim-

ἔτι καὶ Ἀγρίππα· καὶ γὰρ οὗτος ἐπὶ ὕλην ἐπεπόρευτο.

421 γαυρούμενος δὲ ὁ Μηνόδωρος ἐξώκειλέ ποτε τὴν ναῦν ἑκὼν ἐς ἕρμα γῆς ἁπαλὸν σὺν καταφρονήσει καὶ ὑπεκρίνετο αὐτὴν ὑπὸ τοῦ πηλοῦ κατέχεσθαι, μέχρι, τῶν πολεμίων ἐκ τῶν ὁρῶν καταθορόντων ὡς ἐπὶ Μηνοδώρου θήραν ἕτοιμον, ἀνακρουσάμενος ᾤχετο σὺν γέλωτι καὶ τὸν στρατὸν τοῦ Καίσαρος ἀνία κατεῖχε σὺν θαύματι.

422 102. Ὡς δὲ ἱκανῶς ἐπεδέδεικτο, οἷος ἐχθρός τε καὶ φίλος εἴη, Ῥέβιλον μὲν ἑλών, ἄνδρα ἀπὸ βουλῆς, μεθῆκε, μνώμενος ἤδη τὸ μέλλον. Μινδίῳ δὲ Μαρκέλλῳ, τῶν ἑταίρων τινὶ τῶν Καίσαρος, φίλος ἐν τῇ προτέρᾳ γεγονὼς αὐτομολίᾳ, τοῖς μὲν ἀμφ᾽ αὐτὸν ἔφη τὸν Μίνδιον βουλεύειν αὐτομολίαν καὶ προδοσίαν, τοῖς δὲ πολεμίοις προσπελάσας ἠξίου Μίνδιον αὑτῷ συνελ-

423 θεῖν ἔς τινα νησῖδα ἐπὶ λόγοις συνοίσουσι. καὶ συνελθόντι ἔλεγεν, οὐδενὸς ἀκούοντος ἑτέρου, φυγεῖν μὲν ἐς Πομπήιον ὑβριζόμενος ὑπὸ τοῦ τότε ναυάρχου Καλουισίου, τὴν δὲ ναυαρχίαν Ἀγρίππου μεταλαβόντος ἐπανελεύσεσθαι πρὸς Καίσαρα οὐδὲν ἀδικοῦντα, εἰ πίστιν αὐτῷ κομίσειεν ὁ Μίνδιος παρὰ Μεσάλα τοῦ

424 τὴν ἀποδημίαν Ἀγρίππα διοικοῦντος. ἔφη δ᾽ ἐπανελθὼν μὲν ἰάσεσθαι λαμπροῖς τὸ ἁμάρτημα ἔργοις, μέ-

---

68 Perhaps a son of the consul of 45, Gaius Caninius Rebilus, and probably the same Rebilus that Appian mentions (*BCiv.* 4.48.209) as one of the proscribed, who fled to Sicily.

ber—there was complete confusion because of Menodorus. On one occasion, in a spirit of bravado, Menodorus   421
intentionally and contemptuously ran his ship aground on
a sandbank, and pretended it was stuck in the mud, until
his enemies dashed down from the mountains expecting
him to be easy prey. But Menodorus backed his ship
off and disappeared laughing, while distress mixed with
amazement affected Octavian's men.

102. When he had given sufficient evidence of what   422
sort of enemy or friend he would be, now with a mind to
the future, he released a senator he had taken prisoner,
named Rebilus.[68] During his previous period of desertion
Menodorus had associated with Mindius Marcellus, one
of the companions of Octavian, and he now told his own
entourage that Mindius was planning to betray and desert
from his side.[69] Menodorus then approached the enemy
lines and asked Mindius to meet him on a small island with
a view to fruitful discussions. When Mindius arrived at
the meeting, and there was nobody else within earshot,
Menodorus told him that he had fled to Pompeius because   423
he had been insulted by Calvisius, the admiral at the time,
but now that Agrippa had succeeded him in command of
the fleet, he would come back to Octavian, who was in no
way treating him badly, if Mindius would bring him a guarantee of immunity from Messalla, who was directing affairs in Agrippa's absence.[70] He said that on his return he   424
would make amends for his mistake by brilliant exploits,

[69] An inscription records that Marcus Mindius Marcellus was
appointed Prefect of the Fleet by Octavian.

[70] Appian summarizes the career of Marcus Valerius Messalla
Corvinus (consul 31) at *BCiv.* 4.38.159–62.

χρι δὲ τῶν πίστεων λυμανεῖσθαί τινα τῶν Καίσαρος
425 ὁμοίως ἐς τὸ ἀνύποπτον. καὶ ὁ μὲν αὖθις ἐλυμαίνετο,
Μεσσάλας δ' ἐνεδοίασε μὲν ὡς ἐπὶ αἰσχρῷ, ἐνέδωκε
δ' ὅμως, εἴτε πολέμου ταῦτ' εἶναι νομίζων ἀνάγκας
εἴτε καὶ τῆς Καίσαρος γνώμης τι προμαθὼν ἢ τεκμη-
426 ράμενος. καὶ Μηνόδωρος μὲν αὖθις ηὐτομόλει καὶ τὸν
Καίσαρα ἐλθόντα προσπίπτων ἠξίου συγγνῶναί μὴ
λέγοντι τὰς αἰτίας τῆς φυγῆς· ὁ δὲ ἐς μὲν σωτηρίαν
αὐτῷ συνεγίνωσκε διὰ τὰς σπονδὰς καὶ ἀφανῶς ἐφυ-
λάσσετο, τοὺς δὲ τριηράρχους αὐτοῦ μεθίει χωροῦν-
τας ὅποι θέλοιεν.

427   103. Ἑτοίμου δὲ τοῦ στόλου γενομένου, αὖθις ὁ
Καίσαρ ἀνήγετο καὶ ἐς Ἱππώνειον παραπλεύσας δύο
μὲν τέλη πεζῶν Μεσσάλαν ἔχοντα περᾶν ἐκέλευσεν
ἐς Σικελίαν ἐπὶ τὸ Λεπίδου στρατόπεδον καὶ σταθ-
μεύειν ἐς τὸν κόλπον διελθόντα τὸν εὐθὺ Ταυρομενίου,
τρία δ' ἔπεμπεν ἐπὶ Στυλίδα καὶ πορθμὸν ἄκρον ἐφε-
428 δρεύειν τοῖς ἐσομένοις· Ταῦρον δ' ἐς τὸ Σκυλάκιον
ὄρος, ὃ πέραν ἐστὶ Ταυρομενίου, περιπλεῖν ἐκ Τάραντος ἐκέλευε. καὶ ὁ μὲν περιέπλει διεσκευασμένος ἐς
μάχην ὁμοῦ καὶ εἰρεσίαν· καὶ τὰ πεζὰ αὐτῷ παρω-
μάρτει, προερευνώντων τήν τε γῆν ἱππέων καὶ λιβυρ-
νίδων τὴν θάλασσαν. καὶ ὁ Καίσαρ ὧδε ἔχοντι ἐξ
Ἱππωνείου ἐπιδραμὼν ἐπιφαίνεται κατὰ τὸ Σκυλάκιον,
καὶ τὴν εὐταξίαν ἀποδεξάμενος ἐπανῆλθεν ἐς τὸ Ἱπ-
429 πώνειον. ὁ δὲ Πομπήιος, ὥς μοι προείρηται, τάς τε ἐς
τὴν νῆσον ἀποβάσεις ἐφύλασσεν ἁπάσας καὶ τὰς

but that until the proof of immunity arrived he would inflict damage on parts of Octavian's forces as before in order to avoid suspicion. While Menodorus resumed his marauding, Messalla hesitated at such shameful behavior, but he gave in all the same, either because he considered such things necessary in war, or because he had already found out, or guessed, something of Octavian's intentions. So Menodorus again deserted, and, when Octavian arrived, threw himself at his feet and begged forgiveness, without explaining the reasons for his flight. As far as his personal safety was concerned, Octavian forgave him because of the agreement reached, but had him secretly watched; and he released his ship captains, allowing them to go wherever they wanted.

103. When the fleet was ready Octavian again put to sea and sailed along the coast to Hipponium. He ordered Messalla to cross over to Sicily with two legions of infantry to join Lepidus' army, and once he had crossed the straits, to establish his base on the bay opposite Tauromenium. He also sent three legions to Stylis and the head of the channel to keep an eye on developments. He ordered Taurus to sail around from Tarentum to Mount Scylacium, which lies opposite Tauromenium. Taurus did so, having prepared himself for fighting as well as for rowing. His infantry kept pace with him, while cavalry reconnoitered ahead by land and Liburnians by sea. With Taurus thus occupied, Octavian rode over to him from Hipponium and made an appearance at Mount Scylacium, and, having approved the good order of his forces, returned to Hipponium. Pompeius, as I have already said, was guarding all the landing places on the island and keeping his fleet

425

426

427

428

429

ναῦς ἐν Μεσσήνῃ συνεῖχεν ὡς βοηθήσων, ὅποι δεήσειεν.

430   104. Καὶ οἱ μὲν ἐν τούτῳ παρασκευῆς ἦσαν, Λεπίδῳ
δὲ αὖθις ἐκ Λιβύης ἦγον αἱ ὁλκάδες τὰ λοιπὰ τοῦ
στρατοῦ τέλη τέσσαρα. καὶ αὐταῖς ὑπήντα πελάγιος
ἐκ Πομπηίου Παπίας καὶ διέφθειρεν ὡς φιλίως[33] δε-
431   χομένας· ᾤοντο γὰρ σφίσι τὰς Λεπίδου συναντᾶν. αἱ
δὲ βραδέως τε ὑπὸ τοῦ Λεπίδου καθείλκοντο, καὶ
ὕστερον αὐτὰς προσιούσας αἱ ὁλκάδες ὡς καὶ τάσδε
ἄλλας πολεμίας ἐξέκλιναν, ἕως αἱ μὲν ἐκαύθησαν, αἱ
δ᾽ ἐλήφθησαν, αἱ δ᾽ ἀνετράπησαν, αἱ δ᾽ ἐς Λιβύην
432   ἀνέπλευσαν. τοῦ δὲ στρατοῦ δύο μὲν τέλη διώλετο ἐν
τῇ θαλάσσῃ, καί, εἴ τινες αὐτῶν ἐξενήχοντο, καὶ
τούσδε Τισιηνὸς ὁ τοῦ Πομπηίου στρατηγὸς ἐκνέοντας ἐπὶ τὴν γῆν διέφθειρεν· οἱ δὲ λοιποὶ πρὸς Λέπιδον
κατήχθησαν, οἱ μὲν αὐτίκα, οἱ δ᾽ ὕστερον. καὶ Παπίας ἀπέπλευσε πρὸς Πομπήιον.

433   105. Ὁ δὲ Καῖσαρ ἐς μὲν Στρογγύλην, ἣ τῶν πέντε
νήσων ἐστὶ τῶν Αἰόλου, παντὶ τῷ στόλῳ διέπλευσεν
ἐξ Ἱππωνείου, προερευνωμένης αὐτῷ τῆς θαλάσσης·
στρατὸν δὲ ἐπὶ μετώπου τῆς Σικελίας πλέονα ἰδὼν ἔν
τε Πελωριάδι καὶ Μύλαις καὶ Τυνδαρίδι, εἴκασεν αὐτὸν παρεῖναι Πομπήιον καὶ τὰ μὲν ἐνθάδε Ἀγρίππᾳ
434   διαστρατηγεῖν ἐπέτρεψεν. αὐτὸς δὲ εἰς τὸ Ἱππώνειον
αὖθις ἀπέπλει καὶ ἐς τὸ Ταύρου στρατόπεδον ἐξ Ἱππωνείου σὺν τρισὶ τέλεσι μετὰ Μεσσάλα διετρόχα-

---

[33] φιλίως Étienne-Duplessis; φιλίους LBJ; φιλίας P

at Messena, in order to send help wherever it might be needed.

104. While they were making these preparations, trans- 430 port ships were coming back from Africa bringing Lepidus the remaining four legions of his army. Papias went to confront them out at sea, sent by Pompeius, and destroyed them, although they received him in friendly fashion.[71] For they thought it was Lepidus' ships meeting them. 431 These had been launched by Lepidus in leisurely fashion, and when they approached too late, the African transports steered clear of them in the belief that they too were other enemy ships. So some of them were burned, some cap- tured, some capsized, and some sailed back to Africa. Two 432 legions of soldiers died in the sea, and, if there were any who swam away to safety, these too were killed by Pom- peius' general, Tisienus, as they made their way out of the water onto land. The remainder landed at Lepidus' camp, some immediately, others later. Papias sailed back to Pom- peius.

105. Octavian sailed across from Hipponium with his 433 whole fleet to Strongyle,[72] one of the five Aeolian islands, having made a reconnaissance of the sea beforehand. See- ing a large army in front of him on the Sicilian shore both at Pelorus and at Mylae and Tyndaris, he thought it likely that Pompeius himself was there. So he entrusted the command here to Agrippa. He himself sailed back to Hip- 434 ponium again, and from there hurried to Taurus' camp with three legions in the company of Messalla, with the

[71] Papias is generally taken to be the same person as Demo- chares in paragraphs 105–6 below. Dio 49.8 only mentions De- mochares. [72] Present-day Stromboli.

ζεν, ὡς Ταυρομένιον αἱρήσων ἀπόντος ἔτι τοῦ Πομπηίου καὶ τὰς ἐμβολὰς αὐτῷ διχόθεν παρέξων.

435 Ἀγρίππας μὲν οὖν ἀπὸ Στρογγύλης εἰς Ἱερὰν διέπλει
καὶ τῶν Πομπηίου φρουρῶν αὐτὸν οὐχ ὑποστάντων
εἷλε τὴν Ἱερὰν καὶ τῆς ἐπιούσης ἔμελλεν ἐπιχειρήσειν ἐς Μύλας Δημοχάρει τῷ Πομπηίου, τεσσαρά-
436 κοντα ναῦς ἔχοντι· ὁ δὲ Πομπήιος, τὸ βίαιον ὑφορώ-
μενος τοῦ Ἀγρίππα, ἔπεμπε τῷ Δημοχάρει ναῦς
ἄλλας πέντε καὶ τεσσαράκοντα ἀπὸ Μεσσήνης ἐξ-
ελεύθερον ἄγοντα Ἀπολλοφάνη, καὶ αὐτὸς ἐφείπετο
ἄλλαις ἑβδομήκοντα.

437 106. Ἀγρίππας δ' ἔτι νυκτὸς ἐξ Ἱερᾶς ἀνήγετο ταῖς
ἡμίσεσι τῶν νεῶν ὡς Παπίᾳ μόνῳ ναυμαχήσων. ἐπεὶ
δὲ καὶ τὰς Ἀπολλοφάνους εἶδε καὶ τὰς ἑβδομήκοντα
ἑτέρωθι, Καίσαρι μὲν αὐτίκα ἐδήλου Πομπήιον ἐπὶ
τῶν Μυλῶν εἶναι σὺν τῷ πλέονι ναυτικῷ, τὰς δὲ βαρείας αὐτὸς ἦγε κατὰ μέσον καὶ τὸν ἄλλον στόλον ἐξ
438 Ἱερᾶς ἐκάλει κατὰ σπουδήν· ἐσκεύαστο δ' ἀμφοτέροις
πάντα λαμπρῶς, καὶ πύργους ἐπὶ τῶν νεῶν εἶχον
κατά τε πρῷραν καὶ κατὰ πρύμναν. ὡς δὲ αὐτοῖς αἵ
τε παρακελεύσεις, οἷας εἰκὸς ἦν, ἐγεγένηντο καὶ τὰ
σημεῖα κατὰ ναῦν ἦρτο, ἐξώρμων ἐπ' ἀλλήλους, οἱ
μὲν κατὰ μέτωπον, οἱ δ' ἐς περικύκλωσιν, σύν τε βοῇ
439 καὶ ῥοθίῳ νεῶν καὶ καταπλήξει ποικίλῃ. ἦν δὲ καὶ τὰ
σκάφη Πομπηίῳ μὲν βραχύτερα καὶ κοῦφα καὶ ὀξέα
ἐς τὰς ἐφορμήσεις τε καὶ περίπλους, Καίσαρι δὲ
μείζω καὶ βαρύτερα καὶ παρ' αὐτὸ καὶ βραδύτερα,
βιαιότερα δὲ ὅμως ἐμπεσεῖν καὶ τρωθῆναι δυσπαθέ-

intention of capturing Tauromenium while Pompeius was
still absent, and making inroads against him from two
directions. Agrippa, therefore, sailed from Strongyle to   435
Hiera, which he captured when Pompeius' garrison put up
no resistance to him. Next day he was intending to make
an attack at Mylae on the Pompeian commander, Demochares, who had forty ships. But Pompeius suspected   436
Agrippa's violent intention and sent his freedman Apollophanes to Demochares with another forty-five ships, and
followed in person with a further seventy.

106. While it was still dark, Agrippa set sail from Hiera   437
with half his fleet, intending to engage Papias on his
own in a battle. When he saw Apollophanes' ships too,
and the seventy on the other side of him, he immediately
sent word to Octavian that Pompeius was at Mylae with
the greater part of his naval forces. Then he personally
led his heavy ships into the center, and urgently summoned the remainder of his fleet from Hiera. Both sides   438
were magnificently equipped in all respects, and had towers on their ships both on prow and stern. When the customary exhortations had been made and the flags raised
on each ship, they rushed at each other, some head on,
others making a flank attack, and all accompanied by
shouting and spray from the ships and widespread anxiety.   439
The Pompeian vessels were smaller, light, and quick for
attacking and outflanking maneuvers. Those of Octavian
were larger and heavier, and consequently also slower,
yet more powerful in attack and not so easily damaged.

440 στερα. τῶν τε ἀνδρῶν οἱ μὲν ναυτικώτεροι τῶν Καίσαρος ἦσαν, οἱ δὲ σθεναρώτεροι· καὶ κατὰ λόγον οἱ
μὲν οὐκ ἐμβολαῖς, ἀλλὰ μόναις περιόδοις ἐπλεονέ-
κτουν, καὶ ταρσοὺς τῶν μειζόνων ἢ πηδάλια ἀνέκλων
ἢ κώπας ἀνέκοπτον ἢ ἀπεχώριζον ὅλως τὰ σκάφη καὶ
441 ἔβλαπτον ἐμβολῆς οὐχ ἥσσονα· οἱ δὲ τοῦ Καίσαρος
αὐτὰς ἐμβολαῖς ὡς βραχυτέρας ἀνέκοπτον ἢ κατ-
έσειον ἢ διερρήγνυον καί, ὅτε συμπλακεῖεν, ἔβαλλόν
τε ὡς ταπεινοτέρας ἀφ᾽ ὑψηλοῦ καὶ κόρακας ἢ χεῖρας
σιδηρᾶς εὐκολώτερον ἐπερρίπτουν. οἱ δὲ ὅτε βια-
σθεῖεν, ἐξήλλοντο ἐς τὸ πέλαγος, καὶ τούσδε μὲν τὰ
ὑπηρετικὰ τοῦ Πομπηίου περιπλέοντα ἀνελάμβανεν.

442 107. Ὁ δὲ Ἀγρίππας ἵετο μάλιστα εὐθὺ τοῦ Παπίου
καὶ αὐτῷ κατὰ τὴν ἐπωτίδα ἐμπεσὼν κατέσεισε τὴν
ναῦν καὶ ἐς τὰ κοῖλα ἀνέρρηξεν· ἡ δὲ τούς τε ἐν τοῖς
πύργοις ἀπεσείσατο καὶ τὴν θάλασσαν ἀθρόως ἐδέχετο, καὶ τῶν ἐρετῶν οἱ μὲν θαλαμίαι πάντες ἀπελή-
φθησαν, οἱ δ᾽ ἕτεροι τὸ κατάστρωμα ἀναρρήξαντες
ἐξενήχοντο. Παπίας δὲ ἐς τὴν παρορμοῦσαν ἀναλη-
443 φθεὶς αὖθις ἐπήει τοῖς πολεμίοις. καὶ ὁ Πομπήιος ἐξ
ὄρους ἐφορῶν τὰς μὲν ἰδίας μικρὰ ἐπωφελούσας καὶ
ψιλουμένας τῶν ἐπιβατῶν, ὅτε συμπλακεῖεν, Ἀγρίππᾳ
δὲ τὸν ἕτερον στόλον ἐξ Ἱερᾶς προσπλέοντα, ἀναχωρεῖν ἐσήμηνε σὺν κόσμῳ. καὶ ἀνεχώρουν ἐπιόντες τε
444 καὶ ἀναστρέφοντες ἀεὶ κατ᾽ ὀλίγον. Ἀγρίππα δ᾽ ἐπι-
βαρήσαντος αὐτοῖς ἔφευγον, οὐκ ἐς τοὺς αἰγιαλούς,

The Pompeian crews were better sailors than Octavian's, 440
but the latter were stronger. Accordingly, the Pompeian
ships had the advantage not in ramming, but only in ma-
neuverability, and they broke the oar blades and rudders
of the bigger ships, cut off oar handles, or isolated the
enemy's ships entirely, doing them no less harm than if
they had rammed them. Octavian's ships, on the other 441
hand, used their rams to check the smaller enemy vessels
or shatter them or break them apart; and when they came
to close quarters, they threw missiles down on the enemy
from above, as they were lower, and could more easily
throw the "ravens"[73] and grappling irons on them. Whenever the Pompeians were being overpowered, they jumped
into the sea, and Pompeius' tenders sailed round and
picked them up.

107. Agrippa bore straight down on Papias and struck 442
his ship under the catheads, shattering it and breaking into
the hold. The vessel shook off the men in the towers and
took on water everywhere: all the oarsmen on the lower
benches were cut off, but the others broke through the
deck and swam to safety. Papias was transferred onto the
ship moored alongside and resumed his attack on the enemy. Pompeius was looking down from a hill and could see 443
that his own ships were having little effect, and that whenever they came to close quarters with the enemy they were
being denuded of their marines, while on the other side
the rest of Agrippa's fleet was sailing to his assistance from
Hiera. So he gave the signal to withdraw in good order,
and they retired by advancing and constantly pulling back
little by little. When Agrippa pressed them hard, they fled 444

[73] A plank with a spike, for grappling.

ἀλλ᾽ ὅσα τῆς θαλάσσης οἱ ποταμοὶ τεναγώδη πε
ποιήκεσαν.

445   108. Καὶ Ἀγρίππας, κωλυόντων αὐτὸν τῶν κυβερ
νητῶν μεγάλαις ναυσὶν ἐς ὀλίγον ὕδωρ ἐπιπλεῖν,
πελάγιος ἐπ᾽ ἀγκυρῶν ἐσάλευεν ὡς ἐφορμιούμενος
446 τοῖς πολεμίοις καὶ νυκτομαχήσων, εἰ δέοι. τῶν φίλων
δ᾽ αὐτῷ παραινούντων μὴ ἀλόγῳ θυμῷ συμφέρεσθαι
μηδὲ τὸν στρατὸν ἐκτρύχειν ἀγρυπνίᾳ καὶ πόνῳ
μηδὲ πιστεύειν πολυχείμωνι θαλάσσῃ, μόλις ἑσπέρας
447 ἀνεζεύγνυε. καὶ οἱ Πομπηιανοὶ ἐς τοὺς λιμένας παρ
έπλεον, τριάκοντα μὲν τῶν σφετέρων νεῶν ἀποβαλόν
τες, πέντε δὲ καταδύσαντες τῶν πολεμίων καὶ βλά
448 ψαντες ἄλλα ἱκανὰ καὶ βλαβέντες ὅμοια. καὶ αὐτοὺς
ὁ Πομπήιος ἐπαινῶν, ὅτι τηλικαύταις ναυσὶν ἀντ
έσχον, τειχομαχῆσαι μᾶλλον ἔφασκεν ἢ ναυμαχῆσαι
καὶ ὡς νενικηκότας ἐδωρεῖτο, καὶ ἐπήλπιζεν ἐν τῷ
πορθμῷ διὰ τὸν ῥοῦν κουφοτέρους ὄντας περιέσεσθαι
καὶ αὐτὸς ἔφη τι προσθήσειν ἐς τὸ τῶν νεῶν ὕψος.

449   109. Τοῦτο μὲν δὴ τῆς ναυμαχίας τέλος ἦν τῆς περὶ
Μύλας Ἀγρίππᾳ καὶ Παπίᾳ γενομένης· τὸν δὲ Καί
σαρα ὁ Πομπήιος, ὥσπερ ἦν, ὑπολαβὼν ἐς τὸ Ταύρου
στρατόπεδον οἴχεσθαι καὶ ἐπιχειρήσειν τῷ Ταυρο
μενίῳ, μετὰ δεῖπνον εὐθὺς ἐς Μεσσήνην περιέπλει,
μέρος ἐν ταῖς Μύλαις ὑπολιπών, ἵνα αὐτὸν ὁ Ἀγρίπ
450 πας ἔτι παρεῖναι νομίζοι. Ἀγρίππας μὲν δὴ διαναπαύ
σας τὸν στρατόν, ἐς ὅσον ἤπειγεν, ἐς Τυνδαρίδα ἐν
διδομένην ἔπλει· καὶ παρῆλθε μὲν εἴσω, μαχομένων
δὲ λαμπρῶς τῶν φρουρῶν ἐξεώσθη. προσεχώρησαν

not to the beaches, but to the places where the rivers had created shoals in the sea.

108. Agrippa's helmsmen stopped him from sailing into 445 shallow water with his big ships, so he rode at anchor out to sea, intending to blockade the enemy and fight a night engagement, if necessary. But his associates advised him 446 not to be carried away by senseless enthusiasm, nor to wear out his soldiers with work and lack of sleep, nor to trust such a storm-prone sea. So in the evening he reluctantly withdrew. The Pompeians sailed along the coast to 447 their harbors, having lost thirty of their own ships, and sunk five of the enemy's, having inflicted considerable other damage and suffered similar damage in return. Pompeius praised his men for holding off such big ships, 448 saying they had fought a siege against walls rather than a battle against ships; and he rewarded them as though they had been victorious. He encouraged them to believe that, as they were lighter, they would prevail in the straits on account of the current. He also said that he himself would make some addition to the height of his ships.

109. Such was the outcome of the naval battle at Mylae 449 between Agrippa and Papias. Pompeius assumed, correctly, that Octavian had gone to the camp of Taurus and was going to attack Tauromenium. So, directly after supper, he sailed around to Messena, leaving a part of his forces at Mylae in order to make Agrippa think that he was still there. Agrippa, having rested his army to the extent 450 that the urgency of the situation allowed, set sail for Tyndaris, which was in the process of giving up its resistance. Although he got into the town, the garrison fought bril-

δ' ἕτεραι πόλεις αὐτῷ καὶ φρουρὰς ἐδέξαντο· καὶ
451 αὐτὸς ἐπανῆλθεν ἐς Ἱεράν. ὁ δὲ Καῖσαρ ἤδη μὲν ἐς
Λευκόπετραν ἐκ τοῦ Σκυλακίου διεπεπλεύκει, μαθὼν
ἔτι ἀκριβέστερον, ὅτι ὁ Πομπήιος ἐκ Μεσσήνης ἐς
Μύλας οἴχοιτο δι' Ἀγρίππαν· ἐκ δὲ Λευκοπέτρας
ἔμελλε νυκτὸς περᾶν ὑπὲρ τὸν πορθμὸν ἐς τὸ Ταυρο-
452 μένιον. πυθόμενος δὲ περὶ τῆς ναυμαχίας μετέγνω μὴ
κλέπτειν ἔτι τὸν διάπλουν νενικηκώς, ἀλλὰ κατὰ φῶς
θαρροῦντι τῷ στρατῷ περαιοῦσθαι· καὶ γὰρ ἔτι πάν-
453 τως ἡγεῖτο Πομπήιον Ἀγρίππᾳ παραμένειν. κατασκε-
ψάμενος οὖν ἡμέρας τὸ πέλαγος ἐκ τῶν ὁρῶν, ἐπεὶ
καθαρὸν ἔγνω πολεμίων, ἔπλει στρατὸν ἔχων, ὅσον αἱ
νῆες ἐδέχοντο, Μεσσάλαν ἐπὶ τοῦ λοιποῦ καταλιπών,
454 ἕως ἐπ' αὐτὸν αἱ νῆες ἐπανέλθοιεν. ἐλθὼν δ' ἐπὶ τὸ
Ταυρομένιον προσέπεμψε μὲν ὡς ὑπαξόμενος αὐτό, οὐ
δεξαμένων δὲ τῶν φρουρῶν παρέπλει τὸν ποταμὸν τὸν
ὄνομα Ἄμβολον[34] καὶ τὸ ἱερὸν τὸ Ἀφροδίσιον καὶ ὡρ-
μίσατο ἐς τὸν Ἀρχηγέτην, Ναξίων τὸν θεόν, ὡς χάρακα θησόμενος ἐνταῦθα καὶ ἀποπειράσων τοῦ Ταυ-
455 ρομενίου. ὁ δὲ Ἀρχηγέτης Ἀπόλλωνος ἀγαλμάτιόν
ἐστιν, ὃ πρῶτον ἐστήσαντο Ναξίων οἱ εἰς Σικελίαν
ἀπῳκισμένοι.
456   110. Ἐνταῦθα τῆς νεὼς ἐκβαίνων ὁ Καῖσαρ ὤλισθε

34 τὸν Ὀνοβάλαν codd.; τὸν ὄνομα Ἄμβολον Étienne-
Duplessis

194

liantly and he was pushed out. Other towns came over to his side and accepted garrisons. He himself returned to Hiera. In the meantime, Octavian had sailed from Scyla- 451 cium to Leucopetra, having heard even more reliable in- formation that Pompeius had left Messena for Mylae be- cause of Agrippa. He was intending to cross the straits from Leucopetra to Tauromenium by night. But when told 452 about the sea battle, he changed his mind: as victor, he would no longer keep his crossing secret, but would make the passage in daylight with a confident army. For he was still completely convinced that Pompeius was waiting for Agrippa. Accordingly, looking down from the hills on the 453 sea at daybreak and finding that it was clear of enemies, Octavian set sail with as many troops as the ships could carry, leaving Messalla in command of the rest until the fleet returned to him. Arriving at Tauromenium, he sent 454 messengers to announce that he was taking over the town, but when the garrison refused, he sailed on past the outlet of the river Ambolus[74] and the sanctuary of Aphrodite, and anchored at the Archegetes, the god of the Naxians, in- tending to establish his camp there and make an attempt on Tauromenium. The Archegetes is a small statue of 455 Apollo, the first to be erected by those Naxians who settled in Sicily.

110. It was here that when he was disembarking Octa- 456

---

[74] The manuscripts all record an unknown river called the Onobalas. The emendation of the Budé editor gives us the river Ambolus, mentioned by Plutarch as the site of a victory won by the famous fourth-century BC figure Timoleon (*Tim.* 34.1). This is to be identified with the modern Alcantara, which flows to the sea just south of Taormina, ancient Tauromenium.

καὶ ἔπεσε καὶ ἀνέδραμε δι᾽ αὐτοῦ. καὶ αὐτῷ καθιστα-
μένῳ ἔτι τὸ στρατόπεδον Πομπήιος ἐπέπλει στόλῳ
πολλῷ, θαῦμα ἀδόκητον· ᾤετο γὰρ αὐτὸν ἐκπεπο-
457 λεμῆσθαι πρὸς Ἀγρίππα. παρήλαυνε δὲ τῷ Πομπηίῳ
καὶ ἡ ἵππος, ἐς τάχος διερίζουσα τῷ ναυτικῷ, καὶ τὰ
πεζὰ ἑτέρωθεν ἐφαίνετο, ὥστε δεῖσαι μὲν ἅπαντας, ἐν
μέσῳ τριῶν στρατῶν πολεμίων γενομένους, δεῖσαι δὲ
τὸν Καίσαρα, Μεσσάλαν οὐκ ἔχοντα μεταπέμψασθαι.
458 οἱ μὲν οὖν ἱππέες εὐθὺς ἠνώχλουν οἱ Πομπηίου χα-
ρακοποιουμένους ἔτι τοὺς τοῦ Καίσαρος· εἰ δὲ ἐπὶ τοῖς
ἱππεῦσιν οἱ πεζοὶ καὶ τὸ ναυτικὸν ἐφώρμησε, τάχα ἄν
459 τι μεῖζον ἐξήνυστο τῷ Πομπηίῳ. νῦν δὲ ἀπείρως τε
πολέμου, καὶ ὑπ᾽ ἀγνοίας τοῦ θορύβου τῶν Καίσαρος,
καὶ ὄκνου, μὴ μάχης περὶ δείλην ἑσπέραν ἄρχειν, οἱ
μὲν αὐτῶν ἐς Κόκκυνον ἄκραν ὡρμίσαντο, οἱ πεζοὶ δ᾽
οὐκ ἀξιοῦντες ἀγχοῦ τῶν πολεμίων στρατοπεδεύειν ἐς
460 Φοίνικα πόλιν ἀνεχώρουν. καὶ νυκτὸς οἱ μὲν ἀνεπαύοντο, οἱ δὲ τοῦ Καίσαρος τὸν μὲν χάρακα ἐτέλουν,
ὑπὸ δὲ κόπου καὶ ἀγρυπνίας ἐς τὴν μάχην ἐβλά-
461 πτοντο. τέλη δ᾽ ἦν αὐτῷ τρία καὶ ἱππέες χωρὶς ἵππων
πεντακόσιοι καὶ κοῦφοι χίλιοι καὶ κληροῦχοι σύμμα-
χοι χωρὶς καταλόγου δισχίλιοι καὶ ναυτικὴ δύναμις
ἐπὶ τούτοις.

462   111. Τὰ μὲν οὖν πεζὰ πάντα Κορνιφικίῳ παραδοὺς
ὁ Καῖσαρ ἐκέλευσε τοὺς κατὰ τὴν γῆν πολεμίους
ἀπομάχεσθαι καὶ πράσσειν, ὅ τι ἐπείγοι· αὐτὸς δὲ
ταῖς ναυσὶν ἔτι πρὸ ἡμέρας ἀνήγετο ἐς τὸ πέλαγος,
μὴ καὶ τοῦδε αὐτὸν ἀποκλείσαιεν οἱ πολέμιοι.

vian slipped and fell, but quickly got up without assistance. While he was still establishing his camp, Pompeius sailed in with a large fleet, an unexpected sight, since Octavian believed that he had been drawn into battle by Agrippa. Pompeius' cavalry also rode along beside him, striving to 457 keep pace with the fleet, and his infantry appeared on the other side, with the result that all Octavian's men were apprehensive at finding themselves caught in the middle of three enemy forces; and Octavian too was alarmed, as he could not call up Messalla. So Pompeius' cavalry im- 458 mediately began to harass Octavian's men who were still working on the construction of the palisade. If his infantry and fleet had joined the cavalry in the attack, perhaps a more substantial result would have been achieved by Pompeius. But in fact, because his men were inexperi- 459 enced in war and unaware of the confusion among the troops of Octavian, and were hesitant about beginning a battle late in the afternoon, some of his force anchored at the promontory of Coccynus, while the infantry, thinking it unwise to camp near the enemy, withdrew to the town of Phoenix. During the night they rested, while Octavian's 460 men finished their palisade, but were rendered less effec- tive for battle by work and lack of sleep. Octavian had 461 three legions, five hundred cavalry without their horses, one thousand light-armed men, two thousand colonists giving military assistance as volunteers, and besides them his naval force.

111. He therefore put all of his infantry under the com- 462 mand of Cornificius, and ordered him to fight off the en- emy by land and take whatever action was urgent. He himself put to sea with his ships just before daybreak, to prevent the enemy from cutting him off in this place too.

463 καὶ τὸ μὲν δεξιὸν ἐπέτρεπε Τιτινίῳ, τὸ δὲ λαιὸν Κα-
ρισίῳ, λιβυρνίδος δὲ αὐτὸς ἐπέβαινε καὶ περιέπλει
πάντας παρακαλῶν· ἐπὶ δὲ τῇ παρακλήσει τὰ στρα-
τηγικὰ σημεῖα, ὡς ἐν κινδύνῳ μάλιστα ὤν, ἀπέθετο.
464 ἐπαναχθέντος δὲ τοῦ Πομπηίου δὶς μὲν ἐπεχείρησαν
ἀλλήλοις, καὶ τὸ ἔργον ἐς νύκτα ἐτελεύτησεν. ἁλισκομένων δὲ καὶ πιμπραμένων τῶν Καίσαρος νεῶν, αἱ
μὲν ἀράμεναι τὰ βραχέα τῶν ἱστίων ἀπέπλεον ἐς τὴν
Ἰταλίαν, τῶν παραγγελμάτων καταφρονοῦσαι· καὶ
αὐτὰς ἐπ' ὀλίγον οἱ τοῦ Πομπηίου διώξαντες ἐπὶ τὰς
ὑπολοίπους ἀνέστρεψαν, καὶ τῶνδε τὰς μὲν ᾕρουν
465 ὁμοίως, τὰς δὲ ἐνεπίμπρασαν. ὅσοι δ' ἐξ αὐτῶν ἐς τὴν
γῆν ἐσενήχοντο, τοὺς μὲν οἱ ἱππέες οἱ τοῦ Πομπηίου
διέφθειρον ἢ συνελάμβανον, οἱ δ' ἐς τὸ τοῦ Κορνιφικίου στρατόπεδον ἀνεπήδων, καὶ αὐτοῖς ὁ Κορνιφίκιος ἐπιθέουσιν ἐπεκούρει,[35] τοὺς κούφους ἐκπέμπων
μόνους· οὐ γὰρ εὔκαιρον ἐδόκει κινεῖν φάλαγγα δύσ-
θυμον ἀντικαθημένων πεζῶν μεγαλοφρονουμένων, ὡς
εἰκὸς ἦν, ἐπὶ νίκῃ.
466   112. Καίσαρα δ' ἐν τοῖς ὑπηρετικοῖς ἐς πολὺ τῆς
νυκτὸς ἀνακωχεύοντα καὶ βουλευόμενον, εἴτε ἐς Κορνιφίκιον ἐπανέλθοι διὰ μέσων τοσῶνδε ναυαγίων εἴτε
ἐς Μεσσάλαν διαφύγοι, θεὸς ἐς τὸν Ἀβάλαν[36] λιμένα
παρήνεγκε μεθ' ἑνὸς ὁπλοφόρου, χωρὶς φίλων τε καὶ

---

35 ἐπεχείρει codd.; ἐπεκούρει Schweig.
36 Ἀβάλαν codd.; Βαλαρὸν Nissen

He assigned the right wing to Titinius and the left to   463
Carisius, and embarking himself on a Liburnian, sailed
around the whole fleet, encouraging everyone.[75] Having
completed the task of encouragement, he took down his
commander's ensign, regarding himself as being in particular danger. When Pompeius set sail against him, they   464
fought two encounters with each other, the battle ending
with the arrival of night. Among Octavian's ships facing
capture or being set on fire, some raised their short sails
and made for the Italian coast, disregarding their orders.
Pompeius' fleet pursued them for a short distance and
then turned back against the remainder, capturing some
of them, as before, and burning others. Of those crews   465
from the ships who swam ashore, Pompeius' cavalry killed
or captured some, while others clambered up to Cornificius' camp. Cornificius did help them as they ran toward
him, but only sent out his light-armed troops. For he did
not think it was an opportune moment to disturb his
dispirited heavy infantry, when they were facing troops
buoyed up, as was natural, by victory.

112. Octavian spent most of the night anchored among   466
his service vessels, deliberating whether to return to Cornificius through the middle of so many wrecks, or to take
refuge with Messalla. A god brought him to the harbor of
Abala with a single batman and without any associates,

[75] Titinius is otherwise unknown. Carisius is usually identified
with the mint master of 46, Titus Carisius, although there was a
Publius Carisius, legate of Octavian in Spain in the 20s.

467 ὑπασπιστῶν καὶ θεραπόντων. καί τινες ἐκ τῶν ὀρῶν
ἐς πύστιν τῶν γεγονότων καταθέοντες εὗρον αὐτὸν τό
τε σῶμα καὶ τὴν ψυχὴν ἐσταλμένον, καὶ ἐς ἀκάτιον
ἐξ ἀκατίου μεταφέροντες, ἵνα διαλάθοι, μετεκόμισαν
468 ἐς Μεσσάλαν οὐ μακρὰν ὄντα. ὁ δ' εὐθύς, ἔτι ἀθερά-
πευτος, ἔς τε Κορνιφίκιον ἔστελλε λιβυρνίδα καὶ πανταχοῦ διὰ τῶν ὀρῶν περιέπεμπεν, ὅτι σῴζοιτο, Κορνιφικίῳ τε πάντας ἐπικουρεῖν ἐκέλευε καὶ αὐτὸς
469 ἔγραφεν αὐτίκα πέμψειν βοήθειαν. θεραπεύσας δὲ τὸ
σῶμα καὶ ἀναπαυσάμενος ὀλίγον ἐς Στυλίδα νυκτὸς
ἐξῄει, παραπεμπόμενος ὑπὸ τοῦ Μεσσάλα, πρὸς
Καρρίναν τρία ἔχοντα ἐπὶ τοῦ πρόπλου τέλη· καὶ
τῷδε μὲν ἐκέλευσε διαπλεῖν ἐς τὸ πέραν, ἔνθα καὶ
αὐτὸς ἔμελλε διαπλευσεῖσθαι, Ἀγρίππαν δὲ γράφων
ἠξίου κινδυνεύοντι Κορνιφικίῳ πέμπειν Λαρώνιον
470 μετὰ στρατιᾶς ὀξέως. Μαικήναν δ' αὖθις ἐς Ῥώμην
ἔπεμπε διὰ τοὺς νεωτερίζοντας· καί τινες παρακινοῦν-
τες ἐκολάσθησαν. καὶ Μεσσάλαν ἐς Δικαιάρχειαν
ἔπεμπεν, ἄγειν τὸ πρῶτον καλούμενον τέλος ἐς Ἱππώνειον.

471   113. Μεσσάλας δὲ οὗτος ἦν, ὃν οἱ τρεῖς ἐπὶ θανάτῳ
προγεγράφεσαν ἐν Ῥώμῃ, καὶ χρήματα τῷ κτείναντι
καὶ ἐλευθερίαν ἐπικεκηρύχεσαν· ὁ δὲ πρὸς Κάσσιον
καὶ Βροῦτον φυγών, ἀποθανόντων ἐκείνων, τὸν στόλον
472 ἐπὶ σπονδαῖς Ἀντωνίῳ παραδεδώκει. καί μοι τοῦτο

---

76 The manuscripts all name the harbor as Abala, not other-

bodyguards or servants.[76] Certain people who had hurried 467
down from the mountains to hear what had happened,
found him physically and mentally exhausted, and by
transferring him from one skiff to another in order to avoid
detection, brought him to Messalla, who was not far away.
Immediately, and before receiving attention, he dis- 468
patched a Liburnian to Cornificius, and spread the word
all around the mountains that he was safe. He ordered
everyone to assist Cornificius and wrote informing him
that he himself would send help straight away. After at- 469
tending to his own person and taking a little rest, he set
out by night, accompanied by Messalla, for Stylis, where
Carrinas had three legions ready to embark, and ordered
him to sail across to the other side, to the place where he
himself was about to make the crossing. He then wrote to
Agrippa asking him to send Laronius quickly with an army
to Cornificius because he was in danger. He sent Maece- 470
nas again to Rome on account of the political agitators;
and some of these, who were stirring up trouble, were
punished. He also sent Messalla to Dicaearchia to bring
what was called "the First" legion to Hipponium.

113. This was the same Messalla whom the triumvirs 471
had condemned to death on the proscription lists at Rome,
publicly proclaiming money and freedom for the man who
killed him. He had fled to Cassius and Brutus, and, when
they died, had delivered his fleet to Antony in accordance
with their agreement. I have decided to mention this here 472

wise attested. The emendation to Balarus, a place Appian mentioned at *BCiv.* 4.85.361, has merit, although Balarus seems to
have been on the Sicilian side of the straits of Messina, and Octavian is on the Italian mainland.

ἀναμνῆσαι νῦν ἔδοξεν ἐς ζήλωμα τῆς Ῥωμαίων ἀρετῆς, ὅπου Μεσσάλας, μόνον ἔχων ἐν τοσῇδε συμφορᾷ τὸν προγράψαντα, ἐθεράπευεν ὡς αὐτοκράτορα

473 καὶ περιέσῳζε. Κορνιφίκιος δὲ ἀποτρέψασθαι μὲν ἐκ τοῦ χάρακος εὐμαρῶς εἶχε τοὺς πολεμίους, κινδυνεύων δ' ἐξ ἀπορίας ἐς μάχην ἐξέτασσε καὶ προυκα-

474 λεῖτο. Πομπηίου δὲ οὐ συμπλεκομένου μὲν ἀνδράσιν ἐν μόνῃ τῇ μάχῃ τὴν ἐλπίδα ἔχουσιν, παραστήσεσθαι δ' αὐτοὺς τῷ λιμῷ προσδοκῶντος, ὥδευεν ὁ Κορνιφίκιος, ἐν μέσῳ τοὺς ἀπὸ τῶν νεῶν διαφυγόντας ἀνόπλους ἔχων βαλλόμενός τε καὶ χαλεπῶς, ἐν μὲν τοῖς πεδινοῖς ὑπὸ τῶν ἱππέων, ἐν δὲ τοῖς τραχέσιν ὑπὸ τῶν ψιλῶν τε καὶ κούφων, οἳ Νομάδες Λίβυες ὄντες ἠκόντιζόν τε ἐπὶ πλεῖστον καὶ τοὺς ἐπεκθέοντας ὑπέφευγον.

475 114. Τετάρτῃ δ' ἡμέρᾳ μόλις ἐπὶ τὴν ἄνυδρον γῆν ἀφίκοντο, ἣν ῥύακα πυρὸς λέγουσι, ποτὲ μέχρι θαλάσσης κατιόντα,[37] ἐπικλύσαι καὶ σβέσαι τὰ ἐν αὐτῇ νάματα. καὶ αὐτὴν οἱ μὲν ἐπιχώριοι μόνης ὁδεύουσι νυκτός, πνιγώδη τε οὖσαν ἀπ' ἐκείνου καὶ κονιορτοῦ σποδώδους γέμουσαν, οἱ δ' ἀμφὶ τὸν Κορνιφίκιον οὔτε νυκτὸς ἐθάρρουν, ἐν ἀσελήνῳ μάλιστα, ἰέναι διὰ ἀπειρίαν ὁδῶν καὶ ἐνέδρας, οὔτε ἡμέρας ὑπέμενον, ἀλλ' ἀπεπνίγοντο καὶ τὰς βάσεις ὡς ἐν θέρει

476 καὶ καύματι ὑπεκαίοντο, μάλιστα οἱ γυμνοί. βραδύνειν τε οὐ δυνάμενοι διὰ τὴν δίψαν ἐνοχλοῦσαν, οὐ-

---

[37] κατιοῦσαν BJ; κατιόντα Schweig.

as an exemplar of Roman virtue, because, when Messalla had in his power, on his own and in such a disastrous situation, the man who proscribed him, he looked after him as his commanding officer and saved his life. Cornificius 473 was easily able to repel the enemy from his palisade, but, being dangerously short of supplies, he arrayed his army for battle and offered combat. But Pompeius would not 474 engage with men whose sole hope lay in fighting, and expected to reduce them by hunger. So Cornificius, having placed in the center the unarmed men who had escaped from the ships, took to the road, under heavy fire from the cavalry when they were on flat ground, and on rough terrain from the light armed, unencumbered troops; the latter were Numidians from Africa who threw their javelins a great distance and evaded those who ran out against them.

114. On the fourth day, Cornificius managed, with dif- 475 ficulty, to reach the waterless region which they say that a stream of lava, running down to the sea, once covered and dried up the springs in the area.[77] Since then it has been stifling and filled with ash-like dust, and the inhabitants of the country travel on it only at night. Cornificius and his men, however, did not have the confidence to go at night, especially when there was no moon, because they did not know the roads and were afraid of being ambushed; nor could they tolerate it during the day, but found it suffocating, and the soles of their feet were burned (especially those who had no shoes), as they were now in the heat of summer. Unable to go slowly because of the thirst tor- 476

[77] The text is uncertain in this sentence.

δένα ἔτι τῶν βαλλόντων αὐτοὺς ἐπεξῆεσαν, ἀλλ᾽ ἐτι-
477 τρώσκοντο ἀφυλάκτως. ἐπεὶ δὲ καὶ τὰς ἐξόδους τῆς
διακεκαυμένης ἕτεροι κατεῖχον πολέμιοι, ἀμελήσαν-
τες τῶν ἀσθενεστέρων τε καὶ γυμνῶν ἀνεπήδων ἐς
τοὺς αὐχένας οἱ δυνάμενοι τόλμῃ παραβόλῳ καὶ
ἐβιάζοντο τοὺς πολεμίους, ἐς ὅσον εἶχον δυνάμεως.
478 κατεχομένων δὲ καὶ τῶν ἑξῆς αὐχένων ἀπεγίνωσκον
αὐτῶν ἤδη καὶ μεθεῖντο ὑπὸ δίψης καὶ θέρους καὶ
κόπου. προτρέποντος δὲ αὐτοὺς τοῦ Κορνιφικίου καὶ
πηγὴν πλησίον οὖσαν ἐπιδεικνύοντος, οἱ μὲν αὖθις
ἐβιάζοντο, πολλοὺς ἀπὸ σφῶν ἀπολλύντες, ἕτεροι δὲ
τὴν πηγὴν κατεῖχον πολέμιοι, καὶ παντελὴς ἤδη τοὺς
τοῦ Κορνιφικίου κατεῖχον ἀθυμία, καὶ παρίεντο.
479   115. Ὧδε δὲ αὐτοῖς ἔχουσι Λαρώνιος ἐπιφαίνεται
μακρόθεν, ὑπὸ Ἀγρίππου σὺν τρισὶ τέλεσι πεμφθείς,
οὔπω μὲν ἔνδηλος ὤν, ὅτι φίλος εἴη· ὑπὸ δὲ ἐλπίδος
ἀεὶ τοιοῦτον ἔσεσθαι προσδοκῶντες ἀνέφερον αὖθις
480 αὐτῶν.[38] ὡς δὲ καὶ τοὺς πολεμίους εἶδον τὸ ὕδωρ ἀπο-
λιπόντας, ἵνα μὴ γένοιντο ἐχθρῶν ἐν μέσῳ, ἀνέκρα-
γον μὲν ὑπὸ ἡδονῆς, ὅσον ἔσθενον, ἀντιβοήσαντος δ᾽
αὐτοῖς τοῦ Λαρωνίου δρόμῳ τὴν πηγὴν κατέλαβον.
καὶ ὑπὸ μὲν τῶν ἡγεμόνων ἐκωλύοντο πίνειν ἀθρόως·
ὅσοι δὲ ἠμέλησαν, ἔπινον ὁμοῦ καὶ ἀπέθνῃσκον.
481   116. Οὕτω μὲν ἐξ ἀέλπτου Κορνιφίκιος καὶ τοῦ
στρατοῦ τὸ φθάσαν μέρος περιεσώθη πρὸς Ἀγρίπ-

---

[38] αὐτῶν codd.; συντόνως Étienne-Duplessis

menting them, they stopped making sorties against any of those throwing missiles at them, and began to suffer wounds without protecting themselves. Since other enemy troops were in possession of the exits from the scorched land, those who were able abandoned the weaker and the barefoot and charged up into the gorges with reckless daring and overpowered the enemy with their remaining strength. But with the following defiles also occupied by hostile forces, they now began to despair and succumb to thirst and heat and exhaustion. When Cornificius urged them on, however, and pointed out that there was a spring nearby, they again tried to force the issue, taking heavy losses in the process. But because more enemy troops were holding the spring, complete dejection did now take hold of Cornificius' men, and they started to give up. 477

478

115. It was while they were in this state that Laronius makes his appearance in the distance, having been sent by Agrippa with three legions. Although it was not yet clear that he was a friend, they were led by hope into the firm expectation that he would turn out to be one, and once more recovered their spirits. When they saw the enemy abandon the water to avoid finding themselves between two hostile forces, they shouted for joy with all their strength; and when the troops of Laronius shouted in return, they ran and seized the spring. They were ordered by their officers not quench their thirst all in one go; those who ignored the order died while they drank. 479

480

116. This was how Cornificius and the surviving part of his army unexpectedly made their way to safety with 481

παν ἐς Μύλας· ἄρτι δὲ ὁ Ἀγρίππας Τυνδαρίδα εἰλή-
φει, τροφῶν μεστὸν χωρίον καὶ εὐφυῶς ἐς πόλεμον ἐκ
τῆς θαλάσσης ἔχον, καὶ ὁ Καῖσαρ ἐς αὐτὸ τὰ πεζὰ
καὶ τοὺς ἱππέας διεβίβαζεν. ἐγένοντό τε αὐτῷ πάντες
ἐν Σικελίᾳ ὁπλιτῶν μὲν ἐς εἴκοσι καὶ ἓν τέλος, ἱππέες
δὲ δισμύριοι καὶ κοῦφοι πλείους τῶν πεντακισχιλίων.

482 Μύλας δ' ἔτι καὶ τὰ ἐκ Μυλῶν ἐπί τε Ναυλόχους καὶ
Πελωριάδα καὶ τὰ παράλια πάντα φρουραὶ Πομπηίου
κατεῖχον, αἳ φόβῳ μάλιστα Ἀγρίππου πῦρ διηνεκὲς
483 ἔκαιον ὡς ἐμπρήσοντες τοὺς ἐπιπλέοντας. ἐκράτει
δὲ καὶ τῶν στενῶν ἑκατέρων ὁ Πομπήιος. ἀμφὶ δὲ
τὸ Ταυρομένιον καὶ περὶ Μύλας τὰς περιόδους τῶν
ὁρῶν ἀπετείχιζε καὶ τὸν Καίσαρα ἐκ Τυνδαρίδος
ἐς τὸ πρόσθεν ἰόντα ἠνώχλει, μὴ συμπλεκόμενον.
484 Ἀγρίππου δὲ νομισθέντος ἐπιπλεῖν ἐς Πελωριάδα
μετεπήδησεν, ἐκλιπὼν τὰ στενὰ περὶ Μύλας· καὶ ὁ
Καῖσαρ αὐτῶν τε κατέσχε καὶ Μυλῶν καὶ Ἀρτεμι-
σίου, πολίχνης βραχυτάτης, ἐν ᾗ φασι τὰς Ἡλίου
βοῦς γενέσθαι καὶ τὸν ὕπνον Ὀδυσσεῖ.

485 117. Ψευδοῦς δὲ τῆς Ἀγρίππου δόξης φανείσης, ὁ
Πομπήιος ᾔσθετο[39] τῶν στενῶν ἀφῃρημένος καὶ Τισιηνὸν ἐκάλει μετὰ τοῦ στρατοῦ. Τισιηνῷ δ' ὁ Καῖσαρ
ὑπήντα καὶ διημάρτανε τῆς ὁδοῦ περὶ ὄρος τὸ Μυ-
κόνιον, ἔνθα ἄσκηνος ἐνυκτέρευσεν· ὄμβρου τε πολλοῦ καταρραγέντος, οἷος ἐν φθινοπώρῳ γίγνεται, τῶν

---

[39] ᾔσθετο Étienne-Duplessis; ᾔχθετο Schweig.; ᾐσθεὶς codd.

Agrippa at Mylae.[78] Agrippa had recently captured Tyndaris, a stronghold full of provisions and well situated against attack from the sea, and Octavian transported his infantry and cavalry there. He had in Sicily a total of twenty-one legions of infantry, twenty thousand cavalry, and more than five thousand light-armed troops. Pompeius' garrisons still held Mylae and the whole coast from Mylae to Naulochus and Cape Pelorus. They were particularly afraid of Agrippa, and kept fires burning continually to torch any vessels attacking them. Pompeius also controlled both passes. Around Tauromenium and near Mylae he fortified the routes around the mountains, and harassed Octavian as he advanced from Tyndaris, but without engaging him in battle. When it was thought that Agrippa was sailing against him, Pompeius moved his position to Pelorus, abandoning the defiles around Mylae. Octavian occupied them along with Mylae and Artemisium, a very small town, where the cattle of the Sun were to be found and the place where Odysseus fell asleep.[79]

117. When the report about Agrippa turned out to be false, Pompeius was informed[80] that he had lost the defiles, and he called up Tisienus with his army. Octavian went to confront Tisienus, but lost his way near Mount Myconium, where he spent the night without tents. A heavy rainstorm burst over them, the sort that occurs in

[78] As Appian notes himself in this chapter, Mylae was held by Pompeius. The mistake could have been made by a scribe, or, given his geographical weaknesses, by Appian himself.

[79] The famous story in Homer's *Odyssey* (Book 12).

[80] Or perhaps "annoyed" (*echtheto*). The manuscripts mistakenly say "pleased" (*hesthois*).

ὁπλοφόρων τινὲς τὴν νύκτα πᾶσαν ἀσπίδα Κελτικὴν
486 ὑπερέσχον αὐτοῦ. ἐγένοντο δὲ καὶ βρόμοι τῆς Αἴτνης
σκληροὶ καὶ μυκήματα μακρὰ καὶ σέλα περιλάμ-
ποντα τὴν στρατιάν, ὥστε τοὺς μὲν Γερμανοὺς ἐξ
εὐνίων ἀναπηδᾶν ὑπὸ δέους, τοὺς δέ, ἀκοῇ τῶν περὶ
τῆς Αἴτνης λεγομένων, οὐκ ἀπιστεῖν ἐν τοσοῖσδε
487 παραδόξοις ἐμπεσεῖσθαι σφίσι καὶ τὸν ῥύακα. μετὰ
δὲ τοῦτο τὴν πάλαι Λαιστρυγόνων[40] γῆν ἔκειρε, καὶ
Λέπιδος αὐτῷ συνήντετο σιτολογῶν, καὶ Μεσσήνῃ
παρεστρατοπέδευον ἀμφότεροι.

488   118. Γιγνομένων δ' ἀν' ὅλην τὴν Σικελίαν ἀψιμα-
χιῶν πολλῶν, ἔργου δὲ μείζονος οὐδενός, Ταῦρον ὁ
Καῖσαρ ἔπεμψε τὰς ἀγορὰς τοῦ Πομπηίου περικό-
πτειν καὶ τὰς πόλεις τὰς χορηγούσας προκαταλαμ-
489 βάνειν. καὶ τῷδε μάλιστα κάμνων ὁ Πομπήιος ἔκρινε
μάχῃ μείζονι κριθῆναι περὶ ἁπάντων. τὰ μὲν δὴ πεζὰ
τοῦ Καίσαρος ἐδεδίει, ταῖς δὲ ναυσὶν ἐπαιρόμενος
ἤρετο πέμπων, εἰ δέχοιτο ναυμαχίᾳ κριθῆναι. ὁ δὲ
ὠρρώδει μὲν τὰ ἐνάλια πάντα, οὐ σὺν τύχῃ μέχρι
δεῦρο κεχρημένος αὐτοῖς, αἰσχρὸν δὲ νομίσας ἀντει-
490 πεῖν ἐδέχετο. καὶ ὡρίζετο αὐτοῖς ἡμέρα, ἐς ἣν τριακό-
σιαι νῆες ἑκατέρων ἰδίᾳ παρεσκευάζοντο, βέλη τε
παντοῖα φέρουσαι καὶ πύργους καὶ μηχανάς, ὅσας

---

[40] πάλαι Λαιστρυγόνων Étienne-Duplessis; Παλαιστηνῶν
codd.

late autumn, and some of his bodyguard held a Gallic shield over his head the whole night. Harsh cracks came 486 from Etna, and long rumblings and flashes that lit up the army, with the result that the Germans leaped from their sleeping places in fear, while the others, who had heard the stories about Etna, were convinced that in such extraordinary circumstances the lava too would swamp them. After this Octavian ravaged the territory once be- 487 longing to the Laestrygonians,[81] where Lepidus, who was foraging, met him, and they both encamped at Messena.

118. As many skirmishes were taking place all over 488 Sicily, but no major engagement, Octavian sent Taurus to cut off Pompeius' food supplies by first capturing the towns that were provisioning him. This tactic caused Pom- 489 peius particular difficulties, and he decided to stake everything on a major battle. Since he feared Octavian's infantry, but had confidence in his own ships, he sent a message to Octavian inquiring if he would agree to let things be settled by a naval battle. Octavian, although he dreaded all naval operations, which up to this point he had conducted without success, accepted because he thought it cowardly to refuse. They fixed a day, for which each side 490 independently prepared three hundred ships, carrying missiles of all kinds, and towers and whatever machines

---

[81] The manuscripts all have "the territory of the Palestinians." There was an ancient town of Palaeste in Epirus on the east coast of Greece, but none was known in northern Sicily, where the action of the narrative is taking place. As Appian has just made a reference to Homer's *Odyssey*, and Greek tradition located the Laestrygonians in Sicily around Mount Etna, I have adopted the reading of the Budé editor.

491 ἐπενόουν. ἐπενόει δὲ καὶ τὸν καλούμενον ἄρπαγα ὁ
Ἀγρίππας, ξύλον πεντάπηχυ σιδήρῳ περιβεβλημέ-
νον, κρίκους ἔχον περὶ κεραίας ἑκατέρας· τῶν δὲ
κρίκων εἴχετο τοῦ μὲν ὁ ἄρπαξ, σιδήριον καμπύλον,
τοῦ δὲ καλῴδια πολλά, μηχαναῖς ἐπισπώμενα τὸν ἄρπαγα, ὅτε τῆς πολεμίας νεὼς ἐκ καταπέλτου λάβοιτο.

492 119. Ἐλθούσης δὲ τῆς ἡμέρας πρῶτα μὲν ἦν ἐρετῶν
ἅμιλλα καὶ βοή, καὶ βέλη τὰ μὲν ἐκ μηχανῆς, τὰ δ᾽
ἀπὸ χειρῶν, ὅσα λίθοι καὶ πυρφόρα καὶ τοξεύματα.

493 μετὰ δὲ αἱ νῆες αὐταὶ συνερρήγνυντο ἀλλήλαις, αἱ
μὲν εἰς τὰ πλάγια, αἱ δὲ κατ᾽ ἐπωτίδας, αἱ δὲ ἐπὶ τοὺς
ἐμβόλους, ἔνθα μάλιστά εἰσιν αἱ πληγαὶ βίαιοι τινά-
ξαι τε τοὺς ἐπιβάτας καὶ τὴν ναῦν ἀργοτέραν ἐργά-

494 σασθαι. ἄλλαι δὲ ἀλλήλας διεξέπλεον βάλλουσαί τε
καὶ ἀκοντίζουσαι· καὶ τὰ ὑπηρετικὰ τοὺς ἐκπίπτοντας
ἀνελάμβανεν. ἔργα τε χειρῶν ἦν καὶ βία ναυτῶν καὶ
τέχνη κυβερνητῶν καὶ βοαὶ καὶ στρατηγῶν παρακε-

495 λεύσεις καὶ μηχανήματα πάντα. εὐδοκίμει δὲ μάλιστα ὁ ἄρπαξ, ἔκ τε πολλοῦ ταῖς ναυσὶ διὰ κουφότητα
ἐμπίπτων καὶ ἐμπηγνύμενος, ὅτε μάλιστα ὑπὸ τῶν
καλῳδίων ἐφέλκοιτο ὀπίσω· κοπῆναί τε ὑπὸ τῶν
βλαπτομένων οὐκ ἦν εὔπορος διὰ σίδηρον τὸν περι-
έχοντα, καὶ τὸ μῆκος αὐτοῦ δυσεφικτότατα τοῖς
κόπτουσι τὰ καλῴδια ἐποίει· οὐδὲ τὸ μηχάνημά

496 πω προέγνωστο, ὡς δρέπανα δόρασι περιθέσθαι· ἐν
δ᾽ ἐπενόουν ὡς ἐν ἀδοκήτῳ, τὴν ναῦν κρούοντες ἐπὶ
πρύμναν ἀντισπᾶν. τὸ δ᾽ αὐτὸ ποιούντων καὶ τῶν πο-

they could devise. Agrippa devised one called the "grab,"   491
a piece of wood five cubits long encased in iron and having
rings at each end. To one of these rings was attached the
grab itself, a curved piece of iron, to the other numerous
ropes, which pulled in the grab by machine after it had
been fired from a catapult and had hooked an enemy ship.

119. When the day arrived, first there was the rivalry   492
and shouting of the rowers, and the missiles, such as
stones, fireballs, and arrows, some fired by artillery, others
thrown by hand.[82] Next, the ships themselves rammed   493
each other, some amidships, others on the prow, others at
the ram, where the especially violent impact shakes the
marines off and reduces the ship's effectiveness. Others   494
rowed through the opposing line while shooting missiles
and throwing javelins, and service vessels picked up the
men who fell overboard. On display were the combat of
arms and the strength of sailors and the skill of helmsmen
and the shouting of generals, and all types of war machine.
But the "grab" won special recognition. Because it was   495
light it could land on ships from a distance and embed
itself, particularly when it was pulled back by its ropes. As
it was encased in iron, it could not easily be cut by those
who had been hit, and its length made it very difficult to
get at the ropes for anyone trying to cut them. The device
was unknown until then, with the result that they had not
attached sickles to poles. In this unexpected situation, they   496
could only think of one solution, to pull the ship away by
rowing backward. But as the enemy too did the same, the

[82] The battle of Naulochus took place on September 3, 36.

λεμίων ἴση μὲν ἦν ἡ βία τῶν ἀνδρῶν, ὁ δὲ ἅρπαξ
ἐποίει τὸ ἴδιον.

497   120. Ὅτε μὲν οὖν προσπελάσειαν αἱ νῆες, ἐμάχοντο
παντοίως καὶ ἐς ἀλλήλους μεθήλλοντο. καὶ διαγνῶναι
τὸν πολέμιον οὐκ ἦν ἔτι ὁμοίως εὔπορον· ὅπλοις τε
γὰρ ὡς τὰ πολλὰ τοῖς αὐτοῖς ἐχρῶντο καὶ φωνῇ σχεδὸν ἅπαντες Ἰταλῇ, τά τε συνθήματα μιγνυμένων ἐς
ἀμφοτέρους ἐξενήνεκτο, καὶ ἐκ τοῦδε μάλιστα ἐνέδραι
πολλαὶ καὶ ποικίλαι παρὰ ἀμφοῖν, καὶ ἀπιστία πρὸς
τοὺς λέγοντας αὐτὰ ἐπεγίγνετο, ἀγνωσία τε πάντας
ἀλλήλων ἐπεῖχεν ὡς ἐν πολέμῳ καὶ θαλάσσῃ γε-
498   μούσῃ φόνων τε καὶ ὅπλων καὶ ναυαγίων. οὐ γάρ τινα
πεῖραν ἔλιπον, ὅτι μὴ μόνον τὸ πῦρ· τούτου δὲ μετὰ
τοὺς πρώτους ἐπίπλους ἐφείσαντο διὰ τὰς συμπλο-
499   κάς. ὁ δὲ πεζὸς ἑκατέρων στρατὸς ἀπὸ τῆς γῆς μετὰ
φόβου καὶ σπουδῆς ἐς τὴν θάλασσαν ἀφεώρων, ὡς
ἐν τῇδε καὶ αὐτοὶ περὶ τῆς σφῶν σωτηρίας τὴν ἐλπίδα ἔχοντες. διέκρινόν γε μὴν οὐδέν, οὐδ᾽ ἐδύναντο,
καὶ μάλιστα περισκοποῦντες, οἷα νεῶν ἑξακοσίων ἐπὶ
μήκιστον ἐκτεταγμένων καὶ τῆς οἰμωγῆς ἐναλλασσο-
μένης ἀνὰ μέρος ἑκατέρωθεν.

500   121. Μόλις δέ ποτε ταῖς χροιαῖς τῶν πύργων, αἷς
δὴ μόναις διέφερον ἀλλήλων, ὁ Ἀγρίππας συνεὶς
πλέονας ἀπολωλέναι τοῦ Πομπηίου ναῦς ἐθάρρυνε
τοὺς συνόντας ὡς ἤδη κατορθοῦντας· καὶ τοῖς πολεμίοις αὖθις ἐμπεσὼν ἐπέκειτο ἀπαύστως, μέχρι βι-
ασθέντες, ὅσοι μάλιστα κατ᾽ αὐτὸν ἦσαν, τούς τε
πύργους κατέρριψαν καὶ τὰς ναῦς ἐπιστρέψαντες ἐς

force exerted by the men was equal, and the grab did its work.

120. Accordingly, when the ships grappled with each 497 other, all sorts of fighting took place, and the crews boarded each other's vessels. It was no longer as easy to identify the enemy, because, on the whole, both sides used the same weapons and almost all of them spoke Latin, and in the mêlée the watchwords of each side were revealed. As a result, both sides set an unusual number and variety of traps, and there was a lack of trust in those delivering the watchwords. Amid the fighting and the sea filled with corpses, weapons, and the wreckage of ships, everyone was affected by the inability to recognize anyone else. For 498 there was nothing they left untried, with the sole exception of fire. This they avoided, after the first attacks, because the ships were locked together. The infantry of both 499 armies looked out to sea from the land with fear and a keen interest, as it was on this battle that they too based their hope of safety. They did not really make out any details, and could not do so, no matter how hard they looked, given that nearly six hundred ships were arrayed over a very great distance, and the groaning alternated in turn from either side.

121. Using the color of their towers, which was the only 500 thing to differentiate the ships from each other, Agrippa eventually came to realize, with some difficulty, that more of Pompeius' ships had been destroyed, and he began to encourage the men with him, by conveying the message that they were already winning. Falling on the enemy again, he pressed them relentlessly, until those directly confronting him, having yielded to force, tore down their towers, turned their ships, and fled for the straits. Seven-

τὸν πορθμὸν ἔφευγον. καὶ ἔφθασαν ἐσδραμεῖν ἑπτα-
501 καίδεκα νῆες. αἱ δὲ λοιπαί, διακλείσαντος αὐτὰς τοῦ
Ἀγρίππου, αἱ μὲν ἐξώκελλον ἐς τὴν γῆν διωκόμεναι,
καὶ συνεξώκελλον αὐταῖς ὑπὸ ὁρμῆς οἱ διώκοντες ἢ
ὁρμιζομένας ἀπέσπων ἢ ἐνεπίμπρασαν· ὅσαι δὲ ἔτι
κατὰ τὸ πέλαγος ἐμάχοντο, τὰ περὶ αὐτὰς γιγνόμενα
κατιδοῦσαι παρεδίδοσαν ἑαυτὰς τοῖς πολεμίοις. καὶ ὁ
τοῦ Καίσαρος στρατὸς ἐπινίκιον ἠλάλαξεν ἐν τῇ
502 θαλάσσῃ, καὶ ὁ πεζὸς ἀντεβόησεν ἐπὶ τῆς γῆς. οἱ
Πομπηίου δ' ἀνῴμωξαν, καὶ αὐτὸς ἐκ τῶν Ναυλόχων
ἀναθορὼν ἐς τὴν Μεσσήνην ἠπείγετο, οὐδὲν ὑπὸ ἐκ-
πλήξεως περὶ τῶν πεζῶν οὐδ' ἐπισκήψας· ὅθεν καὶ
τούσδε ὁ Καῖσαρ Τισιηνοῦ παραδιδόντος ὑποσπόν-
δους ἐδέχετο καὶ τοὺς ἱππέας ἐπ' αὐτοῖς, τῶν ἱππάρ-
503 χων παραδιδόντων. κατέδυσαν δὲ ἐν τῷ πόνῳ νῆες
Καίσαρος μὲν τρεῖς, Πομπηίου δὲ ὀκτὼ καὶ εἴκοσι,
καὶ αἱ λοιπαὶ κατεφλέχθησαν ἢ ἐλήφθησαν ἢ ἐς τὴν
γῆν ὀκέλλουσαι συνετρίβησαν· αἱ δὲ ἑπτακαίδεκα
μόναι διέφυγον.

504   122. Καὶ ὁ Πομπήιος ἐν ὁδῷ περὶ τῆς μεταγνώμης
τοῦ πεζοῦ πυθόμενος τήν τε ἐσθῆτα ἤλλαξεν ἐς ἰδιώτην ἀπ' αὐτοκράτορος καὶ προύπεμψεν ἐς Μεσσήνην
ἐς τὰς ναῦς ἐντίθεσθαι τὰ δυνατά· παρεσκεύαστο δὲ
505 ἅπαντα ἐκ πολλοῦ. Πλένιόν τε ἐκ Λιλυβαίου, μεθ' ὧν
εἶχεν ὀκτὼ τελῶν, ἐκάλει κατὰ σπουδὴν ὡς μετὰ
τῶνδε φευξόμενος. καὶ Πλένιος μὲν ἠπείγετο πρὸς αὐτόν, αὐτομολούντων δὲ ἑτέρων, φίλων τε καὶ φρουρίων
καὶ στρατῶν, καὶ τῶν πολεμίων ἐς τὸν πορθμὸν

teen of them successfully made their run there first, but 501
of the remainder which Agrippa cut off, some were chased
to land and ran aground, and their pursuers in their rush
ran aground with them, or dragged them off as they rode
at anchor, or set fire to them; while all those who were still
fighting on the open sea surrendered to the enemy when
they saw what was happening around them. At this, Octavian's men on the water raised a chant of victory, and his
infantry shouted out in reply on the land. Pompeius' 502
forces, on the other hand, groaned aloud in disappoint-
ment, and Pompeius himself scurried away from Naulochus and hurried to Messena, without even leaving orders
for his infantry, such was his shock. As a result, Tisienus
surrendered and Octavian received these men too on
agreed terms, as well as the cavalry in addition when their
officers surrendered. Three of Octavian's ships were sunk 503
in the battle, twenty-eight of Pompeius'; the rest of Pompeius' fleet were consumed by fire, captured, or shattered
as they ran aground. Only the seventeen escaped.

122. Pompeius learned of his infantry's defection while 504
he was on the road, and he changed out of his commander
in chief's uniform into the clothes of a private person,
sending ahead to Messena instructions to load everything
possible on the ships, all arrangements having been made
long before. He sent an urgent summons for Plinius to 505
come from Lilybaeum with the eight legions he commanded, intending to flee with them. Plinius hurried to
join him, but, when others, associates and garrisons and
soldiers, began to desert, and the enemy were sailing into

215

ἐσπλεόντων, οὐκ ἀναμείνας οὐδὲ Πλένιον ὁ Πομπήιος
ἐν πόλει καλῶς τετειχισμένῃ, ἔφευγεν ἐκ τῆς Μεσσήνης ἐπὶ τῶν ἑπτακαίδεκα νεῶν ἐς Ἀντώνιον, ὡς ἐξ
506 ὁμοίων αὐτῷ τὴν μητέρα περισεσωκώς. καὶ ὁ Πλένιος
αὐτὸν οὐ καταλαβὼν ἐς τὴν Μεσσήνην παρῆλθε καὶ
κατεῖχε τῆς πόλεως. ὁ δὲ Καῖσαρ αὐτὸς μὲν ἔμεινεν
ἐν τῷ περὶ Ναυλόχους στρατοπέδῳ, Ἀγρίππαν δ᾽
ἐκέλευσε τῇ Μεσσήνῃ παρακαθέζεσθαι· καὶ παρ-
507 εκάθητο σὺν Λεπίδῳ. Πλενίου δὲ πρεσβευομένου περὶ
σπονδῶν Ἀγρίππας μὲν ἠξίου περιμένειν Καίσαρα ἐς
ἕω, Λέπιδος δὲ ἐδίδου τὰς σπονδὰς καὶ τὸν τοῦ
Πλενίου στρατὸν οἰκειούμενος ἑαυτῷ συνεχώρει διαρ-
508 πάσαι τὴν πόλιν μετὰ τοῦ ἄλλου στρατοῦ. καὶ οἱ μὲν
ἐπὶ τῇ σωτηρίᾳ, περὶ ἧς δὴ καὶ μόνης παρεκάλουν,
κέρδος ἀδόκητον εὑρόμενοι, τὴν Μεσσήνην ὅλῃ τῇ
νυκτὶ μετὰ τῶν Λεπίδου διήρπαζον καὶ μετεστρατεύ-
οντο τῷ Λεπίδῳ.

509   123. Ὁ δὲ σὺν τούτοις ἔχων δύο καὶ εἴκοσι τέλη
πεζῶν καὶ ἱππέας πολλοὺς ἐπῆρτο καὶ κρατήσειν
ἐδόκει Σικελίας, πρόφασιν ἔχων, ὅτι πρῶτος ἐπιβαίη
τῆς νήσου καὶ πλέονας πόλεις ἐπαγάγοιτο· ἔς τε τὰ
φρούρια αὐτίκα περιέπεμπε τοὺς παρὰ τοῦ Καίσαρος
ἐλευσομένους μὴ προσίεσθαι καὶ τὰ στενὰ πάντα
510 ἐκρατύνετο. ὁ δὲ Καῖσαρ ἦλθε μὲν τῆς ἐπιούσης καὶ
ἐμέμφετο τῷ Λεπίδῳ διὰ τῶν φίλων, οἳ σύμμαχον
αὐτὸν ἔφασκον ἐλθεῖν Καίσαρι ἐς Σικελίαν, οὐχ
ἑαυτῷ κατακτησόμενον αὐτήν· ὁ δὲ ἀντενεκάλει τῆς
προτέρας τάξεως ἀφῃρῆσθαι καὶ μόνον ἔχειν αὐτὴν

the straits, Pompeius did not even wait for Plinius in what was a well fortified town, but fled from Messena on his seventeen ships to Antony, whose mother, so he reasoned, he had saved in similar circumstances. Although failing to overtake Pompeius, Plinius entered Messena and occupied the town. Octavian himself remained in his camp at Naulochus, and ordered Agrippa to take up position at Messena, which he did in conjunction with Lepidus. When Plinius sent representatives to negotiate a truce, Agrippa's opinion was to wait till morning for the arrival of Octavian, but Lepidus granted terms, and in order to win over Plinius' men for himself, he gave them permission to join the rest of his army in plundering the town. So, having obtained an unexpected bonus, in addition to the personal safety which was all they had actually petitioned for, Plinius' men joined those of Lepidus in plundering Messena the whole night, and then put themselves under the command of Lepidus.

123. Including these men, Lepidus commanded twenty-two legions of infantry and a large body of cavalry. This boosted his confidence and he decided to make himself master of Sicily, advancing the pretext that he was the first to have disembarked on the island and had brought over a considerable number of towns. He immediately circulated orders to the garrisons that they should refuse entry to anyone coming from Octavian, and he seized all the defiles. Octavian arrived the following day, and criticized Lepidus through his associates, who reminded him that he had come to Sicily as an ally of Octavian, not to acquire it for himself. Lepidus countered by claiming that he had been deprived of his former position, now in the

506

507

508

509

510

Καίσαρα βουλομένῳ τε νῦν ἀντιδιδόναι Λιβύην καὶ
511 Σικελίαν ὑπὲρ ἐκείνης. χαλεπαίνων δ' ὁ Καῖσαρ ἦλθε
μὲν καὶ αὐτὸς ὑπὸ ὀργῆς, ὀνειδιῶν τὸν Λέπιδον ἐς
χαριστίαν, διαπειλησάμενοι δὲ ἀλλήλοις διέστησαν,
καὶ αὐτίκα αἵ τε φυλακαὶ διεκρίθησαν καὶ αἱ νῆες
ὥρμουν ἐπ' ἀγκυρῶν· ἐλέχθη γὰρ αὐτὰς ἐπινοεῖν ὁ
Λέπιδος ἐμπρῆσαι.

512   124. Ὁ δὲ στρατὸς ἤχθετο, εἰ πολεμήσουσιν αὖθις
ἐμφύλιον πόλεμον ἕτερον καὶ οὔ ποτε σφᾶς ἐπιλεί-
ψουσιν αἱ στάσεις. οὐ μὴν ἐν ὁμοίῳ Καίσαρα καὶ
Λέπιδον ἐτίθεντο, οὐδὲ οἱ τῷ Λεπίδῳ στρατευόμενοι,
ἀλλὰ καὶ τῆς ἀρετῆς τὸν Καίσαρα ἐθαύμαζον καὶ τὴν
ἀργίαν συνῄδεσαν Λεπίδῳ, καὶ τῆς ἁρπαγῆς αὐτὸν
ἐπεμέμφοντο αὐτῆς, ἐς τὸ ἴσον τοῖς ἡσσημένοις κατα-
513 στάντες. ὧν ὁ Καῖσαρ πυνθανόμενος περιέπεμπε τοὺς
τὰ συμφέροντα παραινέσοντας κρύφα ἑκάστοις. ὡς δὲ
αὐτῷ διεφθάρατο πολλοί, καὶ μάλιστα οἱ γενόμενοι
τοῦ Πομπηίου διὰ δέος τοῦ μήπω τὰς σπονδὰς βεβαίους σφίσιν, εἰ μὴ συνθοῖτο ὁ Καῖσαρ, εἶναι, ἀγνο-
οῦντος ἔτι ταῦτα τοῦ Λεπίδου δι' ἀπραξίαν ὁ Καῖσαρ
ἐπῆλθεν ἐπὶ τὸ στρατόπεδον αὐτοῦ σὺν ἱππεῦσι
πολλοῖς, οὓς πρὸ τοῦ χάρακος καταλιπὼν ἐσῄει μετ'
ὀλίγων, καὶ παριὼν ἐπεμαρτύρετο ἑκάστοις ἄκων ἐς
514 πόλεμον καθίστασθαι. ἀσπαζομένων δὲ αὐτὸν ὡς αὐτοκράτορα τῶν ὁρώντων, οἱ Πομπηιανοὶ πρῶτοι συν-

---

83 After the Battle of Philippi in 42, Octavian and Antony had

Pompeians whose loyalty had been compromised were the first to run over to him and beg him to forgive them. He said that he was astonished that people asking for forgiveness were not yet doing what was in their own best interests. Understanding his meaning, they immediately seized their standards and transferred them to Octavian, while others took down tents.

125. When Lepidus heard the disturbance, he rushed 515 out of his tent to take up arms. There was already some throwing of weapons, and one of Octavian's bodyguards had been killed, and Octavian himself hit in the breastplate, although it did not penetrate to his skin, and he made his escape by running over to the cavalry. One of 516 Lepidus' guard posts jeered him as he ran away, and Octavian could not restrain his anger until he had captured the post with his cavalry and destroyed it. The officers of 517 other guard posts began to transfer their allegiance from Lepidus to Octavian, some immediately, others during the night; some without any attempt being made on them, others, for the sake of appearance, having been mildly harassed by the cavalry. There were some who still re- 518 sisted the attacks and beat them off, for Lepidus was sending reinforcements everywhere. But when the reinforcements themselves defected, the rest of Lepidus' army, even those still well disposed to him, began to change their mind. Again the first to jump ship, unit by 519 unit, were those Pompeians still with him; and when Lepidus armed his other troops to prevent this, those who had been given arms to stop the others took their own standards and joined the rest in going over to Octavian. As they 520 were leaving, Lepidus threatened and begged them and grabbed hold of their standards saying he would not let go,

καὶ οὐ μεθήσειν ἔλεγε, μέχρι τῶν φερόντων αὐτά τις
εἶπε μεθήσειν ἀποθανόντα καὶ δείσας μεθῆκεν.

521   126. Οἱ δὲ ἱππέες τελευταῖοι χωροῦντες ἔπεμψάν
τινα πευσόμενοι τοῦ Καίσαρος, εἰ κτείνωσι Λέπιδον,
522 οὐκέτι ὄντα αὐτοκράτορα· ὁ δὲ ἀπεῖπεν. οὕτω Λέπιδος,
ἀδοκήτῳ πάντων ἀπιστίᾳ συμπεσών, ἔρημος ἐκ τύχης τοσῆσδε καὶ στρατοῦ τοσοῦδε ἐγίγνετο ἐν βρα-
χεῖ. καὶ τὸ σχῆμα ἀλλάξας ἔθει πρὸς τὸν Καίσαρα
523 δρόμῳ, συντρεχόντων ὡς ἐπὶ θέᾳ τῶν ὁρώντων. ὁ δὲ
Καῖσαρ ὑπανέστη τε αὐτῷ προσθέοντι καὶ προσπε-
σεῖν ἐθέλοντα κωλύσας ἔπεμψεν ἐς Ῥώμην, ἐφ᾽ οὗπερ
ἦν σχήματος, ἰδιώτην ἀπ᾽ αὐτοκράτορος, οὐδὲν ἔτι
524 πλὴν ἱερέα ἧς εἶχεν ἱερωσύνης. ὁ μὲν δὴ καὶ αὐτο-
κράτωρ πολλάκις καὶ τῶν τριῶν ἀνδρῶν γενόμενος
ἄρχοντάς τε ἀποφήνας καὶ προγράψας ἐπὶ θανάτῳ
τοσούσδε ὁμοτίμους, ἰδιωτεύων καὶ ἐνίοις τῶν προ-
γραφέντων ἄρχουσιν ὕστερον παριστάμενος διεβί-
ωσε.

525   127. Πομπήιον δὲ ὁ μὲν Καῖσαρ οὐκ ἐδίωκεν οὐδ᾽
ἑτέροις ἐπέτρεπε διώκειν, εἴτε ὡς ἐς ἀλλοτρίαν ἀρχὴν
τὴν Ἀντωνίου φυλασσόμενος ἐμβαλεῖν, εἴτε καραδο-
κῶν τὸ μέλλον καὶ τὰ ἐς αὐτὸν ἐσόμενα ἐξ Ἀντωνίου
καὶ πρόφασιν ἕξων διαφορᾶς, εἰ μὴ δίκαια γίγνοιτο
(οὐ γὰρ ἀνύποπτοί γε ἦσαν ἐκ πολλοῦ διὰ φιλαρχίαν,
ὅτε τοὺς ἄλλους ἐξέλοιεν, ἀλλήλοις διερίσειν), εἴθ᾽, ὡς
αὐτὸς ἔλεγεν ὕστερον ὁ Καῖσαρ, ὅτι μὴ γένοιτο τοῦ
526 πατρὸς ἀνδροφόνος ὁ Πομπήιος. τὴν δὲ στρατιὰν

until one of the standard bearers said he would let go when he was dead. He was frightened by this, and let go.

126. The last to leave were the cavalry, who sent some- 521 one to ask Octavian if they should kill Lepidus, as he was no longer commander in chief. He told them not to. Thus 522 Lepidus, unexpectedly encountering total disobedience, found himself in a short time deprived of such great good fortune and such a mighty army. He changed his clothes and sprinted to Octavian, spectators running along beside him as if they were going at a show. Octavian stood up as 523 Lepidus hurried toward him, prevented him from throwing himself at his feet, although he wanted to, and sent him to Rome in the clothes he was wearing, a private person rather than the commander in chief he had been, of no standing apart from the priesthood he continued to hold. And so this man, who had often commanded armies 524 and as a member of the triumvirate had appointed magistrates and condemned to death so many men of his own rank on the proscription lists, lived the rest of his life as a private citizen, deferring to some of the proscribed who later became magistrates.

127. As for Pompeius, Octavian neither pursued him 525 nor ordered others to do so. This may have been because he was taking care not to encroach on someone else's jurisdiction, that of Antony; or else he was waiting to see what would happen and how Antony would behave toward Pompeius, in order to have an excuse for a dispute if this proved unlawful (for it had long been suspected that because of their love of power Octavian and Antony would quarrel with each other once they had removed the others); or, as Octavian himself said later, it was because Pompeius was not one of his father's murderers. When he 526

συνῆγε, καὶ ἐγένετο αὐτῷ τέλη μὲν ὁπλιτῶν πέντε καὶ
τεσσαράκοντα καὶ ἱππέες δισμύριοι καὶ πεντακισ-
χίλιοι, κοῦφοι δὲ τῶν ἱππέων ὑπὲρ ἡμιολίους μακραί
τε νῆες ἑξακόσιαι· τὸ δὲ τῶν φορτίδων πλῆθος, καί-
527 περ ὂν ἄπειρον, τοῖς δεσπόταις διέπεμπε. καὶ τὸν
στρατὸν ἐπινικίοις ἐδωρεῖτο, τὰ μὲν ἤδη διδούς, τά δὲ
ὑπισχνούμενος, στεφάνους τε καὶ τιμὰς ἅπασιν ἔνε-
μεν καὶ συγγνώμην τοῖς ἡγεμόσιν ἐδίδου τοῦ Πομπηίου.

528   128. Ζήλου δὲ αὐτῷ γέμοντι ἐπὶ τούτοις τὸ δαι-
μόνιον ἐνεμέσησε τοῦ ζήλου, καὶ ὁ στρατὸς ἐστασία-
σεν, ὁ οἰκεῖος αὐτοῦ μάλιστα, ἀπολυθῆναί τε τῆς
στρατείας ἐπειγόμενοι καὶ γέρα λαβεῖν ὅμοια τοῖς ἐν
529 Φιλίπποις ἀγωνισαμένοις. ὁ δὲ ᾔδει μὲν οὐχ ὅμοιον
ἐκείνῳ τόνδε τὸν ἀγῶνα, ὑπισχνεῖτο δ' ὅμως τὰ ἄξια
δώσειν σὺν τοῖς ὑπ' Ἀντωνίῳ στρατευομένοις, ὅτε
κἀκεῖνος ἀφίκηται. περὶ δὲ τῆς ἀστρατείας ὑπεμίμνη-
σκε σὺν ἀπειλῇ τῶν πατρίων νόμων τε καὶ ὅρκων καὶ
530 κολάσεων. οὐκ εὐπειθῶς δὲ ἀκροωμένων ὑφῆκε τῆς
ἀπειλῆς, ἵνα μή τις ἐκ τῶν νεολήπτων στρατῶν ἐπι-
γένοιτο θόρυβος, καὶ ἔλεγεν ἐν καιρῷ τε ἀπολύσειν
σὺν Ἀντωνίῳ, καὶ ἄξειν νῦν οὐκ ἐπ' ἐμφύλια ἔτι, πε-
παυμένα σὺν τύχῃ χρηστῇ, ἐπὶ δ' Ἰλλυριοὺς καὶ
ἕτερα ἔθνη βάρβαρα, σαλεύοντα τὴν μόλις κτηθεῖσαν
531 εἰρήνην, ὅθεν καταπλουτιεῖν αὐτούς. οἱ δ' οὐκ ἔφασαν
αὖθις στρατεύσεσθαι, πρὶν τῶν προτέρων λαβεῖν
γέρα τε καὶ τιμάς. ὁ δὲ οὐκ ἔφη τὰς τιμὰς οὐδὲ νῦν
ἀνατίθεσθαι, πολλὰς δὲ δοὺς προστιθέναι στεφάνους

brought his army together, Octavian had forty-five legions of infantry, twenty five thousand cavalry, half as many more light-armed troops than cavalry, and six hundred warships; and although he had a vast number of merchant vessels, he sent them back to their owners. To the soldiers   527
he awarded payment for their victory, giving some of it now, and promising the rest. He distributed crowns and honors to everyone, and pardoned Pompeius' officers.

128. When he became full of pride at these events, the   528
divinity resented his pride, and his soldiers mutinied, especially his own troops, who demanded to be discharged from service and receive the same privileges as those who fought at Philippi. While Octavian knew that the present   529
war was not like that one, nevertheless he promised to give them what they deserved, along with those serving under Antony, when he too arrived. As for their refusal to serve, he reminded them, in a threatening tone, of their ancestral laws and oaths and punishments. Since they did not listen   530
in a submissive manner, he abandoned his threatening tone to avoid any trouble from the troops he had recently taken over, and said that he would discharge them at the proper time in conjunction with Antony. For the time being, he would lead them not into more civil wars, which had, happily, come to an end, but against the Illyrians and other foreign peoples, who were disturbing the hard-won peace; this would enable him to make the men rich. But   531
they said that they would not serve again until they had received the prizes and honors due from their previous service. Octavian denied that he was postponing the award of honors, even at this moment, but having given many already, said that he would add still more crowns for the

ἔτι τοῖς τέλεσιν ἄλλους καὶ λοχαγοῖς καὶ χιλιάρχοις
περιπορφύρους ἐσθῆτας καὶ βουλευτικὴν ἐν ταῖς πα-
532 τρίσιν ἀξίωσιν. ἔτι δὲ αὐτοῦ τοιάδε προστιθέντος
ἕτερα, ὑπεφώνησε χιλίαρχος Ὀφίλλιος στεφάνους
μὲν καὶ πορφύραν εἶναι παισὶν ἀθύρματα, στρατοῦ δὲ
γέρα χωρία καὶ χρήματα· καὶ τοῦ πλήθους ἐπιβοή-
σαντος, ὅτι ὀρθῶς λέγοι, ὁ μὲν Καῖσαρ ἀπέστη τοῦ
βήματος δυσχεραίνων. οἱ δὲ ἀμφὶ τὸν χιλίαρχον
ἦσαν ἐπαινοῦντές τε καὶ τοῖς οὐ συνισταμένοις αὐτῷ
533 λοιδορούμενοι. ὁ δ' ἔφη καὶ μόνος ἀρκέσειν ἐπὶ οὕτω
δικαίοις. ἀλλ' ὁ μὲν τόδε εἰπὼν ἐς τὴν ἐπιοῦσαν
ἀφανὴς ἦν, καὶ οὐδ', ὅ τι γένοιτο, ἐγινώσκετο.

534   129. Ὁ δὲ στρατὸς οὐκέτι μέν, ὑπὸ δέους, οὐδεὶς
καθ' ἕνα ἐφθέγγετο, κοινῇ δ' ἐβόων, ἀνὰ μέρη συν-
ιστάμενοι, ἀφεθῆναι τῶν στρατειῶν. ὁ δὲ Καῖσαρ
αὐτῶν τοὺς μὲν ἄρχοντας ἐξωμίλει ποικίλως, τῶν δ'
ἐν Φιλίπποις καὶ Μουτίνῃ στρατευσαμένων, ὡς χρο-
νιωτέρων ἄρα ὄντων, ἐδίδου τοῖς θέλουσιν ἀποστρα-
535 τεύεσθαι. καὶ γενομένους ἐς δισμυρίους εὐθὺς ἀπέλυε
καὶ ἐξέπεμπε τῆς νήσου, μὴ διαφθείραιεν ἑτέρους,
τοσόνδε τοῖς ἐκ Μουτίνης μόνοις ἐπειπών, ὅτι σφίσιν
ἀποδώσει τὰ τότε ὑπεσχημένα καίπερ οὕτως ἀπολυ-
536 θεῖσιν. ἐς δὲ τὸ ἄλλο πλῆθος ἐπελθὼν τοὺς μὲν ἀπο-
στάντας ἐμαρτύρετο τῆς ἐπιορκίας, οὐ κατὰ γνώμην
τοῦ αὐτοκράτορος τῆς στρατείας ἀπολυθέντας, τοὺς

---

84 Togas of Roman senators had a broad purple stripe, those
of the equestrian order a narrow one. It seems that Octavian was

legions, and for centurions and military tribunes purple-bordered togas and the rank of senator in their native towns.[84] While he was still distributing other awards of this kind, a military tribune named Ofellius called out in reply that crowns and purple were toys for children, but the privileges due to soldiers were lands and money. The crowd shouted out that what Ofellius said was right, and Octavian angrily stepped down from the tribunal. The men gathered round the tribune, praising him and abusing those who would not stand with him. Ofellius said that he alone would be enough to defend so just a cause, but having made the speech, next day he disappeared, and it was not known what happened.

129. Because they were afraid, the soldiers no longer spoke out individually, but joining together in groups they collectively called for their discharge. Octavian conciliated their leaders in various ways. To those who had served at Philippi and Mutina he granted discharge, for any who wanted it, on the grounds that they had indeed served more than their time. These numbered about two thousand, and he immediately discharged them and sent them off the island, so that they would not subvert the others. He also told only those who were at Mutina that he would give them what had been promised at the time of the campaign, even though they were now being discharged in this way. He then went before the rest of the army and called on them to bear witness that the mutineers had broken their oaths by being discharged from service

offering equestrian status to these officers but without giving them the money (400,000 sesterces) required to automatically qualify for membership of the order.

APPIAN

δὲ παρόντας ἐπῄνει καὶ ἐπήλπιζεν ἀπολύσειν μὲν ταχέως, ὡς μηδενὶ μετανοήσειν,[41] καταπλουτιεῖν δὲ ἀπο-
λύων καὶ νῦν ἐπιδιδόναι δραχμὰς πεντακοσίας ἑκά-
537 στῳ. τοιάδε εἰπὼν Σικελίᾳ μὲν ἐπέβαλλεν ἐσφορὰν
χίλια τάλαντα καὶ ἑξακόσια, στρατηγοὺς δ᾽ ἀπέφαινε
Λιβύης καὶ Σικελίας καὶ στρατὸν ἐς ἑκατέραν διῄρει
καὶ τὰς ναῦς τὰς Ἀντωνίου διέπεμπεν ἐς Τάραντα καὶ
τοῦ λοιποῦ στρατοῦ τὸν μὲν προύπεμπεν ἐς τὴν Ἰταλίαν ἐπὶ νεῶν, τὸν δ᾽ ἐπαγόμενος αὐτὸς ἐκ τῆς νήσου
διεπέρα.

538   130. Ἐρχομένῳ δ᾽ ἥ τε βουλὴ τιμὰς ἐψηφίσατο
ἀμέτρους, ὧν αὐτὸν ἐποίουν κριτήν, ἢ πάσας λαβεῖν
ἢ ὅσας δοκιμάσειε· καὶ ὑπήντων ὅτι πορρωτάτω καὶ
αὐτοὶ καὶ ὁ δῆμος ἐστεφανωμένοι ἔς τε τὰ ἱερὰ καὶ ἐκ
539 τῶν ἱερῶν ἐς τὴν οἰκίαν ἀπιόντα παρέπεμπον. τῆς δ᾽
ἐπιούσης αὐτὸς ἐβουληγόρησέ τε καὶ ἐδημηγόρησε,
τὰ ἔργα καὶ τὴν πολιτείαν ἑαυτοῦ τὴν ἀπ᾽ ἀρχῆς ἐς
τότε καταλέγων· καὶ τὰ εἰρημένα συγγράψας τὸ βι-
540 βλίον ἐξέδωκε. κατήγγελλέ τε εἰρήνην καὶ εὐθυμίαν,
ἐς τέλος τῶν ἐμφυλίων ἀνῃρημένων, καὶ τῶν εἰσφορῶν
τοὺς ἔτι ὀφείλοντας ἀπέλυε καὶ φόρων τελώνας τε καὶ
541 τοὺς τὰ μισθώματα ἔχοντας ὧν ἔτι ὀφείλοιεν. ἐκ δὲ
τῶν ἐψηφισμένων τιμῶν ἐδέχετο πομπήν, ἐτήσιόν τε
ἱερομηνίαν εἶναι, καθ᾽ ἃς ἡμέρας ἐνίκα, καὶ ἐπὶ κίονος

[41] ὡς μηδενὶ μετανοήσειν Viereck; ὅτε μηδενὶ μετανοήσει
codd.

228

against the orders of their commander in chief. He praised those who remained with him, and, to avoid the prospect of anyone changing their mind,[85] encouraged them to hope that he would discharge them soon, saying that when he did so, he would make them rich; for the moment he was giving each man an additional five hundred drachmas. After delivering this speech, Octavian imposed a levy on   537
Sicily of one thousand six hundred talents, appointed governors of Africa and Sicily, allocating troops to each of them, and dispatched Antony's ships to Tarentum. Of his remaining forces, part he embarked on ships and sent ahead to Italy, part he took command of himself and crossed over from the island.

130. While he was on his way to Rome, the senate voted   538
him unlimited honors, leaving him to decide whether to accept them all or just those of which he approved. Wearing garlands, the senators and people went out to meet him at a great distance from the city, and escorted him to the temples and from the temples as he withdrew to his own house. Next day he addressed both the senate and the   539
people, giving a detailed account of his achievements and administration from the beginning to the present time. He wrote down the speeches he had delivered and published them in a pamphlet. He proclaimed Peace and Content-   540
ment, now that the civil wars had finally been brought to an end, and remitted special taxes for those who still owed them, and regular taxes still not paid by the tax collectors and those holding the public contracts. Of the honors   541
voted to him, he accepted an ovation, and annual festival on the anniversary of his victory, and the erection on a

[85] The text is uncertain at this point.

ἐν ἀγορᾷ χρύσεος ἑστάναι μετὰ σχήματος οὗπερ
ἔχων εἰσῆλθε, περικειμένων τῷ κίονι νεῶν ἐμβόλων.
542 καὶ ἕστηκεν ἡ εἰκών, ἐπιγραφὴν ἔχουσα, ὅτι "Τὴν
εἰρήνην ἐστασιασμένην ἐκ πολλοῦ συνέστησε κατά
τε γῆν καὶ θάλασσαν."

543   131. Τοῦ δὲ δήμου τὴν μεγίστην ἱερωσύνην ἐς
αὐτὸν ἐκ Λεπίδου μεταφέροντος, ἣν ἕνα ἔχειν νενόμι-
σται μέχρι θανάτου, οὐκ ἐδέχετο καὶ κτείνειν τὸν Λέ-
544 πιδον ὡς πολέμιον κελευόντων οὐκ ἠνείχετο. ἐς δὲ τὰ
στρατόπεδα πάντα σεσημασμένας ἔπεμψεν ἐπιστο-
λάς, ἐντελλόμενος ἡμέρᾳ μιᾷ πάντας ἀνειλήσαντας
αὐτὰς ἐπιχειρεῖν τοῖς κεκελευσμένοις. καὶ ἦν τὰ ἐπ-
εσταλμένα περὶ τῶν θεραπόντων, ὅσοι παρὰ τὴν στάσιν ἀποδράντες ἐστρατεύοντο, καὶ αὐτοῖς τὴν ἐλευθερίαν ᾔτήκει Πομπήιος, καὶ ἡ βουλὴ καὶ αἱ συνθῆκαι
545 δεδώκεσαν. οἱ δὲ μιᾶς ἡμέρας συνελαμβάνοντο, καὶ
ἀχθέντας αὐτοὺς ἐς Ῥώμην ὁ Καῖσαρ ἀπέδωκεν αὐτῶν τε Ῥωμαίων καὶ Ἰταλῶν τοῖς δεσπόταις ἢ διαδό-
χοις αὐτῶν, ἀπέδωκε δὲ καὶ Σικελιώταις. ὅσους δ' οὐκ
ἦν ὁ ληψόμενος, ἔκτεινε παρὰ ταῖς πόλεσιν αὐταῖς, ὧν
ἀπέδρασεν.

546   132. Τοῦτο μὲν δὴ τῶν τότε στάσεων ἐδόκει τέλος
εἶναι. καὶ ἦν ὁ Καῖσαρ ἐτῶν ἐς τότε ὀκτὼ καὶ εἴκοσι,
καὶ αὐτὸν αἱ πόλεις τοῖς σφετέροις θεοῖς συνίδρυον.
547 ληστευομένης δὲ κατὰ συστάσεις τῆς τε Ῥώμης αὐτῆς καὶ τῆς Ἰταλίας⁴² περιφανῶς καὶ τῶν γιγνομένων
ἁρπαγῇ μετὰ τόλμης ἢ λῃστείᾳ λανθανούσῃ μᾶλλον
ἐοικότων, Σαβῖνος ὑπὸ Καίσαρος αἱρεθεὶς εἰς διόρθω-

column in the Forum of a gilded statue of him in the clothes he wore when he entered the city, with the rams of ships positioned around the column. And the statue was 542 put up, bearing the inscription: "Peace long disturbed by civil discord he restored both on land and sea."

131. When the people wanted to transfer from Lepidus 543 to himself the office of Pontifex Maximus, which it is customary for one person to hold for life, he refused it, and he would not countenance the request to execute Lepidus as a public enemy. He sent sealed letters to all the armies, 544 with instructions that everyone was to open them all on the same day and carry out the orders. These directives related to those slaves who had run away during the civil disorder and joined up as soldiers. Pompeius had asked that they be given their freedom, which both the senate and the terms of the treaty had granted. But they were all 545 arrested on the same day and brought to Rome, where Octavian returned them to their Roman and Italian masters, or their heirs. He also gave back those belonging to Sicilian masters. All those with no one to claim them he executed in the very towns from which they had run away.

132. This seemed, indeed, to mark the end of the civil 546 disturbances of that time, and the towns established a place among their own gods for Octavian, who was now twenty-eight years of age. Since both Rome itself and Italy 547 were being openly raided by groups of bandits, events having the appearance more of brazen pillaging than stealthy burglary, Sabinus was chosen by Octavian to put

---

[42] Ἰταλίας Schweig.; Σικελίας codd.

σιν πολὺν μὲν εἰργάσατο φθόρον τῶν ἁλισκομένων,
ἐνιαυτῷ δ' ὅμως εἰς εἰρήνην ἀφύλακτον ἅπαντα περι-
ήγαγε. καὶ ἐξ ἐκείνου φασὶ παραμεῖναι τὸ τῆς στρα-
548 τιᾶς τῶν νυκτοφυλάκων ἔθος τε καὶ εἶδος. θαυμαζόμε-
νος δὲ ὁ Καῖσαρ ἐπὶ τῷδε ὀξέως οὕτως ἐξ ἀδοκήτου
διωρθωμένῳ πολλὰ τῆς πολιτείας ἐφίει τοῖς ἐτησίοις
ἄρχουσι διοικεῖν κατὰ τὰ πάτρια, καὶ γραμματεῖα,
ὅσα τῆς στάσεως σύμβολα, ἔκαιε, καὶ τὴν ἐντελῆ πολιτείαν ἔλεγεν ἀποδώσειν, εἰ παραγένοιτο ἐκ Παρθυαίων Ἀντώνιος· πείθεσθαι γὰρ κἀκεῖνον ἐθέλειν ἀποθέσθαι τὴν ἀρχήν, τῶν ἐμφυλίων καταπεπαυμένων.
ἐφ' οἷς αὐτὸν εὐφημοῦντες εἵλοντο δήμαρχον ἐς ἀεί,
διηνεκεῖ ἄρα ἀρχῇ προτρέποντες τῆς προτέρας ἀπο-
549 στῆναι. ὁ δὲ ἐδέξατο μὲν καὶ τήνδε, Ἀντωνίῳ δὲ ἐφ'
ἑαυτοῦ περὶ τῆς ἀρχῆς ἐπέστελλεν. ὁ δὲ καὶ Βύβλον
ἀπιόντα πρὸς αὐτὸν ἐντυχεῖν ἐδίδασκεν· ἐς δὲ τὰ ἔθνη
τοὺς ἡγεμόνας αὐτὸς ὁμοίως ἔπεμπε καὶ ἐς Ἰλλυριοὺς
ἐπενόει συστρατεύειν.

550   133. Πομπήιος δ' ἐκ μὲν Σικελίας ἄκρᾳ Λακινίᾳ
προσέσχε καὶ τὸ ἱερὸν τῆς Ἥρας πλουτοῦν ἀναθήμα-
σιν ἐσύλησε, φεύγων ἐς Ἀντώνιον· ἐς δὲ Μιτυλήνην
καταχθεὶς διέτριβεν, ἔνθα αὐτὸν ἔτι παῖδα μετὰ τῆς

---

86 This is probably Gaius Calvisius Calvinus, one of the consuls of 39.   87 The *vigiles* (the watchmen) were officially
instituted by Augustus in AD 6. They were primarily concerned
with fire protection but also functioned as a sort of police force.

88 It is generally thought more likely that, as Dio says

the situation right.[86] Sabinus inflicted extensive slaughter on those he captured, but nevertheless in the space of a year brought secure peace to all parts. It is from this time, they say, that the custom of maintaining a corps of night watchmen, and the form it takes, has persisted.[87] Admired   548 for restoring order so quickly and unexpectedly, Octavian delegated much of the government business to the annual magistrates for them to administer in the traditional manner. He also began to burn all written evidence of the civil discord, and said that he would give up control of the entire governance of the state, when Antony got back from Parthia. For he was convinced that Antony, too, would be willing to lay down his office, now that the civil wars were at an end. The people applauded him for this and chose him tribune for life, no doubt to encourage him with a permanent magistracy to give up his previous one.[88] But   549 he took this one in addition, and wrote himself to Antony about their magistracy. Antony gave instructions to Bibulus, who was leaving him to meet with Octavian, and, like Octavian, he also personally sent out governors to the provinces, while intending to join the campaign against the Illyrians.[89]

133. On leaving Sicily in his flight to Antony, Pompeius   550 landed at the Lacinian promontory and robbed the sanctuary of Hera, which was rich in dedications. He put in at Mytilene and spent some time there: it was here that when

(49.15.5–6), Octavian was given the inviolability (*sacrosanctitas*) rather then the full powers of the tribune at this point.

[89] Appian has already identified Lucius Calpurnius Bibulus, son of Julius Caesar's colleague as consul in 59, as a frequent intermediary between Octavian and Antony: see *BCiv.* 4.38.162.

μητρὸς ὑπεξέθετο ὁ πατήρ, Γαΐῳ Καίσαρι πολεμῶν,
551 καὶ ἡττηθεὶς ἀνέλαβεν. Ἀντωνίου δὲ πολεμοῦντος ἐν
Μηδίᾳ Μήδοις τε καὶ Παρθναίοις, γνώμην ὁ Πομπήιος ἐποιεῖτο ἑαυτὸν ἐπανελθόντι ἐπιτρέψαι. ἐπεὶ δ᾽
ἐπύθετο ἡσσῆσθαι Ἀντώνιον καὶ τὸ συμβὰν ἡ φήμη
μειζόνως μετέφερεν, αὖθις ἦν ἐν ἐλπίσιν ὡς ἢ διαδε-
ξόμενος Ἀντώνιον, εἰ τέθνηκεν, ἢ μεριούμενος ἐπανελ-
θόντι· ἐνθύμιός τέ οἱ συνεχὲς ἦν Λαβιηνὸς οὐ πρὸ
552 πολλοῦ τὴν Ἀσίαν ἐπιδραμών. ὧδε δὲ ἔχοντι ἀγγέλλεται Ἀντώνιος εἰς Ἀλεξάνδρειαν ἐπανελθών. καὶ τεχνάζων ἔτι ἐπ᾽ ἀμφότερα διεπρεσβεύετο πρὸς ⟨Ἀντώ-
νιον⟩, αὐτόν[43] ἐπιτρέπων ἐκείνῳ καὶ φίλον εἶναι διδοὺς
καὶ σύμμαχος, ἔργῳ δὲ τὰ Ἀντωνίου κατασκεπτόμε-
553 νος. ἔς τε Θρᾴκην καὶ ἐς τὸν Πόντον ἔπεμπεν ἑτέρους
κρύφα πρὸς τοὺς ἑκατέρων δυνάστας ἐπινοῶν, εἰ μὴ
κρατεῖ τῶν ἐνθυμουμένων, διὰ τοῦ Πόντου φυγεῖν ἐς
554 Ἀρμενίαν. ἔπεμπε δὲ καὶ ἐς Παρθναίους, ἐλπίσας ἐς
τὰ λοιπὰ τοῦ πολέμου τοῦ πρὸς Ἀντώνιον αὐτοὺς δέ-
ξεσθαι προθύμως στρατηγὸν Ῥωμαῖόν τε καὶ παῖδα
Μάγνου μάλιστα. τάς τε ναῦς ἐπεσκεύαζε καὶ τὸν ἐν
αὐταῖς στρατὸν ἐγύμναζεν, ὑποκρινόμενος ἢ δεδιέναι
Καίσαρα ἢ Ἀντωνίῳ τάδε παρασκευάζειν.
555   134. Ὁ δὲ Ἀντώνιος πυθόμενος μὲν εὐθὺς ἀμφὶ
τοῦ Πομπηίου, στρατηγὸν ἐπ᾽ αὐτῷ Τίτιον ᾕρητο καὶ

[43] πρὸς Ἀντώνιον, αὐτόν Étienne-Duplessis; πρὸς αὐτόν
codd.

he was still a boy, his father, while at war with Gaius Caesar, had left him for safety with his mother, and had collected him after being defeated.[90] As Antony was waging   551
war in Media against the Medes and the Parthians, Pompeius decided to hand himself over to him on his return. But when he heard that Antony had been defeated—and rumor exaggerated what had happened—his hopes once more revived, either of succeeding Antony, if he was dead, or of sharing power with him when he returned; and Labienus, who had overrun Asia not long before, was constantly on his mind.[91] Such was his state of mind when he   552
is given the news that Antony had returned to Alexandria. Continuing to entertain both schemes, he sent a deputation to Antony, handing himself over and giving the impression that he was a friend and ally, when in reality he was spying on Antony's affairs. He sent other envoys se-   553
cretly to Thrace and Pontus, to the rulers of both countries, with the intention of escaping to Armenia through Pontus, if he failed to achieve his plans. He also sent a   554
mission to the Parthians, in the hope that for the rest of their war against Antony they would enthusiastically welcome a Roman general, especially a son of Pompey the Great. He refitted his ships and drilled the soldiers on board, pretending either to be afraid of Octavian, or to be making these preparations for Antony.

134. Immediately on hearing the news about Pompeius, Antony appointed Titius as general to oppose him,   555

[90] Plutarch (*Pomp.* 74.1) and other sources indicate that it was his stepmother, Cornelia, not his mother, Mucia, who was with the young Pompeius in Mytilene.

[91] On Quintus Labienus, see above, 65.276 with note 50.

ναῦς καὶ στρατὸν ἐκ Συρίας λαβόντα ἐκέλευε πολεμοῦντι μὲν τῷ Πομπηίῳ πολεμεῖν κατὰ κράτος, ἐπι-
556 τρέποντα δὲ αὐτὸν Ἀντωνίῳ μετὰ τιμῆς ἄγειν. ἐλθοῦσι δὲ τοῖς πρέσβεσιν ἐχρημάτιζεν, ἀγγέλλουσιν
οὕτως· "Ἡμᾶς Πομπήιος ἔπεμψεν οὐκ ἀπορῶν μὲν ἐς
Ἰβηρίαν, εἰ πολεμεῖν ἐγνώκει, διαπλεῦσαι, φίλην οὖσαν αὐτῷ πατρόθεν καὶ συλλαβοῦσαν ἔτι ὄντι νεω-
τέρῳ καὶ καλοῦσαν ἐπὶ ταῦτα καὶ νῦν, αἱρούμενος δὲ
εἰρηνεύειν τε σὺν σοὶ καὶ πολεμεῖν, εἰ δεήσειεν, ὑπὸ
557 σοί. καὶ τάδε οὐ νῦν πρῶτον, ἀλλ' ἔτι κρατῶν Σικελίας καὶ τὴν Ἰταλίαν πορθῶν, ὅτε σοι τὴν σὴν μη-
558 τέρα περισώσας ἔπεμπε, προύτεινε. καὶ εἰ ἐδέξω, οὔτ'
ἂν ὁ Πομπήιος ἐξέπεσε Σικελίας (οὐ γὰρ ἂν Καίσαρι
τὰς ναῦς κατ' αὐτοῦ παρέσχες), οὔτ' ἂν σὺ ἥττησο ἐν
Παρθυαίοις, Καίσαρός σοι τὸν στρατὸν οὐ πέμψαν-
τος, ὃν συνέθετο· ἐκράτεις δ' ἂν ἤδη πρὸς οἷς εἶχες
559 καὶ τῆς Ἰταλίας. οὐ δεξάμενον δέ σε ταῦτα, ἐν καιρῷ
τότε μάλιστ' ἄν σοι γενόμενα, ἀξιοῖ καὶ νῦν μὴ πολλάκις ὑπὸ Καίσαρος ἐνεδρευθῆναι λόγοις τε καὶ τῷ
γενομένῳ κήδει, μνημονεύοντα, ὅτι Πομπηίῳ τε κη-
δεύων μετὰ συνθήκας ἐπολέμησεν ἄνευ προφάσεως,
καὶ Λέπιδον κοινωνὸν ὄντα τῆς ἀρχῆς τὸ μέρος
ἀφείλετο καὶ οὐδέτερα αὐτῶν ἐνείματό σοι.

---

92 Marcus Titius (suffect consul 31) had a long career, first as
a supporter of Marc Antony, whom he abandoned before the
battle of Actium, and then with Octavian/Augustus. He gave the
order for the execution of Sextus Pompeius (although perhaps on
Antony's instructions).

and ordered him to get ships and troops from Syria, and to make war with all his might if Pompeius made war, and to treat him with honor if Pompeius surrendered himself to Antony.[92] When a delegation arrived from Pompeius, Antony gave them an audience at which they deliver the following message: "Pompeius sent us at a time when, if he had decided to wage war, he was not lacking the opportunity to sail to Iberia, which is well disposed to him in memory of his father, assisted him when he was still young, and even now extends the invitation to go there. He prefers, however, to be at peace with you, or, if it should prove necessary, wage war under your command. The present occasion is not the first time he has made this proposition. He did so when he was still in control of Sicily and ravaging Italy, and sent your mother to you after saving her life. If you had accepted, Pompeius would not have been driven out of Sicily (for you would not have provided Octavian with the ships to use against him), nor would you have been defeated in Parthia as a result of Octavian failing to send you the troops as agreed; and you would now be master of Italy in addition to what you already held. Although you did not accept this offer, made at what would have been a particularly opportune moment for you, Pompeius now asks you not to be repeatedly trapped by Octavian's words and by the marriage connection you made with him, but to remember that, in spite of being connected to Pompeius by marriage and of having an agreement with him, Octavian attacked him without pretext, and also deprived Lepidus, who was his partner, of his share of power, and divided the benefits of neither action with you.

556

557

558

559

560   135. "Λοιπὸς δ' ἐς τὴν περιπόθητον αὐτῷ μοναρχίαν σὺ νῦν ὑπολείπῃ· ἤδη γάρ σοι καὶ ἐν χερσὶν ἦν,
561 εἰ μὴ Πομπήιος ἔτι ἦν ἐν μέσῳ. καὶ τάδε εἰκὸς μὲν
καὶ σὲ προορᾶν ἐπὶ σεαυτοῦ, προφέρει δέ σοι καὶ
Πομπήιος ὑπὸ εὐνοίας, αἱρούμενος ἄνδρα ἄκακον καὶ
μεγαλόφρονα ἀντὶ ὑπούλου τε καὶ δολεροῦ καὶ φιλο-
562 τέχνου. οὐδὲ ἐπιμέμφεταί σοι τῆς δόσεως τῶν νεῶν,
ἃς ἐπ' αὐτὸν Καίσαρι ἔδωκας ὑπ' ἀνάγκης, ἀντιλα-
βεῖν στρατὸν ἐς Παρθυαίους δεόμενος, ἀλλ' ὑπο-
μιμνήσκει, τὸν οὐ πεμφθέντα στρατὸν προφέρων.
563 συνελόντι δὲ εἰπεῖν, Πομπήιος ἑαυτὸν ἐπιτρέπει σοι
μετὰ τῶν νεῶν, ἃς ἔτι ἔχει, καὶ τοῦ στρατοῦ, πιστο-
τάτου γε ὄντος αὐτῷ καὶ οὐδ' ἐν τῇ φυγῇ καταλιπόν-
τος, εἰρηνεύοντι μὲν μέγα κλέος, εἰ τὸν Μάγνου παῖδα
περισῴζοις, πολεμοῦντι δὲ μοῖραν ἱκανὴν ἐς τὸν ἐσόμενον πόλεμον, ὅσον οὔπω παρόντα."

564   136. Τοιαῦτα τῶν πρέσβεων εἰπόντων, ὁ Ἀντώνιος
τὰς ἐντολὰς αὐτοῖς ἐξέφερεν, ἃς ἐντείλαιτο Τιτίῳ· καὶ
εἰ τῷ ὄντι ταῦτα φρονοίη Πομπήιος, ἥξειν αὐτὸν ἔφα-
565 σκεν παραπεμπόμενον ὑπὸ Τιτίου. ἅμα δὲ ταῦτα ἐγίγνετο, καὶ οἱ πεμφθέντες ἐς Παρθυαίους ὑπὸ τοῦ Πομπήιου ἐλήφθησαν ὑπὸ τῶν Ἀντωνίου στρατηγῶν καὶ
ἐς Ἀλεξάνδρειαν ἤχθησαν. καὶ ὁ Ἀντώνιος ἕκαστα
μαθὼν ἐκάλει τοὺς τοῦ Πομπήιου πρέσβεις καὶ τοὺς
566 ληφθέντας αὐτοῖς ὑπεδείκνυεν. οἱ δὲ καὶ ὡς παρῃ-
τοῦντο νέον ἄνδρα ἐν συμφοραῖς ἐσχάταις ὑπὸ δέους,
εἰ ἄρα μὴ προσοῖτο φιλίως αὐτὸν ὁ Ἀντώνιος, ἀναγ-
κασθέντα καὶ τῶν ἀεὶ Ῥωμαίοις ἐχθίστων ἀποπειρᾶ-

135 "You are now the only one left standing between 560
him and the monarchy he so ardently desires: indeed he
would already have been at blows with you, if Pompeius
were not still in the way. You can probably foresee these 561
things for yourself, but Pompeius also draws them to your
attention out of goodwill, because he prefers a guileless
and magnanimous man to an insincere and treacherous
and scheming one. Nor does he blame you for the gift of 562
the ships to be used against Pompeius which you made to
Octavian under force of necessity because you needed to
exchange them for troops to attack the Parthians, but he
mentions it to highlight the fact that the troops were not
sent. To summarize, Pompeius is entrusting himself to you 563
along with the ships still in his possession and with his
army, which is totally loyal to him and did not abandon
him even in his flight. If you keep the peace, you will get
great credit for saving the son of Pompey the Great; and
if you wage war, you will acquire a substantial resource for
the coming war, which has all but started."

136. When the ambassadors had finished this speech, 564
Antony disclosed to them the orders he had given to Titius, and said that if these were really Pompeius' intentions, he would come in person escorted by Titius. While 565
this was happening, the messengers sent by Pompeius to
the Parthians were captured by Antony's commanders and
brought to Alexandria. After he had heard everything,
Antony summoned Pompeius' envoys and showed them
the captured men. Even in this situation, they begged 566
forgiveness for a young man in a desperate crisis, forced
by fear that Antony would not treat him in a friendly fashion into making approaches even to those who had always
been Rome's deadliest enemies. They said that as soon as

239

σαι· δηλώσειν τ' αὐτὸν αὐτίκα, ὅτε μάθοι τὰ Ἀντωνίου,
μηδὲν ἔτι πείρας ἢ μηχανῆς δεόμενον. οἷς ὁ Ἀντώνιος
ἐπίστευσεν, ὢν καὶ τὰ ἄλλα αἰεὶ τὸ φρόνημα ἁπλοῦς
καὶ μέγας καὶ ἄκακος.

567   137. Ἐν τούτῳ δὲ Φούρνιος, ὁ τῆς Ἀσίας ἡγούμενος
Ἀντωνίῳ, τὸν Πομπήιον ἐλθόντα μὲν καὶ ἀτρεμοῦντα
ἐδέχετο, οὔτε κωλύειν ἀξιόμαχος ὢν οὔτε πω τὴν γνώμην εἰδὼς τὴν Ἀντωνίου· γυμνάζοντα δὲ τὸν στρατὸν
ὁρῶν κατέλεγέ τινας ἐκ τῶν ὑπηκόων καὶ Ἀηνόβαρβον ἄρχοντα γείτονος στρατοῦ καὶ Ἀμύνταν ἑτέρωθεν
568   ἐκάλει κατὰ σπουδήν. συνελθόντων δ' ὀξέως, ὁ Πομπήιος ἐμέμφετο, εἰ πολέμιον ἡγοῦνται τὸν πρέσβεις
ἐς Ἀντώνιον ἀπεσταλκότα καὶ τὰ παρ' ἐκείνου περι-
μένοντα. καὶ ταῦτα λέγων Ἀηνόβαρβον ὅμως ἐπενόει
συλλαβεῖν ἐκ προδοσίας Κουρίου τινὸς τῶν ἀμφὶ τὸν
Ἀηνόβαρβον, ἐλπίζων ἐς ἀντίδοσιν αὐτοῦ μεγάλην
569   ἕξειν μοῖραν Ἀηνόβαρβον. γνωσθείσης δ' οὖν τῆς
προδοσίας, Κούριος μὲν ἐν τοῖς παροῦσι Ῥωμαίων
ἐλεγχθεὶς ἀπέθανε, Πομπήιος δὲ Θεόδωρον ἐξελεύθε-
ρον, ὃς μόνος οἱ συνῄδει τὸ βούλευμα, ὡς ἐξειπόντα
570   ἔκτεινεν. οὐκέτι δὲ τοὺς ἀμφὶ τὸν Φούρνιον λήσειν
ἐλπίσας, Λάμψακον ἐκ προδοσίας κατέλαβεν, ἣ πολλοὺς εἶχεν Ἰταλοὺς ἐξ ἐποικίσεως Γαΐου Καίσαρος,
καὶ μισθοῖς μεγάλοις εὐθὺς ἐστράτευε τοὺς Ἰταλούς.
571   ἤδη δὲ ἔχων ἱππέας τε διακοσίους καὶ πεζοὺς τρία

---

93 For Gaius Furnius, see above, 30.116 with note 28.
94 Gnaeus Domitius Ahenobarbus (consul 32) was governor

he learned Antony's intentions, he would demonstrate that he had no further need of trial or stratagem. Antony believed them, since he was at all times and in all respects a man of uncomplicated and magnanimous and guileless character.

137. In the meantime, Furnius, who was governing the province of Asia for Antony, received Pompeius, as he caused no trouble when he arrived, and Furnius neither had sufficient strength to keep him out, nor yet knew what Antony had decided.[93] But when he saw Pompeius drilling his troops, he enrolled some of his provincial subjects, and urgently summoned Ahenobarbus, who commanded a neighboring army, and from the other direction, Amyntas.[94] They came quickly, but Pompeius complained that they were treating him as an enemy, although he had sent a mission to Antony and was waiting to hear back from him. Even as he was saying this, he was planning to grab Ahenobarbus through the treachery of a certain Curius, one of Ahenobarbus' entourage, in the hope that Ahenobarbus would prove a valuable asset in exchange for himself. In fact, the treachery was discovered, and Curius was convicted before the Romans present and put to death, while Pompeius executed his freedman, Theodorus, for revealing the plan, to which he alone was privy. No longer expecting to keep his intentions secret from Furnius and his staff, Pompeius captured Lampsacus by treachery. The town contained many Italians since the time of Gaius Caesar's colonial settlement, and he immediately enlisted these Italians on high wages. As he now had two hundred

567

568

569

570

571

of Pontus and Bithynia; for Amyntas, king of the region that on his death became the province of Galatia, see above, note 58.

τέλη, ἐπεχείρησε Κυζίκῳ κατά τε γῆν καὶ διὰ θαλάσσης. οἱ δὲ αὐτὸν ἑκατέρωθεν ἀπεκρούσαντο· καὶ γάρ
τις ἦν ἐν τῇ Κυζίκῳ στρατὸς οὐ πολὺς Ἀντωνίῳ,
φύλακες τῶν ἐκεῖ τρεφομένων αὐτῷ μονομάχων. ἐς δὲ
τὸν Ἀχαιῶν λιμένα ἐπανελθὼν ἐσιτολόγει.

572   138. Φουρνίου δὲ οὐκ ἄρχοντος μὲν χειρῶν, ἀεὶ δ᾽
αὐτῷ παραστρατοπεδεύοντος σὺν ἱππεῦσι πολλοῖς
καὶ σιτολογεῖν οὐκ ἐῶντος οὐδὲ προσποιεῖσθαι τὰς
πόλεις, ὁ Πομπήιος ἱππέας οὐκ ἔχων ἐπεχείρησε τῷ
τοῦ Φουρνίου στρατοπέδῳ κατὰ μέτωπον καὶ κατόπιν
573   ἐκ περιόδου λαθών. ὅθεν ὁ Φούρνιος ἐς τὸν Πομπήιον
ἐπεστραμμένος ὑπὸ τῶν ὄπισθεν ἐξεβλήθη τοῦ στρατοπέδου. καὶ φεύγοντας αὐτοὺς διὰ τοῦ Σκαμανδρίου
πεδίου διώκων ὁ Πομπήιος ἔκτεινε πολλούς· καὶ γὰρ
574   ἦν τὸ πεδίον ὑγρὸν ἐξ ὄμβρων. οἱ δὲ περισωθέντες
τότε μὲν ὑπεχώρουν, οὐκ ὄντες ἀξιόμαχοι. προσδεχο-
μένων <. . .>[44] δὲ ἀπό τε Μυσίας καὶ τῆς Προποντίδος
καὶ ἑτέρωθεν, οἱ πενόμενοι διὰ τὰς συνεχεῖς εἰσφορὰς
ἐμισθοφόρουν ἀσμένως τῷ Πομπηίῳ κατὰ δόξαν
575   μάλιστα τῆς ἐν Ἀχαιῶν λιμένι γενομένης νίκης. ἱπ-
πικοῦ δ᾽ ἀπορῶν ὁ Πομπήιος, καὶ παρ᾽ αὐτὸ βλαπτό-
μενος ἐν ταῖς προνομαῖς, ἐπύθετο ἴλην ἱππέων Ἰταλι-
κὴν ἐς Ἀντώνιον χωρεῖν, ὑπὸ Ὀκταουίας χειμεριζούσης
ἐν Ἀθήναις ἀπεσταλμένην· καὶ εὐθὺς ἔπεμπέ τινας ἐς
διαφθορὰν τῆς ἴλης μετὰ χρυσίου. ἀλλὰ τούσδε μὲν

----

[44] Lacunam indicavi; alii alia prop.

cavalry and three legions of infantry, he attacked Cyzicus by land and sea, but the inhabitants repulsed him on both fronts, because Antony had a small force in Cyzicus guarding the gladiators who were being looked after there for him. Pompeius retired to the Harbor of the Achaeans and collected provisions.[95]

138. Furnius refused to initiate combat, but by continually stationing a large body of cavalry beside Pompeius, he prevented him from foraging or winning the towns to his cause. Pompeius had no cavalry, so he made a frontal assault on the camp of Furnius, and a secret one from the rear after circling around. As a result, Furnius, who was facing Pompeius, was driven out of his camp by those attacking from the rear. Pompeius pursued his men, and killed many of them, as they fled across the plain of the Scamander, which was waterlogged after rain. The survivors withdrew for the time being, as they were not combat fit. Although ⟨help?⟩ was expected[96] from Mysia, the Propontis, and elsewhere, the inhabitants, impoverished by the constant exactions, gladly signed up with Pompeius as mercenaries, particularly because of the reputation he gained for the victory achieved at the Harbor of the Achaeans. But in lacking cavalry Pompeius was consequently hampered in foraging. So, when he heard that a troop of Italian horse was making its way to Antony, dispatched by Octavia who was spending the winter in Athens, he immediately sent some men with gold to bribe

572

573

574

575

95 The Harbor of the Achaeans was named from the Homeric story of the Greek siege of Troy. Its exact location near Troy is not known.

96 The text is unsatisfactory at this point, and the meaning is not clear. It is tempting to think that something is missing.

ὁ τῆς Μακεδονίας ἡγούμενος Ἀντωνίῳ συνέλαβε καὶ
τὸ χρυσίον τοῖς ἱππεῦσι διένειμεν·

576   139. Ὁ δὲ Πομπήιος Νίκαιάν τε καὶ Νικομήδειαν
καταλαβὼν ἐχρηματίζετο λαμπρῶς, καὶ ἐς μεγάλα
577   ταχέως αὐτῷ πάντα ηὔξετο παρ' ἐλπίδα. Φουρνίῳ δὲ
οὐ μακρὰν παραστρατοπεδεύοντι πρῶται μὲν ἧκον ἐκ
Σικελίας, ἦρος ἀρχομένου, νῆες ἑβδομήκοντα, ὅσαι
περιεσώθησαν ἐξ ὧν Ἀντώνιος ἐκεχρήκει κατὰ Πομπηίου Καίσαρι (μετὰ γὰρ τὸ Σικελικὸν ἔργον αὐτὰς
ὁ Καῖσαρ ἀπέλυσεν), ἧκεν δὲ καὶ ἐκ Συρίας Τίτιος
ἑτέραις ἑκατὸν εἴκοσι ναυσὶ καὶ στρατῷ πολλῷ, καὶ
578   κατῆραν ἅπαντες ἐς Προκόννησον. δείσας οὖν ὁ Πομπήιος τὰς ναῦς ἐνέπρησε καὶ τοὺς ἐρέτας ὥπλισεν, ὡς
579   ἄμεινον ὁμοῦ πᾶσι κατὰ τὴν γῆν συνοισόμενος. Κάσσιος δὲ ὁ Παρμήσιος καὶ Νασίδιος καὶ Σατορνῖνος
καὶ Θέρμος καὶ Ἀντίστιος ὅσοι τε ἄλλοι τῶν ἀξιολό-
γων ἔτι τῷ Πομπηίῳ παρῆσαν φίλοι, καὶ ὁ τιμιώτα-
τος αὐτῷ Φάννιος καὶ ὁ κηδεστὴς αὐτοῦ Πομπηίου
Λίβων ὡς εἶδον αὐτὸν οὐδὲ Τιτίου παρόντος, ὅτῳ τὰ
περὶ αὐτὸν Ἀντώνιος ἐπιτρέπει, παυόμενον τοῦ πρὸς
τὸν ἀμείνονα πολέμου, ἀπέγνωσαν αὐτοῦ καὶ πράξαν-
τες ὑπὲρ ἑαυτῶν πίστιν ἐς Ἀντώνιον μετῆλθον.

---

97 For Cassius of Parma, see above, 2.4 with note 1. Coins
establish that Quintus Nasidius held a naval command for Sextus
Pompeius. For Saturninus and Libo, see above, 52.217 with note
40. Quintus Minucius Thermus, an honest man according to Cicero (*Att.* 11.1.2, 2.3), was governor of Asia in 51/50, sided with
Pompey against Julius Caesar, was reconciled with him after

the squadron. But Antony's governor of Macedonia caught these men and divided up their gold among the horsemen.

139. Having captured Nicea and Nicomedia, however, 576 Pompeius got dazzling amounts of money, and contrary to expectations, his whole situation improved greatly and fast. But for the benefit of Furnius, who was camped not 577 far away, first there arrived from Sicily at the beginning of spring the seventy ships that had been saved from the ones Antony had lent Octavian to use against Pompeius (for after the war in Sicily Octavian had released them); then Titius arrived from Syria with one hundred and twenty additional ships and a large army; and they all landed at Proconnesus. Alarmed at this, Pompeius burned his ships 578 and armed his rowers, in the belief that it would turn out better if they were all together on land. Cassius of Parma 579 and Nasidius and Saturninus and Thermus and Antistius and all the other distinguished men who still supported Pompeius, including his most valued associate, Fannius, and Pompeius' father-in-law, Libo, when they saw that, even after the arrival of Titius, to whom Antony entrusts the job of dealing with Pompeius, he did not desist from fighting against superior forces, they despaired of him, and, after arranging a guarantee for themselves, went over to Antony's side.[97]

Pharsalus, but was proscribed in 43. A certain Gaius Antistius Reginus served as one of Julius Caesar's legates in Gaul in 53, and Appian (*BCiv.* 4.40.168) mentions a Reginus among the proscribed: it is not clear whether they are all the same man. Gaius Fannius (praetor before 54) supported Pompey against Julius Caesar, governed Asia, and took refuge with Sextus Pompeius in 43 (*BCiv.* 4.84.354).

580 140. Ὁ δ' ἔρημος ὢν ἤδη φίλων ἐς τὰ μεσόγαια
τῆς Βιθυνίας ἀνεχώρει, λεγόμενος ἐς Ἀρμενίους ἐπείγεσθαι. καὶ αὐτόν, νυκτὸς ἀναζεύξαντα ἀφανῶς, ἐδίωκεν ὅ τε Φούρνιος καὶ ὁ Τίτιος, καὶ ἐπ' ἐκείνοις Ἀμύν-
581 τας. συντόνῳ δὲ δρόμῳ περὶ ἑσπέραν καταλαβόντες
ἐστρατοπέδευσαν ἕκαστος ἐφ' ἑαυτοῦ περὶ λόφῳ τινί,
ἄνευ τάφρου καὶ χάρακος, ὡς ἐν ἑσπέρᾳ καὶ κόπῳ.
582 ὧδε δὲ αὐτοῖς ἔχουσιν ὁ Πομπήιος νυκτὸς ἐπέθετο
πελτασταῖς τρισχιλίοις καὶ πολλοὺς ἔκτεινεν εὐναζο-
μένους ἔτι καὶ ἀναπηδῶντας· οἱ δὲ καὶ γυμνοὶ πάμπαν
583 αἰσχρῶς ἔφευγον. καὶ δοκεῖ τότε ὁ Πομπήιος ἅπαντι
τῷ στρατῷ νυκτὸς ἐπελθὼν ἢ τῆς γε τροπῆς γενομένης ἐπαγαγὼν τάχ' ἂν αὐτῶν ἐντελῶς ἐπικρατῆσαι.
νῦν δ' ὁ μὲν καὶ ταῦτα θεοῦ βλάπτοντος ὑπερεῖδε καὶ
οὐδὲν ἐπ' ἔργῳ τοιῷδε πλέον ἢ αὖθις ἐς τὸ μεσόγαιον
584 ἐχώρει· οἱ δ' ἁλισθέντες εἵποντο καὶ σιτολογοῦντα
ἠνώχλουν, ἕως κινδυνεύων ὑπὸ τῆς ἀπορίας ἠξίωσεν
ἐς λόγους ἐλθεῖν Φουρνίῳ, φίλῳ τε Μάγνου γεγενο-
μένῳ καὶ ἀξιώσει προύχοντι τῶν ἄλλων καὶ βεβαιο-
τέρῳ τὸν τρόπον.

585 141. Ποταμὸν δ' ἐν μέσῳ λαβὼν ἔλεγε μέν, ὅτι
πρεσβεύσαιτο πρὸς Ἀντώνιον, ἐπετίθει δ', ὅτι τροφῶν
ἐν τοσούτῳ δεόμενος καὶ ἀμελούμενος ὑπὸ αὐτῶν,
586 τάδε ἐργάσαιτο. "Ὑμεῖς δὲ εἰ μὲν Ἀντωνίου γνώμῃ
πολεμεῖτέ μοι, κακῶς ὁ Ἀντώνιος ὑπὲρ ἑαυτοῦ βου-
λεύεται, τὸν ἐπιόντα πόλεμον οὐ προορῶν· εἰ δὲ τὴν
Ἀντωίου γνώμην φθάνετε, μαρτύρομαι καὶ παρακαλῶ

140. Now without supporters, Pompeius withdrew into 580
the interior of Bithynia, and was said to be pressing on for
Armenia. He broke camp at night without being seen, but
Furnius and Titius set off in pursuit, and Amyntas as well.
Toward evening they caught up with him after an unre- 581
lenting chase, and encamped near a hill, each on his own,
without ditch or palisade, because it was evening and they
were exhausted. While they were in this state, Pompeius 582
made a night attack on them with three thousand light-
armed troops, and killed many who were still asleep or
jumping up from their sleeping place. Others even ran
away, in a completely disgraceful manner, without their
weapons. And it seems that, if on this occasion Pompeius 583
had made a night attack with his whole army, or had at
least followed up the rout that took place, he would perhaps have been completely victorious over them. But as it
was, a divinity led him astray, and he scorned this opportunity too, achieving nothing more from such a success
than a resumption of his advance into the interior. His 584
enemies, having regrouped, followed him and harried his
foraging expeditions, until, under threat from lack of supplies, he asked to enter discussions with Furnius, who had
been an associate of Pompey the Great, and was of higher
rank and more reliable character than the others.

141. Taking up position with a river between them, 585
Pompeius said that he had sent an embassy to Antony,
adding that, because he needed provisions in the meantime, and was receiving no help from them, he had acted
in the way he had. "If you are fighting me in accordance 586
with the decision of Antony, then in failing to foresee the
coming war, Antony is making a poor job of consulting his
own interests. If, on the other hand, you are anticipating

247

περιμεῖναι τὴν πρεσβείαν μου τὴν ἐς Ἀντώνιον ἀπ-
εσταλμένην ἢ λαβόντας ἄγειν ἤδη πρὸς αὐτόν. ἐπι-
τρέψω δ' ἐμαυτὸν ἐγὼ σοὶ μόνῳ, Φούρνιε, τοσοῦτον
ἐς πίστιν αἰτήσας, ὅτι με σῶον ἄξεις ἐς Ἀντώνιον."

587 ὁ μὲν οὕτως εἶπεν, Ἀντωνίῳ τε θαρρῶν ὡς ἀγαθῷ τὴν
φύσιν καὶ μόνα τὰ ἐν μέσῳ δεδιώς· ὁ δὲ Φούρνιος
αὐτὸν οὕτως ἠμείψατο· "Ἐπιτρέποντος μὲν ἦν ἑαυτὸν
Ἀντωνίῳ χωρεῖν ἐς αὐτὸν ἐξ ἀρχῆς ἢ περιμένειν ἀτρεμοῦντα ἐν Μιτυλήνῃ τὰς ἀποκρίσεις, πολεμοῦντος δέ,
ἃ πεποίηκας ἅπαντα· τί γὰρ αὐτὰ δεῖ πρὸς εἰδότα

588 λέγειν; εἰ δὲ νῦν μετέγνωκας, μὴ συγκρούειν μὲν ἡμᾶς
τοὺς στρατηγοὺς ἐς ἀλλήλους, Τιτίῳ δὲ σαυτὸν
ἐπιτρέπειν· Τιτίῳ γὰρ ἐπιτέτραπται τὰ περὶ σὲ ὑπὸ
Ἀντωνίου· καὶ πίστιν, ἣν αἰτεῖς παρ' ἡμῶν, ἔνι σοι
καὶ Τίτιον αἰτεῖν. κεκέλευσται δ' ὑπὸ Ἀντωνίου πολεμοῦντα μέν σε κατακανεῖν, ἐγχειρίζοντα δὲ πέμπειν
ἐς αὐτὸν ἐντίμως."

589   142. Ὁ δὲ Πομπήιος Τιτίῳ μὲν ἀχαριστίας ὠργί-
ζετο, τὸν πόλεμον τόνδε ὑποδεξαμένῳ πολεμήσειν
πρὸς αὐτόν· ἁλόντα γὰρ αὐτὸν αἰχμάλωτον περισε-

590 σώκει. ἐπὶ δὲ τῇ ὀργῇ καὶ ἠδόξει, Πομπήιος ὤν, ἐπὶ
Τιτίῳ γενέσθαι, οὐκ ἐπιφανεῖ πάνυ ἀνδρί, καὶ ὑπώ-
πτευεν αὐτὸν ὡς οὐ βέβαιον ἔς τε τὸν τρόπον ὑπονοῶν καί τινα συγγινώσκων ἐς αὐτὸν ὕβριν παλαιὰν

591 πρὸ τῆς εὐεργεσίας. Φουρνίῳ δ' αὖθις ἑαυτὸν ἐπέτρεπε
καὶ δέξασθαι παρεκάλει. ὡς δ' οὐκ ἔπειθεν, ὁ δὲ καὶ
Ἀμύντᾳ ἔλεγεν ἑαυτὸν ἐπιτρέψειν. τοῦ Φουρνίου δὲ
φήσαντος οὐδ' Ἀμύνταν ἂν δέξασθαι τόδε ὕβριν ἔχον

Antony's decision, then I protest and implore you to wait for the embassy I sent to Antony; or apprehend me and bring me to him now. I will surrender myself to you alone, Furnius, asking only for your assurance that you will conduct me to Antony in safety." Pompeius spoke in these 587 terms because he had confidence in Antony as a man of good nature, and he was afraid only of what would happen in the meantime. Furnius replied to him as follows: "A man intending to hand himself over to Antony would have gone to him at the very beginning, or waited calmly in Mytilene for his answer; a man intending to make war would have done exactly what you have done. Why do you find it necessary to tell me what I already know? But if you 588 have now changed your mind, don't set us generals against each other, just surrender to Titius. For he was the one given the task of dealing with you by Antony. And the assurance you ask of me, you can also ask of Titius. His orders from Antony were to kill you if you made war, but if you place yourself in his hands to send you to him with honor."

142. Pompeius was angry with Titius for his ingratitude 589 in undertaking to fight this war against him, for he had saved his life when he had been taken prisoner. As well as 590 being angry, he considered it beneath his dignity that a Pompeius should be in the power of Titius, who was not a man of distinction at all. He was also suspicious that Titius was unreliable, both distrusting his character and being aware of an old offense he had committed against him before the service he had rendered. So he tried a second 591 time to surrender to Furnius, and begged that he would receive him. When Furnius refused, he said that he would even hand himself over to Amyntas. But Furnius said that not even Amyntas would accept such an insult against the

ἐς τὸν ἐξ Ἀντωνίου τὸ πᾶν ἐπιτετραμμένον, διελύθη-
592 σαν. καὶ τοῖς μὲν ἀμφὶ τὸν Φούρνιον δόξα ἦν, ὅτι ὁ
Πομπήιος ἐξ ἀπορίας τῶν παρόντων ἑαυτὸν ἐς τὴν
ἐπιοῦσαν ἡμέραν ἐκδώσει τῷ Τιτίῳ· ὁ δὲ νυκτὸς τὰ
συνήθη πυρὰ καίεσθαι καταλιπὼν καὶ τοὺς σαλ-
πιγκτὰς σημαίνειν τὰ διαστήματα τῆς νυκτός, ὥσπερ
ἦν ἔθος, ἔλαθε μετὰ τῶν εὐζώνων ὑπεξελθὼν τοῦ
στρατοπέδου, οἷς οὐδὲ αὐτοῖς προεῖπεν, οἷ χωρήσειν
593 ἔμελλεν. ἐπενόει δ᾽ ἐπὶ θάλασσαν ἐλθὼν ἐμπρῆσαι τὸ
τοῦ Τιτίου ναυτικόν. καὶ τάχα ἂν ἔδρασεν, εἰ μὴ
Σκαῦρος αὐτομολήσας ἀπ᾽ αὐτοῦ τὴν μὲν ἔξοδον ἐμή-
νυσε καὶ τὴν ὁδόν, ἣν ἐφέρετο, τὴν δ᾽ ἐπίνοιαν οὐκ
594 ᾔδει. τότε δὴ χιλίοις καὶ πεντακοσίοις ἱππεῦσιν
Ἀμύντας ἐδίωκε τὸν Πομπήιον ἱππέας οὐκ ἔχοντα. καὶ
ἐς τὸν Ἀμύνταν οἱ τοῦ Πομπηίου πλησιάσαντα μετ-
εχώρουν, οἱ μὲν ἀποδιδράσκοντες, οἱ δὲ καὶ φανερῶς.
595 μονούμενος οὖν ὁ Πομπήιος καὶ δεδιὼς ἤδη τὰ οἰκεῖα,
ἑαυτὸν ἄνευ σπονδῶν ἐνεχείρισεν Ἀμύντᾳ, ὁ Τιτίῳ
μετὰ σπονδῶν ἀδοξήσας.

596   143. Οὕτω μὲν ἑάλω Πομπήιος Σέξτος, ὁ λοιπὸς
ἔτι παῖς Πομπηίου Μάγνου, νεώτερος μὲν ὑπὸ τοῦ
πατρὸς ἀπολειφθεὶς καὶ ὑπὸ τοῦ ἀδελφοῦ μειράκιον
ἤδη, λαθὼν δ᾽ ἐπ᾽ ἐκείνοις ἐς πολὺ καὶ κρύφα λῃ-
στεύων ἐν Ἰβηρίᾳ, μέχρι, πολλῶν συνδραμόντων ἐς
αὐτὸν ἐπιγνωσθέντα εἶναι Πομπηίου παῖδα, ἐλῄστευέ
τε φανερώτερον, καὶ μετὰ Γάιον Καίσαρα ἐπολέμησεν

man appointed by Antony to deal with the whole matter, and they went their separate ways. It was the opinion of Furnius' staff that, because of his current lack of supplies, Pompeius would hand himself over to Titius the next day. But when it was dark, Pompeius left the customary fires burning, and the trumpets sounding the watches of the night as usual, while he slipped out of the camp unnoticed with his light-armed troops, without telling even them where he was intending to go. He had in mind to make for the coast and set fire to Titius' naval force. He might have succeeded if Scaurus had not deserted from him and given information on his departure and the route he was taking, although he did not know Pompeius' plan.[98] Then Amyntas, with one thousand five hundred cavalry, pursued Pompeius, who had no cavalry. When Amyntas approached, Pompeius' men went over to him, some escaping unobtrusively, others openly. So Pompeius, deserted and already afraid of his own troops, the man who had thought it unworthy to surrender to Titius with conditions, surrendered to Amyntas unconditionally.

143. This was how Sextus Pompeius was captured, the last living son of Pompey the Great. He had lost his father when he was a boy, and his brother while still an adolescent. After that he lay low for a long time and secretly operated as a bandit in Iberia, until many rushed to join him when he was recognized as a son of Pompey, and he more openly carried out bandit raids. After the death of Gaius Caesar, he waged war energetically: he collected a

---

[98] Marcus Aemilius Scaurus was son of the Scaurus defended (unsuccessfully) by Cicero in 53. His mother was Mucia, who had been married to Pompey the Great. He was, therefore, a half brother of Sextus Pompeius.

ἐγκρατῶς καὶ στρατὸν ἤγειρε πολὺν καὶ ναῦς καὶ
χρήματα, καὶ νήσους εἷλε, καὶ θαλασσοκράτωρ τῆς
ἀμφὶ τὰς δύσεις θαλάσσης ἐγένετο, καὶ τὴν Ἰταλίαν
περιήνεγκεν ἐς λιμὸν καὶ τοὺς ἐχθροὺς ἐς συμβάσεις,
597 ἃς ἤθελε. τὸ δὲ μέγιστον, ἐπίκουρος ἐν ταῖς προγρα-
φαῖς τῇ πόλει πανώλεθρα πασχούσῃ γενόμενος περι-
έσωσεν ἄνδρας ἀρίστους τε καὶ πολλούς, οἳ τότε δι᾽
αὐτὸν ἦσαν ἐν τῇ πατρίδι. ὑπὸ δὲ θεοβλαβείας αὐτὸς
οὔ ποτε ἐπεχείρησε τοῖς πολεμίοις, πολλὰ τῆς τύχης
εὔκαιρα παρεχούσης, ἀλλ᾽ ἠμύνετο μόνον.

598 144. Καὶ Πομπήιος μὲν τοιόσδε γενόμενος ἑαλώκει,
Τίτιος δὲ τὸν μὲν στρατὸν αὐτοῦ μετεστράτευσεν
Ἀντωνίῳ, αὐτὸν δὲ Πομπήιον, τεσσαρακοστὸν ἔτος
βιοῦντα, ἐν Μιλήτῳ κατέκανεν, εἴτε δι᾽ αὐτοῦ, μηνίων
ἄρα τῆς ποτὲ ὕβρεως καὶ ἀχάριστος ἐς τὴν ἔπειτα
εὐεργεσίαν γενόμενος, εἴτε καὶ ἐπιστείλαντος Ἀντω-
599 νίου. εἰσὶ δ᾽ οἱ Πλάγκον, οὐκ Ἀντώνιον λέγοντες ἐπι-
στεῖλαι, καὶ νομίζουσιν ἄρχοντα Συρίας, καὶ ταῖς
ἐπιστολαῖς ἐπιτετραμμένον ἐς τὰ ἐπείγοντα ἐπιγρά-
600 φειν τὸν Ἀντώνιον καὶ τῇ σφραγῖδι χρῆσθαι. καὶ
Πλάγκον δὲ γράψαι νομίζουσιν οἱ μὲν συνειδότος
Ἀντωνίου καὶ αἰδουμένου γράψαι διὰ ὄνομα τοῦ Πομπηίου καὶ διὰ Κλεοπάτραν, εὔνως ἔχουσαν τῷ Πομπηίῳ διὰ τὸν πατέρα Μάγνον, οἱ δὲ αὐτὸν ἐφ᾽ ἑαυτοῦ
Πλάγκον, τάδε αὐτὰ συνιδόντα καὶ φυλαξάμενον, μὴ
τὴν αἰσίαν⁴⁵ Ἀντωνίου καὶ Καίσαρος ἐς ἀλλήλους
αἰδῶ Πομπήιος καὶ Κλεοπάτρα Πομπηίῳ συνεργοῦσα
ἀνατρέψαιεν.

large army and ships and money, and captured islands, and became master of the western sea, and reduced Italy to starvation, and forced his enemies to come to terms of his choosing. Most important, he brought assistance to Rome   597 during the proscriptions when it was suffering complete destruction, and saved the lives of many nobles who at the time of his surrender were living in their native land because of him. But afflicted by some divine madness, he never personally took the offensive against his enemies, although fate provided many good opportunities; and he remained solely on the defensive.

144. So Pompeius was captured after such a career.   598 Titius transferred his army to Antony, and had Pompeius himself executed at Miletus in the fortieth year of his life, either on his own authority, because he was angry, I suppose, at the old insult and ungrateful for his subsequent service, or because Antony gave the order. There are even   599 those who say that it was not Antony but Plancus who issued the order: they believe that as governor of Syria he had been given permission, in cases of urgency, to sign letters in Antony's name and use his seal. Of those who   600 think that Plancus wrote the order, some believe that Antony was complicit, but was ashamed to write it himself because of Pompeius' name and because of Cleopatra, who was well disposed to Pompeius on account of his father, Pompey the Great; others think that Plancus acted on his own, conscious of these very things, to make sure that Pompeius and Cleopatra working with him, did not disturb the proper respect that Antony and Octavian had for each other.

---

45 αἰτίαν codd.; αἰσίαν Viereck

601   145. Ἀλλὰ Πομπήιος μὲν ἐτεθνήκει, Ἀντώνιος δὲ αὖθις ἐς Ἀρμενίαν ἐστράτευε, καὶ ὁ Καῖσαρ ἐπὶ Ἰλλυριούς, οἳ τὴν Ἰταλίαν ἐλήστευον, οἱ μὲν οὐχ ὑπακούσαντές πω Ῥωμαίων, οἱ δ᾽ ἐν τοῖς ἐμφυλίοις ἀπο-

602 στάντες. καί μοι ἔδοξε τὰ Ἰλλυρικά, οὔτε ἀκριβῶς γενόμενά μοι γνώριμα οὔτε συντελοῦντα μῆκος ἰδίας συγγραφῆς οὔτε χώραν ἔχοντα ἑτέρωθι λεχθῆναι,[46] τοῦ χρόνου, καθ᾽ ὃν ἐλήφθησαν, συνάγοντος αὐτὰ ἐς τέλος, προαναγράψαι καὶ ὑποθεῖναι αὐτὰ τῇ ὁμόρῳ Μακεδονικῇ.

[46] Lacunam post λεχθῆναι indic. Étienee-Duplessis

145. After the death of Pompeius, Antony conducted a   601
second campaign against Armenia, and Octavian attacked
the Illyrians, who were plundering Italy, some of whom
had never been subject to Rome, while others had re-
volted during the civil wars. Because Illyrian affairs are   602
not familiar to me in detail, and are not of sufficient length
to require their own book, and there is no other place for
them to be recounted, I decided to write them up in an
earlier book, the period when they were conquered bringing the account to an end, and to append them to the
history of neighboring Macedonia.[99]

[99] The text of this last sentence is far from certain, and there
may well be something missing. The meaning is reasonably clear.

FRAGMENTA HISTORIAE
ROMANAE

1 *Bas.* 1a. *Excerpta anonymi Byzantini* Treu 1880 pp. 36.10–37.29. See Appian vol. 1 (LCL 2), pp. 32–37.

2 ἀνεζεύγνυ· ἀνέστρεφεν. Ἀππιανός· ὁ δὲ μετὰ πολλῆς λείας ἀνεζεύγνυ. (*Suda,* α 2225)

3 Ἐγχρόνων· οὐ πρὸ πολλοῦ χρόνου συντεθεισῶν. Ἀππιανός· κατεφρόνουν τῶν σπονδῶν ἔτι ἐγχρόνων οὐσῶν. (*Suda,* ε 190)

4 Ἐδοκίμαζεν· ἔκρινε . . . καὶ Ἀππιανός· ὁ δὲ ἐπὶ τὰς οἰκίας χωρῶν συνελάμβανεν, ὅσους ἐδοκίμαζεν. ἀντὶ τοῦ ἔκρινεν ἐτάσεως εἶναι ἀξίους. (*Suda,* ε 245)

5 Ἐπαφρόδιτος· ἐπίχαρις, ἡδύς. Ἀππιανός· καὶ τὴν ἐν πᾶσιν ἐπαφροδισίαν ὑπεραίρων ἐσεμνολόγει περὶ ἑαυτοῦ. (*Suda,* ε 2003)

FRAGMENTS OF THE
ROMAN HISTORY

1 *Bas.* 1a. *Excerpta anonymi Byzantini* Treu 1880 pp. 36.10–37.29. See Appian vol. 1 (LCL 2), pp. 32–37.

2 He withdrew: [meaning] "he retired." Appian [writes]: He withdrew with a great quantity of booty. (*Suda*, α 2225)

3 Recent: [meaning] "made not long before." Appian [writes]: They were contemptuous of the peace terms although they were still recent. (*Suda*, ε 190)

4 He saw fit: [meaning] "he made a judgment" . . . Also Appian [writes]: Making his way to their houses, he arrested all those he wanted to examine. Meaning, "those he decided deserved to be put on trial." (*Suda*, ε 245)

5 Charming: [meaning] "pleasant, sweet." Appian [writes]: And exaggerating his charm in all matters, he spoke pompously about himself. (*Suda*, ε 2003)

APPIAN

6 Θησαυρούς. Ἀππιανός· ὅπλα τε πολλὰ καὶ σῖτον ἡτοιμάζετο καὶ θησαυροὺς ἐποίει. καὶ Θησαυροφυλάκιον. (*Suda*, θ 362)

7 Ἱλαρός· εὔχαρις, ἀστεῖος, ἡδύς. Ἀππιανός· σὺν βοῇ ἱλαρᾷ καὶ θορύβῳ χρηστῷ παρέπεμπον αὐτὸν καὶ θαρρεῖν ἐκέλευον. ἐπέπρεπε δὲ αὐτῷ μάλιστα τὸ τῆς ψυχῆς ἱλαρόν. (*Suda*, ι 294)

8 Οἷ· περισπωμένως ἀντὶ τοῦ ἑαυτῷ, ὀξυτόνως δὲ τὸ οὗτοι. Ἀππιανός· ἐπεὶ δὲ ἦν οἷ τὸ κακὸν τέχνης κρεῖττον καὶ μέντοι καὶ ἐπικουρίας τῆς ἐκ θνητῶν συμμάχων δυνατώτερον. (*Suda*, οι 3)

9 Οἰστρεῖ· ἐρεθίζει, ἐκμαίνει. Ἀππιανός· τῷ ὄντι πᾶσιν οἰστρώδης ἐνέπιπτεν ὁρμὴ καὶ προθυμία κατὰ τῶν βαρβάρων. (*Suda*, οι 178)

10 Πιθανούς· τοὺς εὐπειθεῖς. Ἀππιανός· ἕνα δ' αὐτῶν πιστὸν καὶ πιθανὸν εἰς τὸ ἔργον, ἐντυχόντα τοῖς ὑπάτοις ἐν ἀπορρήτῳ, πίστιν αἰτῆσαι. (*Suda*, π 1574)

11 Πρόσριζα· σὺν ταῖς ῥίζαις. Ἀππιανός· τὰ δένδρα ἔκοπτε πρόσριζα, τοῦ μὴ πάλιν φῦναι. (*Suda*, π 2800)

6 Treasuries. Appian [writes]: He made ready a large supply of arms, and grain, and constructed treasuries. Also [attested], "treasury guard post." (*Suda, θ* 362)

7 Joyous: [meaning] "charming, witty, sweet." Appian [writes]: With a joyous shout and the applause of well-wishers, they provided an escort for him and urged him to be of good spirit. What was particularly conspicuous about him was the sweetness of his soul.[1] (*Suda, ι* 294)

8 For him: meaning, with a circumflex accent, "for oneself," but with an acute accent "these." Appian [writes]: Since his misfortune was too strong for his skill, and in fact more powerful even than the help of mortal allies. (*Suda, οι* 3)

9 It stings: [meaning] "it rouses, maddens." Appian [writes]: In fact, everyone experienced a stinging urge and eagerness to take on the barbarians. (*Suda, οι* 178)

10 Obedient: [meaning] "ready to obey." Appian [writes]: One of them who was reliable and prepared to do the job met the consuls in secret and asked for an assurance. (*Suda, π* 1574)

11 By the roots: [meaning] "roots and all." Appian [writes]: He was cutting the trees at the roots, to prevent them growing again. (*Suda, π* 2800)

---

[1] It is not known from which author the last sentence comes.

12 Ὦσατο ἑαυτόν· κατέβαλεν ἀπὸ τοῦ ἵππου. Ἀππιανός· οὐ μὴν ἔφθασε τρῶσαι, συναρπασάντων αὐτὸν τῶν ὑπασπιστῶν. ἢ παρενέβαλεν εἰς κίνδυνον ἑαυτόν. (*Suda*, ω 218)

13 χρηματίζειν· ὁ αὐτὸς (i.e., Ἀππιανὸς) δευτέρῳ Αἰγυπτιακῶν· πρεσβείαις ὁ Καῖσαρ ἐχρημάτισεν. (*Anecd.* Bekker p. 179.21 = Περὶ Συντάξεων No. 34 Gaillard)

14 ἐπισκήπτω· Ἀππιανὸς τρίτῳ Αἰγυπτιακῶν· ἐπισκήπτω σε τῆς ἀξιώσεως. (*Anecd.* Bekker p. 139.29 = Περὶ Συντάξεων No. 6 Gaillard)

15 χρῶμαι· τὸ κατὰ χρῆσίν τι λαβεῖν, αἰτιατικῇ. Ἀππιανὸς ϛʹ.[1] ἃς δὲ ἐχρησάμην παρὰ Ἀντωνίου ναῦς. (*Anecd.* Bekker p. 179.19 = Περὶ Συντάξεων No. 33 Gaillard)

[1] Ἀππιανὸς ϛʹ recte Gaillard; Ἀππιανὸς κʹ Schweig.

12 He pushed himself away: [meaning] "he threw himself down off his horse." Appian [writes]: He did not even have time to inflict a wound, before the hypaspists seized him.[2] Or, "he put himself in danger." (*Suda*, ω 218)

13 To conduct business: the same author (i.e., Appian) [writes] in the second book of his *Egyptian History*: Caesar busied himself with embassies. (*Anecd.* Bekker p. 179.21 = *On Syntax* No. 34 Gaillard)

14 I call on: Appian [writes] in the third book of his *Egyptian History*: I call on you for the sake of your dignity. (*Anecd.* Bekker p. 139.29 = *On Syntax* No. 6 Gaillard)

15 I borrow: [meaning] "to take something on loan," with the accusative. Appian [writes] in Book 6:[3] But the ships I borrowed from Antony. (*Anecd.* Bekker p. 179.19 = *On Syntax* No. 33 Gaillard)

[2] The quotation from Appian does not contain the words being explained.

[3] Appian's sixth book is the Iberian book, but the citation clearly refers to the ships Octavian borrowed from Antony in 37 (App. *BCiv.* 5.95.396). As Gaillard 2002, l–li, has shown, the manuscript does cite Book 6 of Appian, and not Book 20, as Schweighäuser suggested; and Appian can only be referring to the sixth book in the *Civil War* sequence, that is, the first book of his *Egyptian History*.

16 συνηδόμενοι· γενικῇ. Ἀππιανὸς τετάρτῳ Αἰγυπτια-
κῶν· συνηδόμενοι τῶν γεγονότων. (*Anecd.* Bekker
p. 174.14 = Περὶ Συντάξεων No. 30 Gaillard)

17 τούτου δὲ τοῦ χρησμοῦ μέμνηται καὶ Ἀππιανὸς ἐν
τῷ εἰκοστῷ δευτέρῳ λόγῳ τῆς Ῥωμαϊκῆς ἱστορίας
αὐτοῦ. (Zonar. 11.16 T3 p. 50.15 Dindorf)

18 ⟨Τραϊανὸς⟩ ἐστράτευσε μέντοι ἐπὶ Δάκας, ἢ Δα-
κοὺς κατὰ Ἴωνας, ὡς ὁ Ἀππιανὸς ἐν τῷ εἰκοστῷ
τρίτῳ λόγῳ τῆς Ῥωμαϊκῆς ἱστορίας φησί. (Zonar.
11.21 T3 p. 65.27 Dindorf)

19 περὶ Ἀράβων μαντείας. Ἀππιανός φησι τῷ τέλει
τοῦ κδʹ βιβλίου. φεύγοντί μοί ποτε τοὺς Ἰουδαίους
ἀνὰ τὸν πόλεμον τὸν ἐν Αἰγύπτῳ γενόμενον καὶ ἰόντι
διὰ τῆς Πετραίας Ἀραβίας ἐπὶ ποταμόν, ἔνθα με
σκάφος περιμένον ἔμελλε διοίσειν ἐς Πηλούσιον,
Ἄραψ ἀνὴρ δʼ ἡγεῖτό μοι τῆς ὁδοῦ νυκτός, οἰομένῳ
πλησίον εἶναι τοῦ σκάφους κρωζούσης ἄρτι πρὸς
ἕω κορώνης ἔφη συνταραχθείς· "Πεπλανήμεθα." καὶ
2 κρωζούσης αὖθις εἶπεν· "Ἄγαν πεπλανήμεθα." θορυ-
βουμένῳ δέ μοι καὶ σκοποῦντι, εἴ τις ὁδοιπόρος
ὀφθήσεται, καὶ οὐδένα ὁρῶντι ὡς ἐν ὄρθρῳ ἔτι πολλῷ
καὶ γῇ πολεμουμένῃ, τὸ τρίτον ὁ Ἄραψ τοῦ ὀρνέου

16 Delighted with: with the genitive. Appian [writes] in his fourth book of *Egyptian History*: Delighted with events. (*Anecd.* Bekker p. 174.14 = *On Syntax* No. 30 Gaillard)

17 Appian too mentions this oracle in the twenty-second book of his *Roman History*. (Zonar. 11.16 T3 p. 50.15 Dindorf)

18 (Trajan), however, campaigned against the Dacians, or Daci, according to the Ionians, as Appian says in his twenty-third book of *Roman History*. (Zonar. 11.21 T3 p. 65.27 Dindorf)

19 Concerning Arab divination. Appian says at the end of his 24th book: Once, when I was fleeing from the Jews during the war that took place in Egypt,[4] and traveling through Arabia Petraea to a river, where a waiting boat was due to take me across to Pelusium, an Arab man was my guide on the road one night. I thought we were near the boat, when a crow cawed just as dawn was breaking, and my guide was confused, and said, "We are lost." When the crow cawed again, he said, "We are completely lost." I was 2 worried and checked if anyone was to be seen on the road, but I saw nobody, as was to be expected when it was still very early and we were in a war zone. But when the Arab heard the bird for a third time, he was pleased and said,

[4] Appian is referring to the Jewish revolt of AD 115 to 117, which spread from Cyrene into Egypt, Mesopotamia, and Judaea.

APPIAN

3 πυθόμενος εἶπεν ἡσθείς, "Ἐπὶ συμφέροντι πεπλανήμεθα καὶ ἐχόμεθα τῆς ὁδοῦ." ἐγὼ δὲ ἐγέλων μέν, εἰ
καὶ νῦν ἐξόμεθα τῆς πλανώσης, καὶ ἀπεγίνωσκον
ἐμαυτοῦ, πάντων πολεμίων ὄντων, οὐκ ὄν μοι δυνατὸν
οὐδ᾽ ἀναστρέψαι διὰ τοὺς ὄπισθεν, οὓς δὴ καὶ φεύγων
ἠρχόμην, ὑπὸ δ᾽ ἀπορίας εἱπόμην ἐκδοὺς ἐμαυτὸν τῷ
4 μαντεύματι. οὕτω δὲ ἔχοντί μοι παρὰ δόξαν ἕτερος
ποταμὸς ἐκφαίνεται, ὁ ἀγχοτάτω μάλιστα τοῦ Πηλου-
σίου, καὶ τριήρης ἐς τὸ Πηλούσιον παραπλέουσα, ἧς
ἐπιβὰς διεσωζόμην· τὸ σκάφος δέ, ὅ με ἐν τῷ ἑτέρῳ
ποταμῷ ὑπέμεινεν, ὑπὸ Ἰουδαίων ἐλήφθη. τοσοῦτον
ὠνάμην τῆς τύχης καὶ τοσοῦτον ἐθαύμασα τοῦ μαν-
5 τεύματος. οὗτοι μὲν οὖν εἰσι θρησκευτικοί, μαντικοί,
γεωργοί, φαρμάκων ἐπιστήμονες, οὓς εἰκὸς ἐν Αἰγύπτῳ γῆν εὑρόντας ἀγαθὴν οἷα γεωργοὺς καὶ ἔθνος
ὁμοίως θεοσεβές τε καὶ μαντικὸν καὶ φαρμάκων οὐκ
ἄπειρον οὐδ᾽ ἄστρων ἐμμεῖναι χαίροντας ὡς παρ᾽
ὁμοίοις. (Codex Paris. Suppl. Gr. 607A)

20 ἄρχω. γενικῇ . . . Ἀππιανὸς δὲ δοτικῇ· διεχρήσατο
Νέρων, ὅτε ἦρχε Ῥωμαίοις. (*Anecd.* Bekker p. 120.24 =
Περὶ Συντάξεων No. 2 Gaillard)

21 ἀμελητέα. γενικῇ τὸ πρᾶγμα, τὸ δὲ πρόσωπον
δοτικῇ . . . καὶ Ἀππιανός· ἀλλήλων ἠμέλουν. (*Anecd.*
Bekker p. 129.26 = Περὶ Συντάξεων No. 4 Gaillard)

264

"It was to our advantage that we got lost and we are now 3
on the right road." As for me, I could only laugh at the
prospect of remaining lost, and despaired of my life, since
I was surrounded by enemies and could not even go back,
considering those in our rear from whom I had, of course,
set out to escape. Not knowing what to do, I surrendered
myself to the prophecy and followed my guide. Such was 4
my state of mind when, unexpectedly, another river ap-
pears, very close to Pelusium, and a trireme sailing past
on its way to Pelusium, which I boarded and was thus
rescued. On the other hand, the boat which was waiting
for me on the other river, was captured by the Jews. That
is how much fate helped me and how much I admired the
prophecy. These Arabs are, in general, pious prophets and 5
farmers, skilled in medicines, and it is fitting that having
found in Egypt a good land, being as they are farmers
and a people likewise both god-fearing and prophetic and
with considerable expertise in medicines and stars, they
live there happily, finding themselves among likeminded
people. (Codex Paris. Suppl. Gr. 607A)

20 I rule. With the genitive . . . But Appian uses it with
the dative: Nero was killed (?) when he was ruler of the
Romans. (*Anecd.* Bekker p. 120.24 = *On Syntax* No. 2
Gaillard)

21 Things to be ignored. With the genitive of the thing,
and dative of the person . . . And Appian [writes]: They
ignored each other. (*Anecd.* Bekker p. 129.26 = *On Syntax*
No. 4 Gaillard)

22 ἐξέδραμεν. γενικῇ. Ἀππιανός· ἐξέδραμε τοῦ δανει-
στοῦ. (*Anecd.* Bekker p. 146.5 = Περὶ Συντάξεων No. 11
Gaillard)

23 κουφίζω καὶ ἐπικουφίζω. γενικῇ. Ἀππιανός· ὅσα
δὲ ὅμως ἐπικουφιεῖ τῆς ἀνίας, αἰτεῖτε καὶ λαμβάνετε
προσιόντες. (*Anecd.* Bekker p. 154.17 = Περὶ Συντάξεων
No. 18 Gaillard)

24 συμπλεκόμενος. δοτικῇ. ὁ αὐτός (i.e., Ἀππιανός)·
συμπλεκόμενος αὐτῇ. (*Anecd.* Bekker p. 174.9 = Περὶ
Συντάξεων No. 28 Gaillard)

25 Παρὰ Ἀππιανοῦ Φρόντωνι. οὐδὲ σήμερον ἐδυνήθην
σε ἰδεῖν, διὰ τὴν γαστέρα νυκτὸς ἐνοχλοῦσαν ἕως
ἄρτι κοιμηθείς. ἃ δὲ ἀγρυπνῶν ἠπόρουν, οὐ κατέσχον
οὐδ᾽ ἀνεβαλόμην, ἀλλ᾽ ἐκ πολλῶν ὀλίγα σοι γέγραφα.
σὺ δέ, εἰ μὲν δίκαιά ἐστιν, ὡς δικαίοις, εἰ δὲ σχο-
λαστικά, ὡς ἁπλοῖς, εἰ δὲ μή, ἀλλ᾽ ἔμοιγε ὡς λυπου-
2 μένῳ καὶ παρακαλοῦντι πείσθητι καὶ εἶξον. εἰκὸς
ἕπεσθαι τοῖς κοινοῖς τὰ ἰδιωτικά· εὐθύνομεν γοῦν τὰ
ἴδια πρὸς ἐκεῖνα, καὶ ὁ νόμος οὕτω κελεύει. πῶς οὖν
αἱ μὲν πόλεις οὐκ ὀκνοῦσι λαμβάνουσαι παρὰ τῶν
διδόντων ἀναθήματά τε καὶ χρήματα καὶ ἀργύριον

---

[5] The subject of this letter is a gift of two slaves Appian has
sent to Fronto, who has returned them. Appian is now sending
them again, with a letter providing arguments why Fronto should

22 He escaped. With the genitive. Appian [writes]: he escaped his creditor. (*Anecd.* Bekker p. 146.5 = *On Syntax* No. 11 Gaillard)

23 I lighten, and, I relieve. With the genitive. Appian [writes]: Nevertheless, whatever will relieve you of your sorrow, just ask for it, and come and get it. (*Anecd.* Bekker p. 154.17 = *On Syntax* No. 18 Gaillard)

24 Becoming involved with. With the dative. The same author (i.e., Appian) [writes]: Becoming involved with her. (*Anecd.* Bekker p. 174.9 = *On Syntax* No. 28 Gaillard)

25 From Appian to Fronto.[5] I could not see you today either, as owing to stomach problems during the night, I stayed in bed until just now. What I was puzzling over while lying awake I am not holding back or putting off, but have written you a few out of my many thoughts. As for you, if they are right, let yourself be persuaded to yield to them as right; if they are pedantic treat them as honest; otherwise, at least let yourself be persuaded to yield to me, as I have a grievance and come to you with a request. It is fitting that personal matters follow the way of public affairs. At any rate, we direct our private affairs according to public ones, and the law requires us to do this. How is it, then, that states do not hesitate to accept dedications and property and gold itself from both citizens and strang-

accept them. For the most recent text of this letter, see Van den Hout 1988, 142–43.

αὐτὸ[2] πολιτῶν τε καὶ ξένων, ἤδη δέ τινας καὶ αὐτούς
πως ὑποδιδόντας, φίλος δὲ δὴ[3] παρὰ φίλου λαβεῖν

3 ὀκνεῖ παρακαλοῦντος; καὶ οἱ θεοὶ δὲ τῷ νόμῳ τῶν
πόλεων προσίενται[4] ταῦτα παρὰ τῶν ἀνδρῶν, καὶ
δεικνύουσιν οἱ θησαυροὶ τῶν θεῶν. καὶ οἱ φίλοι δὲ ἐκ

4 τῶν διαθηκῶν λαμβάνειν οὐκ ὀκνοῦσιν. καὶ διὰ τί οὖν
ἐκ μὲν διαθήκης ἄν τις λάβοι, παρὰ δὲ τῶν περιόντων
οὐ λάβοι, ὅποτε καὶ μεῖζον ταῦτ' ἔχει τὸ δεῖγμα τῆς
προθυμίας; οἱ μὲν γὰρ ἄλλον ἄλλου προτιθέασιν, οἳ
δὲ περιόντες ἑαυτῶν τοὺς φίλους προτιθέασιν. καὶ
ἥδιον παρὰ τοῦ περιόντος λαβεῖν, ὅτι προτιθέασιν.

5 καὶ ἥδιον παρὰ τοῦ περιόντος λαβεῖν, ὅτι καὶ μαρτυ-
ρῆσαι περιόντι δυνατόν ἐστι καὶ ἀμείψασθαι. πάλιν
ξένιον μὲν οὔτε θεοῖς οὔτε πόλει πέμπεται, τὰ σεμνό-
τερα δ' ἀεὶ τοῖς σεμνοτέροις. ἀλλ' οὐκ εἰσὶ ταῦτα
βαρύτερα λαμβάνειν; τί γάρ ἐστι φιλίας καὶ τιμῆς
βαρύτερον, ὧν οὐδ' ἴσως γ' ἄρειον οὐδέν ἐστιν; τί δὲ

6 καὶ βαρὺ ἦν ὅλως ἢ τί ἂν ἐγὼ βαρὺ ἔχοιμι; οὐδ' ἂν
μὲν ἐργασαίμην οὐδὲν οὐδὲ πριαίμην οὐδέποτε, † δέον
τινὰ μισθὸν ἴσον †[5] ἐξ οἴκου, φασίν, ἐς οἶκον μετελ-
θεῖν.[6] ἐννόησον δὲ κἀκεῖνο, ὅση μὲν ἡδονὴ τῷ πέμψαντι
ληφθέντων, ὅση δὲ λύπη μὴ ληφθέντων ἐπιγίγνεται.[7]
εἰ τὸ καθαρὸν <. . .> καὶ μετὰ πολὺ[8] προσιέναι σοι.
πιστεύοις δὲ δίκαιον εἶναι τὸν νόμον τῶν τε πόλεων
καὶ θεῶν καὶ φίλων <. . .> φίλων δὲ οὐ τοσοῦτον

---

[2] αὐτοπολιτῶν Van den Hout
[3] δὴ om. Van den Hout

ers, and now in some cases a sort of gift of themselves, but a friend shrinks from accepting a gift from a friend when he requests it? Even the Gods follow the law of states and accept these gifts from men, as the treasuries of the Gods testify. And friends too do not hesitate to accept bequests. So, why should a person accept a bequest, but not accept something from the living, when the latter is an even greater proof of affection? For in the first case people are prioritizing one person over another, but the living are prioritizing their friends over themselves. And it is more pleasant to receive a gift from a living person, because it is possible both to acknowledge it to a living person and to give in return. No minor gift is exchanged with Gods or cities, but nobler things are always for more noble beings. But are these latter more onerous to accept? For what can be more onerous than friendship and honor, than which there is perhaps nothing finer? And what was there here that was onerous at all, or what should I count as onerous? I could not do anything nor ever buy anything, that necessitated an equivalent return, passing, as they say, from house to house. Consider this point too, what pleasure acceptance gives the sender, and what pain results from nonacceptance. If the pure ⟨. . .⟩ even after a long time come to you. Please believe that the law of Gods and cities and friends is a just one ⟨. . .⟩ but as friends do not parade

3

4

5

6

---

⁴ προστίθενται Van den Hout

⁵ τι ἅμα μισθὸν ἔχον Van den Hout

⁶ μετατεθέν Van den Hout

⁷ εἰσγίγνεται, Van den Hout

⁸ πο⟨. . .⟩ Van den Hout

ἐπιδεικνύντων θράσος εὐνοίας, ἀλλὰ κρυπτόντων[9] ὑπὸ δέους, ἔπεμψα τὸ[10] πρὶν ἐπιτρέψῃς. σὺ δὲ μὴ δεύτερον ἀποπέμψῃς,[11] ᾧ γε ἔδει μηδ' ἅπαξ. (Viereck-Roos 537–38)

[9] καὶ τούτων Van den Hout
[10] εἴ επέμψα τώ Van den Hout
[11] μὴ δευτερώσῃς Van den Hout

such a boldness of goodwill, but from diffidence conceal it, I have sent my gift before you gave permission. Do not send back my gift a second time, as you ought not to have done even the first time.

INDEX

INDEX

Apollophanes (admiral of Sextus Pompeius), *BCiv.* 5.84.356, 105.436–106.437

Aponius (proscribed), *BCiv.* 4.26.112–13

Appian of Alexandria, *Praef.* 15.61–62; *Syr.* 50.252; *BCiv.* 1.38.172; 2.86.362, 90.380; *Frag.*19

Appian way, *BCiv.* 1.69.314

Appius (lieutenant of Octavian), *BCiv.* 5.98.407–9

Appius (proscribed), *BCiv.* 4.44.185, 51.222

Appuleius, M. (cos. 20), *BCiv.* 3.63.259; 4.46.197, 75.316

Appuleius, P. (tr. pl. 43; proscribed), *BCiv.* 3.93.384; 4.40.166

Appuleius Saturninus, L. (tr. pl. 103, 100), *BCiv.* 1.28.127–32.145

Apsarus (river in Armenia), *Mith.* 101.465

Apsus (river). *See* Alor

Apuleius (bandit), *Ib.* 68.289

Aquileia (town in Gaul), *Ill.*18.52; *BCiv.* 3.97.401

Aquillius, M'. (cos. 129), *Mith.* 12.39, 57.231; *BCiv.* 1.22.92

Aquillius, M'. (cos 101), *Mith.* 11.34, 21.80, 112.544

Aquillius Crassus, M'. (pr. 43; proscribed), *BCiv.* 3.93.384, 94.386

Aquinus, M. (conspirator against Caesar), *BCiv.* 2.119.500

Aquitania, *BCiv.* 5.92.386

Arabia/Arabs, *Praef.* 2.4, 9.35; *Syr.* 32.167, 51.256, 55.281; *Mith.* 106.498, 114.556; *BCiv.* 2.71.294; 4.88.373; *Frag.* 19.1–5

Arabio (son of Masinissa), *BCiv.* 4.54.230–56.242, 83.349

Arachosia (ruled by Seleucus), *Syr.* 55.281

Aradians (in Phoenician island), *BCiv.* 4.61.262; 5.9.35

Araxes (river), *Mith.* 103.480

Arcadians, *Syr.* 41.213–14

Arcathias (son of Mithridates), *Mith.* 17.63, 18.64–69, 35.137, 41.156

Archelaus (general of Mithridates), *Mith.* 17.62, 18.64–69, 27.106, 28.108–29.115, 30.117–41.159, 42.160–45.176, 49.194–97, 50.198–202, 54.215–55.224, 58.239–40, 64.268, 114.560, 121.597

Archelaus (priest at Comana), *Mith.* 114.560, 121.597

Archelaus of Rhodes (tutor of Cassius), *BCiv.* 4.67.283–70.299

Ardaei (Illyrian people), *Ill.* 3.7, 10.29

Ardea (town in Latium), *Ital.* 8.5; *BCiv.* 2.50.205

Areacidae (Numidian people), *Lib.* 33.139

Ares, *Lib.*133.632; *Bas.* 1.1, 1a.6

Aretas (king of Nabataean Arabs), *Mith.* 106.498, 117.576

Arethusa (town in Syria), *Syr.* 57.298

INDEX

6.18, 24.91, 26.97, 78.320;
4.1.1, 5.18, 58.248, 74.313–
75.316, 87.368–88.373,
106.445, 108.455, 120.506,
134.565; 5.1.1, 2.4, 2.6, 4.16,
52.216, 55.230, 65.276,
133.551, 137.567

Asinius Hereius (Italian general
in Social War), *BCiv.*
1.40.181

Asinius Pollio, C. (cos. 40),
BCiv. 2.40.162, 45.185–86,
46.187, 82.346; 3.46.190,
74.304, 81.331, 97.399;
4.12.46, 27.114, 84.352;
5.20.80, 31.120–33.132,
35.141, 50.208–12, 61.257,
64.272

Aspis (town in Africa), *Lib.*
3.14, 110.519

Asprenas. *See* Nonius

Assyrians, *Praef.* 9.34; *Lib.*
87.412

Astacus (town in Syria), *Syr.*
57.298

Astapa (town in Baetica), *Ib.*
33.132–36

Asyla (gold mines near
Philippi), *BCiv.* 4.106

Atabyrius, shrine of, *Mith.*
26.103

Ateius (lieutenant of Antony),
BCiv. 5.33.130, 50.208

Atella (town in Campania),
Hann. 48.210

Athamanes (Epirote people),
Mac. 3.1; *Syr.* 13.50–52,
17.71

Athena, *Lib.* 133.632; *Mith.*
53.212–23

Athens/Athenian/Attica, *Praef.*
8.29; *Hann.* 39.169; *Lib.*
87.408–9; *Mac.* 4.1–2, 7.1;
Syr. 45.233, 68.361; *Mith.*
8.24, 28.108–10, 30.118–
39.152, 83.373–74, 95.435;
BCiv. 2.15.56, 50.205, 70.293,
75.315, 88.368; 5.7.30, 11.43,
52.217, 53.219, 75.320,
76.322–24, 78.333, 93.387,
138.575

Atia (mother of Octavian),
BCiv. 3.10.34, 13.43–14.49,
23.89, 91.376, 92.380

Atilius (proscribed), *BCiv.*
4.30.129–31

Atilius, P. (leg. of Pompey in pirate war), *Mith.* 95.434

Atilius Regulus, M. (cos. 267,
256), *Lib.* 3.11–4.15; *Sic.*
2.2–3

Atilius Regulus, M. (cos. 227,
217), *Hann.* 16.68

Atilius Serranus, C. (pr. 218),
Hann. 5.18–19

Atilius Serranus, C. (cos. 106),
BCiv. 1.72.332

Atilius Serranus, Sex. (cos.
136?; prefect of fleet), *Lib.*
114.543

Atintani (people of Illyria), *Ill.*
7.20, 8.23

Atlas (mountain in Mauritania),
Num. 5.2

Attalus (ruler of Paphlagonia),
Mith. 114.560

INDEX

301

INDEX

India, *Lib.* 71.324; *Syr.* 56.288,
57.298; *Mith.* 89.407; *BCiv.*
2.149.622, 153.642, 154.647;
5.9.37
Indibilis (Celtiberian prince),
Ib. 37.147, 38.156–57
Indus river, *Syr.* 55.281–82
Inquilinus (lodger; name ap-
plied to Cicero by Catiline),
BCiv. 2.2.5
Intercatia (town in Spain), *Ib.*
53.222, 54.229, 55.231
Interfrurini (Illyrian people),
Ill. 16.47
Interrex, BCiv. 1.98.457
Io, *Mith.* 101.468
Ionia/Ionians, *Praef.* 2.6, 2.7,
3.9, 3.10, 9.36; *Mac.* 4.2, 18.4;
Syr. 1.2, 6.23, 29.147, 51.259;
Mith. 20.77, 21.82, 118.581;
BCiv. 1.76.347; 2.49.202,
71.294, 89.373; 3.2.4;
4.60.258, 63.271, 82.345;
5.65.276; *Frag.* 18
Ionian sea/gulf, *Praef.* 3.9, 3.10,
5.15, 14.55, 14.56; *Hann.*
8.34, 8.35; *Lib.* 87.409; *Ill.*
1.1, 3.7, 7.17, 8.24, 12.35;
Syr. 15.65, 16.70, 29.144,
63.333; *Mith.* 95.435,
112.542; *BCiv.* 1.5.20,
39.175, 49.211, 50.216,
66.303, 109.509; 2.38.151,
41.166, 49.200, 49.201,
150.625; 3.9.30, 10.35, 24.92,
27.104, 30.119, 63.260,
64.262, 96.396; 4.3.8, 58.248,
63.271, 65.276, 70.297,
94.393, 99.415, 115.479,

116.488, 122.513, 123.515,
127.530; 5.2.8, 4.15, 8.32,
26.104, 55.230, 61.259, 65.274
Ipsus (town in Phrygia), *Syr.*
55.279
Isauria (in Asia Minor), *Mith.*
75.326
Isauricus. *See* Servilius
Isis (apparition at Rhodes),
Mith. 27.105
Issa (island in Illyria), *Ill.* 7.17–
21
Ister (Danube), *Praef.* 4.15;
Mac. 18.1, 2; *Ill.* 1.1, 3.5,
5.14, 6.15, 6.16, 14.40, 22.65,
22.66; *Mith.* 15.54, 69.293
Isthmian games. *See* games
Istrians (Illyrian people), *Ill.* 8
Istrus (town in Mysia), *Ill.* 30.85
Itucca (town in Spain), *Ib.*
66.282, 67.284, 67.287
Ituraea in Syria, *Mith.* 106.499;
BCiv. 5.7.31
Iulius Caesar, C. (cos. 59, 48,
46–44), *Celt.* 1.6, 15.1, 17a;
Sic. 7.1, *Ib.* 102.442; *Lib.*
136.645; *Ill.* 15.44, 28.81,
29.84; *Mith.* 121.596–98;
BCiv. 1.4.12–16, 104.487;
2.1.1, 6.20–21, 8.26–15.54,
17.61–19.68, 23.87–36.145,
38.149–50, 40.159–43.174,
47.191–49.201, 52.212–
154.649; 3.1.1–35.141,
38.154, 40.164, 44.179,
50.216–57.238, 60.246–
62.256, 63.259, 64.262,
66.270, 73.298–87.358,
88.363, 94.391, 95.392,

INDEX

315

341